CURRENT PERSPECTIVES ON JOB-STRESS RECOVERY

RESEARCH IN OCCUPATIONAL STRESS AND WELL BEING

Series Editors: Pamela L. Perrewé and
Daniel C. Ganster

Recent Volumes:

RESEARCH IN OCCUPATIONAL STRESS AND
WELL BEING   VOLUME 7

CURRENT PERSPECTIVES ON JOB-STRESS RECOVERY

EDITED BY

SABINE SONNENTAG
University of Konstanz, Germany

PAMELA L. PERREWÉ
Florida State University, USA

DANIEL C. GANSTER
University of Arkansas, USA

Emerald

JAI

United Kingdom – North America – Japan
India – Malaysia – China

JAI Press is an imprint of Emerald Group Publishing Limited
Howard House, Wagon Lane, Bingley BD16 1WA, UK

First edition 2009

Copyright © 2009 Emerald Group Publishing Limited

Reprints and permission service
Contact: booksandseries@emeraldinsight.com

British Library Cataloguing in Publication Data
A catalogue record for this book is available from the British Library

ISBN: 978-1-84855-544-0
ISSN: 1479-3555 (Series)

Awarded in recognition of
Emerald's production
department's adherence to
quality systems and processes
when preparing scholarly
journals for print

INVESTOR IN PEOPLE

CONTENTS

v

LIST OF CONTRIBUTORS

Torbjörn Åkerstedt	Stress Research Institute, Stockholm University and Clinical Neuroscience, Karolinska Institutet, Stockholm, Sweden
Fabienne T. Amstad	Department of Work and Organizational Psychology, University of Bern, Bern, Switzerland
Arnold B. Bakker	Institute of Psychology, Erasmus University Rotterdam, Rotterdam, The Netherlands
Shoshi Chen	Faculty of Management, Tel Aviv University, Israel
Evangelia Demerouti	Department of Social and Organizational Psychology, Utrecht University, Utrecht, The Netherlands
Dalia Etzion	Faculty of Management, Tel Aviv University, Israel
Sabine A. E. Geurts	Work and Organizational Psychology, Radboud University Nijmegen, Nijmegen, The Netherlands
Ivona Hideg	Rotman School of Management, University of Toronto, Ontario, Canada
Göran Kecklund	Stress Research Institute, Stockholm University, Stockholm, Sweden
Peter M. Nilsson	Department of Clinical Sciences, University of Lund, Malmö University Hospital, Malmö, Sweden

Norbert K. Semmer	Department of Work and Organizational Psychology, University of Bern, Bern, Switzerland
Sabine Sonnentag	Department of Psychology, University of Konstanz, Konstanz, Germany
Toon W. Taris	Work and Organizational Psychology, Radboud University Nijmegen, Nijmegen, The Netherlands
Töres Theorell	Institute for Stress Research, Stockholm University, Stockholm, Sweden
John P. Trougakos	Department of Management – Scarborough, Rotman School of Management, University of Toronto, Ontario, Canada
Mina Westman	Faculty of Management, Tel Aviv University, Israel

FOREWORD

For decades research on occupational stress and well-being has been dominated by studies that demonstrated the negative effects of job stressors and lack of resources on employee health and well-being. Although this body of research is highly important and informative, it offers only limited insight into the processes that offset and "undo" the stress process. During recent years, researchers have paid increasing attention to such processes that reduce and reverse the effects of stress (i.e., recovery processes). This 7th volume of *Research in Occupational Stress and Well Being* is devoted to this growing research area on job stress recovery. The volume includes seven excellent chapters that provide state-of-the-art overviews on this theme, identify research gaps, and provide inspiring suggestions for further research.

The first chapter of this volume by Sabine Sonnentag and Sabine A. E. Geurts discusses methodological issues in recovery research. These authors explain why it is important to differentiate between recovery settings (e.g., work breaks, free evenings, vacations), recovery processes (i.e., activities and experiences), and recovery outcomes (e.g., affect, job-performance). They describe how to design and conduct various types of recovery studies, including (quasi-)experiments, diary studies, and longitudinal studies.

In the second chapter, John P. Trougakos and Ivona Hideg focus on momentary work recovery that takes place during breaks within workdays. The authors argue that work breaks affect psychological resources, particularly regulatory and affective resources that, in turn, influence workplace outcomes. They further suggest that workplace factors (job demands and job control) and individual difference variables (extraversion and neuroticism) moderate the relationship between work breaks and the resulting resource level.

The next chapter, authored by Evangelia Demerouti, Arnold B. Bakker, Sabine A. E. Geurts, and Toon W. Taris, deals with recovery at the day level. These authors summarize the empirical literature on diary studies of recovery and relate these studies to research on need for recovery. They propose that the recovery potential of activities pursued at home after work affect employees' psychological and energetic state at bedtime. Specifically, the recovery potential of activities should buffer the relationship between job-induced strain and a person's recovery state at bedtime.

The fourth chapter, authored by Fabienne T. Amstad and Norbert K. Semmer, discusses recovery in the specific context of the work–family interface. Amstad and Semmer start with an overview of the work and family literature from a macro (i.e., mainly person level) perspective. The core of their chapter then focuses on a micro-level perspective that describes transitions from one life domain (e.g., work) to the other life domain (e.g., family) over the course of a day. The authors suggest that recovery processes influence coping with stressful events within each life domain and at the transition point between the two domains.

In the fifth chapter, Mina Westman, Dalia Etzion, and Shoshi Chen examine business trips from a recovery perspective. They discuss business trips within a stress framework and describe in detail how business trips might impact travelers and their families. By differentiating among various phases (before, during, and after the trip), these authors delineate both the positive and negative outcomes of business trips.

The next chapter by Torbjörn Åkerstedt, Peter Nilsson, and Göran Kecklund reviews sleep as a crucial recovery process. The authors explain why sleep is important for the restoration of basic processes of the central nervous system, and they describe factors that affect the regulation of sleep and sleepiness. They summarize empirical evidence on the physiological consequences of sleep. Their chapter puts sleep in a broader societal context and discusses causes and consequences of sleep disturbances in modern societies.

The final chapter, authored by Töres Theorell, discusses recovery in the context of basic anabolic and catabolic processes at work. This chapter provides research evidence on the physiology of anabolic processes and their consequences. It demonstrates how recovery can influence basic bodily functions (including at the cell level) and how lack of recovery can impair such basic processes. Theorell summarizes findings from a broad range of empirical studies that illustrate the core propositions of his chapter.

As a whole, these chapters demonstrate the importance and the viability of this emerging research area on job stress recovery. They illustrate that knowledge on recovery processes helps us to better understand the work stress process and its consequences. We hope that you enjoy volume 7 of *Research in Occupational Stress and Well Being* and that it inspires you to think in a new way about job stress and how to reduce its damaging effects.

Sabine Sonnentag
Pamela L. Perrewé
Daniel C. Ganster
Editors

METHODOLOGICAL ISSUES IN RECOVERY RESEARCH

Sabine Sonnentag and Sabine A. E. Geurts

ABSTRACT

This chapter describes methodological issues that are relevant for research on recovery. We aim to provide an overview of methodological approaches that have been or can be used in recovery research, and to provide methodological guidelines that researchers may use in assessing the process of recovery. We argue that studies on recovery must be explicit about recovery settings, recovery processes (i.e., activities and experiences) and recovery outcomes. We describe typical operationalizations of these three perspectives and focus in more detail on potential measures of recovery outcomes. We give an overview of research designs including experiments and quasi-experiments, diary studies, and longitudinal field studies. We conclude by pointing to remaining challenges for researchers in the area of recovery.

INTRODUCTION

Research in the field of work and health has consistently demonstrated the adverse impact of psychosocial job stressors on individuals' health and well-being. Longitudinal research guided by the influential Job Demand–Job

Current Perspectives on Job-Stress Recovery
Research in Occupational Stress and Well Being, Volume 7, 1–36
Copyright © 2009 by Emerald Group Publishing Limited
All rights of reproduction in any form reserved
ISSN: 1479-3555/doi:10.1108/S1479-3555(2009)0000007004

Control model has demonstrated that being exposed to psychosocial risk factors at work (i.e., high psychological demands and low job control) is associated with increased levels of physical and psychological health problems across time (Belkic, Landsbergis, Schnall, & Baker, 2004). Research inspired by the Effort–Reward Imbalance model provided evidence that a combination of high effort expended at work and low job rewards (e.g., low career prospects, poor job security) is related to subjective health complaints, coronary heart disease, and absenteeism (Van Veghel, De Jonge, Bosma, & Schaufeli, 2005).

In the past decade, the awareness has risen that *recovery* plays a crucial intervening role in the relationship between stressful work characteristics on the one hand, and health, well-being and performance capability on the other hand, and that stress-related psychophysiological processes are important ingredients of the recovery process. Geurts and Sonnentag (2006) propose that the essence of recovery is that "the psychophysiological systems that were activated during work will return to and stabilize at a baseline level, that is, a level that appears in a situation in which no special demands are made on the individual" (p. 483). Accordingly recovery is a process of psychophysiological unwinding that is the opposite of the activation of psychophysiological systems that has occurred during exposure to stressful work conditions. Exposure to high job demands or stressors activates several bodily stress systems, in particular the Sympathetic–Adrenal–Medullary (SAM) system and the Hypothalamic–Pituitary–Adrenal (HPA) system, resulting in neuroendocrine responses (e.g., elevated excretion levels of catecholamines and cortisol) and cardiovascular responses (e.g., elevated blood pressure (BP) and heart rate (HR) levels). As the occurrence of these stress-related physiological reactions is normally adaptive and short-lived, it does not necessarily pose a serious risk for health and well-being. However, when these physiological stress reactions occur repeatedly or over prolonged times, and no longer return to their baseline levels after exposure to the immediate stressor has ended, they become potentially harmful as they may disturb the organism's precarious homeostatic balance. This homeostatic balance (also called "allostasis"; McEwen, 1998) refers to the balance between the sympathetic nervous system being dominant during the mobilization of energy (e.g., in response to stressors) and the parasympathetic nervous system being in control during rest and relaxation (e.g., sleep). Parasympathetic activity has the important aim to restore the undesirable and potentially destructive effects of sympathetic arousal (e.g., by slowing down the HR). A disturbed sympathetic–parasympathetic balance will manifest itself in chronic over-activity or inactivity of crucial bodily systems (e.g., the immune system; McEwen (1998) refers to this pathological outcome as "allostatic load"), as well as in disturbed affective processes and deteriorated performance capabilities. Health, well-being, and performance are, thus, seriously at risk when individuals do not completely recover from acute stress-related physiological reactions.

Earlier research and practical interventions addressing rest breaks (Tucker, 2003), work hours (Harma, 2006), shift work (Smith, Folkard, & Fuller, 2003), and work-life balance (Geurts & Demerouti, 2003) have – at least implicitly – acknowledged the important role of recovery in protecting employee health, well-being, and performance capabilities. However, as yet, the topic of recovery has received only limited scientific attention. As far as research on this topic exists, it is characterized by a wide variety of perspectives and measurements. As a consequence, the process of recovery is not yet well understood (Geurts & Sonnentag, 2006; Zijlstra & Sonnentag, 2006).

The focus of this contribution is on methodological issues that are relevant for recovery research. We aim to provide an overview of methodological approaches that have been or can be used in recovery research, and to provide methodological guidelines that researchers may use in assessing the process of recovery. In the next section on measurement issues, we will first discuss various perspectives on recovery. More concretely, we will discuss the various recovery settings (e.g., free evenings, free weekends, vacations), and the perspective on recovery as a process and as an outcome. In this section, we will also discuss the various types of recovery outcomes (i.e., psychological (self-reported) outcomes, physiological outcomes, and behavioral outcomes). In the next section, we will present possible study designs (i.e., (quasi-)experimental, diary studies, and longitudinal surveys). We will finish this chapter with some conclusions about future research on recovery.

MEASUREMENT ISSUES

In this section, we will describe how to assess recovery. As the recovery phenomenon can be approached from different angles, we will first characterize these different perspectives. Then, we will present specific measures and measurement approaches for assessing the outcomes of recovery processes.

Perspectives on Recovery

Studies on recovery can assess various facets of recovery, namely the recovery settings, recovery as a process, and recovery as an outcome.

Recovery Settings
Recovery researchers may want to assess the temporal and situational *settings* in which recovery is assumed to occur. Such settings include work breaks (see Trougakos and Hideg in this volume), free evenings (Sonnentag, 2001), weekends (Fritz & Sonnentag, 2005), vacations (Westman & Eden, 1997), and sabbaticals (Davidson, 2006). Typical studies on recovery settings compare a person's state while (or after) being in such recovery situation with their states outside (or before) such a situation. For example, a study by Westman and Eden (1997) compared employees' burnout scores before, during, and after a two-week vacation. Although, in general, research on vacation as a recovery setting is scarce, some studies compared job stress indicators (e.g., work demands), health indicators (e.g., psychosomatic complaints), and job attitudes (e.g., job satisfaction) before and after a vacation period (for a systematic review on vacation studies, cf. De Bloom et al., 2009). In a similar vein, Fritz and Sonnentag (2005) compared health and performance indicators across a weekend period. Research using physiological indicators, for instance, compared urinary cortisol levels in truck drivers during working days and during rest days (Kuiper, Van der Beck, & Meijman, 1998). Variants of this approach may not only compare a vacation situation with a nonvacation situation, but might also want to distinguish between various types of vacations, for example, with respect to location or geographical region (Strauss-Blasche et al., 2004; Strauss-Blasche, Reithofer, Schobersberger, Ekmekcioglu, & Marktl, 2005).

Recovery as a Process
Studies focusing on recovery as a *process* aim at the assessment of the mechanisms assumed to underlie the recovery phenomenon. The most basic distinction refers to passive versus active mechanisms underlying the recovery process. A perspective focusing on passive recovery refers to relief from job demands and other stressors. A more active perspective on recovery addresses processes other than just the absence of demands or stressors crucial for recovery to occur. It reflects the active engagement in potentially recovering activities and experiences (Geurts & Sonnentag, 2006).

With respect to activities that are assumed to support the recovery process, studies have assessed how much time individuals have spent on specific and potentially recovering activities such as hobbies, sport, socializing, and low-effort activities (Rook & Zijlstra, 2006; Sonnentag, 2001; Van Hooff, Geurts, Kompier, & Taris, 2007a; Winwood, Bakker, & Winefield, 2007). Also studies that measure the amount of sleep individuals get regularly or during particular nights fall into this category (Cropley, Dijk, & Stanley, 2006; Van Hooff et al., 2007a). Studies that assess hours of overtime (i.e., during time that "should" be devoted to recovery) indirectly provide information on (lack of) recovery. For instance, a recent study among a large-sized heterogeneous sample of Dutch full time employees showed that involuntary overtime work was associated with relatively high fatigue and low satisfaction (Beckers et al., 2008). Similarly, research on the use of job-related communication technologies adds to our understanding of factors that might impede recovery processes (Boswell & Olson-Buchanon, 2007; Eden, 2001).

When interested in recovery as a process, researchers might not only be interested in activities but also in specific attributes associated with these activities. It has been argued that it is not the activities themselves, but the psychological experiences attached to these activities that are relevant for recovery (Sonnentag & Fritz, 2007). For example, one person likes to play soccer with a group of friends, whereas the other person prefers to watch a movie, but both "switch off" from their work while engaging in these activities and feel refreshed afterwards.

Sonnentag and Fritz (2007) distinguished between four distinct recovery experiences: psychological detachment from work, mastery, relaxation, and experiencing control. Psychological detachment from work implies to gain mental distance from one's job. When detaching oneself psychologically from one's job one refrains from job-related activities and job-related thoughts. In people's everyday experience, psychological detachment is often experienced as "switching off." Mastery experiences imply to address new challenges (e.g., doing a hiking tour in the mountains), to learn something new (e.g., practicing a new language), or to broaden one's horizon (e.g., traveling to a foreign country). Mastery experiences refer to the notion that recovery processes are not necessarily effortless. Recovery may require some kind of effort investment, but the demands are different from the demands one is facing at the job. Relaxation refers to processes characterized by low sympathetic activation. It can occur both at a physical level (e.g., by reducing one's physical activity) or at a mental level (e.g., by engaging in a kind or purposeful relaxation exercise such as meditation).

Relaxation experiences are also possible when listening to music, reading a novel etc. Control refers to self-determination during off-job time. It implies that one experiences discretion in the choice of one's activities. For example, deciding about when and how to do a specific activity can result in recovery.

Studies using between-person and within-person data showed that the four recovery experience dimensions can be clearly differentiated empirically (Sonnentag, Binnewies, & Mojza, 2008; Sonnentag & Fritz, 2007). Closely related – but not identical – to lack of psychological detachment are processes such as worry (Brosschot, Van Dijk, & Thayer, 2007) and rumination (Cropley & Purvis, 2003).

In addition to the four dimensions suggested by Sonnentag and Fritz (2007), one can think of other experiences that are helpful for recovery to occur. Such experiences may include the experience of pleasure or the experience of meaning, or lack of experiences that may negatively affect the recovery process such as experiences of effort. For instance Van Hooff et al. (2007a) showed among faculty members that those who experienced their work activities as effortful, also experienced their nonwork activities as effortful, and showed significantly higher levels of fatigue and more sleep complaints than individuals who did not experience their work and home activities as effortful. In addition, one could argue that the dimensions proposed so far may be too broad, and that, for example, it may be useful to distinguish between physical and mental relaxation. Also further refinement might be needed with respect to the concept of psychological detachment. For example, one might argue that lack of psychological detachment impairs well-being but only if job-related thoughts have a negative valence (e.g., when thinking about negative events that happened at work). Job-related thoughts with a positive valence (e.g., when thinking about a recent success at work) may help to improve one's well-being (Fritz & Sonnentag, 2005).

During sleep fatigue is reduced and resources are restored (see also Åkerstedt, Nilsson, and Kecklund in this volume). Therefore, studies that focus on sleep and do not only assess sleep duration, but also sleep quality, measure process aspects of recovery (Scott & Judge, 2006; Van Hooff et al., 2007a). At the same time, sleep duration and sleep quality can also be seen as an outcome of recovery (see next section).

Also environmental psychology has developed theoretical frameworks that are specific about the experiences that provide opportunities for recovery and restoration. Kaplan (1995) described restorative environments as environments that offer – among other aspects – fascination, a feeling of being away, and compatibility between the features of the environment and one's own preferences. Research has shown that natural environments (i.e., nature areas) largely meet the requirements for such restorative environments (Kaplan, 1995), but that also other environments such as museums have a restorative potential (Hartig, Mang, & Evens, 1991; Hartig, Evans, Jamner, Davis, & Gärling, 2003; Kaplan, Bardwell, & Slakter, 1993).

Recovery as an Outcome
Recovery may not only be studied in terms of the specific setting, regarding when and where it occurs, or in terms of the processes that eventually lead to a state of being recovered. Researchers may also want to examine recovery as an outcome. This perspective focuses on recovery as the result of a successful or less successful recovery process. For example, a person's affective state, specific physiological parameters (e.g., cardiovascular parameters such as BP or HR, and neuroendocrine parameters such as catecholamines or cortisol), and also performance scores are typically used as outcomes of recovery (these outcomes will be discussed in more detail in the next section).

One important issue with respect to recovery as an outcome refers to the differentiation between absolute levels versus relative levels of the recovery outcomes. When one is interested in a specific recovery outcome (e.g., a person's affective state before starting a new working day), one may assess the absolute level of this outcome (e.g., level of state positive and negative affect in the morning) or a relative level of this outcome. Such a relative score might capture the change in the outcome variable since the stressor ended (e.g., increase in state positive affect since the end of the last working day) or an outcome score relative to a person-specific comparison value (e.g., state affect during a typical off-job situation such as the weekend or a vacation).

Whereas absolute levels are often easier to obtain and may incorporate valuable information about a person's affective, cardiovascular or neuroendocrine state at a given moment, they are rather far away from the conceptual core of recovery – defined as a process opposite to the strain process during which important indicators of the organism's functioning return to their baseline levels (Craig & Cooper, 1992). Moreover, absolute levels of affect and physiological data may be influenced by all kinds of other variables that have nothing to do with recovery (e.g., a person's dispositional affectivity or health status).

Change scores that represent the difference in affective or physiological states between the start of a recovery period (e.g., end of a working day or the first day of a vacation) and the end of a recovery period (e.g., the morning before heading off for work or days in the second half of the vacation) reflect more closely the core of the recovery concept, namely the "undoing" of the strain process. In practical terms, such change scores can be attained by using difference scores or residuals in a multiple regression equation. For example, one could assess a person's level of fatigue before and after a recovery period and then subtract the postrecovery fatigue score from the prerecovery score (fatigue recovery = $fatigue_{pre}-fatigue_{post}$) or by regressing the postrecovery fatigue score on the prerecovery fatigue score and regarding the residual as an indicator of recovery. Of course, it has to be taken into account that such change scores can also be influenced by factors other than recovery (e.g., circadian rhythm). Whenever possible, these other factors should be controlled for.

Another way to conceptualize relative recovery scores refers to the discrepancy between the recovery outcome (e.g., affective or physiological states) at the end of the recovery period and a baseline level of affect or physiological indicators. Thus, here the recovery score is expressed relative to the baseline level of the respective indicator. This perspective on recovery measures is most closely linked to the conceptualization of recovery as "return to the baseline." However, in practical terms, it is very difficult to assess a person's baseline level of the respective indicator. For example, with respect to some physiological data (e.g., HR) one might want to assess the level immediately after a person's awakening. This approach, however, assumes that the HR in the early morning before getting up reflects the true baseline, in other words, that full recovery occurred during the night. This is an assumption that is often not warranted.

Considering the practical problems in assessing a true baseline, most recovery studies might want to opt for a recovery score that relates the recovery outcome after the recovery period to the respective measure before the onset of the recovery period, for example, by using difference scores or residuals. In addition, one could also opt to assess within-person effects in a repeated measures design.

Combinations of Context, Process, and Outcomes
Of course, researchers might also want to combine these various perspectives (setting, process, outcomes) into one single study. For example, one might want to examine if the recovery experiences differ between weekends and vacations and if these differences result in differences with respect to affective states, physiological outcomes or performance outcomes. In fact, most studies on recovery incorporate a combination of two or more facets. When combining the various facets, however, it is important to clearly distinguish among them and not to blur setting with process or process with outcome. For example, in a recent study on recovery during a

short respite such as a long weekend, Kühnel, Sonnentag, and Westman (in press) analyzed (i) if work engagement increased after the respite, and (ii) if psychological detachment from work during the weekend played a role in the degree to which work engagement increased after the respite. In this particular study, the weekend period refers to the setting dimension, work engagement can be considered an outcome of the recovery process, and psychological detachment refers to "recovery as a process."

Types of Recovery Outcomes

Various outcome variables can be used as indicators of a successful or less successful recovery process. Globally, we can distinguish among three types of recovery outcomes: psychological (e.g., fatigue, affect, sleep quality), physiological (e.g., cardiovascular and neuroendocrine) and behavioral (e.g., performance). To adequately capture the outcomes of the recovery process, we should use measurements that are sensitive for subtle fluctuations in the recovery process across time. In recovery research, the observation period sometimes covers a relatively long period (e.g., months or years), for instance, when the long-term impact of high strain jobs and incomplete recovery on health and well-being is investigated (Gump & Matthews, 2000; Kivimäki et al., 2006; Van Hooff et al., 2005). For instance, Kivimäki et al. (2006) showed in a prospective cohort study that industrial workers (initially free of overt cardiovascular disease), who reported insufficient recovery during free weekends, showed an elevated risk of cardiovascular death more than 20 years later. However, in recovery research observation periods are often shorter covering a period of several weeks, for instance, across a vacation period (Westman & Eden, 1997), or of several hours or days, for instance, when recovery from a stressful workday or workweek is studied (Sonnentag, 2001; Van Hooff et al., 2007a). A general guideline is that when observation periods are short, researchers should utilize "momentary" measures of recovery or adapt more general recovery measures in such a way that they become appropriate for day-level research. In the next paragraphs, we will elaborate on each category of recovery outcomes.

Psychological Recovery Outcomes

Many researchers assess individuals' level of recovery directly by asking the individuals themselves how they feel after a (stressful) work period and after a recovery period. Individuals may respond in terms of, for instance, their state of recovery, their level of fatigue, other affective states, and their sleep quality.

Recovery State. A measure that is widely used to assess the present recovery state is the *Need for Recovery scale* (De Croon, Sluiter, & Frings-Dresen, 2006; Van Veldhoven & Broersen, 2003). This questionnaire assesses a person's wish for being – temporarily – relieved from any demands in order to replenish his or her energy resources. Need for recovery is experienced as "feelings of 'wanting to be left in peace for a while', or 'wanting to lay down for a while'" (Sluiter, Frings-Dresen, Van der Beek, & Meijman, 2001, p. 29). The *Intershift recovery scale* taps a similar experience (Winwood, Winefield, Dawson, & Lushington, 2005). As these recovery measures were originally not developed for day-level purposes, adjustments for capturing day-level fluctuations in need for recovery have been proposed (Sonnentag & Zijlstra, 2006). In addition to a person's need for recovery, the state of feeling actually recovered can also be assessed more directly ("This morning, I feel well rested"; Binnewies, Sonnentag, & Mojza, 2009).

Fatigue Level. Conceptually, "fatigue" is inversely related to "recovery state" and often similar items are used to capture it. Research, however, indicates that fatigue is still distinct from recovery (Jansen, Kant, & van den Brandt, 2002). Fatigue is often measured in a way that reflects how fatigued people generally feel. Examples are the *Fatigue Assessment Scale* (FAS, example item: "I am bothered by fatigue"; Michielsen, De Vries, & Van Hecke, 2003) and the exhaustion subscale of the *Utrecht Burnout Scale* (UBOS; Schaufeli & van Dierendonck, 2000). However, such general measures are not suitable to capture a person's current recovery state, unless they are adapted for day-level measurement (e.g., "Today I experienced fatigue"). The *Experienced Load Scale* (Van Veldhoven, De Jonge, Broersen, Kompier, & Meijman, 2002) was developed as a momentary measure of fatigue by asking workers, for instance, to what extent they felt mentally tired during the first and last hour of a specific working day. Recently, Van Hooff, Geurts, Taris, and Kompier (2007b) tested the validity of a *single-item fatigue measure* on the day level (respondents answered with a report mark to the question "How fatigued do you currently feel") by relating it to the well-validated six-item fatigue measure of the *Profile of Mood States* (POMS; McNair, Lorr, & Droppelman, 1971). They concluded that the single-item fatigue measure was psychometrically equivalent to the multiple-item fatigue measure, and thus, that the report mark is a valid and useful tool to measure day-level fatigue.

Other Affective States. Because stressful work conditions often lead to impaired mood, restoration of the disturbed emotional state is one of the core functions of recovery. However, the precise role of affective states in the recovery process is not yet disentangled. High positive and low negative affective states may be considered outcomes of a successful recovery process with a favorable change in affective state demonstrating that recovery has occurred. However, we might as well consider affective state as an antecedent or a facilitator of the recovery process. For instance, Fredrickson, Mancuso, Branigan, and Tugade (2000) provided evidence, in line with the broaden-and-build theory of positive emotions (Fredrickson, 1998), that positive emotions facilitate the recovery process by downregulating cardiovascular reactivity that was triggered by negative emotions. In this particular study (Fredrickson et al., 2000), negative and positive affect appeared to be an antecedent and a facilitator of cardiovascular recovery outcomes, respectively (see further explanation below).

A widely used measure of negative and positive affect is the *Positive and Negative Affect Schedule* (PANAS; Watson, Clark, & Tellegen, 1988). Watson and his coworkers propose that Negative Affect and Positive Affect are two broad, general, and only weakly related dimensions that are each composed of various, related, but differentiable, emotions with, for instance, fear, sadness, hostility, and guilt as negative emotions, and with, for instance, joviality, self-assurance, and attentiveness as positive emotions. Although the PANAS is often used as a trait measure of Negative Affect and Positive Affect ("Thinking about yourself and how you normally feel, to what extent do you generally feel ... "), it can also be applied as a state measure (e.g., "To what extent do you feel ... at this moment"). In addition to positive and negative affect as broad affective dimensions, one could also assess the discrete emotions as recovery outcomes. For example, Watson and Clark (1994) suggest fear, hostility, guilt, and sadness to be basic negative emotions, and joviality, self-assurance, and attentiveness to be basic positive emotions. In addition, they differentiate between four other affective states namely shyness, fatigue, serenity, and surprise.

A related measure of affective states is the earlier discussed POMS. The POMS covers, besides "fatigue" (feeling tired), other dimensions of mood, that is, "depression," "anger," "(loss of) vigor," and "tension." Also the POMS has been used both as a trait measure (e.g., "To what extent do you [feel tired] over the last few days including today," supposedly reflecting how people generally feel, although the period of reflection is still relatively short) and as a state measure (e.g., "To what extent do you [feel tired] at this moment?").

Sleep Quality. Sleep quality can be conceptualized both as a recovery process (i.e., a mechanism that reduces fatigue and supports restoration of resources; see previous section) and as a recovery outcome. Most obviously, successful recovery during a free evening should improve sleep quality. Sleep quality covers various aspects such as difficulties with falling asleep, difficulties with sleeping through, and early awakening. Adequate sleep scales for day-to-day measurements are the *Sleep Quality Scale* (Van Veldhoven, De Jonge, Broersen, Kompier, & Meijman, 2002; Van Hooff et al., 2007a; e.g., "Last night I woke up several times") and a *subjective sleep scale* (Åkerstedt, Hume, Minors, & Waterhouse, 1994; slightly adapted by Cropley et al., 2006; e.g., "Did you sleep throughout the night"). The *Sleep Wake Experience List* (SWEL; Van Diest, 1990) has been used to measure both the incidence and the severity of sleep complaints over the last three months. Also other measures of sleep quality as the Pittsburgh Sleep Quality Index (Buysse, Reynolds, Monk, Berman, & Kupfer, 1989) can be adapted for use in day-level studies (Sonnentag et al., 2008).

Physiological Recovery Outcomes

Recovery is an important part within the field of physiological research on stress. Usually a differentiation is made between two physiological phenomena related to the stress process: reactivity and recovery (Linden, Earle, Gerin, & Christenfeld, 1997). Reactivity refers to the physiological responses that occur while the stressful event is actually occurring. Recovery refers to processes during the poststressor period, when physiological strain indicators return to their baseline levels. As we discussed earlier, slow recovery may manifest itself in the prolonged elevation of physiological indicators after the stressor has ended (a phenomenon also known as the "slow unwinding"). In this section, we will first discuss the neuroendocrine measures, that is, catecholamines (noradrenaline and adrenaline as main outcomes of the SAM system) and cortisol (as main actor of activity of the HPA system). Next, we will discuss cardiovascular indicators, that is, HR and BP, which can be considered more secondary and manifest outcomes of activity of the SAM system. We will discuss the use of these measures both in laboratory and field settings. Neuroendocrine measures are taken generally through (intrusive) blood samples and urinary samples (with the latter, of course, being less inconvenient for participants). Cortisol can be derived, in addition to blood and urinary samples, more easily through saliva samples.

Neuroendocrine Measures. Catecholamine and cortisol levels are extensively studies in laboratory settings, mostly in response to a stressful task or event (see Sonnentag & Fritz, 2006, for a review). As catecholamines are secreted very instantly through the SAM system in response to a stressor, catecholamine recovery also may occur relatively quickly, that is, a few minutes after termination of the stressor (Linden et al., 1997). However, there are indications that after exposure to a stressful task or event (in particular, anger-provoking situations), catecholamine levels (and particularly adrenaline) remain elevated for quite some time (e.g., for 1 or 2 h) after the stressor has ended (Linden et al., 1997). As cortisol is the main stress indicator in the somewhat slower operating HPA system, it takes normally 20 min after exposure to the stressor before cortisol can be observed in saliva, and it takes 40–60 min before elevated levels have returned to their baseline or prestressor levels (with the higher the cortisol reactivity, the longer it takes before cortisol levels have stabilized; Dickerson & Kemeny, 2004). The use of cortisol measures as outcomes of recovery might be problematic because the return to prestressor levels seems to be depend on very stable (individual) characteristics (Pruessner, Hellhammer, & Kirschbaum, 1999).

Also field studies examined catecholamine and cortisol recovery (for a review, see Sonnentag & Fritz, 2006). In field research, neuroendocrine measures are generally taken during (work) load at daytime and during recovery at evening/night time. Catecholamine and cortisol levels are generally higher during daytime (as compared to evening time) and during working days (as compared to rest days). Of particular interest is to what extent catecholamine and cortisol levels remain elevated during free periods (e.g., free evenings or free weekends) after a work period (e.g., a day or a week), indicating incomplete recovery. Again, one might assume that it is difficult to use cortisol as an outcome indicator of recovery as cortisol secretion follows a strong circadian rhythm (high and rising levels in the early morning, a gradual decrease during the day and the lowest levels in the first part of the night) and therefore the impact of relief from daily stressors on this circadian rhythm can hardly be detected. A recent study, however, demonstrated that decline in cortisol across the day can be used as a recovery indicator, at least in women (Saxbe, Repetti, & Nishina, 2008).

Cardiovascular Measures. Physiological reactivity to and recovery from stressors may also manifest itself in cardiovascular outcomes. Prolonged elevated HR and BP levels indicate sustained sympathetic activation and, thus, delayed or incomplete recovery (Rau, Georgiades, Fredrikson, Lemne, & de Faire, 2001; Rau & Triemer, 2004). Information about parasympathetic activation and its crucial function of restoring the negative effects of sympathetic arousal can also be deduced from the HR, namely from the Heart Rate Variability (HRV) which is associated with respiration. During inhaling HR increases, whereas during exhaling HR decreases (the so-called "Respiratory Sinus Arrhythmia," RSA). The difference between the maximum HR during inhaling and the minimum HR during exhaling is a measure of parasympathetic activation with high differences (high HRV) indicating stronger parasympathetic and thus restorative activation. Low HRV is considered a marker of low parasympathetic activation and thus indicative of disturbed restorative functions and incomplete recovery (Gerin, Davidson, Christenfeld, Goyal, & Schwartz, 2006). Both in field and laboratory settings, HR and HRV (together with motor activity) can be recorded continuously by ambulatory monitoring (e.g., De Geus, Willemsen, Klaver, & Van Doornen, 1995). Systolic and diastolic BPs can be measured on an interval basis (e.g., every 15 min), for instance with a BP monitor on the nondominant arm (e.g., Vrijkotte, Van Doornen, & De Geus, 2000) or by continuous beat-to-beat measures, for instance, by using the Finapres, a noninvasive method using an inflatable finger cuff on the third finger of the nondominant hand (e.g., Gerin et al., 2006). In both the laboratory and field setting, one way to analyze HR, HRV and BP data is to average these parameters over the baseline period, the stress period and the recovery period (for a detailed discussion on the measurement and analysis of cardiovascular recovery measures, see Linden et al. (1997)).

Other Physiological Measures. Of course, one might also think of other physiological measures such as electromyographic indicators (EMG), skin conductance or assessment of skin temperature (Burns, 2006; Veldhuizen, Gaillard, & de Vriese, 2003). However, these measures are not so often used in applied settings.

Behavioral Recovery Outcomes
One behavioral outcome of a successful recovery process is that workers perform adequately when returning back to work after a period of rest. During free time, individuals do not only recover from strain build up at work, but may reload their "personal batteries" (i.e., psychological resources) as well, which may manifest itself in higher job performance after the free period. Job performance can be seen as a multidimensional concept (Campbell, McCloy, Oppler, & Sager, 1993). For instance, Fritz and Sonnentag (2005) focused on task performance (i.e., behaviors that are recognized by formal reward systems and are part of the formal job requirements) and proactive behaviors at work, that is, taking personal

initiative (e.g., taking initiative in improving the work circumstances; Frese, Fay, Hilburger, Leng, & Tag, 1997) and pursuit of learning (e.g., searching for situations in which one can develop new knowledge and skills; Sonnentag, 2003).

A recent study examined job performance following work breaks in a very specific sample, namely cheerleader instructors (Trougakos, Beal, Green, & Weiss, 2008). Trougakos and his coworkers conceptualized "affective delivery" (i.e., acting with spirit/enthusiasm, energy, alertness and sincerity) as a core aspect of job performance in this sample and used ratings of video recordings as the performance indicator. This study showed that the quality of affective delivery after work breaks increased when these cheerleader instructors had engaged in respite break activities (e.g., napping, relaxing, socializing) as opposed to chore activities (e.g., working with customers, running errands).

Particularly with respect to task performance one should carefully choose the performance indicators that allow the detection of even minimal changes in performance. As completing work tasks is a high priority in many jobs, people most probably try to uphold their performance level even when they are not optimally recovered. For example, when workers are not in a fully recovered state, they may use compensatory effort in order to not fall behind in their performance (Binnewies et al., 2009; Hockey, 1997). Therefore, the effects of recovery on task performance are quite difficult to detect, and manifestations of compensatory effort or strain should be simultaneously taken into account. Thus, task performance as such might not always be a good outcome indicator of recovery.

STUDY DESIGNS

Recovery research can be done with various study designs. In this section, we will discuss how to implement recovery studies by following (quasi-) experimental designs, diary study approaches and longitudinal designs.

Quasi-Experimental and Experimental Designs

For examining the "outcomes" of recovery occasions, quasi-experimental and particularly experimental designs are rather straightforward study-design options. Shadish, Cook, and Campbell (2001) define an experiment as "a study in which an intervention is deliberately introduced to observe its effects" (p. 12). True or randomized experiments are experiments in which study participants are randomly assigned to two or more study conditions. Quasi-experiments are experiments where such a random assignment is lacking.

With respect to recovery research, true experiments are rather rare – but not impossible. Quasi-experiments are much more common. In typical quasi-experimental recovery research, study participants are observed (or more often: surveyed) during a recovery episode and during a nonrecovery episode. Because of their more frequent use in recovery research, we will first discuss quasi-experimental designs and then move to experimental designs.

Quasi-Experiments
In the context of recovery research, quasi-experimental studies typically examine affect, (mental) health, or attitudes before, during and after a re-covery episode, for example, a free weekend, a vacation, or even a sabbatical. In addition, before and after the recovery episode, job performance measures also can be assessed. Typical examples of such quasi-experimental studies comprise a study by Fritz and Sonnentag (2005) examining recovery during the weekend, the vacation study by Westman and Eden (1997) mentioned earlier in this chapter and an impressive study on recovery during sabbaticals (Davidson, 2006).

Quasi-experimental designs are not limited to just one measurement point before, during and after a recovery episode. More comprehensive designs may include even more measurement points. For example, Westman and Eden (1997) realized two measurement points before a vacation, one during the vacation and two after the vacation. Using several measurement points before the recovery episode allows for the investigation of potential anticipation effects, using two or three measurement points after the recovery episode enables the researchers to address potential fade-out effects over time.

For drawing conclusions based on these types of quasi-experimental designs with just one study group that spent time on the recovery episode, it may be useful to not just collect data from the persons who spent time on the recovery episode, but also from persons in a control group that continued to work during the same period of time. Otherwise, it is difficult to conclude that positive changes after the recovery episode happened because of the recovery episode. For example, changes on study participants' outcomes might have occurred because of a change in weather (or other processes unrelated to the recovery episode) or because of methodological artifacts. For example, Etzion and her coworkers conducted a quasi-experimental study with two measurement points and two study groups (Etzion, Eden, & Lapidot, 1998). However, the inclusion of a control group in recovery research also encounters problems. As the recovery process may be influenced by a wide variety of variables (i.e., personality, work and family situation), it is very difficult to standardize these variables for the recovery group and the control group. In other words, it is very likely that the two groups may differ on variables that may be relevant in the recovery process. It may be for this reason that recovery studies, which are using control groups, are very rare overall. For example, De Bloom et al. (2009) conducted a systematic review of vacation studies and found that only two out of eight vacation studies used a control group. With respect to other recovery settings (i.e., weekend or free evenings) control groups are even more difficult to study.

Strictly speaking, strong causal interferences can only be drawn from a true experimental procedure that randomly assigns study participants to the various study groups – a condition that might be very difficult to implement with respect to typical recovery episodes such as vacations. We will discuss true experimental designs later in this section.

When planning recovery studies with measurement points before and after a recovery episode, decisions have to be made with respect to the exact timing of the measurements. When should the premeasures, and when should the postmeasures be taken? The premeasure has to be scheduled at a time when affect (or other outcome measures) is not yet potentially influenced by the recovery episode to come. For example, with respect to a vacation study, it should be ruled out that study participants are already in a good mood because they are looking forward to going on vacation – or that they are fatigued and stressed because they have to prepare many things before the beginning of the vacation (e.g., finishing work tasks, packing the bags). Thus, in order to get an idea of a person's recovery state in a normal (regular) workweek, a measurement point somewhat distal to the vacation might be preferable over a measurement point immediately before the vacation. Measurements during a normal workweek relatively long before the vacation period can then be considered baseline measures. Effects of vacation itself as well as potential anticipation and fade-out effects can be detected by making within-person comparisons with this baseline measure. This approach would make the use of a control group not necessary as each person is compared to his or her own baseline level (keeping most potentially disturbing variables like personality, family situation and nature of work under control). Similarly, when examining recovery during weekends, measurements at Friday afternoons might not represent the best preweekend measures as then weekend anticipation might already play a role. Instead measurements at a regular workday somewhere in the middle of the workweek would provide the best baseline with which to compare the weekend effects.

However, when explicitly interested in vacation (or weekend) anticipation, a measurement point rather close to the recovery episode is important. For example, Westman and Eden (1997) realized two prevacation measurement points, one six weeks before the vacation (in order to assess "true" prevacation states) and three days before the vacation (to test vacation anticipation).

With respect to postrecovery measures, the timing of the assessment is also crucial. Often, one is interested in the immediate outcomes of the recovery episode, and in such cases it is recommended to assess affect, performance, or other outcomes just after the termination of the recovery episode and before potential daily (job) stressors start to exert their influence on the person again. However, one might argue that at the end of the recovery period, one already anticipates the next working days or weeks and that this anticipation already reduces the recovery effect. For instance, Rook and Zijlstra demonstrated that sleep quality already decreased on Sunday nights. Similarly, Van Hooff et al. (2007a) showed among faculty members that those who experienced their work activities as effortful, reported lower motivation to start the next working week after a free weekend. Therefore, one might consider measuring the outcomes of the recovery processes even before anticipation of work takes place. Moreover, one might also be interested in long-term outcomes of recovery processes and might want to examine how long recovery effects persist. Particularly with respect to recovery during vacations, fade-out processes have been proposed (Westman & Eden, 1997). To capture vacation fade-out, it is useful to assess the outcome measure two to four weeks after the end of the vacation.

Another important decision to be made refers to the question of whether measures should be taken during the recovery episode (e.g., vacation or a free weekend). To assess whether changes in affect, well-being and similar outcome variables may be caused by the recovery episode, it is useful to have an indication if affect, well-being and such outcomes changed during the recovery episode. For example, if one assumes that levels of exhaustion are reduced after a recovery episode, exhaustion should most probably already show a reduction during the recovery episode. However, it might be difficult to draw inferences from such an approach. In addition to the fact that no causal conclusion can be drawn from nonexperimental studies, it has to be considered that recovery might not be reflected in an immediate decrease in exhaustion. It may be that feelings of exhaustion remain high during the first phase of the vacation, but decline towards the end of a vacation. Then, high exhaustion scores would be observed when taking the measures during the first days of the vacation. Moreover, not all recovery outcomes can be adequately measured during a recovery episode. For example, it does not make much sense to assess job-related tension during a vacation. However, when researchers are interested in affective states, in the activities people engage in, or in the specific experiences they have during a recovery episode, it is useful to assess these affective states, activities and experiences during the recovery episode (Fritz & Sonnentag, 2006), thereby facing the challenge of not putting a burden on the participants during the recovery episode.

It is important to note that the setting and other conditions for completing the measures should be identical before and after the recovery episode. For example, study participants should respond to surveys either at the workplace or at home before and after the recovery episode. When it comes to the assessment of physiological data, comparability of the measurement situation is particularly critical. Also the time of the day of data collection should be identical before and after the recovery episode not only for physiological measures as they follow a strong circadian rhythm, but also for psychological measures (people are generally in different moods immediately after awakening than when they come home from work or just before going to bed). Consequently, not all types of recovery settings can be equally well examined with a quasi-experimental pre–post design. Since one cannot simply compare affect or physiological parameters immediately after work (prerecovery) with affect or physiological parameters at bedtime or in the next morning (postrecovery), this approach is less suitable for addressing recovery during free evenings of regular work weeks.

Experiments
Recovery research can also build on true experiments with random assignment of study participants to study conditions. In fact, true experiments would be highly needed in recovery research in order to establish causality. However, true experiments are (still) rather rare. Random assignment of study participants to various experimental conditions is most feasible in a laboratory research context, but also field experiments are an option.

An experimental research tradition relevant for recovery is sleep research (see also Åkerstedt, Nilsson, and Kecklund in this volume). To gain a better understanding about the processes and outcomes of sleep as a recovery mechanism, a typical approach in sleep research is to prevent study participants from sleeping. Sleep prevention studies, often implemented with experimental designs, showed that severe sleep loss impairs human functioning (Pilcher & Huffcutt, 1996). Thus, because it is difficult to experimentally manipulate long and good sleep, one tries to draw inferences about recovery by sleep from studies manipulating the lack of sleep. Also studies in the tradition of environmental psychology used experimental designs to examine the effects of various environmental contexts on recovery (Bodin & Hartig, 2003; Hartig et al., 2003).

When designing a true experiment on recovery, one has to decide about the most appropriate recovery manipulation. One of the core conceptual and theoretical questions is whether to operationalize recovery as the absence of any demand (or stressor) or as a more specific recovery process (e.g., psychological detachment from demands, relaxation, or exposure to a natural environment). These questions and the associated decisions are far from being trivial. For example, with respect to the first option, one should try to ensure that the manipulation is really just the absence of a demand – and does not at the same time pose additional demands on the study participant (e.g., when assigning a "distraction" task). In addition, the choice of an adequate control group is crucial. For example, one might choose exposure to a demand or a stressor as the control manipulation. However, the problem with such an approach is that it is difficult to decide if any differences found between the experimental and the control group are due to the absence of a demand in the experimental group or presence of another demand in the control group. Thus, in the end, the outcomes of such a study could also be interpreted as the effects of different demands, and not as the effects of recovery. Such ambiguities, however, can be reduced when following the second option of directly manipulating specific recovery processes. When designing a true experiment on recovery, it is important to have a stressor phase before manipulating recovery. It is necessary that before the onset of the recovery manipulation, study participants show strain reactions caused by the stressor. Without such a stressor phase, by definition, no recovery can occur.

Intervention Studies as Experiments and Quasi-Experiments
Also intervention studies can be designed as true experiments or quasi-experiments. Mostly, vacations and free weekends occur as "natural" events

in most people's lives and researchers can track changes in affect, mental health, or performance as co-occurring during or after vacations or free weekends. In addition to these observations of such "natural" recovery episodes, researchers can also actively implement recovery experiences in intervention efforts. The outcomes of such intervention efforts can be evaluated by using quasi-experiments or even true experiments.

For example, such intervention efforts might imply providing a "recovery training" for persons experiencing high levels of job stress. During such a training, participants can learn how to relax and how to increase positive experiences during free time (Weh, 2006; Weh & Sonnentag, 2007). Another option for a recovery intervention could refer to organizational efforts that aim at increasing recovery. Changing the break regime within the organization or providing better break facilities (e.g., for engaging in sport during lunch break or quiet rooms for relaxation or meditation) are typical examples of such organization-based interventions that potentially increase recovery. In practical terms, one should try to ensure that following the intervention program is not an additional burden for the participants (e.g., because it adds to their already busy schedules).

When evaluating the benefits of such interventions in a quasi-experiment, it is important to collect data before and after the intervention. Again, adequate timing of the measurement points is crucial. Particularly, with respect to the postintervention measure one should try not only to assess short-term outcomes, but also to look at the long-term changes, as some of the positive effects might take time to unfold – but also because some of the effects might be only short-lived. Here, one has to carefully monitor if study participants still use and adhere to the interventions implemented; in addition, it is important to assess other changes in the organization and in people's lives to rule out alternative explanations for changes in the outcome – or to account for a lack of any change. Ideally, also here the study design should include a control group. However, particularly within organizational settings, this is difficult to implement. Semmer (2006) provides some guidelines about issues to be considered in intervention studies.

In most cases, intervention studies follow a quasi-experimental approach because it is difficult to randomly assign persons to the invention (i.e., experimental) and the control condition. However, implementing waiting control groups to which participants are randomly assigned is a way to increase methodological rigor. Nevertheless, particularly in field settings, it will be difficult to hold all conditions and processes – except the manipulation – constant for all study participants over longer periods of time.

Diary Studies

When researchers are interested in examining relatively short-term recovery processes in field settings they may want to use diary study designs. We refer here to diary studies as a broad category of study designs that include measurements over a period of several (consecutive) days in the participants' natural environment (Bolger, Davis, & Rafaeli, 2003). Most often, there is more than one measurement occasion per day (e.g., in the morning, after work, at bedtime).

More fine-grained assessments with more frequent measurements per day can be done by using the experience-sampling methodology (Csikszentmihalyi & LeFevre, 1989; Minor, Glomb, & Hulin, 2005) or ecological momentary assessments that include the registration of physiological indicators (Stone & Shiffman, 2002). The approach of asking people to report on fixed (e.g., every hour) or random (e.g., on various unpredictable) time points during the (working) day is known as the *Experience Sampling Method*. This approach is an intensive but fruitful way of measuring temporal fluctuations during the course of the (working) day not only in thoughts (thought sampling), but also in events (event sampling) and in mood (mood sampling). With fixed or stratified random time intervals during the (work)day, workers are asked, after hearing a signal (e.g., a beep) to report about what thoughts have occurred to them since the last beep, what happened since the last beep and how they felt just before the beep. One of the major advantages of this approach is that researchers do not have to rely on the (possibly biased) retrospective recall of experiences (for a detailed discussion on this approach, see Beal and Weiss (2003) and Reis and Gable (2000)).

Another option is to move the level of analysis from the day level to the week level. Such an approach would imply the assessment of recovery processes and outcomes over several weeks with one or more assessments per week. Again, it is important to keep the time of measurement (especially time of the day) as constant as possible during the observation period in order to prevent that the effects could easily be explained by diurnal or weekly rhythms.

When planning a diary study there are several issues to consider. The most crucial ones refer to the data collection protocol, the measures to be taken, the data collection devices and the data analysis issues. We will cover these issues in this section.

Data Collection Protocols

One major advantage of the diary approach is that it allows for assessing "life as it is lived" (Bolger et al., 2003, p. 579). Therefore, one should strive to collect the data in close temporal connection to the events or experiences one is interested in. Thus, assessing retrospective data once a day would be too "rough" when being interested in the processes occurring during the day. Here, an experience sampling approach might be most appropriate (Reis & Gable, 2000), but also implementing three to four measurement occasions per day may provide interesting data. Reis and Gable (2000) provide an overview of more specific recording protocols (interval-contingent (i.e., time-contingent), signal-contingent, event-contingent; see also Bolger et al. (2003)).

Often, one might strive for sampling as many days per person as possible. Indeed, there are impressive studies – although not necessarily about recovery – that succeeded in assessing diary data over the course of several months (Fuller et al., 2003). However, when planning data collection one should be realistic about the number of days that are feasible for study participants and that do not compromise compliance. Moreover, one should take into consideration that the collection of diary data over longer courses of time may constitute an intervention in itself (Burt, 1994) that may have an impact on the study findings. Therefore, in most cases, collection periods should not be longer than two to four weeks (cf. also Burt, 1994; Wheeler & Reis, 1991). Reis and Gable (2000) suggest that when one measurement per day is taken, each measurement period should not exceed 5–7 min. As it is often desirable to have more measurement occasions per day, one should strive for even shorter assessment durations.

Measures
It is rather self-evident that measures taken in diary studies should be short, as it is not feasible that study participants respond to 15-item measures of each of several constructs several times per day. Nevertheless, reliability and validity of the measures must not be compromised. Thus, pilot testing is often needed. Researchers do not agree whether one-item measures should be used. Recently, one-item measures with good face validity have been developed (Sonnenschein, Sorbi, van Doornen, Schaufeli, & Maas, 2007; Van Hooff et al., 2007b). For example, Van Hooff et al. (2007b) demonstrated that a single-item measure of fatigue was equally valid as a well-tested 6-item fatigue measure, making it a very useful and attractive tool to measure day-level fatigue. Nevertheless, the construct validity of many diary measures should still be demonstrated (Bolger et al., 2003).

Data Collection Devices
Another important question to be answered when planning a diary study refers to data collection devices, or as Green and coworkers termed it

"paper or plastic?" (Green, Rafaeli, Bolger, Shrout, & Reis, 2006). Nowadays researchers can choose between paper-based and electronic data collection devices. Paper-based instruments are usually small booklets that study participants carry with them over the course of data collection. Typical electronic data collection devices comprise pocket computers or mobile phones. One can expect that during the years to come, more technical innovations may become available for data collection purposes (Song, Foo, & Uy, 2008). In addition to such paper-based and electronic devices that study participants carry with them, diary studies may be also implemented through the internet or a company intranet. Data collection through the internet or an intranet requires that study participants have easy access to the internet or the intranet at all required measurement occasions. For example, employees who work at many different locations (without internet or intranet access at every location) may not be able to provide reliable data; in addition – and more specific for research on recovery – data collection through the internet requires that all study participants have internet facilities in their homes and are willing to use them there at bedtime, or in the early morning right after awakening, or right before leaving home, or right after coming home. A major advantage of electronic data collection devices (and data collection through the internet) is that compliance with the study protocol (i.e., exact time of responding to the diaries) can be tracked.

Approaches to Data Analysis
Diary studies offer multiple opportunities for analyzing the data, depending on the specific research question pursued. Maybe the two most straightforward options for data analysis refer to within-person analysis that focuses at day-level processes and to between-person analysis that tries to capture changes within persons over the period of several days. Most of the existing recovery studies using the diary approach followed the first option. Typically, these studies aim to predict within-person variation in recovery outcomes from variables indicating specific recovery activities or processes (Sonnentag & Bayer, 2005; Sonnentag & Natter, 2004) or aim at predicting work-related variables from recovery outcomes (Bakker, Van Emmerik, Geurts, & Demerouti, 2008; Sonnentag, 2003).

The data structure with days nested within persons asks for a statistical procedure that takes the interdependence of data into account. Hierarchical linear modeling (also known as the multi-level modeling) meets this requirement and is often used in recovery studies (Bryk & Raudenbush, 1992; Snijders & Bosker, 1999).

To focus on within-person processes and to rule out between-person variance in predictor variables, predictor variables can be centered at the specific person mean (for centering decisions in multi-level research, see Hofmann and Gavin (1998)). This approach involves the comparison of several days with one another within the same person; differences between persons are neglected. For example, a study using such a centering procedure can provide an answer to the question of whether people feel better at bedtime on days *when* they have detached from their job during the evening (as opposed to days when they have not detached). But the study will be mute about the question of whether people who detach more from work will generally feel better. If one wishes to address the latter question in diary research, data should be centered around the grand mean.

The second option of analyzing trajectories of change over several days promises answers to different types of questions. For example, it is interesting to know if well-being or job performance gradually deteriorate over the course of a working week when lack of recovery accumulates over the course of this week. One might also want to know if specific person or work situation variables have an impact on the trajectories of change over the course of one or more weeks. These kinds of questions can be answered with growth curve modeling approaches (Duncan, 1999). One of the prerequisites for taking advantage of this analysis is that one has at least three consecutive data points for all study participants. More complex research questions require more data points. As an alternative to growth curve modeling, one might also consider conducting time series analysis to capture change over time (Fuller et al., 2003).

An additional interesting option for improving our understanding of the recovery phenomenon refers to the combination of within-person and between-person data. In less technical terms, testing interactions between chronic working conditions or personality variables on the one hand and specific recovery events or processes on the other is very promising. For example, Semmer, Grebner, and Elfering (2004) provided examples how the different kind of data might be combined.

Longitudinal Studies

Until now, most research on job stress recovery is correlational or quasi-experimental in nature, or it examines short-term processes with diary approaches (Demerouti, Taris, & Bakker, 2007; Gump & Matthews, 2000; Kivimäki et al., 2006). To learn more about whether recovery has long-term benefits, longitudinal studies covering longer observation periods are needed. For example, a research question to be addressed in such a longitudinal study could be if specific recovery experiences (e.g., psychological detachment from one's work during leisure time) are related to an increase in psychological well-being over time or if specific recovery experiences may even buffer the negative consequences of highly stressful jobs.

Longitudinal studies should at least have two measurement occasions; the "initial" levels of the variables included as outcome variables should be assessed so that it is possible to examine change in the outcome variable over time (and therefore exclude some alternative interpretations). However, we should realize that these "initial" levels will at the same time be the outcome of changes that have happened before the researchers started to measure these levels. In other words, initial levels are never true initial levels as if individual life has just started (Kasl & Jones, 2003).

A core question in the design of longitudinal studies refers to the best time lag by which the several measurement waves should be separated (Mitchell & James, 2001). Often, time lags in longitudinal research seem to be chosen rather arbitrarily and often seem to be too long to detect any change (Dormann, 2007). Therefore, it is highly important to come up with theoretical models about how long specific processes need to unfold (Mitchell & James, 2001; Taris & Kompier, 2003). With respect to recovery, these models are still lacking. Research on lack of recovery suggests that recovery takes place within several time frames, with some happening within very short time frames such as hours (Linden et al., 1997), and others having their effects unfold over much longer periods such as weeks, months (Demerouti et al., 2007; Van Hooff et al., 2005) or even years (Kivimäki et al., 2006).

Longitudinal studies put substantial demands on researchers who are planning and conducting such a study. For example, it is necessary to include measures that prevent participant dropout and to exclude (or at least track) external factors influencing the processes to be studied. Specific approaches to data analysis such as structural equation modeling ask for relatively large sample sizes. Reviews of typical problems encountered in longitudinal research (and ways to overcome them) are available (Taris & Kompier, 2003; Zapf, Dormann, & Frese, 1996).

Combination of Several Approaches

It is important to note that the various study design options described in this section must not be seen in isolation. Of course, all kinds of combinations are possible. For example, one might think about conducting a quasi-experimental study on vacations and combine this design with the use of diaries, implying that the pre- and post-measurements are not taken once or twice before and after the vacation, but on a daily basis over the course of one or two weeks before and after the vacation. Similarly, one can also imagine having a diary study covering one or two weeks nested in a "true" longitudinal study.

CONCLUSIONS AND IMPLICATIONS FOR FUTURE RECOVERY STUDIES

In this chapter, we have provided an overview of the most important methodological issues within recovery research. In this section, we will highlight some of the points that are most relevant for researchers who want to learn more about recovery.

As described in this chapter, we believe that it is particularly important to differentiate between various specific perspectives on recovery: recovery setting, recovery processes and recovery outcomes. In real life, recovery setting, recovery processes and recovery outcomes are closely linked. Researchers should be explicit about the perspective they take in their specific study and the question they want to answer. For instance, if one interested in the effects of spending time in a specific potentially recovery-providing setting (e.g., a vacation) or is one interested in the recovery process itself (i.e., the mechanisms that lead to unwinding and the restoration of strained resources) or does one mainly focus on specific recovery outcomes such as affective state or level of physiological activation? It must not be taken for granted that in a prototypical recovery setting (e.g., during a vacation) recovery processes (e.g., detachment from work) or positive outcomes (e.g., reduction of strain) will occur. Most probably, empirical studies on recovery will combine at least two of the perspectives; ideally, one might strive for an integration of the three perspectives. For example, one might want to examine the recovery processes occurring during weekends that lead to increased positive affect at the beginning of the next working week.

When it comes to study designs, many options are available that have specific advantages and disadvantages; thus, there is no one best way to design a recovery study. We suggest using a range of different study design options in a research program. For example, for examining long-term outcomes of (lack of) recovery, longitudinal field studies covering longer observation periods are most appropriate; for investigating the effects of specific underlying recovery mechanisms on physiological indicators, controlled laboratory studies are better suited. Daily surveys might be most suitable for assessing recovery cycles in people's everyday lives. We believe that the combination of the various design approaches will help to arrive at a more comprehensive picture of the recovery phenomenon. It will be a great challenge in future studies to integrate findings from the distinct research settings, implying that findings referring to different time frames and different indicators of recovery outcomes have to be combined into one overall picture.

It is crucial to have sensitive measures to assess recovery processes and recovery outcomes; until now, most recovery-process measures are self-report instruments. Within some study contexts it might be desirable to have assessments provided by significant others or to use more objective measures. A first attempt to use spouse reports of psychological detachment from work has been undertaken (Sonnentag & Kruel, 2006). However, the question remains as to whether people can provide valid assessment of others' recovery processes – beyond pure reports of activities. If one wants to move beyond ratings and if one strives for collecting more objective data on recovery processes, for example physiological data, one should realize that disentangling the recovery *process* from the recovery *outcome* will not be possible.

With respect to outcome measures of recovery, several aspects are important. First, recovery-outcome measures should be sensitive enough to capture small changes in strain (i.e., recovery) levels in a reliable way. Second, it is necessary to have measures that properly reflect the time frame of the specific recovery setting; for example, recovery outcomes after a free weekend might be more subtle (and therefore more difficult to detect) than recovery outcomes after a two-week vacation. Maybe, recovery outcomes resulting from different recovery settings not only differ in magnitude, but also in quality. For example, spending an evening with friends in a nice restaurant might increase positive affect and might restore affective resources, but may not be sufficient for physiological resources that need longer times off in order to recover. Here, not only methodological refinements, but also more conceptual work is needed. Third, measures of recovery outcomes ideally address both physiological and psychological (e.g., affective) aspects of recovery. As our knowledge about recovery processes is still very limited it must not be taken for granted that psychological recovery in terms of affective changes mirrors physiological recovery of, for instance, the cardiovascular system. Low agreement between the various indicators of recovery outcomes might not necessarily reflect poor measurement, but might point to more complex underlying processes.

When it comes to more practical measurement issues, it is particularly important to have reliable and valid measures that can be used in field settings with repeated measurements; technical devices that assess both psychological as well as physiological indicators will help a lot. However, also the fanciest technical devices do not make the need for proper measurement development obsolete.

Analyzing complex recovery data is still a challenge for many researchers. In our view, two aspects warrant particular attention. First, it is important to differentiate between between-person and within-person processes – and ideally to combine these two processes in one study. Recovery processes and associated recovery outcomes differ between persons; for example, person A may be healthier and perform better at work because he or she enjoys better recovery processes than person B. In addition, person A may feel better and be more active at work after weekends that he or she spends in the mountains or at the seaside as opposed to weekends spent at home. To make things even more complex, it might be that within-person variation exists only for persons who already are relatively better off, whereas others cannot take advantage of the small benefits of favorable recovery processes (Sonnentag & Niessen, 2008). Hierarchical linear modeling approaches allow for testing more complex patterns (Snijders & Bosker, 1999). Second, we suggest that researchers should also pay more attention to cyclical processes. When thinking about recovery in the more traditional way, we assume that recovery processes precede and predict recovery outcomes such as affect or low physiological strain. However, most probably recovery "outcomes" may also influence subsequent recovery processes. For example, when feeling energetic and lively after a satisfying weekend, one may decide to spend the evenings during the week also in a more active way or to exercise more. This activity in turn probably fosters future recovery outcomes. To examine such more complex processes, (multi-level) structural equation modeling offers a promising approach.

Without doubt, methodological issues are of paramount importance to move research on recovery forward. If we do not succeed in disentangling the complexities of various recovery indicators and time frames, and if we are not able to shed at least some light on the causality issue, our knowledge about recovery will remain rather limited. At the same time, proper methodology helps little when conceptual and theoretical questions are not addressed adequately. Moreover, as we have tried to illustrate in this last section, decisions about the most appropriate methodology are very closely intertwined with the concepts and theories underlying the notion of recovery. Therefore, improvements in research methodologies must go hand in hand with conceptual refinements and further developments of theoretical approaches to recovery.

REFERENCES

Åkerstedt, T., Hume, K., Minors, D., & Waterhouse, J. (1994). The meaning of good sleep: Longitudinal study of polysomnography and subjective sleep quality. *Journal of Sleep Research, 3*, 152–158.

Bakker, A. B., van Emmerik, I. H., Geurts, S. A. E., & Demerouti, E. (2008). *Recovery turns job demands into challenges: A diary study on work engagement and performance.* Working Paper. Erasmus University Rotterdam.

Beal, D. J., & Weiss, H. M. (2003). Methods of ecological momentary assessment in organizational research. *Organizational Research Methods, 6*, 440–464.

Beckers, D. G. J., Van der Linden, D., Smulders, P. G. W., Kompier, M. A. J., Taris, T. W., & Geurts, S. A. E. (2008). Voluntary or involuntary? Control over overtime and rewards for overtime in relation to fatigue and work satisfaction. *Work & Stress, 22*, 33–50.

Belkic, K. L., Landsbergis, P. A., Schnall, P. L., & Baker, D. (2004). Is job strain a major source of cardiovascular disease risk? *Scandinavian Journal of Work, Environment and Health, 30*, 85–128.

Binnewies, C., Sonnentag, S., & Mojza, E. J. (2009). Daily performance at work: Feeling recovered in the morning as a predictor of day-level job performance. *Journal of Organizational Behavior, 30*, 67–93.

Bodin, M., & Hartig, T. (2003). Does the outdoor environment matter for psychological restoration gained through running? *Psychology of Sport and Exercise, 4*, 141–153.

Bolger, N., Davis, A., & Rafaeli, E. (2003). Diary methods: Capturing life as it is lived. *Annual Review of Psychology, 54*, 579–616.

Boswell, W. R., & Olson-Buchanon, J. B. (2007). The use of communications technologies after hours: The role of work attitudes and work–life conflict. *Journal of Management, 33*, 592–610.

Brosschot, J. F., Van Dijk, E., & Thayer, J. F. (2007). Daily worry is related to low heart rate variability during waking and the subsequent nocturnal sleep period. *International Journal of Psychophysiology, 63*, 39–47.

Bryk, A. S., & Raudenbush, S. W. (1992). *Hierarchical linear models: Application and data analysis methods.* Newbury Park, CA: Sage.

Burns, J. W. (2006). Arousal of negative emotions and symptom-specific reactivity in chronic low back pain patients. *Emotion, 6*, 309–318.

Burt, C. D. B. (1994). Prospective and retrospective account-making in diary entries: A model of anxiety reduction and avoidance. *Anxiety, Stress and Coping: An International Journal, 6*, 327–340.

Buysse, D. J., Reynolds, C. F., Monk, T. H., Berman, S. R., & Kupfer, D. J. (1989). Pittsburgh sleep quality index (PSQI). *Psychiatry Research, 28*, 193–213.

Campbell, J. P., McCloy, R. A., Oppler, S. H., & Sager, C. E. (1993). A theory of performance. In: E. Schmitt, W. C. Borman, & Associates (Eds), *Personnel selection in organizations* (pp. 35–70). San Francisco: Jossey-Bass.

Craig, A., & Cooper, R. E. (1992). Symptoms of acute and chronic fatigue. In: A. P. Smith & D. M. Jones (Eds), *Handbook of human performance* (Vol. 3, pp. 289–339). London: Academic Press.

Cropley, M., Dijk, D.-J., & Stanley, N. (2006). Job strain, work rumination and sleep in school teachers. *European Journal of Work and Organizational Psychology, 15*, 181–196.

Cropley, M., & Purvis, L. J. M. (2003). Job strain and rumination about work issues during leisure time: A diary study. *European Journal of Work and Organizational Psychology, 12*, 195–207.

Csikszentmihalyi, M., & LeFevre, J. (1989). Optimal experience in work and leisure. *Journal of Personality and Social Psychology, 56*, 815–822.

Davidson, O. B. (2006). *Sabbatical leave as "time out" from chronic job stress: Embedding stress-respite research within conservation of resources theory.* Unpublished Dissertation, Tel Aviv University, Tel Aviv.

De Bloom, J., Kompier, M. A. J., Geurts, S. A. E., De Weerth, C., Taris, T., & Sonnentag, S. (2009). Do we recover from vacation? Meta-analysis of vacation effects on health and well-being. *Journal of Occupational Health, 51*(1), 13–25.

De Croon, E. M., Sluiter, J. K., & Frings-Dresen (2006). Psychometric properties of the need for recovery after work scale: Test–retest reliability and sensitivity to detect change. *Occupational and Environmental Medicine, 63*, 202–206.

De Geus, E. J. C., Willemsen, G. H. M., Klaver, C. H. A. M., & Van Doornen, L. J. P. (1995). Ambulatory measurement of respiratory sinus arrhythmia and respiration rate. *Biological Psychology, 41*, 205–227.

Demerouti, E., Taris, T. W., & Bakker, A. B. (2007). Need for recovery, home–work interference and performance: Is lack of concentration the link? *Journal of Vocational Behavior, 71*, 204–220.

Dickerson, S. S., & Kemeny, M. E. (2004). Acute stressors and cortisol responses: A theoretical integration and synthesis of laboratory research. *Psychological Bulletin, 130*, 355–391.

Dormann, C. (2007). Sustainable WO-psychology research: An illusion? Why short-term effects matter more! *Presentation at the Eighth European Congress of Work and Organizational Psychology.*

Duncan, T. E. (1999). *An introduction to latent variable growth curve modeling: Concepts, issues, and applications.* Mahwah, NJ: Erlbaum.

Eden, D. (2001). Job stress and respite relief: Overcoming high-tech tethers. In: P. L. Perrewé & D. C. Ganster (Eds), *Research in occupational stress and well-being: Exploring theoretical mechanisms and perspectives* (pp. 143–194). New York: JAI Press.

Etzion, D., Eden, D., & Lapidot, Y. (1998). Relief from job stressors and burnout: Reserve service as a respite. *Journal of Applied Psychology, 83*, 577–585.

Fredrickson, B. L. (1998). What good are positive emotions? *Review of General Psychology, 2*, 300–319.

Fredrickson, B. L., Mancuso, R. A., Branigan, C., & Tugade, M. M. (2000). The undoing effect of positive emotions. *Motivation and Emotion, 24*, 237–258.

Frese, M., Fay, D., Hilburger, T., Leng, K., & Tag, A. (1997). The concept of personal initiative: Operationalization, reliability and validity in two German samples. *Journal of Occupational and Organizational Psychology, 70*, 139–161.

Fritz, C., & Sonnentag, S. (2005). Recovery, health, and job performance: Effects of weekend experiences. *Journal of Occupational Health Psychology, 10*, 187–199.

Fritz, C., & Sonnentag, S. (2006). Recovery, well-being, and performance-related outcomes: The role of workload and vacation experiences. *Journal of Applied Psychology, 91*, 936–945.

Fuller, J. A., Stanton, J. M., Fisher, G. G., Spitzmüller, C., Russell, S. S., & Smith, P. C. (2003). A lengthy look at the daily grind: Time series analyses of events, mood, stress, and satisfaction. *Journal of Applied Psychology, 88*, 1019–1033.

Gerin, W., Davidson, K. W., Christenfeld, N. J. S., Goyal, T., & Schwartz, J. E. (2006). The role of angry rumination and distraction in blood pressure recovery from emotional arousal. *Psychosomatic Medicine, 68*, 64–72.

Geurts, S. A. E., & Demerouti, E. (2003). Work/non-work interface: A review of theories and findings. In: M. J. Schabracq (Ed.), *The handbook of work and health psychology* (pp. 279–312). Chichester, UK: Wiley.

Geurts, S. A. E., & Sonnentag, S. (2006). Recovery as an explanatory mechanism in the relation between acute stress reactions and chronic health impairment. *Scandinavian Journal of Work, Environment and Health, 32*, 482–492.

Green, A. S., Rafaeli, E., Bolger, N., Shrout, P. E., & Reis, H. T. (2006). Paper or plastic? Data equivalence in paper and electronic diaries. *Psychological Methods, 11*, 87–105.

Gump, B. B., & Matthews, K. A. (2000). Are vacations good for your health? The 9-year mortality experience after the multiple risk factor intervention trial. *Psychosomatic Medicine, 62*, 608–612.

Harma, M. (2006). Working hours: Associations to work stress, recovery and health. *Scandinavian Journal of Work Environment and Health, 32*, 502–514.

Hartig, T., Evans, G. W., Jamner, L. D., Davis, D. S., & Gärling, T. (2003). Tracking restoration in natural and urban field settings. *Journal of Environmental Psychology, 23*, 109–123.

Hartig, T., Mang, M., & Evens, G. W. (1991). Restorative effects of natural environment experience. *Environment and Behavior, 23*, 3–26.

Hockey, G. R. J. (1997). Compensatory control in the regulation of human performance under stress and high workload: A cognitive-energetical framework. *Biological Psychology, 45*, 73–93.

Hofmann, D. A., & Gavin, M. B. (1998). Centering decisions in hierarchical linear models: Implications for research in organizations. *Journal of Management, 24*, 623–641.

Jansen, N. W. H., Kant, I., & van den Brandt, P. A. (2002). Need for recovery in the working population: Description and associations with fatigue and psychological distress. *International Journal of Behavioral Medicine, 9*, 322–340.

Kaplan, S. (1995). The restorative benefits of nature: Toward an integrative framework. *Journal of Environmental Psychology, 15*, 169–182.

Kaplan, S., Bardwell, L. V., & Slakter, D. B. (1993). The museum as a restorative environment. *Environment and Behavior, 25*, 725–742.

Kasl, S. V., & Jones, B. A. (2003). An epidemiological perspective on research design, measurement, and surveillance strategies. In: J. C. Quick & L. E. Tetrick (Eds), *Handbook of occupational health psychology* (pp. 379–398). Washington, DC: American Psychological Association.

Kivimäki, M., Leino-Arjas, P., Kaila-Kangas, L., Lukkonen, R., Vahtera, J., Elovainio, M., Härmä, M., & Kirjonen, J. (2006). Is incomplete recovery from work a risk marker of cardiovascular death? Prospective evidence from industrial employees. *Psychosomatic Medicine, 68,* 402–407.

Kühnel, J., Sonnentag, S., & Westman, M. (in press). Does work engagement increase after a short respite? The role of job involvement as a double-edged sword. *Journal of Occupational and Organizational Psychology.* DOI: 10.1348/096317908X349362.

Kuiper, J. I., Van der Beck, A. J., & Meijman, T. F. (1998). Psychosomatic complaints and unwinding of sympathoadrenal activation after work. *Stress Medicine, 14,* 7–12.

Linden, W., Earle, T. L., Gerin, W., & Christenfeld, N. (1997). Physiological stress reactivity and recovery: Conceptual siblings separated at birth? *Journal of Psychosomatic Research, 42,* 117–135.

McEwen, B. S. (1998). Stress, adaptation, and disease: Allostasis and allostatic load. *Annals of the New York Academy of Sciences, 840,* 33–44.

McNair, D. M., Lorr, M., & Droppelman, L. F. (1971). *Edits manual for the profile of mood states.* San Diego, CA: Educational and Industrial Testing Service.

Michielsen, H. J., De Vries, J., & Van Hecke, G. L. (2003). Psychometric qualities of a brief self-rated fatigue measure: The fatigue assessment scale (fas). *Journal of Psychosomatic Research, 54,* 345–352.

Minor, A. G., Glomb, T. M., & Hulin, C. (2005). Experience sampling mood and its correlates. *Journal of Occupational and Organizational Psychology, 78,* 171–193.

Mitchell, T. R., & James, L. R. (2001). Building better theory: Time and the specification of when things happen. *Academy of Management Review, 26,* 530–547.

Pilcher, J. J., & Huffcutt, A. I. (1996). Effects of sleep deprivation on performance: A meta-analysis. *Sleep, 19,* 318–326.

Pruessner, J. C., Hellhammer, D. H., & Kirschbaum, C. (1999). Low self-esteem, induced failure and the adrenocortical stress response. *Personality and Individual Differences, 27,* 477–489.

Rau, R., Georgiades, A., Fredrikson, M., Lemne, C., & de Faire, U. (2001). Psychosocial work characteristics and perceived control in relation to cardiovascular rewind at night. *Journal of Occupational Health Psychology, 6,* 171–181.

Rau, R., & Triemer, A. (2004). Overtime in relation to blood pressure and mood during work, leisure, and night time. *Social Indicators Research, 67,* 51–73.

Reis, H. T., & Gable, S. L. (2000). Event-sampling and other methods for studying everyday experience. In: T. H. Reis & M. C. Judd (Eds), *Handbook of research methods in social and personality psychology* (pp. 190–222). New York: Cambridge University Press.

Rook, J. W., & Zijlstra, F. R. H. (2006). The contribution of various types of activities to recovery. *European Journal of Work and Organizational Psychology, 15,* 218–240.

Saxbe, D. E., Repetti, R. L., & Nishina, A. (2008). Marital satisfaction, recovery from work, and diurnal cortisol among men and women. *Health Psychology, 27,* 15–25.

Schaufeli, W. B., & Van Dierendonck, D. (2000). *UBOS, Utrechtse Burnout Schaal.* The Netherlands, Lisse: Swets & Zeitlinger B.V.

Scott, B. A., & Judge, T. A. (2006). Insomnia, emotions, and job satisfaction: A multilevel study. *Journal of Management, 32,* 622–645.

Semmer, N. K. (2006). Job stress interventions and the organization of work. *Scandinavian Journal of Work Environment and Health, 32,* 515–527.

Semmer, N. K., Grebner, S., & Elfering, A. (2004). Beyond self-report: Using observational, physiological, and situation-based measures in research on occupational stress. In: P. L. Perrewé & D. C. Ganster (Eds), Research in Occupational Stress and

Well-being. *Emotional and physiological processes and positive intervention strategies* (Vol. 3, pp. 207–263). Amsterdam: JAI.

Shadish, W. R., Cook, T. D., & Campbell, D. T. (2001). *Experimental and quasi-experimental designs for generalized causal inference.* Boston: Houghton Mifflin.

Sluiter, J. K., Frings-Dresen, M. H. W., van der Beek, A. J., & Meijman, T. F. (2001). The relation between work-induced neuroendocrine reactivity and recovery, subjective need for recovery, and health status. *Journal of Psychosomatic Research, 50,* 29–37.

Smith, C. S., Folkard, S., & Fuller, J. A. (2003). Shiftwork and working hours. In: J. C. Quick & L. E. Tetrick (Eds), *Handbook of occupational health psychology* (pp. 163–183). Washington, DC: American Psychological Association.

Snijders, T. A. B., & Bosker, R. J. (1999). *Multilevel analysis. An introduction to basic and advanced multilevel modeling.* London: Sage.

Song, Z., Foo, M.-D., & Uy, M. A. (2008). Mood spillover and crossover among dual-earner couples: A cell phone event sampling study. *Journal of Applied Psychology, 93,* 443–452.

Sonnenschein, M., Sorbi, M. J., van Doornen, L. J. P., Schaufeli, W. B., & Maas, C. J. M. (2007). Electronic diary evidence on energy erosion in clinical burnout. *Journal of Occupational Health Psychology, 12,* 402–413.

Sonnentag, S. (2001). Work, recovery activities, and individual well-being: A diary study. *Journal of Occupational Health Psychology, 6,* 196–210.

Sonnentag, S. (2003). Recovery, work engagement, and proactive behavior: A new look at the interface between non-work and work. *Journal of Applied Psychology, 88,* 518–528.

Sonnentag, S., & Bayer, U.-V. (2005). Switching off mentally: Predictors and consequences of psychological detachment from work during off-job time. *Journal of Occupational Health Psychology, 10,* 393–414.

Sonnentag, S., Binnewies, C., & Mojza, E. J. (2008). Did you have a nice evening? A day-level study on recovery experiences, sleep, and affect. *Journal of Applied Psychology, 93,* 674–684.

Sonnentag, S., & Fritz, C. (2006). Endocrinological processes associated with job stress: Catecholamine and cortisol responses to acute and chronic stressors. In: P. L. Perrewé & D. C. Ganster (Eds), *Research in organizational stress and well-being: Employee health, coping and methodologies* (pp. 1–59). Amsterdam: Elsevier.

Sonnentag, S., & Fritz, C. (2007). The recovery experience questionnaire: Development and validation of a measure assessing recuperation and unwinding at work. *Journal of Occupational Health Psychology, 12,* 204–221.

Sonnentag, S., & Kruel, U. (2006). Psychological detachment from work during off-job time: The role of job stressors, job involvement, and recovery-related self-efficacy. *European Journal of Work and Organizational Psychology, 15,* 197–217.

Sonnentag, S., & Natter, E. (2004). Flight attendants' daily recovery from work: Is there no place like home? *International Journal of Stress Management, 11,* 366–391.

Sonnentag, S., & Niessen, C. (2008). Staying vigorous until work is over: The role of trait vigor, day-specific work experiences and recovery. *Journal of Occupational and Organizational Psychology, 81,* 435–458.

Sonnentag, S., & Zijlstra, F. R. H. (2006). Job characteristics and off-job activities as predictors of need for recovery, well-being, and fatigue. *Journal of Applied Psychology, 91,* 330–350.

Stone, A. A., & Shiffman, S. (2002). Capturing momentary, self-report data: A proposal for reporting guideline. *Annals of Behavioral Medicine, 24*, 236–243.

Strauss-Blasche, G., Reithofer, B., Schobersberger, W., Ekmekcioglu, C., & Marktl, W. (2005). Effect of vacation on health: Moderating factors of vacation outcome. *Journal of Travel Medicine, 12*, 94–101.

Strauss-Blasche, G., Riedmann, B., Schobersberger, W., Ekmekcioglu, C., Riedmann, G., Waanders, R., Fries, D., Mittermayr, M., Marktl, W., & Humpeler, E. (2004). Vacation at moderate and low altitude improves perceived health in individuals with metabolic syndrome. *Journal of Travel Medicine, 11*, 300–306.

Taris, T. W., & Kompier, M. A. J. (2003). Challenges in longitudinal designs in occupational health psychology. *Scandinavian Journal of Work Environment and Health, 29*, 1–4.

Trougakos, J. P., Beal, D. J., Green, S. G., & Weiss, H. M. (2008). Making the break count: An episodic examination of recovery activities, emotional experiences, and positive affective displays. *Academy of Management Journal, 51*, 131–146.

Tucker, P. (2003). The impact of rest breaks upon accident risk, fatigue and performance: A review. *Work and Stress, 17*, 123–137.

Van Diest, R. (1990). Subjective sleep characteristics as coronary risk factors, their association with Type A behaviour and vital exhaustion. *Journal of Psychosomatic Research, 34*, 415–426.

Van Hooff, M. L. M., Geurts, S. A. E., Kompier, M. A. J., & Taris, T. W. (2007a). Workdays, in-between workdays and the weekend: A diary study on effort and recovery. *International Archives of Occupational and Environmental Health, 80*, 599–613.

Van Hooff, M. L. M., Geurts, S. A. E., Kompier, M. A. J., Taris, T. W., Dikkers, J. S. E., & Houtman, I. L. D. (2005). Disentangling the causal relationships between work-home interference and employee health. *Scandinavian Journal of Work, Environment and Health, 31*, 15–29.

Van Hooff, M. L. M., Geurts, S. A. E., Taris, T. W., & Kompier, M. A. J. (2007b). "How fatigued do you currently feel?" Convergent and discriminant validity of a single-item fatigue measure. *Journal of Occupational Health, 49*, 224–234.

Van Veghel, N., De Jonge, J., Bosma, H., & Schaufeli, W. B. (2005). Reviewing the effort-reward imbalance model: Drawing up the balance of 45 empirical studies. *Social Science & Medicine, 60*, 1117–1131.

Van Veldhoven, M., & Broersen, S. (2003). Measurement quality and validity of the "need for recovery scale". *Occupational and Environmental Medicine, 60*, i3–i9.

Van Veldhoven, M., De Jonge, J., Broersen, S., Kompier, M., & Meijman, T. F. (2002). Specific relationships between psychosocial job-conditions and job-related stress: A three level analytic approach. *Work & Stress, 16*, 207–228.

Veldhuizen, I. J. T., Gaillard, A. W. K., & de Vriese, J. (2003). The influence of mental fatigue on facial EMG activity during a simulated workday. *Biological Psychology, 63*, 59–78.

Vrijkotte, T. G. M., Van Doornen, L. J. P., & De Geus, E. J. C. (2000). Effects of work stress on ambulatory blood pressure, heart rate, and heart rate variability. *Hypertension, 35*, 880–886.

Watson, D., & Clark, L. A. (1994). The PANAS-X. Manual for the positive and negative affect schedule. University of Iowa.

Watson, D., Clark, L. A., & Tellegen, A. (1988). Development and validation of brief measures of positive and negative affect: The panas-scales. *Journal of Personality and Social Psychology, 54*, 1063–1070.

Weh, S.-M. (2006). *Förderung individueller Erholungsprozesse: Ergebnisse einer Trainingsevaluation.* Dissertation, Technische Universität Braunschweig, Braunschweig.

Weh, S.-M., & Sonnentag, S. (2007). Positive experiences off the job: Results from an intervention study on changes in psychological well-being. Paper presented at the Annual Meeting of the Academy of Management, August, 2007, Philadelphia, PA.

Westman, M., & Eden, D. (1997). Effects of a respite from work on burnout: Vacation relief and fade-out. *Journal of Applied Psychology, 82,* 516–527.

Wheeler, L., & Reis, H. T. (1991). Self-recording of everyday life events: Origins, types, and uses. *Journal of Personality, 59,* 339–354.

Winwood, P. C., Bakker, A. B., & Winefield, A. H. (2007). An investigation of the role of non-work time behavior in buffering the effects of work strain. *Journal of Occupational and Environmental Medicine, 49,* 862–871.

Winwood, P. C., Winefield, A. H., Dawson, D., & Lushington, K. (2005). Development and validation of a scale to measure work-related fatigue and recovery: The occupational fatigue exhaustion recovery scale (OFER). *Journal of Occupational and Environmental Medicine, 47,* 594–606.

Zapf, D., Dormann, C., & Frese, M. (1996). Longitudinal studies in organizational stress research: A review of the literature with reference to methodological issues. *Journal of Occupational Health Psychology, 1,* 145–169.

Zijlstra, F. R. H., & Sonnentag, S. (2006). After work is done: Psychological perspectives on recovery from work. *European Journal of Work and Organizational Psychology, 15,* 129–138.

MOMENTARY WORK RECOVERY: THE ROLE OF WITHIN-DAY WORK BREAKS

John P. Trougakos and Ivona Hideg

ABSTRACT

Drawing from research on personal resources (e.g., Baumeister, Bratslavsky, Muraven, & Tice, 1998; Fredrickson, 1998) and the episodic nature of work (Beal, Weiss, Barros, & MacDermid, 2005), we examine research and theory relevant to the study of momentary recovery in the workplace. Specifically, we propose that the nature of within workday breaks influences the levels of psychological resources, which in turn influence various workplace outcomes. First, we discuss the momentary approach to studying workplace breaks and consequent resource levels. In doing so, we distinguish between two types of breaks, respites and chores; and we detail two types of psychological resources, regulatory and affective resources. Consequences of psychological resource levels on emotional exhaustion and performance are considered. We also explore possible moderators of the proposed relationships; we discuss job and individual characteristics, and motivation to perform. Finally, we conclude the chapter with a brief discussion on future research and possible applications of the momentary approach to work recovery in organizations.

Current Perspectives on Job-Stress Recovery
Research in Occupational Stress and Well Being, Volume 7, 37–84
Copyright © 2009 by Emerald Group Publishing Limited
All rights of reproduction in any form reserved
ISSN: 1479-3555/doi:10.1108/S1479-3555(2009)0000007005

INTRODUCTION

Employees today are experiencing escalating work demands; and levels of stress, exhaustion, and burnout are becoming increasingly problematic for employees and organizations alike (e.g., Elkin & Rosch, 1990; Fletcher, 1991; Van der Hek & Plomp, 1997). Understanding how employees recover from work therefore is commensurately important, and is directing a burgeoning area of research in organizational behavior and work psychology. One manifestation of this area is the study of employees' breaks from work, including the role of work vacations (e.g., Fritz & Sonnentag, 2006; Westman & Eden, 1997), weekends (Fritz & Sonnentag, 2005), and end of day activities (e.g., Sonnentag, 2001; Sonnentag & Zijlstra, 2006) in relation to employees' job performance, exhaustion, and well-being, among other outcomes. Yet, until recently (Trougakos, Beal, Green, & Weiss, 2008), the majority of work in this area has generally ignored the behavior of employees *during* their workdays. That is, the relationship between work recovery and employee use of within workday breaks has received little attention. This absence is surprising considering that people spend anywhere from a third to a half of their day at their place of work. During this time they are likely to have formally scheduled breaks such as lunch or coffee breaks, as well as various types of informal breaks such as time at the water cooler, a stroll around the office to socialize, or even taking an opportunity to sneak a quick peek at the newspaper.

This chapter examines how episodic within-day work breaks impact recovery. We will discuss the elements of momentary work recovery, focusing on the episodic within-person processes involved in recovery. In doing so, we first discuss an approach emphasizing the episodic nature of the workday. Second, we discuss different types of work breaks by reviewing the previous literature on break activities and recovery; moreover, we distinguish between two general types of break activities, respites and chores. Next, we touch on various theories of personal resources. By focusing on the ebb and flow of episodic psychological resources, we consider how the nature of break activities (respites versus chores) influences recovery either by restoring or depleting resources necessary to complete subsequent episodes of performance. Furthermore, we look at how momentary resource levels might impact important work-relevant outcomes, including task and affective performance, as well as stress-related outcomes such as emotional exhaustion. Finally, we discuss some potential moderators of the interrelations between breaks, momentary resource levels, and outcomes, and suggest implications of the momentary approach for studying breaks and recovery for future research.

THE EPISODIC PERSPECTIVE

To properly examine the components of within workday recovery, we must first discuss the episodic perspective within which we frame our discussion and detail the importance of employing this perspective to study work recovery. Similar to Barker (1963) and Beal, Weiss, Barros, and MacDermid (2005), we view people's daily lives as a stream of experience made up of discrete episodes that have a "coherent, thematic organization and are associated with specific people, occurrences, and goals. For example, individuals get up, have breakfast, go to work, have lunch, take a break, and otherwise engage in all manner of compartmentalized, coherent activities" (Beal et al., 2005, p. 1055). Drawing on Barker's work, Beal and colleagues suggest that the continuous flow of daily work behavior can be divided into natural units. These units, referred to as "behavior episodes," are natural units of work activity that have a recognizable thematic coherence. This perspective suggests that the construction of behavior episodes is organized around goals, personal strivings, or preferred states (Barker, 1963; Craik, 2000). Research has supported the notion that both actors and observers structure streams of behavior episodically, by and large agreeing on the breakpoints for these episodes (Dickman, 1963; Newtson, 1973; Newtson & Engquist, 1976).

Applying this framework to the study of work breaks and work recovery seems, in theory, to be a relatively natural extension of this paradigm. Though we must be cautious not to oversimplify daily patterns of human behavior, categorizing the nature of time people devote to their various daily activities does not need to account for how every moment is spent in order to provide useful insight into how these patterns of behavior impact work recovery. For example, a common sequence of daily episodes might include waking up, preparing for work, traveling to work, engaging in an initial work activity, taking a break from this activity, continuing work on the initial activity, taking a lunch break, changing to a new work activity, traveling back home, eating dinner, engaging in a leisure activity, and ultimately going to sleep in order to repeat a similar cycle the following workday. Although there can be many variations within each day and from one day to the next, working under the assumption that behavior can be "chunked" provides us some advantages in understanding work recovery.

First, an episodic perspective emphasizes variability within a person across different episodes. A great deal of recent research in social and organizational psychology has emphasized the utility of examining within-person changes both in important work outcomes as well as predictors that traditionally were conceived and studied as stable constructs (Fleeson, 2001, 2004; Miner & Hulin, 2006; Moskowitz, Brown, & Côté, 1997). There is no reason to believe that work recovery is a stable phenomenon, yet the dominant paradigm often leads to between-person (i.e., stable) comparisons of recovery. This is not to say that all recovery research is mired in the static view that some people are better "recoverers" than others; indeed there are many good examples of dynamic treatments of the topic (e.g., Fritz & Sonnentag, 2006; Westman & Eden, 1997). Nevertheless, our episodic framework focuses explicitly on within-person variability and suggests that there likely is meaningful change that occurs within a day across multiple episodes.

A second advantage of the episodic perspective is that by identifying the key characteristics of particular episodes, we can obtain an understanding of recovery that is rooted in what is likely the most fundamental level of analysis. That is, studies at more macro levels of analysis require participants to mentally aggregate across multiple instances of the events of interest. Even asking someone to describe the breaks, work activities, and accompanying states that occur over the course of a day necessitates some calculation across multiple instances of rest and work on the part of the participant. As our understanding of such processes is rather limited (cf. Fredrickson & Kahneman, 1993; Schreiber & Kahneman, 2000), it seems prudent to at least initially examine the process on an episode-by-episode basis. If such an analysis reveals that people simply compute averages of the various moments of their lives, then perhaps a more macro approach would be justified. If, however, the initial findings are any indication, then this seems unlikely (Fredrickson, 2000; Robinson & Clore, 2002). Given this state of affairs, our approach identifies the characteristics of each performance episode and the characteristics of antecedent and subsequent break episodes, devising a richer and more potent depiction of how resources are depleted and recovered throughout the day.

A third important aspect of utilizing an episodic approach to study work recovery is that we are able to capture the fleeting nature of the processes associated with work recovery and thus better understand its depths and limitations. At a basic level, this perspective allows us to consider the simple yet unknown issue of what form the time course of recovery and depletion takes. Is there a peak of recovered resources followed by a steep depletion, or do breaks simply flatten out an otherwise slowly declining pattern of resources over the course of a day? Beyond the simple trajectories of resource levels, there are the additional questions of influence on subsequent states and behaviors to examine. For example, does a break from work have an influence only on the immediately subsequent performance episode, or does the effect persist and decay into later episodes? If so, which types of break activities result in the longest decays? Also, is there a tradeoff between the immediate level of resources restored and the duration of their benefit? That is, if one expends a great deal of restored resources immediately after taking a break, will the duration of recovery be attenuated? All of these questions are as of yet unanswered, but fit well within the purview of an episodic perspective of work recovery.

Several of these points also speak to another benefit of employing an episodic perspective to study work recovery: greater accuracy in measurement of the behaviors and phenomena of interest. When asked to recall what one did sometime in the past, a common response might be "I cannot remember what I ate for breakfast let alone what I did last week!" As time passes between an experience and the reporting of that experience, people's recollections of the event incorporate less information from the actual episode and increasingly reflect stable attributes of the person (Robinson & Clore, 2002). For instance, if someone was asked what effect the coffee break they had last week had on their work recovery it is unlikely that they would remember the event let alone be able to accurately assess the efficacy of the break for subsequent experiences. By employing an episodic approach, we can capture something much closer to immediate experience, allowing a reduction of interfering memory biases.

As we stated earlier, our discussion of episodic work recovery is not intended to suggest that research on work recovery has not employed some elements of the episodic framework. In fact, it can be argued that research in the area of work recovery has employed a few aspects of the episodic perspective. For example, some research in this area has employed repeated measure within-person analysis, allowing for examination of behavioral patterns and comparisons of behaviors across time (Trougakos et al., 2008). Furthermore, whether focusing on vacation, weekend, end of day, or within workday breaks, prior research has examined how discrete periods of time in people's lives influence recovery as well as other associated outcomes. What we suggest, however, is that more explicitly grounding research on recovery within an episodic experience framework, both methodologically as well as theoretically, will aid research in the area to develop a clearer picture of recovery processes and outcomes, especially those involved in daily work recovery. With this in mind, the focus of our chapter is on the momentary processes and outcomes involved in daily work recovery, which we propose take place within the context of quotidian experience.

WORK BREAKS

Work breaks represent a period of time during which work-relevant tasks are not required or expected (Trougakos et al., 2008). Like others examining work recovery phenomena (e.g., Eden, 2001; Sonnentag, 2001; Sonnentag & Zijlstra, 2006), we suggest that taking a break from work is necessary for recovery. Moreover, in order for a break to result in recovery, people must utilize this time to engage in activities that reduce demands on personal resources and allow the opportunity for these resources to be recovered. As we pointed out in the introduction of this chapter, work recovery research has studied many different kinds of work breaks including vacations (e.g., Fritz & Sonnentag, 2006; Westman & Eden, 1997), weekends (Fritz & Sonnentag, 2005), end of workday (e.g., Sonnentag, 2001; Sonnentag & Zijlstra, 2006), as well as within workday breaks (Trougakos et al., 2008). Each of these lines of research has found support for the general premise that breaks do indeed relate to recovery (typically measured as levels of stress and well-being), with the general caveat being that breaks are used to engage in activities that are not taxing and are enjoyable. As such, it seems that the real key to recovery lies in the types of activities people engage in during their work breaks. We suggest that the nature of breaks will have consequences for the levels of resources throughout a workday. Before we discuss the nature of break activities in more detail (respites versus chores), let us first examine some of the most common types of breaks that have received attention in the work recovery literature so that we can better understand the context in which people engage in break activities.

Vacations

Research on the impact of vacations has generally supported the notion that taking a break from work aids in recovery (Fritz & Sonnentag, 2005; Westman & Eden, 1997; Westman & Etzion, 2001). For example, studies examining the effects of vacation on well-being found that vacation resulted in decreased stress levels (Eden, 1990) as well as in lower levels of burnout after vacation compared to before (Westman & Eden, 1997;

Westman & Etzion, 2001). Furthermore, the positive effects of vacation on well-being were determined by the activities employees engaged in during vacation, with relaxing and non-taxing activities being most likely to have a positive impact (Fritz & Sonnentag, 2006). In addition, research has indicated that vacation may reduce the effort employees need to exert in order to perform on return to work, providing that employees engaged in relaxing or non-taxing vacation activities (Fritz & Sonnentag, 2006). Furthermore, the general consensus of this research is that the positive effects of vacation are short lived and fade-out within days or weeks of returning to work (Fritz & Sonnentag, 2006).

Weekends and End-of-Day Breaks

Similar to vacation research, studies exploring the impact of weekends and end-of-day suggest that effective use of these times to relieve the burdens associated with work are vital for recovery. Although little research has specifically focused on the role of weekends in recovery, the work that does exist indicates that non-work demands and a lack of social activities during weekends resulted in greater burnout and lower well-being (e.g., Fritz & Sonnentag, 2005). At the day level, samples of the research indicate that feelings of recovery relate to work engagement and proactive behavior (Sonnentag, 2003), and engaging in recovery activities is positively related to well-being, whereas work-related activities are negatively related to well-being (Sonnentag, 2001; Sonnentag & Natter, 2004). Furthermore, engaging in unfavorable end-of-day activities resulted in employees reporting a higher need for recovery and greater fatigue (Sonnentag & Zijlstra, 2006). In summary, after-work-time and weekends generally serve to aid recovery and well-being, again assuming that these employees utilize these periods to engage in stimulating, restful activities, or low demand activities.

Within-Day Work Breaks

Relatively little organizational research has specifically focused on the study of within-day work breaks, especially in the context of work recovery. In a very general sense, the formal study of within-day work breaks in modern organizations dates back to Mayo (1933) and the Hawthorne Studies. This research was intended to examine how work was organized and how this in turn related to work strain and employee productivity, among other things.

Since then, the primary domain for exploring the role of within-day work breaks has been the ergonomics literature. Researchers in this area have explored the role of what they call micro-breaks as a means to alleviate musculoskeletal discomfort and strain associated with prolonged or repeated office-related tasks (e.g., Fisher, Andres, Airth, & Smith, 1993; Henning, Jacques, Kissel, Sullivan, & Alteras-Webb, 1997; McLean, Tingley, Scott, & Rickards, 2001; Tucker, 2003). This line of research has mostly examined (a) frequency of work breaks (Boucsein & Thum, 1997; Dababneh, Swanson, & Shell, 2001), (b) timing of work breaks (Boucsein & Thum, 1997; Henning, Kissel, & Maynard, 1994; Henning et al., 1997; McLean et al., 2001), and (c) length of work breaks (Lisper & Eriksson, 1980). Overall, these studies suggest that breaks can be effective in fighting fatigue effects and increasing productivity, but many unanswered questions still remain in this area such as understanding how the content of work breaks impact recovery as well as establishing the nature of the various underlying processes responsible for these effects (Tucker, 2003).

To our knowledge, only one published study in the area of work recovery has specifically focused on the role of within-day work breaks in the recovery process (Trougakos et al., 2008). Studying a group of service employees, this research found that the types of activities people engage in during their daily work breaks has implications for the emotions they report experiencing as well as performance of affective displays while interacting with customers. The results of this study reveal that the nature of activities employees engage in during breaks is important in the recovery process, with restful and enjoyable activities seemingly providing greater recovery.

An examination of the research for each of the different types of work breaks reveals a relatively clear commonality: it seems that to properly understand momentary work recovery, one must take into account the nature of the activities people engage in during their within-day work breaks. For each of the different types of work breaks studied, we can generally conclude that activities that removed or reduced demands, work related or otherwise, tended to result in more positive outcomes. On the other hand, activities that failed to curb these demands, tended to have negative consequences for employees. These conclusions make it clear that the recovery process hinges on the exact nature of the activities people partake in during breaks. This is especially likely to be the case for within workday breaks as employees are unlikely to have the opportunity to completely detach themselves from work for extended periods as is the case with breaks of longer duration such as weekends or vacations.

The Nature of Work Break Activities within a Workday

As we have already discussed, work breaks are a vital component of the recovery process. As one can imagine, there are many behaviors that might relieve the burdens associated with work and just as many that might not. We begin our discussion of break activities by broadly describing what types of activities and behaviors generally help foster recovery and what types of behaviors reduce or inhibit recovery. For the moment, we make the assumption that people have freedom of choice when selecting what activities to engage in during work breaks. As we already mentioned, we distinguish between two general types of activities people might engage in during work breaks: respites and chores. In the next sections, we will outline what we consider to be respites and chores, and how they aid or impede momentary work recovery processes.

Respites

We began this chapter with the simple notion that in order to recover from the negative effects of work, people need to have work breaks. However, as our discussion has made evident, simply taking a break may not be enough. What seems to be important is how people use their breaks. More specifically, it seems that in order to recover, people need to use their break time to engage in activities that stop the demands associated with work. That is, stopping one work task in favor of another, or in favor of a non-work-related task that is nevertheless burdensome, is unlikely to result in recovery. For recovery to be successful, "an individual's well-being improves, and resources drawn upon during the strain process are restored" (Sonnentag & Natter, 2004, p. 368). Thus, in order to recover, people must use their breaks to engage in respite activities. We define *respite activities* as break activities that involve either low effort or preferred choice. These types of activities cease the depletion of personal resources necessary for effective work functioning and well-being, and provide people with personal resources that can aid effective work functioning and well-being.

Let us further examine the two specific characteristics that help define activities as respites: the amount of effort involved in the activity and the degree to which the activity was a preferred choice. Low effort activities aid recovery because they stop the continued depletion of resources by relieving the demand and strain associated with work and provide one with the opportunity to restore depleted resources. Examples of low effort respite activities might include relaxation, sitting quietly, and sleep. Preferred choice activities can also aid recovery by providing people with the opportunity to recover and gain resources depleted during work, but these activities may function in a slightly different manner. These types of respite activities provide people with the opportunity to engage in activities they may find enjoyable, thus serving to energize them. When employees engage in activities they prefer compared to work-related activities or even non-preferred non-work activities, the need to regulate behavior is reduced, which leads to increase in positive feelings and higher subjective well-being (Fritz & Sonnentag, 2005; Miner, Glomb, & Hulin, 2005; Sonnentag & Zijlstra, 2006; Trougakos et al., 2008). Even activities that may be physically tiring, such as exercising, could serve as a respite if this is indeed the person's preferred choice. A basic premise here is that people do not have to "make" or "force" themselves to engage in preferred choice activities, thus reducing regulatory burden. This notion, to be more fully detailed shortly, is supported by findings suggesting that personal resources can be depleted when people make a choice to engage in non-preferred activities (Moller, Deci, & Ryan, 2006). Also, as we will discuss later in this chapter, examples of preferred-choice respite activities may differ from person to person; however, generally speaking, these activities involve an interruption of non-preferred activities in favor of activities that an individual would rather do, such as spending time with friends, enjoying a game of some type, or reading an enjoyable book.

Chores

In contrast to respite activities, *chore activities* are those break activities that continue to draw on the resources utilized during work and thus do not allow employees to recover from the negative effect of work. These activities continue the depletion of personal resources necessary for effective work functioning and well-being, and they fail to provide people with opportunity to recover personal resources that can aid effective work functioning and well-being. Sonnentag (2001) has noted that activities representing either continuing to work (e.g., continuing to work with customers, or preparing for future work episodes) or engaging in other effortful tasks (e.g., running errands) generally require increased behavior regulation. Whether focused on work-relevant tasks or not, this effortful regulation results in resource depletion (Baumeister, Bratslavsky, Muraven, & Tice, 1998). In addition, chore activities typically are not preferred behaviors, and as a result interfere with people being able to engage in preferred activities. This can result in decreased positive feelings and increased negative feelings (Trougakos et al., 2008), which can reduce well-being and effective work functioning. Examples of chore activities might include switching one work task in favor of another, running errands, having a disagreement with a friend, or doing household chores. Of course, as is the case with respite activities, we must note that certain activities may be chores for some people but not to others. For example, some people view cooking as a burdensome household chore, whereas others enjoy cooking and find it relaxing. In the work place, some people may consider a quick trip to a mall for some shopping during the lunch hour as a relaxing and reenergizing change of scenery, whereas others may experience it as a tiring chore that must be done. Regardless of what someone's personal preferences are, the general goal for people seeking to recover from work is to avoid chores during breaks and try to use these opportunities to engage in respites. The purpose of doing so is to preserve and replenish personal resources.

PERSONAL RESOURCES

The central premise of this chapter revolves around the assumption that, by and large, work is effortful and thus depleting to individuals' momentary levels of resources. We use the term *work* to refer to those tasks, both implicit and explicit, that employees must carry out in order to fulfill the requirements of their job. Work has the capacity to drain us both physically as well as mentally. Furthermore, certain non-work activities, such as doing household chores or running errands, are also likely to have a similar effect on us. Generally, resource depletion theories (e.g., Baumeister et al., 1998) emphasize that workers have a limited amount of "personal resources" that allow them to complete the variety of taxing activities they engage in throughout the day.

The concept of personal resources has been applied to many areas of organizational behavior and psychology. Of course, research on work recovery is usually based on the notion of limited personal resources. Some of these conceptualizations are particularly applicable to the study of work recovery including workload and work processes (Meijman & Mulder, 1998), stress (Hobfoll, 1998), affective states (Fredrickson, 1998), and behavior regulation (Muraven & Baumeister, 2000). Each of these limited resource perspectives has similarities as well as some differences. Moreover, the extent to which these different perspectives apply to and have been utilized in the study of work recovery also varies.

Two theories of work stress and work processes utilizing the concept of limited personal resources have been predominately featured in the work recovery literature. The first of these, Meijman and Mulder's (1998) effort-recovery model focuses on the depleting effect of employees' efforts to manage their workloads. The general premise behind this theory is that when employees expend effort on work it results in load reactions, which deplete employees' energy resources. Recovery occurs by temporarily removing the demands the employees face.

The second theory of limited personal resources typically featured in research on work recovery is Hobfoll's (1989, 1998) conservation of resources theory. Conservation of resources theory considers the general relationship between stress and well-being. This theory suggests that people seek to possess and protect personal resources, which include object resources (e.g., money), condition resources (e.g., tenure), personal characteristics (e.g., skills), and energies (which tend to serve in the acquisition of the other resources). The main tenet of this theory is that resource loss impacts stress experiences because resource loss is more salient than is resource gain. Another important tenet of this theory is that individuals with more resources are less vulnerable to resource loss because the abundance of resources begets even more resources. Conversely, those with fewer resources are more vulnerable to resource loss. To break the resource loss cycle, an individual has to engage in a period of relaxation in order to regroup or achieve more resources (Hobfoll & Shirom, 2001).

Beyond the current domain of work recovery, the notion that affective states can serve as resources for people in work settings has been mentioned in various theories. One recent theory seems to have exhibited reasonable success in establishing this notion. Fredrickson's (1998) broaden and build theory of positive emotion suggests that when people experience positive emotions, such as joy, interest, contentment, and love, their momentary action-thought repertoire is broadened. This then results in the building of personal resources, which results in numerous positive outcomes (Fredrickson, 2001). Because of the episodic nature of emotional experiences and states (Beal et al., 2005), this theory is especially relevant to the perspective we adopt in examining daily work recovery.

Another theory of particular pertinence to the current discussion is the concept of regulatory resource or "ego" depletion advanced by Muraven and Baumeister (2000). This theory suggests that people have a central and limited psychological resource that determines one's ability to regulate behavior at any given moment. Each time we engage in some sort of self-control or self-regulatory behavior, this central resource is depleted, making future regulatory efforts increasingly difficult. Although relatively little is known about how these resources are recovered, researchers have recently begun to explore the underlying mechanisms involved in this process (e.g., Gailliot et al., 2007; Tice, Baumeister, Shmueli, & Muraven, 2007). For example, recent laboratory research suggests that affective states seem to impact the recovery process (Tice et al., 2007) as does the consumption of nutrients like glucose (Gailliot et al., 2007). Moreover, a recent field study applying regulatory resource theory has found that low effort activities during work breaks improve job performance, whereas work-related activities and other effortful tasks do not (Trougakos et al., 2008).

As our discussion of these different perspectives of resource depletion indicates, the precise nature of these resources varies somewhat from theory to theory. However, a common feature is that engaging in effortful tasks (i.e., work or similar activities) is particularly draining of these resources. And though these theories provide much utility to the study of work recovery, not all of them capture the nuances of ongoing recovery processes as they unfold during workdays. In particular, though the first two theories make mention of some of the episodic demands employees face, they do not specifically discuss the nature of the momentary processes involved in recovery. Rather, these theories focus more on general levels of resources over longer time periods. For instance, in the effort-recovery model, the exact nature of resources is somewhat vague and as such it is not completely clear how we would conceptualize this in relation to momentary recovery processes. As for Hobfoll's perspective, resources are relatively broadly conceptualized (e.g., status, money), and are unlikely to be attained during a coffee or lunch break, making it a more appropriate approach to utilize when examining resiliency and longer term recovery from work rather than momentary recovery within a workday.

Thus, although these theories are well suited for understanding factors that result in general stress levels, it is slightly more difficult to apply these theories to momentary work recovery. Since we are approaching work recovery from an episodic perspective, our focus is on momentary resource levels. As such, our discussion focuses on two theories of momentary psychological resources: Baumeister and colleagues' (1998) theory of regulatory resources and Fredrickson's (1998) perspective on affect as a personal resource. Our primary focus in this chapter is the nature and replenishment of momentary psychological resources depleted when people engage in work. Let us now consider these resources in more detail.

PERSONAL RESOURCES ASSOCIATED WITH MOMENTARY RECOVERY

Momentary Regulatory Resources

According to a limited resource model of behavior regulation, prolonged regulation of behavior depletes regulatory resources available for subsequent regulation and can be mentally and physically taxing (Baumeister et al., 1998; Muraven & Baumeister, 2000). Although research is supportive of the regulatory resource concept, the exact nature of these resources is somewhat unclear. Researchers have likened self-regulatory capacity to a psychological "muscle" (Muraven, Tice, & Baumeister, 1998). With extended periods of use, the regulatory "muscle" fatigues and functions less effectively, until eventually it begins to fail. To prevent regulatory failure, people must take a break from effortful regulation in order to replenish the resources needed for future behavior regulation (Muraven & Baumeister, 2000). This is exemplified when we consider how an employee might feel on a typical workday. Assuming reasonable rest the previous evening, the employee starts the day feeling energized and able to easily concentrate on and complete his or her routine work tasks. As the day progresses, the ability to concentrate and sustain effort on work tasks may start to diminish, the employee may be more prone to making mistakes, and it may take longer to complete work tasks. To combat this, organizations usually have work breaks, such as lunch breaks, structured into employees' workdays.

Although there is uncertainty as to the nature of regulatory resources, it does seem that the nature of the breaks people take is important if replenishment is to occur. Researchers suggest that in order to recover depleted regulatory resources, it is necessary to avoid other forms of regulation (Beal et al., 2005; Hobfoll, 1998; Meijman & Mulder, 1998; Muraven & Baumeister, 2000). Baumeister et al. (1998) have emphasized that *all* acts of self-regulation utilize the same resource; thus, if replenishment is to occur, one must lessen the amount of regulation, no matter the particular task. For instance, ceasing one job task in favor of another is unlikely to restore depleted resources if behavior regulation continues in the new task.

In support of this notion, laboratory studies repeatedly find evidence that a wide range of activities result in subsequent decrements in one's ability to regulate behavior. The shared factor across this wide array of tasks is that they all require regulation. Thus, it matters not whether one is squeezing a hand grip, regulating emotional expression, or completing an effortful editing task, the result is that one's ensuing attempts at regulation of any kind will suffer (e.g., Baumeister et al., 1998; Muraven et al., 1998). The primary mechanisms involved in studies of regulatory resource depletion are the extent to which someone is engaging in a behavior that one does not ideally wish to engage in, or on the other hand, actively inhibiting a dominant or preferred behavior. Therefore, momentary regulatory resource recovery can occur in two possible ways, either by stopping a task that depletes regulatory resources, or engaging in a preferred behavior.

When individuals engage in tasks that require focused attention (i.e., a task one does not ideally wish to engage in and or one that requires high levels of attention and regulation in order to maintain focus), they must employ the use of self-control, which according to limited regulatory resource theory (Baumeister, Vohs, & Tice, 2007) is effortful and can deteriorate over time. Studies support the notion that acts of volition, such as self-regulation, function as a limited resource, which is impaired by prior exertion (e.g., Baumeister et al., 1998; Muraven et al., 1998). As such, one act of volition will have a negative impact on succeeding acts of volition. For example, it has been shown that when people regulate emotions and engage in subsequent tasks that require self-regulation, they perform with less persistence and more poorly when compared to people who have not had to use their regulatory capacity before performing the task (Baumeister et al., 1998; Muraven et al., 1998). Since self-regulation acts as a finite resource, the greater the level of self-regulation utilized, the greater the capacity is depleted, so those who must continually draw on this reserve deplete it to the point that self-regulation becomes more and more difficult. After a certain point of exertion, the capacity to continue to regulate at an optimal level declines and eventually it is theorized that complete regulation failure is inevitable. Therefore, when one stops all tasks that require focused attention, the burden placed on the self's capacity to regulate is removed thus allowing recovery to occur. In other words, in order to stop the depletion of regulatory resources people must take a break, with the ultimate form of recovery occurring through sleep as the burden of regulation is completely removed and the body resets the regulatory system.

In contrast with the notion of preventing regulatory resource loss by *refraining from* engaging in certain behaviors, people may be able to conserve regulatory resources by *taking part in* certain behaviors. Experiencing work recovery is associated with and conceptualized as a positive outcome (Sonnentag & Zijlstra, 2006; Trougakos et al., 2008). This suggests that regulatory resource loss may also be prevented through the active engagement in *preferred* behaviors. A possible means for this to occur might therefore involve the extent to which someone is actively engaging in (as opposed to actively inhibiting) a dominant or preferred behavior (Higgins, 1997). That is, people can reduce or prevent resource loss by engaging in activities that they find enjoyable and have a very strong desire to engage in. The main premise behind this line of reasoning is that when people engage in behaviors they enjoy, they do not need to "force" themselves to partake in and focus on these activities. Rather, engaging in these behaviors is relatively easy from a regulatory perspective as they represent activities that people truly wish to do. In fact, it may be that people deplete resources by refraining from engaging in these preferred activities, and switching to preferred activities relieves regulatory burden (Baumeister, Heatherton, & Tice, 1994).

Evidence from empirical research supports the idea that choice can impact regulatory resource levels (Vohs et al., 2008), and preferred choice activities do seem, at the very least, to reduce regulatory burden compared to non-preferred choice activities (Moller et al., 2006). Supporting this line of reasoning, studies examining preferred choice and exercise reveal that engaging in a more preferred exercise resulted in lower perceived exertion, lower fatigue, and greater momentary well-being when compared to a non-preferred exercise condition (Parfitt & Gledhill, 2004). Moreover, research by Moller and colleagues (2006) demonstrated that in contrast with a forced choice situation, people who have choice of autonomy do not experience regulatory resource depletion. Therefore, just as stopping activities that involve engaging in the active inhibition of preferred behavior (i.e., self-regulation) should aid regulatory resource replenishment, break activities that involve the active engagement in preferred behavior seems to prevent regulatory resource loss and might allow for resource recovery.

To conclude our examination of regulatory resources, we must address two interesting questions this discussion raises. First, to what extent do within-day work breaks actually foster resource recovery or simply resource preservation? Resource replenishment is the restoration of the regulatory resources people need to regulate their behavior. Resource preservation, on the other hand, represents people's attempts to either cease behaviors that deplete regulatory resources, or to engage in behaviors that are neutral with regard to regulatory resources, to preserve remaining resources for future use. From a conceptual standpoint, the difference between resource recovery and resource preservation is relatively simple, the first involves regaining lost resources, the second preventing further loss of resources. However, practically, disentangling these concepts has been far less clear. Theories of regulatory resources primarily address the notion of depletion, focusing on what happens when depletion occurs and how depletion is stopped, not necessarily addressing the manner in which resources are recovered. This brings us to the second issue we must address, what exactly is being recovered when one is attempting to restore regulatory resources? Unfortunately, relatively little work exists that can definitively address either of these issues, although recent research addressing how resources might be recovered may provide at least partial answers to both questions.

In a novel study, Gailliot and colleagues (2007) have found support for the role of glucose in the operation of self-regulation. Research on brain physiology supports the notion that effortful brain functioning, such as that involved in self-regulation, can consume relatively large levels of glucose (Benton, 1990; Benton, Owens, & Parker, 1994). On the basis of this, Gailliot and colleagues proposed that people's blood glucose levels should impact self-regulation.

In a series of experiments, they demonstrated that effortful self-regulation resulted in a decrease in blood glucose levels. That is, blood glucose levels were lower for people after they engaged in tasks that required high amounts of self-regulation when compared to people who did not engage in tasks that had a high regulatory demand, demonstrating that glucose can be depleted through self-regulation. Furthermore, decreases in blood glucose due to regulation on an initial high regulation task resulted in decreased regulatory capacity on a second task, supporting the notion that decreased glucose levels could impair subsequent regulation. Finally, they established a causal link between glucose and self-regulatory capacity by showing that decrements in regulatory capacity could be restored by consuming glucose. Although this research cannot conclude that glucose is the sole, or even the primary mechanism involved in regulatory resource recovery, the evidence to date seems to indicate that this is at least one avenue worthy of further exploration.

The research on glucose and self-regulation also provides further insight into whether or not work breaks replenish resources or prevent further depletion. As we have already suggested in this chapter, recovery may be dependent on what people do on their work breaks. On the basis of Gailliot and colleagues (2007) work, it would seem logical that if people eat something during their breaks this may help recover resources. However, Muraven and Baumeister (2000) suggest that regulatory strength is at its maximum after a period of rest, and if the rest is not sufficient, regulatory resources become depleted over time. In fact, sleep and rest seem to aid self-regulation independent of nutrient intake (Baumeister et al., 1994). Therefore, work breaks that allow people to rest should also aid recovery, first by reducing or removing the regulatory burdens and second by allowing psychological systems to restore or reset. For simplicity sake, we take the point of view that when resources are depleted recovery is hindered. Therefore, we argue that whether one is merely stemming the tide of resource depletion, or actually recovering resources, either through calorie consumption or some other means, the act of taking a break from activities that deplete resources is central to the recovery process. Further, we leave the question about what specifically is being recovery in this process to future research.

Momentary Affective Resources

Although there are various types of affective experiences people can have (Watson, 1988; Watson, Wiese, Vaidya, & Tellegen, 1999; Weiss & Cropanzano, 1996), the ones which are typically characterized as the most episodic in nature, and thus most appropriate for the current discussion, are emotional experiences (Beal et al., 2005). Emotional experiences are conceptualized as short-lived punctuated affective states individuals experience in relation to specific events (Frijda, 1993) and often are classified as positive or negative (Shaver, Schwartz, Kirson, & O'Connor, 1987). This ephemeral nature of emotional experiences makes it most likely that these affective states will coincide with the momentary processes associated with within-day work breaks (Trougakos et al., 2008). Although the study of emotion in the workplace has garnered more attention recently, the role of emotions in the work recovery process has received relatively little attention (for an exception, see Trougakos et al., 2008). Despite this lack of research, there is considerable evidence to suggest a prominent role for emotions in the process of work recovery, especially at the within-day level.

Weiss and Cropanzano (1996) suggest that the affective states associated with events employees experience during their workday impacts subsequent work attitudes and behaviors. This notion has received increasing support in the organizational literature (e.g., Bono, Foldes, Vinson, & Muros, 2007; Grandey, Tam, & Brauburger, 2002; Kelly & Barsade, 2001; Trougakos et al., 2008). At its most basic level, this framework suggests that when employees experience negative events they experience negative emotions, and when they experience positive events they experience positive emotions. For example, if an employee uses break time to joke around with friends this event is likely to result in the experience of positive emotions such as happiness or joy, depending on how funny the jokes being told are! On the basis of this logic, we suggest that the activities employees engage in during work breaks will function as affective events, often resulting in employees experiencing discrete emotions, which we suggest employees can utilize as a resource to impact future work outcomes.

Although there are a handful of examples of researchers treating affective experiences as personal resources (e.g., Marks, 1977; Repetti, 1987; Rothbard, 2001) perhaps the most relevant theory supporting our conceptualization of how emotions can serve as a type of personal resource is illustrated by Fredrickson's (1998, 2001) broaden and build theory of positive emotion. Fredrickson's research describes the impact of positive emotion on people's behavior. Specifically, the broaden and build perspective states that "certain discrete positive emotions – including joy, interest, contentment, pride, and love – although phenomenologically distinct, all share the ability to broaden people's momentary thought-action repertoires and build their enduring personal resources" (Fredrickson, 2001, p. 219). The primary tenet of this research is that positive emotions facilitate approach behavior, motivating people to engage in their environment and partake in activities. Therefore, when people experience positive emotions, these emotions can be utilized as a resource, helping direct attention and effort toward work-related tasks, as well as impacting attitudes and personal well-being.

Fredrickson's broaden and build theory dovetails well with Weiss and Cropanzano's affective events theory. Taken together, these perspectives indicate that break activities should have an impact on individuals' emotional states such that enjoyable or restful activities should generally result in positive experiences and should therefore result in an increased experience of positive emotional states. On the other hand, engaging in demanding or non-enjoyable activities might result in less pleasant experiences and therefore lead to fewer positive emotional experiences. Therefore, the positive emotions people experience can be utilized akin to a resource during the time period immediately following the break.

Although limited research has been conducted on this specific relationship, some support for this notion has been found. Specifically, Trougakos et al. (2008) found that service employees who reported using breaks to partake in relaxing activities also reported greater levels of positive emotional experiences. Engaging in work-related activities during breaks was related to lower levels of positive emotional experiences. Moreover, positive emotions also seemed to aid employee performance in the episodes immediately following breaks. As such, the emotions people experience as a result of their break activities function as affective resources that can impact their subsequent work and personal outcomes. Importantly, we are not arguing that a change in emotional state is equivalent to the recovery of regulatory resources. Rather, the generation of emotions is considered to be a separate, although possibly related, process which can provide an affective resource which employees can draw on during subsequent periods of work. For example, the sense of accomplishment employees feel after completing a workout during lunch may expand thought-action repertoires (Fredrickson, 2001); thus, carrying over to aid in the completion of a work project, or the happiness associated with hearing a coworker tell a funny joke may aid in the display of organizationally prescribed positive emotion to customers.

Physiological Resources

We would be remiss if we did not at least briefly touch on physiological resources in order to acknowledge the role these resources play in the recovery process. Physiological resources typically refer to the physical energy that an individual possesses at any given moment that can be directed toward work tasks. As such, we conceptualize physiological resources primarily in a biological sense. Simply put, people have a finite capacity to physically exert themselves, and at some point this capacity is depleted. Although different people have different physiological capacities, ultimately everyone has a limit, beyond which point they are physically unable to continue without physically replenishing themselves. In this case, recovery occurs by consuming food energy, resting, and sleeping. Eating, in particular, may be relevant in daily work settings where breaks often involve having lunch or getting a coffee or a snack. Of course, these types of activities are common to all people as we all must eat and sleep to maintain biological functioning, and people generally stop working before physiological resources are completely depleted, lest they suffer serious health consequences. Thus, although we acknowledge that physiological resources are an important factor in people's on-going work recovery, a full discussion of the nature of the physiological resources involved in work recovery is beyond the scope of this chapter. We do note, however, that each of the resources we have discussed does not function completely independently. We already have discussed some evidence for this interdependence while detailing the role of glucose in regulatory resource replenishment. As such, let us briefly touch on the relationships between these different types of personal resources.

The Relationship between Momentary Personal Resources

Although we alluded to the relationship between the different personal resources occasionally throughout this chapter, we have generally considered each independently. Of course, disentangling these resources from one another is much easier to achieve in theory than in practice. In actuality, the relationship between these resources is likely rather complex and it is difficult to separate the role of each in the recovery process. It is reasonable to assume that each of these resources is interrelated, and likely often function in conjunction. Our earlier discussion of the research by Gailliot and colleagues (2007) regarding glucose and self-regulation is one example of just such an interrelation. Furthermore, the experience of positive emotions appears to impact regulatory resource levels (Tice et al., 2007). This research indicates that positive emotional experiences off-set regulatory resource depletion such that those people who are depleted and then experience positive emotion perform equally well on subsequent regulatory tasks as those who are not initially depleted (Tice et al., 2007). However, it is also noted that the mechanism involved in this process is somewhat unclear. It could be that positive emotions improve regulatory resources, or it simply could be that the activation associated with positive emotion provides the necessary resources to perform on subsequent tasks. Nevertheless, whether positive emotion replenishes regulatory resources or, simply serves to compensate for depleted regulatory resources, that these processes seem to overlap in some manner appears evident.

Furthermore, one can envision a situation in which people who have recovered their regulatory resources feel upbeat and positive. On the other hand, people who have depleted their regulatory resources may feel negatively. This could be exacerbated if negative feelings have to be regulated, as is the case in many work settings where positive emotional displays are the norm (Hochschild, 1983). Regulation of emotion can deplete regulatory resources (Baumeister et al., 1998), which in turn might lead to continued experiences of negative affect. In addition, having to engage in behavior that requires regulatory effort means that people are likely not engaging in preferred choice activities. This may result in negative affective experiences (Trougakos et al., 2008), dissatisfaction (Higgins, 1997), and decreased feelings of well-being (Parfitt & Gledhill, 2004). In contrast, engaging in activities that are people's preferred choice could lead to positive emotional experiences, as people are likely to choose activities they find enjoyable. Similarly, because people try to maintain positive emotional states (Isen & Simmonds, 1978; Wegener & Petty, 1994), they may be likely to pursue activities that aid regulatory resource recovery if these activities are responsible for the initial positive affective state. Thus, one can envision numerous variations of cycles of resource recovery or depletion.

To further complicate matters, not only might we expect complex relationships between the different types of personal resources, but there are a host of other variables that can influence the process of momentary resource recovery. Recall from our earlier discussion on work break activities, we made the assumption that people have freedom of choice when selecting activities. Of course, as was the case with the different personal resources, this is a rather simplistic view, as the real world is not easily constrained by such assumptions. Also recall, we mentioned that people's perceptions of what might be considered a respite or a chore is likely to differ from person to person and that some activities may aid recovery more for some compared to others. Bearing these points in mind, we now consider some factors that might moderate the relationship between break activities and resource recovery.

MODERATORS OF THE BREAK ACTIVITY–RESOURCE LEVEL RELATIONSHIP

In this chapter, we have suggested that different break activities will have consequences for levels of personal resources. Specifically, respite activities lead to resource replenishment and thus to higher levels of resources, whereas chore activities lead to resource depletion and thus to lower levels of resources. However, this relationship has boundaries defined by different individual and situational characteristics. Employees differ in terms of their personal characteristics, non-work life, and the job context itself. These differences may play an important role in the way psychological resources are depleted and replenished in the workplace.

In the next sections, we discuss two categories of moderators of the relationship between break activities and levels of resources: job characteristics and personal characteristics. Two job characteristics that are likely to have a significant impact on personal resource levels and recovery processes are job demands and job control. Job demands should impact how much resources employees need to invest in work tasks, and job control should influence when and how employees recover their resources. As for personal characteristics, previous research on personality, cognitive appraisals, and reactions to daily stressors has mostly examined Extraversion and Neuroticism (Grant & Langan-Fox, 2007; Lee-Baggley, Preece, & DeLougis, 2005). Given the literature focus on these two traits, our discussion on the moderating role of personality on the relationship between break activities and levels of resources will be constrained to Extraversion and Neuroticism.

Job Demands

Job demands refer to physical, psychological, social, and organizational features of the job that require sustained effort expenditure and thus it is associated with certain physiological and psychological costs (Bakker & Demerouti, 2006; Mauno, Kinnunen, & Ruokolainen, 2007). Frequently encountered job demands are heavy workload, time pressure, role ambiguity, and role conflict (Mauno et al., 2007; Sonnentag & Zijlstra, 2006). Previous research has shown that job demands tend to have detrimental effects on employee well-being (for reviews, see Kahn & Byosiere, 1992; Sonnentag & Frese, 2003). In addition, previous research has shown that job demands have direct effects on need for recovery – an emotional state in which individuals feel that they cannot continue with current demands and activities and thus they need a break (Sonnentag & Zijlstra, 2006). Supporting the notion that job demands could impact the relationship between breaks and resource levels, a study conducted by Sonnentag and Zijlstra (2006) revealed that as employees experienced higher job demands they also experienced higher need for recovery indicating that their resources were depleted.

When employees experience high job demands, they usually struggle to find enough "hours in a day" to manage and complete all of the required tasks. On the one hand, high job demands require more effort and investment of one's resources into tasks, which consequently leads to higher resource expenditure (Hockey, 1996). On the other hand, the struggle for time usually leads to working during scheduled breaks or taking shorter breaks. Therefore, on average, employees experiencing high job demands are likely to engage in more chore activities (e.g., work activities, or running errands over lunch because they will have to work late) compared to employees experiencing low job demands. Consequently, this should lead to greater regulatory resource depletion and thus lower levels of resources. Also, high job demands, and especially high workload, is positively related to negative effects (e.g., Geurts, Kompier, Roxburgh, & Houtman, 2003;

Repetti, 1993; Rothbard, 2001), which suggests a decreased likelihood of experiencing positive emotions and greater depletion of resources as employees must work to conceal and repair negative affective states. Thus, the evidence presented from previous research on job demands and its effects on employees' resource levels suggests that employees with high job demands may have chronically low levels of both regulatory as well as affective resources.

How do job demands impact the relationship between the break activity and resource levels? It seems that quick respites (e.g., a coffee break) for employees with high job demands may not be sufficient for recovery. People with high job demands are unlikely to experience the same degree of recovery when compared to those with low job demands as breaks are used less effectively and thoughts of work often might consume these individuals during off-work time (Sonnentag & Kruel, 2006), reducing the effectiveness of a break even when activities that would typically be recovering are engaged in. As a result, short breaks may not be sufficient to undo the effects of excessively high job demands. It seems that these employees would require a greater period of relief in order to allow for both physical and mental disassociation from work. As such, these employees may need an extended break such as a few days vacation in order to restore their resource levels.

Job Control

Job control refers to an employee's opportunity to influence his or her job activities and make decisions about the job (Frese, 1989). Numerous previous studies have shown that job control is associated with beneficial outcomes such as higher well-being (e.g., Daniels & Guppy, 1994; Jackson, 1983; Karasek, 1979). Given that job control plays an important role for employee's experience of the work place and consequent well-being, it is important to explore the role of job control in the processes of resource depletion and replenishment.

Job control may influence the relationship between break activities and levels of resources in at least two ways. First, job control implies that employees have discretion over when and for how long they can take breaks. When employees have high job control and they experience tiredness, they can switch to work on less demanding tasks or take a break (Jackson, Wall, Martin, & Davids, 1993). Furthermore, because employees with high job control have greater flexibility in determining how they structure their workday, these individuals may have more options in choosing a preferred break activity. For example, an employee might want to attend a yoga class during the lunch break and unwind, but that activity may require a lunch break of an hour and fifteen minutes. An employee with high job control may have the flexibility to take an extended lunch, making the yoga class a viable option for recovery. The low job control employee, on the other hand, is unlikely to be able to extend his or her lunch break beyond the company scheduled one-hour time frame. On the basis of this discussion, employees with high job control are (a) more likely to take breaks when they really need them, and (b) more likely to engage in preferred choice activities, resulting in greater replenishment compared to employees with low job control.

This discussion rests on the notion that employees can effectively use discretionary breaks to replenish their resources. However, past research on micro-breaks has produced equivocal results. On the one hand, previous research showed that employees manage fatigue most effectively when they can adjust their break periods to coincide with their fatigue periods (Feyer & Williamson, 1995). The same findings have been observed with employees in computer-based work where rigid breaks (preplanned by the company) were associated with the disruption of work flow (Henning et al., 1994) and increased emotional strain (Boucsein & Thum, 1997). Thus, these findings suggest that employees with high control over scheduling their breaks would use breaks efficiently. However, on the other hand, some research suggests that employees without formally scheduled breaks may overwork themselves and fail to take a break when they need it (McLean et al., 2001). When breaks occur at the point at which the employees are overworked, the breaks may not function effectively in replenishing resources (McLean et al., 2001). Thus, these findings suggest that employees with high job control over scheduling their work breaks may not use the breaks efficiently.

The research on micro-breaks has mostly involved employees with highly repetitive and routine tasks (e.g., machine operators), and we suggest that job control may be more important for employees with less repetitive tasks (e.g., knowledge workers). Knowledge workers tend to be involved in several projects at the same time and have different agendas and different deadlines each day. They may benefit from flexible break scheduling for several reasons. First, it may be very difficult and counter-productive to set-up breaks at the exact same time every day when each day may require different scheduling of work tasks. For example, having a rigidly scheduled lunch break may preclude an employee from organizing an important business lunch with a client that may bring more business to a company.

Second, knowledge workers may occasionally need to work long hours to finish a project, and may not have the luxury of taking extended breaks during these times. Being forced to take a break when they have important deadlines may make employees facing these types of situations even more drained, tired, and upset. Thus, we suggest that job control in scheduling one's daily breaks may be especially important to knowledge workers, although future research is needed to confirm if the potential impact, either positive or negative, of job control.

Second, employees with high job control may experience the same events differently from employees with low job control, and thus, the same break activity (e.g., working during the lunch break) may have different consequences for resource depletion. Specifically, employees with high job control may deplete fewer resources than employees with low job control while engaging in the same activity. Evidence for this notion comes from research on the ameliorative psychological effects of control (Glass, Reim, & Singer, 1971; Glass & Singer, 1973). In their study, Glass and Singer exposed participants to either controllable or uncontrollable noise. The participants who were exposed to controllable noise experienced lower levels of frustration and performed better at a postnoise task. There are a few reasons why control may reduce resource depletion and consequent job stress. One reason is that the mere belief in personal control determines reactions to stress and job demands (Averill, 1973; Miller & Norman, 1979). In Glass and Singer's (1973) study, participants in the controllable noise condition were told that they could stop aversive noise at any time by pressing a button. However, nobody pressed the button, and thus they endured the same amount and intensity of the aversive noise as the participants in the uncontrollable noise condition. Still, participants in the controllable noise condition had lower levels of frustration and performed better at a postnoise task. Thus, it seems that the mere belief in control has a powerful ameliorative effect. On the basis of these findings, job control may also influence how draining certain activities are for employees, that is, the same activity (e.g., working during lunch time) may be more resource depleting for employees with low job control than for employees with high job control.

Individual Differences

As already noted in this chapter, individuals differ in the way they perceive, experience, and appraise situations. The same situation may be experienced completely differently by two individuals. For example, consider having a lunch with members of one's work group. Generally, this break activity could be classified as a respite, as long as it does not involve engaging in work-related tasks. Some individuals, however, may find this type of activity especially recovering. For example, highly extraverted individuals that enjoy being in the company of other people, may experience this lunch more so as a respite and experience greater replenishment of their resources compared to less extraverted people. However, some individuals, those who are more introverted, may perceive and experience this lunch as a chore, resulting in greater depletion of resources. Thus, individual differences play an important role in how different break activities are appraised, and consequently that appraisal may lead to different resource levels. Also, individuals differ in how much stress, as well as positive and negative effects they experience, which also has implications for resource levels. In this section, we explore the moderating role of personality in the recovery process by specifically discussing Extraversion and Neuroticism.

Extraversion refers to the degree to which people are enthusiastic, talkative, assertive, and energetic (McCrae & John, 1992). Previous research has found that individuals high on Extraversion compared to individuals low on Extraversion have a general positive appraisal tendency (Gallagher, 1990; Hemenover & Dienstbier, 1996); perceive that they have high and adequate coping abilities (Penley & Tomaka, 2002); experience more positive emotions and experience daily stressors as challenges (Gallagher, 1990). Extraversion may influence the relationship between break activities and resource levels in three ways. First, given that extraverts have positive appraisal tendencies, a chore break may not be experienced as highly draining. In support of this notion, a vast literature on the effects of extraversion on stress suggests that extraversion is negatively related to stress and positively related to well-being in the workplace (e.g., Goodwin & Engstrom, 2002; Grant & Langan-Fox, 2007; Judge, Heller, & Mount, 2002).

Second, extraverts may prefer more social types of respites such as a group lunch or a coffee break with work colleagues. These social types of respites may not only serve as a respite but also to secure social support during demanding times. In addition, extraverts are more likely to socialize with work colleagues in general, which expands their social network and the possibility to secure help from that network when needed. Furthermore, extraverts are more likely to explicitly seek support when they need it and moreover they know where to seek that help – they are more aware of existing resources in other employees and feel more comfortable to approach them (Amirkhan, Risinger, & Swickert, 1995; Vollrath, Torgersen, & Alnæs, 1995; Watson & Hubbard, 1996). Thus, when extraverts engage in chore activities, these activities may be less depleting because they can turn to their social support network to help them during demanding times.

Third, previous research has shown that extraversion is related to positive emotions and affect (e.g., DeNeve & Cooper, 1998; Diener, Suh, Lucas, & Smith, 1999; Lucas & Fujita, 2000). Considering our conceptualization of emotions as a psychological resource, it follows that extraverts experience higher levels of affective resources in general. Moreover, as we suggested, affective resources are interrelated with other psychological resources, which suggests that extraverts may be able to fend off depletion of personal resources in general more effectively. This notion that individuals who have high level of resources attract even more resources is also consistent with broader theories applied to work recovery such as the conservation of resources theory (Hobfoll, 1998).

This discussion of extraversion suggests that individuals scoring low on Extraversion (introverts) may react differently than extraverts to some possible break activities. For example, introverts may not be able to recover their resources during a group lunch rather it may exhaust them even more. We suggest that introverts may need different types of breaks than extraverts in order to replenish their resources (e.g., reading a book during the lunch break). Also, because organizations are inherently social entities (Parsons, 1951), we suggest that replenishment may be more difficult for introverts in many organizational settings, especially those that require frequent social interaction (e.g., customer service or sales jobs). As such, introverts need to be especially cognizant of the types of break activities that aid their replenishment while at work in order to ensure that they can alleviate the potential strain that social situations pose for them. However, past research suggests that individuals chose and stay in occupations and organizations that suit their personalities (e.g., Johansson, 1970; Schaubroeck, Ganster, & Jones, 1998). Thus, although introverts may have more difficulties recovering their resources than extroverts in organizational contexts in general, once in a position or organization that suits their personality they should be able to recover their resources, although to what extent when compared to extraverts is unclear.

Neuroticism refers to the degree to which people experience negative emotions such as anxiety, hostility, depression, vulnerability, and impulsiveness (McCrae & John, 1992). Previous research has found that individuals high on Neuroticism compared to individuals low on

Neuroticism have negative general appraisal tendency (Gallagher, 1990; Hemenover & Dienstbier, 1996), are more prone to experiences of stressful events and perceive daily stressor as unpleasant (Kling, Ryff, Love, & Essex, 2003), and have difficulties coping with daily stressors (Gunthert, Cohen, & Armeli, 1999). In addition, individuals high on Neuroticism experience higher levels of interpersonal conflicts (Bolger & Schilling, 1991; Gunthert et al., 1999).

Neuroticism may influence the relationship between break activities and resource levels in two ways. First, individuals high on Neuroticism may perceive more stressors and be less able to cope with them than individuals low on Neuroticism throughout a regular workday. These increased experiences of daily stressors will lead to faster depletion of resources. In addition, these stressors increase negative effects, which is also related to neuroticism (e.g., Gallagher, 1990; Gunthert et al., 1999). Furthermore, because it is typically inappropriate to openly display negative emotions in the workplace (Hochschild, 1983), more neurotic individuals are more likely to have to engage in effortful emotion regulation, which also depletes regulatory resources (Grandey, 2000; Gross, 1998). In general, individuals high on Neuroticism experience more stressful events in the workplace and outside of work, which consequently leads to more negative effects and lower level of resources. Therefore, in any given workday individuals high on Neuroticisms may have lower levels of psychological resources.

Another possibility is that individuals high on Neuroticism appraise and experience their break activities differently from individuals low on Neuroticism. For example, consider an employee high on Neuroticism that is having lunch with his or her work group, and the group leader does not talk much to that employee throughout the lunch. This employee is likely to perceive this encounter more negatively than neutral. The negative appraisal may lead to resource depletion instead of replenishment as neurotic individuals struggle with trying to regulate their thoughts and behaviors as well as the negative emotions associated with such an appraisal. Therefore, the same break activity may be appraised differently between individuals high and low on Neuroticism, resulting in differential effects on levels of psychological resources.

A concept inversely related to Neuroticism, called "toughness" (Dienstbier, 1989), may provide insight into why people high in Neuroticism, as well as others who lack this, seem to be predisposed to the negative effects of work stress. Dienstbier (1989) describes how some people approach potentially stressful situations as challenges, and do not fully experience the negative consequences associated with stress, including decreased production of stress hormones. Dienstbier suggest that toughness allows people to endure trying situations by viewing them as challenges, which once conquered, result in positive feelings of accomplishment. Neurotic individuals seem to be especially lacking in this toughness and as a result, they are more likely to be negatively impacted by the demands of work.

Furthermore, Dienstbier suggests that toughness can be developed through repeated exposure to demanding situations, such as physical exercise. Over time, by approaching difficult situations as challenges, people develop toughness, allowing them to deal more effectively with similar situations in the future. In fact, the notion of toughness is consistent with Baumeister and colleagues' (e.g., Baumeister et al., 1994, 1998; Muraven et al., 1998) conceptualization of regulatory resources as a muscle that can be strengthened with repeated use. Although empirical research has yet to test the notion that regulatory resources function in this manner, it is highly suggestive of a potential individual difference that could also moderate the role of break activities in the recovery process. People higher in toughness, or its regulatory resource equivalent, might require shorter breaks, fewer breaks, or possibly different kinds of breaks, as the demands associated with work may not negatively impact these individuals to the same extent.

CONSEQUENCES OF PERSONAL RESOURCE LEVELS

Thus far we have focused on the antecedents of personal resource levels. However, personal resource levels can also have important consequences for various workplace outcomes. In this section, we will consider the consequences of resource levels on the following outcomes: stress and emotional exhaustion, task performance, affective performance, and organizational citizenship behaviors (OCBs). Of course this is not a comprehensive list of potential outcomes; however, this set of workplace outcomes is particularly sensitive to changes within a workday, in particular, changes in people's resource levels. In general, we suggest that higher levels of personal resources would have positive consequences for an array of organizational and individual outcomes.

Stress and Emotional Exhaustion

Research on respites, stress, and well-being has recognized the role of resources and their depletion and replenishment in consequent stress experiences (e.g., Sonnentag, 2001; Westman & Eden, 1997; Westman & Etzion, 1995). However, this line of research has never explicitly examined whether resource levels are mechanisms through which break activities (e.g., daily breaks, vacations) influence stress and well-being. This lack of empirical assessment and examination of levels of resources is partially due to measurement challenges. Thus, measuring an individual's levels of psychological resources and directly examining the relation between levels of resources and stress should be a priority for future research. We seek to help guide future endeavors in this area by theorizing on the relation between level of resources in a workday and a specific form of stress – emotional exhaustion.

Although, there are various indicators of stress and strain used in the literature, such as psychological well-being, burnout, physiological health, and emotional exhaustion, for the purposes of this discussion, we concentrate on emotional exhaustion. We do so because in momentary, within-day processes, emotional exhaustion will be more influenced by daily fluctuations in resource levels than will be overall psychological well-being or a person's overall health that develops over an extended period of time and remains stable. Emotional exhaustion is the core component of burnout (Maslach, 1982), and it refers to being emotionally exhausted by one's work, which is accompanied by psychological and emotional drain and physical fatigue (Wright & Cropanzano, 1998, p. 486).

We suggest that low levels of resources will lead to high emotional exhaustion. One reason for this suggestion is that when resources get depleted individuals are less able to deal with stress. The recognition of the importance of resources in dealing with stress goes back to one of the most influential stress theories, the transactional theory of stress postulated by Lazarus and Folkman (1984). The transactional theory of stress suggests that personal and social resources play an important role in stress appraisal and consequent coping with stress. Lazarus and Folkman theorized that resources available to individuals determine their reaction to stress and their employed coping strategies. In other words, if resources are exhausted or lacking, individuals would perceive stressors as a threat, whereas if they have resources they would perceive them as a challenge. Experiencing stressors as a threat would lead to employment of maladaptive coping strategies, which has detrimental effects on health and well-being.

Furthermore, Lazarus and Folkman (1984) distinguished between two sets of coping strategies, problem- and emotion-focused strategies. The problem-focused strategies involve actively dealing with problems (e.g., defining problems, seeking solutions), whereas emotion-focused strategies involve avoiding or distancing oneself from problems. Individuals with low levels of resources (especially regulatory) may be more likely to employ emotion-focused coping strategies because of their temporary inability to focus and solve problems. In turn, avoiding problems can lead to more problems and uncertainty, and consequently to the experience of emotional exhaustion. Furthermore, if affective resources are depleted, this would lead to the experience of negative effect. Negative effect has consequences for how situations and events are appraised. Specifically, negative effect leads to more negative interpretations of events (Hemenover & Dienstbier, 1996), which further leads to emotional exhaustion. Thus, levels of resources influence peoples' appraisal and coping strategies, which in turn leads to emotional exhaustion.

One other way in which lower levels of resources lead to emotional exhaustion may lie in the relationship between resource levels and task performance. Specifically, when individuals experience low levels of resources their performance is likely to diminish and they may feel that they cannot accomplish everything they ought to, or would like to accomplish in a given workday. This inability may lead to feelings of frustration and diminished feelings of control over their situations, giving rise to negative emotions (Shechtman & Horowitz, 2006) and ultimately to emotional exhaustion. It should be noted that it is quite possible that the relationship may be the other way around, that is, when individuals experience emotional exhaustion, they are unable to focus on their tasks and thus their performance suffers. One of the few empirical studies that examined the relationship between emotional exhaustion and job performance has found a negative relation between the two (Wright & Cropanzano, 1998). However, it was not possible to establish causality in this study because all data were collected at the same point in time.

Performance

To understand the within-day nature of resource depletion of job performance, let us once again consider Beal and colleagues (2005) episodic performance model. This model suggests that a regular workday consists of *performance episodes*, which are defined as "behavioral segments that are thematically organized around organizationally relevant goals and objectives" (p. 1055). It is argued that the variation in performance across work episodes in a workday is influenced by regulating attention to the focal tasks in a given episode. As we have already detailed, this regulation of attention results in regulatory resource depletion. Furthermore, they suggest that affective experiences can create additional cognitive demands on an individual, which in turn also depletes resources as people struggle to stay focused on the task at hand. As people's resources are depleted, greater effort is required to maintain performance during a given episode. If this process continues, performance levels degrade and ultimately become unacceptable.

We extend this line of reasoning in suggesting that low levels of resources should have negative effects on multiple facets of job performance within a workday. Past research on ego depletion has found that even after one episode of self-regulation, performance on subsequent tasks suffers, presumably because regulatory resources were depleted during the previous task. For example, Baumeister and colleagues (1998) conducted a series of laboratory experiments in which they found that (a) when participants engaged in a task that required resisting eating chocolate and instead eating radishes, subsequent performance on a difficult puzzle task was impaired; (b) when participants gave a counter attitudinal speech, they were more likely to give up on a subsequent puzzle solving tasks; and (c) when participants engaged in self-regulatory activities, they became more passive on subsequent tasks requiring regulation. Therefore, Baumeister and colleagues demonstrated that regulatory resources are used for many different activities and their initial use impairs performance on subsequent tasks. This occurs even when subsequent tasks may not be related to the initial task, supporting the idea that all acts of regulation draw on a common resource of self-regulation. Taken together, regulatory resource theory and the episodic process model of performance, suggest that individuals' levels of resources fluctuate within a workday, which in turn impact episodic job performance. When individuals experience low levels of resources, they have difficulties focusing attention on a task and in being more active in relation to the task (e.g., experience passivity). This is especially true if the previous job performance episode also involved more self-regulation. Furthermore, not only do we expect resource levels to impact task performance, but this process should function in a similar manner with regard to other types of job performance.

Affective Performance

In addition to performance of job tasks, many occupations require employees to engage in affective performance. Namely, the service sector requires its employees to display organizationally desired emotions (Hochschild, 1983), most often happiness, and thus the expression of emotion has become a part of many such jobs (Wichroski, 1994). The consequences of displaying organizationally desired behaviors have been examined in the literature on emotional labor. Emotional labor can be defined as the effort and control needed to display organizationally desired emotions (Morris & Feldman, 1996). Furthermore, it has been suggested that maintaining appropriate emotional displays is taxing and requires adequate levels of personal resources (Grandey, 2000). Thus, similar to task performance, affective display performance is affected by personal resource levels, such that lower levels of resources leads to poor quality of affective display. Although empirical results are limited, resource replenishment does indeed seem to influence the quality of positive affective display (Trougakos et al., 2008).

Of course there are various factors that could influence the relationship between personal resource levels and performance of emotional displays. For example, emotional labor often involves using one of two emotion regulation strategies: (1) *surface acting* – changing external expression of emotion while the internal state is unchanged or (2) *deep acting* – changing the actual internal experience of emotion (Grandey, 2000; Hochschild, 1983). Previous research has found that surface acting is related to strain and emotional exhaustion, whereas deep acting is not related to strain (Grandey, 2003; Gross, 1998). One explanation in the literature for the effect of surface acting on strain is that surface acting involves displaying emotions that are not internalized and thus there is a conflict between genuinely felt emotions and displayed emotions, which leads to emotional dissonance (Morris & Feldman, 1996). The other explanation is that suppressing truly felt emotion, or maintaining emotion that is not truly felt requires effort and control, which in turn depletes one's resources (Hochschild, 1983; Wharton, 1993). Indeed, research on resource depletion supports the notion that effortful regulation of emotion can deplete regulatory resources (Baumeister et al., 1998). Therefore, regulating emotion while engaging in affective performance should be related to resource depletion, and this can have consequences on job performance.

Organizational Citizenship Behaviors

The final type of job performance we discuss is OCBs. OCBs are defined as workplace behaviors that are discretionary, not explicitly required or rewarded by an organization, and in aggregate they promote organizational effectiveness (Organ, 1988). Hence, the presence of OCBs enables employees and organizations to function more smoothly. On the basis of our previous discussion, low levels of resources should also lead to low exhibition of OCBs. To explain the relationship between the levels of resources and OCBs, it is useful to distinguish between two general categories of OCBs (1) behaviors directed at the organization directly (e.g., staying extra hours to finish or improve a report), and (2) behaviors directed at individuals (e.g., helping new employee to find his or her way around) (Organ & Konovsky, 1989; Williams & Anderson, 1991).

The mechanisms behind the relationship between people's regulatory resources and OCBs directed at the organization (OCB-O) are similar to the mechanisms behind the relationship between psychological resources and task performance. The main distinction between task performance and OCB-Os is that task performance is an officially required and formally rewarded work activity, whereas OCB-Os are activities that go beyond the call of duty. However, the mechanisms for performing job tasks and OCB-Os are the same – an employee needs to invest certain amounts of energy, effort, and resources to perform them. When the level of regulatory resources is low, attention is decreased and passivity is increased, which leads to lower job performance. Furthermore, individuals seek to protect resources when there is a threat of resource loss (Hobfoll, 1998); and thus, we suggest that when regulatory resources are low, employees will be more likely to concentrate on job required tasks while abandoning performing any non-essential, non-rewarded activities such as OCB-Os.

The mechanisms behind the relationship between regulatory resources and OCBs directed at individuals (OCB-I) are generally similar to the mechanisms for OCB-Os. However, whether or not someone with depleted resources engages in OCB-I or not is likely to be influenced by a host of factors, including how well they know the person seeking help (motivation to help) as well as the complexity of the task. Presumably, the better an individual knows the person seeking help and the less complex the nature of the request is, thus requiring less effort, it is more likely that the employee will help the fellow coworker even under conditions of depleted resources. Overall, however, the message here is that employees are more likely to help when they have high levels of resources than when they have low levels of resources.

In addition to regulatory resources, affective resources might also play a role in the performance of OBC-I. There is much evidence to suggest that positive emotional affective experiences serve as a resource that can facilitate OCBs. Previous research has found that positive mood fosters prosocial behaviors in various settings (e.g., George, 1991; George & Bettenhausen, 1990; Rosenhan, Salovey, & Hargis, 1981). One account for this relationship is that individuals who are experiencing positive emotional states perceive stimuli around them in a more positive light (e.g., Bower, 1981; Carson & Adams, 1980; Clark & Teasdale, 1985) and are more attracted to other people (e.g., Bell, 1978; Gouaux, 1971; Mehrabian & Russell, 1975). Thus, they will be more likely to help their fellow coworkers.

In addition, previous research suggests that individuals in a positive mood strive to prolong their mood state, and helping others can serve to achieve this goal (e.g., Isen, Shalker, Clark, & Karp, 1978). The notion of people trying to maintain positive emotional states ties to our discussion of preferred choice activities. We suggested previously that engaging in activities that individuals preferred would lead to more positive effect. By helping their coworkers they maintain their positive emotional states and thus build their personal resources. In turn, higher levels of personal resources lead to more helping behaviors. Thus, high levels of helping behaviors (OCB-I) may be the consequence of high resource levels, but helping behaviors may also act as a preferred activity that contributes to building more personal resources. In other words, there is likely a positive feedback loop between affective resources and helping behaviors in the workplace.

MOTIVATION AS A MODERATOR OF THE RELATIONSHIP BETWEEN RESOURCE LEVELS AND OUTCOMES

Thus far, we have considered how low levels of momentary psychological resources should lead to negative outcomes such as poor job performance and high levels of emotional exhaustion. We have also pointed out a few factors that could potentially influence some of the relationships we have discussed. However, there are numerous other factors that might impact these relationships. In particular, individuals' behaviors are strongly influenced by their motivation (Bandura, 1986), and under some circumstances, motivation may be strong enough to counteract the effects of depleted resources.

A major thrust of motivation research in the workplace has been to examine factors that lead to greater job performance (e.g., Campbell &

Pritchard, 1976; Kanfer, 1992). Therefore, the focus of our discussion on motivation as a moderator will be on the relationship between resource levels and job performance. However, there are extensions that we can make about the impact of motivation on the relationship between resource levels and stress-related outcomes as well. Therefore, although we will focus on job performance, we will also briefly address the impact of motivation on stress.

Work Motivation

Work motivation can be defined as the extent to which people are willing to persist in achieving a certain goal (Locke & Latham, 2004). It has long been recognized that job performance does not only depend on one's abilities and skills, but it also depends on one's motivation to perform (Locke, 2000). Work motivation has been of interest to organizational scholars at least since the Hawthorne studies in the 1930s (e.g., Latham & Budworth, 2007), which spawned a correspondingly large literature on the subject. In the next sections, we describe how work motivation may also qualify the relationship between resource levels and job performance. The basic premise here is that daily job performance may remain relatively high despite low levels of resources because some individuals are motivated to continue performing at high levels.

Every job-related task aims to accomplish a certain goal, and the nature of those goals may have important consequences for the relationship between resource levels and job outcomes (e.g., performance and stress levels). According to goal-setting theory, higher (more difficult), more specific, and sophisticated goals lead to higher outcomes (Latham & Locke, 1991). Difficult and specific goals may be perceived as more challenging and important (e.g., Drach-Zahavy & Erez, 2002), and more challenging and important goals are usually associated with tangible rewards such as pay and intangible rewards such as satisfaction and pride associated with accomplishing a difficult and important goal. In turn, when employees are experiencing high levels of resource depletion, they may feel that continuing to work on those goals will be beneficial for them and thus they increase focus and effort in order to continue to work as effectively as possible. However, if employees perceive that the goals set are "not worthy" of their further effort and energy, performance may wane and eventually they may cease to work on the task altogether.

A study conducted by Muraven and Slessareva (2003) offers evidence that depleted employees may continue to work and perform when they perceive that their tasks and goals are important and beneficial. They examined whether motivation can offset negative consequences of resource depletion. In series of laboratory experiments, they found that (a) depleted participants who were working on a self-control task continued to work on the task when they believed that they could help others (important task) compared to depleted participants who did not believe that the task could help others (unimportant task); (b) also, depleted participants performed better when they believed that they would have personal benefits from the task when compared to depleted participants who did not believe they could benefit from the task. The authors offered an interesting plausible explanation for their findings: individuals are motivated to conserve their limited regulatory resources and as their resources become depleted, they are more likely to cease activities involving regulatory resources not because it is more difficult to exercise self-control, but because they want to preserve their resources. However, if they are strongly motivated to continue using their regulatory resources, that is, benefits are higher than associated costs of resource depletion, they will continue with activities that deplete regulatory resources.

In addition, having a clear direction and goals when resources are low also has implications for individuals' levels of stress and well-being. Previous research has examined the influence of role ambiguity on stress. Role ambiguity refers to lack of clear goals and direction, which increases individual's levels of stress (Posig & Kickul, 2003). Previous research has found that role ambiguity is positively related to stress and specifically to emotional burnout (e.g., Lee & Ashforth, 1996; Posig & Kickul, 2003). When individuals experience low levels of resources, clear goals and directions help them to know where they need to direct their remaining energy and how they can accomplish their goals, which will ultimately lead to less stress and emotional exhaustion. Also, when resources are depleted, it may be very difficult to prioritize existing goals and formulate new goals. Having clear goals allows individuals to perform predetermined tasks and thus maintain performance when resource levels are low. In other words, when resource levels are low, employees may perform well by working on predetermined and more mundane tasks (e.g., entering data into a spreadsheet) and avoiding more complex tasks that call for defining goals.

Goals also differ in terms of their origin; goals can be either internally (self) imposed or externally imposed (e.g., imposed by a manager). The concept of the origin of goals (self imposed versus externally imposed) can be mapped onto the concept of autonomous and controlled motivation postulated in the self-determination theory of motivation (Gagné & Deci, 2005; Ryan & Deci, 2000). Autonomous motivation refers to acting volitionally and having a choice, whereas controlled motivation refers to lack of choice and a feeling of pressure to perform a task. Furthermore, intrinsic motivation may represent autonomous motivation – engaging in an activity because it is inherently interesting and enjoyable. Extrinsic motivation may represent controlled motivation – engaging in an activity because it leads to some tangible outcomes such as rewards or avoiding punishment (Ryan & Deci, 2000). When employees define their goals, they are more likely to be intrinsically motivated. Intrinsically motivated employees will perform better because they enjoy their work and enjoyment makes task completion easier. This enjoyment associated with pursuing an intrinsically interesting task is closely tied to a type of respites that we discussed earlier in this chapter – preferred choice activities. When employees engage in an activity they prefer they decrease the use of self-regulatory resources, which has consequences on job performance and well-being (Fritz & Sonnentag, 2005; Miner et al., 2005; Trougakos et al., 2008). In addition, because engaging in an intrinsically motivated task often results in experiencing enjoyment, a positive emotional experience, this can result in an increase in affective resources. Thus, engaging in work tasks which are intrinsically motivating can lead to two processes. First, less regulatory resources are consumed, and thus, less resource depletion is experienced. Second, it fosters more resource building, specifically building and replenishment of affective resources. In turn, the combination of greater regulatory resources and replenishment of affective resources may lead to higher performance levels and higher levels of well-being.

CONCLUDING THOUGHTS

Research in the area of work recovery has primarily focused on how people use their time outside of typical work hours. However, the average person probably spends anywhere from seven to ten hours on the job each workday. Considering the time people spend at work, within-day work breaks provide excellent opportunities for momentary recovery. Yet despite the ubiquitous nature of within-day work breaks, little research has systematically examined the role of these breaks in the recovery process. With this in mind, we focused on the role of within-day work breaks in people's daily recovery in order to help develop a more comprehensive picture of work recovery. It is important to note that in no way are we presuming to have covered all of the factors involved in momentary daily recovery. Rather, the aim of this chapter has been to serve as an initial discussion of this understudied area of work recovery, with the intention to review relevant prior findings and bring together some of the relevant theories with the hopes of stimulating future research in the area.

Specifically, the notion of limited personal resources has been central to the study of work recovery, yet prior conceptualization of resources have not adequately accounted for the processes involved in within-day recovery. We suggest that in order to better understand these processes, applying an episodic approach along with more micro-level theories of personal resources, in conjunction with the traditional recovery theories, should prove useful in advancing this area of study. Furthermore, future research in the area of work recovery would be well served to bear in mind that there are numerous individual differences and situational factors that might impact recovery. Exploring these variables is likely to result in an understanding that activities leading to work recovery are not a "one size fits all" proposition. Therefore, in order to maximize the prescriptive utility of this stream of research, a broader understanding of individual and contextual differences is necessary.

Finally, it is important to note that the effects of various types of work breaks, and the activities people engage in during these breaks, are unlikely completely independent phenomena, although research often treats them as such. That is, what we do before we go to work, during our within-day work breaks, and after work, are all likely to be interrelated in some manner. We have little doubt that people's daily resource levels are impacted by the cumulative effects of all opportunities for recovery. It is therefore likely that a host of outcomes are similarly impacted. Understanding the intricacies of these relationships, both over the course of a single workday, as well as over greater periods of time, is an important step to develop a more comprehensive understanding of the processes and outcomes associated with work recovery.

ACKNOWLEDGMENTS

The authors would like to acknowledge Sabine Sonnentag and Daniel Ganster for their helpful reviews and feedback on this chapter. We would also like to recognize Daniel Beal for his insights and comments. Finally, J. P. Trougakos would like to thank Panagiotis Ioannis for invaluable help in providing real life insights into some of the topics covered in this chapter. This research was funded by Social Sciences and Humanities Research Council of Canada grant number 410-2008-0505.

REFERENCES

Amirkhan, J. H., Risinger, R. T., & Swickert, R. J. (1995). Extraversion: A "hidden" personality factor in coping? *Journal of Personality, 63,* 189–212.

Averill, J. R. (1973). Personal control over aversive stimuli and its relationship to stress. *Psychological Bulletin, 80,* 286–303.

Bakker, A. B., & Demerouti, E. (2006). The job demands-resources model: State of the art. *Journal of Managerial Psychology, 22,* 309–328.

Bandura, A. (1986). The explanatory and predictive scope of self-efficacy theory. *Journal of Social & Clinical Psychology, 4,* 359–373.

Barker, R. G. (Ed.) (1963). *The stream of behavior.* East Norwalk, CT: Appleton-Century-Crofts.

Baumeister, R. F., Bratslavsky, E., Muraven, M., & Tice, D. M. (1998). Ego depletion: Is the active self a limited resource? *Journal of Personality and Social Psychology, 74,* 1252–1265.

Baumeister, R. F., Heatherton, T. F., & Tice, D. M. (1994). *Losing control: How and why people fail at self-regulation.* San Diego, CA: Academic Press.

Baumeister, R. F., Vohs, K. D., & Tice, D. M. (2007). The strength model of self-control. *Current Directions in Psychological Science, 16,* 351–355.

Beal, D. J., Weiss, H. M., Barros, E., & MacDermid, S. M. (2005). An episodic process model of affective influences on performance. *Journal of Applied Psychology, 90,* 1054–1068.

Bell, P. A. (1978). Affective state, attraction, and affiliation: Misery loves happy company, too. *Personality and Social Psychology Bulletin, 4,* 616–619.

Benton, D. (1990). The impact of increasing blood glucose on psychological functioning. *Biological Psychology, 30,* 13–19.

Benton, D., Owens, D. S., & Parker, P. Y. (1994). Blood glucose influences memory and attention in young adults. *Neuropsychologia, 32,* 595–607.

Bolger, N., & Schilling, E. A. (1991). Personality and the problems of everyday life: The role of neuroticism in exposure and reactivity to daily stressors. *Journal of Personality, 59,* 355–386.

Bono, J. E., Foldes, H. J., Vinson, G., & Muros, J. P. (2007). Workplace emotions: The role of supervision and leadership. *Journal of Applied Psychology, 92,* 1357–1367.

Boucsein, W., & Thum, M. (1997). Design of work/rest schedules for computer work based on psychophysiological recovery measures. *International Journal of Industrial Ergonomics, 20,* 51–57.

Bower, G. H. (1981). Mood and memory. *American Psychologist, 36,* 129–148.

Campbell, J. P., & Pritchard, R. D. (1976). Motivation theory in industrial and organizational psychology. In: M. D. Dunnette (Ed.), *Handbook of industrial and organizational psychology* (pp. 63–130). Chicago: Rand McNally.

Carson, T. P., & Adams, H. E. (1980). Activity valence as a function of mood change. *Journal of Abnormal Psychology, 89,* 368–377.

Clark, D. M., & Teasdale, J. D. (1985). Constraints on the effects of mood on memory. *Journal of Personality and Social Psychology, 48*, 1595–1608.

Craik, K. H. (2000). The lived day of an individual: A person-environment perspective. In: W. B. Walsh, K. H. Craik & R. H. Price (Eds), *Person-environment psychology: New directions and perspectives* (2nd ed., pp. 233–266). Mahwah, NJ: Lawrence Erlbaum Associates Publishers.

Dababneh, A. J., Swanson, N., & Shell, R. L. (2001). Impact of added rest breaks on the productivity and well being of workers. *Ergonomics, 44*, 164–174.

Daniels, K., & Guppy, A. (1994). Occupational stress, social support, job control, and psychological well-being. *Human Relations, 47*, 1523–1544.

DeNeve, K. M., & Cooper, H. (1998). The happy personality: A meta-analysis of 137 personality traits and subjective well-being. *Psychological Bulletin, 124*, 197–229.

Dickman, H. R. (1963). The perception of behavioral units. In: R. G. Barker (Ed.), *The stream of behavior: Explorations of its structure and content* (pp. 23–41). East Norwalk, CT: Appleton-Century-Crofts.

Diener, E., Suh, E. M., Lucas, R. E., & Smith, H. L. (1999). Subjective well-being: Three decades of progress. *Psychological Bulletin, 125*, 276–302.

Dienstbier, R. A. (1989). Arousal and physiological toughness: Implications for mental and physical health. *Psychological Review, 96*, 84–100.

Drach-Zahavy, A., & Erez, M. (2002). Challenge versus threat effects on the goal–performance relationship. *Organizational Behavior and Human Decision Processes, 88*, 667–682.

Eden, D. (1990). Acute and chronic job stress, strain, and vacation relief. *Organizational Behavior and Human Decision Processes, 45*, 175–193.

Eden, D. (2001). Vacations and other respites: Studying stress on and off the job. In: C. L. Cooper & I. T. Robertson (Eds), *International review of industrial and organizational psychology* (Vol. 16, pp. 121–146). New York: Wiley.

Elkin, A. J., & Rosch, P. J. (1990). Promoting mental health at the workplace: The prevention side of stress management. *Occupational Medicine: State of Art Review, 5*, 739–754.

Feyer, A. M., & Williamson, A. M. (1995). Work and rest in the long distance road transport industry in Australia. *Work and Stress, 9*, 198–205.

Fisher, D. L., Andres, R. O., Airth, D., & Smith, S. S. (1993). Repetitive motion disorders: The design of optimal rate-rest profiles. *Human Factors, 35*, 283–304.

Fleeson, W. (2001). Toward a structure- and process-integrated view of personality: Traits as density distributions of states. *Journal of Personality and Social Psychology, 80*, 1011–1027.

Fleeson, W. (2004). Moving personality beyond the person-situation debate: The challenge and the opportunity of within-person variability. *Current Directions in Psychological Science, 13*, 83–87.

Fletcher, B. C. (1991). *Work, stress, disease and life expectancy*. Chichester, England: Wiley.

Fredrickson, B. L. (1998). What good are positive emotions? *Review of General Psychology, 2*, 300–319.

Fredrickson, B. L. (2000). Extracting meaning from past affective experiences: The importance of peaks, ends, and specific emotions. *Cognition & Emotion, 14*, 577–606.

Fredrickson, B. L. (2001). The role of positive emotions in positive psychology: The broaden-and-build theory of positive emotions. *American Psychologist, 56*, 218–226.

Fredrickson, B. L., & Kahneman, D. (1993). Duration neglect in retrospective evaluations of affective episodes. *Journal of Personality and Social Psychology, 65*, 45–55.

Frese, M. (1989). Human computer interaction within an industrial psychology framework. *Applied Psychology: An International Review, 38*, 29–44.

Frijda, N. H. (1993). Moods, emotion episodes, and emotions. In: M. Lewis & J. M. Haviland (Eds), *Handbook of emotions* (pp. 381–403). New York: Guilford Press.

Fritz, C., & Sonnentag, S. (2005). Recovery, health, and job performance: Effects of weekend experiences. *Journal of Occupational Health Psychology, 10*, 187–199.

Fritz, C., & Sonnentag, S. (2006). Recovery, well-being, and performance-related outcomes: The role of workload and vacation experiences. *Journal of Applied Psychology, 91*, 936–945.

Gagné, M., & Deci, E. L. (2005). Self-determination theory and work motivation. *Journal of Organizational Behavior, 26*, 331–362.

Gailliot, M. T., Baumeister, R. F., DeWall, C. N., Maner, J. K., Plant, E. A., Tice, D. M., Brewer, L. E., & Schmeichel, B. J. (2007). Self-control relies on glucose as a limited energy source: Willpower is more than a metaphor. *Journal of Personality and Social Psychology, 92*, 325–336.

Gallagher, D. J. (1990). Extraversion, neuroticism and appraisal of stressful academic events. *Personality and Individual Differences, 11*, 1053–1057.

George, J. M. (1991). State or trait: Effects of positive mood on prosocial behaviors at work. *Journal of Applied Psychology, 76*, 299–307.

George, J. M., & Bettenhausen, K. (1990). Understanding prosocial behavior, sales performance, and turnover: A group-level analysis in a service context. *Journal of Applied Psychology, 75*, 698–709.

Geurts, S. A. E., Kompier, M. A. J., Roxburgh, S., & Houtman, I. L. D. (2003). Does work–home interference mediate the relationship between workload and well-being? *Journal of Vocational Behavior, 63*, 532–559.

Glass, D. C., Reim, B., & Singer, J. E. (1971). Behavioral consequences of adaptation to controllable and uncontrollable noise. *Journal of Experimental Social Psychology, 7*, 244–257.

Glass, D. C., & Singer, J. E. (1973). Experimental studies of uncontrollable and unpredictable noise. *Representative Research in Social Psychology, 4*, 165–183.

Goodwin, R., & Engstrom, G. (2002). Personality and the perception of health in the general population. *Psychological Medicine, 32*, 325–332.

Gouaux, C. (1971). Induced affective states and interpersonal attraction. *Journal of Personality and Social Psychology, 20*, 37–43.

Grandey, A. A. (2000). Emotional regulation in the workplace: A new way to conceptualize emotional labor. *Journal of Occupational Health Psychology, 5*, 95–110.

Grandey, A. A. (2003). When "the show must go on": Surface acting and deep acting as determinants of emotional exhaustion and peer-rated service delivery. *Academy of Management Journal, 46*, 86–96.

Grandey, A. A., Tam, A. P., & Brauburger, A. L. (2002). Affective states and traits in the workplace: Diary and survey data from young workers. *Motivation and Emotion, 26*, 31–55.

Grant, S., & Langan-Fox, J. (2007). Personality and the occupational stressor–strain relationship: The role of the big five. *Journal of Occupational Health Psychology, 12*, 20–33.

Gross, J. J. (1998). The emerging field of emotion regulation: An integrative review. *Review of General Psychology, 2*, 271–299.

Gunthert, K. C., Cohen, L. H., & Armeli, S. (1999). The role of neuroticism in daily stress and coping. *Journal of Personality and Social Psychology, 77*, 1087–1100.

Hemenover, S. H., & Dienstbier, R. A. (1996). Prediction of stress appraisals from mastery, extraversion, neuroticism, and general appraisal tendencies. *Motivation and Emotion, 20,* 299–317.

Henning, R. A., Jacques, P., Kissel, G. V., Sullivan, A. B., & Alteras-Webb, S. M. (1997). Frequent short rest breaks from computer work: Effects on productivity and well-being at two field sites. *Ergonomics, 40,* 78–91.

Henning, R. A., Kissel, G. V., & Maynard, D. C. (1994). Compensatory rest breaks for VDT operators. *International Journal of Industrial Ergonomics, 14,* 243–249.

Higgins, E. T. (1997). Beyond pleasure and pain. *American Psychologist, 52,* 1280–1300.

Hobfoll, S. E. (1989). Conservation of resources: A new attempt at conceptualizing stress. *American Psychologist, 44,* 513–524.

Hobfoll, S. E. (1998). *Stress, culture, and community: The psychology and philosophy of stress.* New York: Plenum Press.

Hobfoll, S. E., & Shirom, A. (2001). Conservation of resources theory: Applications to stress and management in the workplace. In: R. T. Golembiewski (Ed.), *Handbook of organizational behavior* (2nd ed., pp. 57–80). New York: Marcel Dekker.

Hochschild, A. (1983). *The managed heart.* Berkeley, CA: University of California Press.

Hockey, G. R. J. (1996). Energetical-control processes in the regulation of human performance. In: W. Battmann & S. Dutke (Eds), *Processes of the molar regulation of behavior* (pp. 271–287). Lengerich, Germany: Pabst Science Publishers.

Isen, A. M., Shalker, T. E., Clark, M., & Karp, L. (1978). Affect, accessibility of material in memory, and behavior: A cognitive loop? *Journal of Personality and Social Psychology, 36,* 1–12.

Isen, A. M., & Simmonds, S. F. (1978). The effect of feeling good on a helping task that is incompatible with good mood. *Social Psychology, 41,* 346–349.

Jackson, P. R., Wall, T. D., Martin, R., & Davids, K. (1993). New measures of job control, cognitive demand, and production responsibility. *Journal of Applied Psychology, 78,* 753–762.

Jackson, S. E. (1983). Participation in decision making as a strategy for reducing job-related strain. *Journal of Applied Psychology, 68,* 3–19.

Johansson, C. B. (1970). Strong vocational interest blank introversion–extraversion and occupational membership. *Journal of Counseling Psychology, 17,* 451–455.

Judge, T. A., Heller, D., & Mount, M. K. (2002). Five-factor model of personality and job satisfaction: A meta-analysis. *Journal of Applied Psychology, 87,* 530–541.

Kahn, R. L., & Byosiere, P. (1992). Stress in organizations. In: M. D. Dunnette & L. M. Hough (Eds), *Handbook of industrial and organizational psychology* (Vol. 3, pp. 571–650). Palo Alto, CA: Consulting Psychologists Press.

Kanfer, R. (1992). Work motivation: New directions in theory and research. In: C. L. Cooper & I. T. Robertson (Eds), *International review of industrial and organizational psychology* (Vol. 7, pp. 1–53). New York: Wiley.

Karasek, R. (1979). Job demands, job decision latitude, and mental strain: Implications for job redesign. *Administrative Science Quarterly, 24,* 285–306.

Kelly, J. R., & Barsade, S. G. (2001). Mood and emotions in small groups and work teams. *Organizational Behavior and Human Decision Processes, 86,* 99–130.

Kling, K. C., Ryff, C. D., Love, G., & Essex, M. (2003). Exploring the influence of personality on depressive symptoms and self-esteem across a significant life transition. *Journal of Personality and Social Psychology, 85,* 922–932.

Latham, G. P., & Budworth, M. (2007). The study of work motivation in the 20th century. In: L. L. Koppes (Ed.), *Historical perspectives in industrial and organizational psychology* (pp. 353–381). Mahwah, NJ: Lawrence Erlbaum Associates Publishers.

Latham, G. P., & Locke, E. A. (1991). Self-regulation through goal setting. *Organizational Behavior and Human Decision Processes, 50*, 212–247.

Lazarus, R. S., & Folkman, S. (1984). *Stress, appraisal, and coping.* New York: Springer.

Lee-Baggley, D., Preece, M., & DeLongis, A. (2005). Coping with interpersonal stress: Role of big five traits. *Journal of Personality, 73*, 1141–1180.

Lee, R. T., & Ashforth, B. E. (1996). A meta-analytic examination of the correlates of the three dimensions of job burnout. *Journal of Applied Psychology, 81*, 123–133.

Lisper, H., & Eriksson, B. (1980). Effects of the length of a rest break and food intake on subsidiary reaction-time performance in an 8-hour driving task. *Journal of Applied Psychology, 65*, 117–122.

Locke, E. A. (2000). Motivation, cognition, and action: An analysis of studies of task goals and knowledge. *Applied Psychology: An International Review, 49*, 408–429.

Locke, E. A., & Latham, G. P. (2004). What should we do about motivation theory? Six recommendations for the twenty-first century. *Academy of Management Review, 29*, 388–403.

Lucas, R. E., & Fujita, F. (2000). Factors influencing the relation between extraversion and pleasant affect. *Journal of Personality and Social Psychology, 79*, 1039–1056.

Marks, S. R. (1977). Multiple roles and role strain: Some notes on human energy, time, and commitment. *American Sociological Review, 42*, 921–936.

Maslach, C. (1982). *Burnout: The cost of caring.* Englewood Cliffs, NJ: Prentice Hall.

Mauno, S., Kinnunen, U., & Ruokolainen, M. (2007). Job demands and resources as antecedents of work engagement: A longitudinal study. *Journal of Vocational Behavior, 70*, 149–171.

Mayo, E. (1933). *The human problems of an industrialized civilization.* Glenview, IL: Scott Foresman.

McCrae, R. R., & John, O. P. (1992). An introduction to the five-factor model and its applications. *Journal of Personality, 60*, 175–215.

McLean, L., Tingley, M., Scott, R. N., & Rickards, J. (2001). Computer terminal work and the benefit of microbreaks. *Applied Ergonomics, 32*, 225–237.

Mehrabian, A., & Russell, J. A. (1975). Environmental effects on affiliation among strangers. *Humanitas, 11*, 219–230.

Meijman, T. F., & Mulder, G. (1998). Psychological aspects of workload. In: P. J. D. Drenth, H. Thierry & C. J. de Wolff (Eds), *Handbook of work and organizational psychology, Vol. 2: Work psychology* (pp. 5–33). Hove, England: Psychology Press.

Miller, I. W., & Norman, W. H. (1979). Learned helplessness in humans: A review and attribution-theory model. *Psychological Bulletin, 86*, 93–118.

Miner, A. G., Glomb, T. M., & Hulin, C. (2005). Experience sampling mood and its correlates at work. *Journal of Occupational and Organizational Psychology, 78*, 171–193.

Miner, A. G., & Hulin, C. L. (2006). Multimethods in industrial and organizational psychology: Expanding "methods" to include longitudinal designs. In: M. Eid & E. Diener (Eds), *Handbook of multimethod measurement in psychology* (pp. 429–439). Washington, DC: American Psychological Association.

Moller, A. C., Deci, E. L., & Ryan, R. M. (2006). Choice and ego-depletion: The moderating role of autonomy. *Personality and Social Psychology Bulletin, 32*, 1024–1036.

Morris, J. A., & Feldman, D. C. (1996). The dimensions, antecedents, and consequences of emotional labor. *Academy of Management Review, 21*, 986–1010.

Moskowitz, D. S., Brown, K. W., & Côté, S. (1997). Reconceptualizing stability: Using time as a psychological dimension. *Current Directions in Psychological Science, 6*, 127–131.

Muraven, M., & Baumeister, R. F. (2000). Self-regulation and depletion of limited resources: Does self-control resemble a muscle? *Psychological Bulletin, 126*, 247–259.

Muraven, M., & Slessareva, E. (2003). Mechanism of self-control failure: Motivation and limited resources. *Personality and Social Psychology Bulletin, 29*, 894–906.

Muraven, M., Tice, D. M., & Baumeister, R. F. (1998). Self-control as a limited resource: Regulatory depletion patterns. *Journal of Personality and Social Psychology, 74*, 774–789.

Newtson, D. (1973). Attribution and the unit of perception of ongoing behavior. *Journal of Personality and Social Psychology, 28*, 28–38.

Newtson, D., & Engquist, G. (1976). The perceptual organization of ongoing behavior. *Journal of Experimental Social Psychology, 12*, 436–450.

Organ, D. W. (1988). *Organizational citizenship behavior: The good soldier syndrome.* Lexington, MA: Lexington Books.

Organ, D. W., & Konovsky, M. (1989). Cognitive versus affective determinants of organizational citizenship behavior. *Journal of Applied Psychology, 74*, 157–164.

Parfitt, G., & Gledhill, C. (2004). The effect of choice of exercise mode on psychological responses. *Psychology of Sport and Exercise, 5*, 111–117.

Parsons, T. (1951). *The social system.* New York: Free Press.

Penley, J. A., & Tomaka, J. (2002). Associations among the big five, emotional responses and coping with acute stress. *Personality and Individual Differences, 32*, 1215–1228.

Posig, M., & Kickul, J. (2003). Extending our understanding of burnout: Test of an integrated model in nonservice occupations. *Journal of Occupational Health Psychology, 8*, 3–19.

Repetti, R. L. (1987). Linkages between work and family roles. *Applied Social Psychology Annual, 7*, 98–127.

Repetti, R. L. (1993). Short-term effects of occupational stressors on daily mood and health complaints. *Health Psychology, 12*, 125–131.

Robinson, M. D., & Clore, G. L. (2002). Belief and feeling: Evidence for an accessibility model of emotional self-report. *Psychological Bulletin, 128*, 934–960.

Rosenhan, D. L., Salovey, P., & Hargis, K. (1981). The joys of helping: Focus of attention mediates the impact of positive affect on altruism. *Journal of Personality and Social Psychology, 40*, 899–905.

Rothbard, N. P. (2001). Enriching or depleting? The dynamics of engagement in work and family roles. *Administrative Science Quarterly, 46*, 655–684.

Ryan, R. M., & Deci, E. L. (2000). Self-determination theory and the facilitation of intrinsic motivation, social development, and well-being. *American Psychologist, 55*, 68–78.

Schaubroeck, J., Ganster, D. C., & Jones, J. R. (1998). Organization and occupation influences in the attraction–selection–attrition process. *Journal of Applied Psychology, 83*, 869–891.

Schreiber, C. A., & Kahneman, D. (2000). Determinants of the remembered utility of aversive sounds. *Journal of Experimental Psychology, 129*, 27–42.

Shaver, P., Schwartz, J., Kirson, D., & O'Connor, C. (1987). Emotion knowledge: Further exploration of a prototype approach. *Journal of Personality and Social Psychology, 52*, 1061–1086.

Shechtman, N., & Horowitz, L. (2006). Interpersonal and noninterpersonal interactions, interpersonal motives, and the effect of frustrated motives. *Personality and Social Psychology Bulletin, 32,* 1126–1139.

Sonnentag, S. (2001). Work, recovery activities, and individual well-being: A diary study. *Journal of Occupational Health Psychology, 6,* 196–210.

Sonnentag, S. (2003). Recovery, work engagement, and proactive behavior: A new look at the interface between nonwork and work. *Journal of Applied Psychology, 88,* 518–528.

Sonnentag, S., & Frese, M. (2003). Stress in organizations. In: W. C. Borman, D. R. Ilgen & R. J. Klimoski (Eds), *Handbook of psychology: Industrial and organizational psychology* (Vol. 12, pp. 453–491). Hoboken, NJ: Wiley.

Sonnentag, S., & Kruel, U. (2006). Psychological detachment from work during off-job time: The role of job stressors, job involvement, and recovery-related self-efficacy. *European Journal of Work and Organizational Psychology, 15,* 197–217.

Sonnentag, S., & Natter, E. (2004). Flight attendants' daily recovery from work: Is there no place like home? *International Journal of Stress Management, 11,* 366–391.

Sonnentag, S., & Zijlstra, F. R. H. (2006). Job characteristics and off-job activities as predictors of need for recovery, well-being, and fatigue. *Journal of Applied Psychology, 91,* 330–350.

Tice, D. M., Baumeister, R. F., Shmueli, D., & Muraven, M. (2007). Restoring the self: Positive affect helps improve self-regulation following ego depletion. *Journal of Experimental Social Psychology, 43,* 379–384.

Trougakos, J. P., Beal, D. J., Green, S. G., & Weiss, H. M. (2008). Making the break count: An episodic examination of recovery activities, emotional experiences, and positive affective displays. *Academy of Management Journal, 51,* 131–146.

Tucker, P. (2003). The impact of rest breaks upon accident risk, fatigue and performance: A review. *Work & Stress, 17,* 123–137.

Van der Hek, H., & Plomp, H. N. (1997). Occupational stress management programmes: A practical overview of published effect studies. *Occupational Medicine, 47,* 133–141.

Vohs, K. D., Baumeister, R. F., Schmeichel, B. J., Twenge, J. M., Nelson, N. M., & Tice, D. M. (2008). Making choices impairs subsequent self-control: A limited-resource account of decision making, self-regulation, and active initiative. *Journal of Personality and Social Psychology, 94,* 883–898.

Vollrath, M., Torgersen, S., & Alnæs, R. (1995). Personality as long-term predictor of coping. *Personality and Individual Differences, 18,* 117–125.

Watson, D. (1988). Intraindividual and interindividual analyses of positive and negative affect: Their relation to health complaints, perceived stress, and daily activities. *Journal of Personality and Social Psychology, 54,* 1020–1030.

Watson, D., & Hubbard, B. (1996). Adaptational style and dispositional structure: Coping in the context of the five-factor model. *Journal of Personality, 64,* 737–774.

Watson, D., Wiese, D., Vaidya, J., & Tellegen, A. (1999). The two general activation systems of affect: Structural findings, evolutionary considerations, and psychobiological evidence. *Journal of Personality and Social Psychology, 76,* 820–838.

Wegener, D. T., & Petty, R. E. (1994). Mood management across affective states: The hedonic contingency hypothesis. *Journal of Personality and Social Psychology, 66,* 1034–1048.

Weiss, H. M., & Cropanzano, R. (1996). Affective events theory: A theoretical discussion of the structure, causes and consequences of affective experiences at work. In: B. M. Staw & L. L. Cummings (Eds), *Research in organizational behavior: An annual series of analytical essays and critical reviews* (Vol. 18, pp. 1–74). Greenwich, CT: JAI Press.

Westman, M., & Eden, D. (1997). Effects of a respite from work on burnout: Vacation relief
    and fade-out. *Journal of Applied Psychology, 82*, 516–527.
Westman, M., & Etzion, D. (1995). Crossover of stress, strain and resources from one spouse to
    another. *Journal of Organizational Behavior, 16*, 169–181.
Westman, M., & Etzion, D. (2001). The impact of vacation and job stress on burnout and
    absenteeism. *Psychology & Health, 16*, 595–606.
Wharton, A. S. (1993). The affective consequences of service work: Managing emotions on the
    job. *Work and Occupations, 20*, 205–232.
Wichroski, M. A. (1994). The secretary: Invisible labor in the workworld of women. *Human
    Organization, 53*, 33–41.
Williams, L. J., & Anderson, S. E. (1991). Job satisfaction and organizational commitment as
    predictors of organizational citizenship and in-role behaviors. *Journal of Management,
    17*, 601–617.
Wright, T. A., & Cropanzano, R. (1998). Emotional exhaustion as a predictor of job
    performance and voluntary turnover. *Journal of Applied Psychology, 83*, 486–493.

DAILY RECOVERY FROM WORK-RELATED EFFORT DURING NON-WORK TIME

Evangelia Demerouti, Arnold B. Bakker,
Sabine A. E. Geurts and Toon W. Taris

ABSTRACT

The aim of this chapter is to provide a literature review on daily recovery during non-work time. Specifically, next to discussing theories that help us understand the process of recovery, we will clarify how recovery and its potential outcomes have been conceptualized so far. Consequently, we present empirical findings of diary studies addressing the activities that may facilitate or hinder daily recovery. We will pay special attention to potential mechanisms that may underlie the facilitating or hindering processes. Owing to the limited research on daily recovery, we will review empirical findings on predictors and outcomes of a related construct, namely need for recovery. We conclude with an overall framework from which daily recovery during non-work time can be understood. In this framework, we claim that daily recovery is an important moderator in the process through which job characteristics and their related strain may lead to unfavorable states on a daily basis.

Current Perspectives on Job-Stress Recovery
Research in Occupational Stress and Well Being, Volume 7, 85–123
Copyright © 2009 by Emerald Group Publishing Limited
All rights of reproduction in any form reserved
ISSN: 1479-3555/doi:10.1108/S1479-3555(2009)0000007006

INTRODUCTION

Job demands have shown a tendency to increase, to such a degree that work-related stress and burnout have become a serious and pervasive problem in many countries. Whereas there is a considerable literature on the consequences of high demands within the workplace (among others, Bakker & Demerouti, 2007; Lee & Ashforth, 1996), there has been less emphasis on the role of *recovery* from the associated strain during non-work time. In particular, few studies have examined the significance of different types of behavior during non-work time and its relative contribution to recovery from work strain. This is surprising because, all other things being equal, it is plausible that a worker who is well (versus poorly) recovered from a previous work period is more likely to be engaged with work in a subsequent work period, with presumed benefits in improving employee performance at work (Bakker, 2009; Demerouti & Cropanzano, 2009).

In this chapter, we argue that adequate recovery on a daily basis is crucial for the maintenance of well-being and job performance. Recovery may occur in the context of work and non-work (Geurts & Sonnentag, 2006). The first is referred to as *internal* recovery and occurs during short breaks from work. The second is called *external* recovery and may occur during after-work hours, during weekends, and during longer periods of respite like vacation. In the present chapter, we focus specifically on external recovery. Although many European employees have long recovery time during vacations, it seems that daily recovery is more crucial for health and well-being. The point is that the salutary effects of vacations fade out quickly (De Bloom et al., 2009). Specifically, levels of burnout and well-being have been found to return rapidly to prevacation levels after returning to work (Westman & Eden, 1997; Westman & Etzion, 2001). Therefore, recovery that takes place daily after work or during the weekend may well be more important for protecting well-being and performance (Sonnentag, 2001, 2003).

The goal of this chapter is to provide insight in the process of daily recovery by discussing (i) theories that help us understand the process of re-covery, (ii) the concept of recovery and its potential outcomes, (iii) empirical studies addressing activities that may facilitate or hinder daily recovery, (iv) potential mechanisms that may underlie the facilitating or hindering processes, and (v) empirical findings on predictors and outcomes of need for recovery. We conclude with an overall framework from which daily recovery during non-work time can be understood.

THEORETICAL FRAMEWORK

It has been well-established that unfavorable work situations adversely affect individuals' health and well-being. Particularly work situations characterized by high job demands and low job resources (e.g., low job control) are associated with the development of physical and psychological health complaints across time (for reviews, see Belkic, Landsbergis, Schnall, & Baker, 2004; De Lange, Taris, Kompier, Houtman, & Bongers, 2003). In the linkage between exposure to unfavorable work situations and adverse health and well-being, stress-related physiology seems to play a crucial mediating role (Geurts & Sonnentag, 2006). In principle, stress-related physiological activation in response to job stressors is reversible and short-lived, and is, therefore, not harmful for employee health. However, when stress-related activation occurs repeatedly or prolongs during potential recovery time, relationships with serious disease (e.g., hypertension) across time and overall mortality have been demonstrated (among others, Stewart, Janicki, & Kamarack, 2006). Unfortunately, our knowledge about how to undo these negative "short-term" effects in order to prevent negative long-term consequences is still limited. Geurts and Sonnentag (2006) recently argued that recovery may help to explain how stressfull working conditions and the related acute load reactions of employees may impair their health in the long run. Later, we briefly discuss three models that may explain the role of recovery.

Effort-Recovery Model

The crucial role of incomplete recovery from stress can be understood from the perspective of Effort-Recovery theory (E-R theory, Meijman & Mulder, 1998). Its core assumption is that effort expenditure at work is unavoidably associated with, in principle adaptive, acute load reactions (e.g., accelerated heart rate, elevated blood pressure levels, and fatigue). Effort is mobilized by activation of the Sympathetic–Adrenal–Medullary (SAM) system which – by secretion of catecholamines (adrenalin and noradrenalin) – regulates cardiovascular activity (i.e., sympathetic activation). Under very stressful circumstances, the Hypothalamic–Pituitary–Adrenal (HPA) system with the "stress hormone" cortisol as its main actor, may be activated as well in order to mobilize supplementary effort needed to deal with the stressful situation (Clow, 2001). Under optimal circumstances, the stress-related acute load reactions return to prestressor levels during after-work hours, and recovery is completed before the next working period starts. In this situation health is not at risk. However, when the stress-related acute load reactions prolong or re-occur during after-work hours (i.e., sustained sympathetic activation), recovery is incomplete (Geurts & Sonnentag, 2006). As a consequence, the worker will start the next working period while being in a suboptimal condition, and will have to invest compensatory effort in order to perform adequately at work. The resulting increased intensity of load reactions will in turn initiate an even higher demand on the subsequent recovery process, and thus result in an accumulative process developing into chronic load reactions (or "allostatic load" according to McEwen's (1998) allostatic load theory), such as chronically elevated heart rate, hypertension, chronic fatigue, and persistent sleep problems (Sluiter, Frings-Dresen, Van der Beek, & Meijman, 2001).

An important question is under what circumstances the crucial process of daily recovery is hampered by prolongation or re-occurrence of stress-related acute load reactions during after-work hours. One condition is the prolonged exposure to work demands or the new exposure to effortful demands. According to Geurts and Sonnentag (2006), particularly the prolonged exposure to work demands (e.g., daily overtime work) is a risk factor as a demand is made on the *same* psycho-physiological systems that were already activated on the job. Particularly these systems should unwind and return to their baseline levels. In addition, the continued exposure to stressful demands (irrespective of being work-related or not) is a serious risk because of the high sympathetic (cardiovascular) activation associated with the stress exposure. From the perspective of recovery after work, it seems important that people engage in activities that appeal to other systems than already used during work, and that are not (again) stressful. Another condition that hampers the quality of recovery after work is the difficulty to psychologically detach from job stressors. Even when people are not exposed to (new) stressful demands after work, cognitive processes may be responsible for the prolongation or reactivation of stress-related physiological activation, such as rumination about past stressors and anticipation of future stressors, a phenomenon referred to as "perseverative cognition" (Brosschot, Pieper, & Thayer, 2005).

Conservation of Resources Theory

A second theory that may be helpful to describe how people may act during after-work hours in order to recover from stressful work is *Conservation of Resources* (COR) theory (Hobfoll, 1998, 2002). Its core assumption is that people strive to obtain, retain, protect, and build resources that are important to them, and that stress develops when valued resources are threatened, lost, or not gained after having invested in them. Resources refer here to a heterogeneous category including personal characteristics (e.g., self-esteem), object resources (e.g., clothing), condition resources (e.g., a good marriage), and energy resources (e.g., the level of vigor) that are either valued in themselves, or that serve as a means of obtaining other valued resources. Since resources such as self-esteem and vigor may be lost or threatened in an unfavorable work situation, employees will attempt to restore their resources during after-work hours. This can be realized, for instance, by engaging in leisure activities that may refill their batteries (energy) or will contribute to their self-esteem. After discussing the concept of recovery (third section), we discuss activities and experiences (fifth section) during after-work hours that may hamper or facilitate the recovery process.

Bakker, Van Emmerik, Geurts, and Demerouti (2008) conducted a diary study to test the predictions of the E-R and COR theories. Specifically, they investigated the role of daily recovery in the relationship between daily job demands, work engagement, and performance. Data were collected among 53 fulltime working assembly line employees through daily surveys over two consecutive working weeks (10 working days) that were interrupted by a two-day weekend period. Recovery was assessed in the morning before participants went to work. Job demands, work engagement, and perfor-mance were assessed immediately after work. Results revealed that daily work engagement is a function of recovery in-between working days, and that daily work engagement, in turn, is a predictor of daily performance. Additionally, results suggest that recovery turns job demands into challenges: only if employees recovered sufficiently in-between work periods, daily job demands were positively related to work engagement. Thus, recovery moderated the relationship between job demands and work engagement. This study nicely illustrates the principles of E-R and COR theories, and emphasizes the importance of recovery for work engagement and performance, on a day-to-day basis. High effort expended at work is not damaging for health or well-being as long as employees have the opportunity to recover from load effects built up during the working day (see also Geurts & Sonnentag, 2006; Totterdell, Spelten, Smith, Barton, & Folkard, 1995).

Allostatic Load Model

In ergonomics, cardiovascular parameters have been introduced to evaluate the consequences of having been exposed to workload and strain (e.g.,

Luczak, 1987; Schnall, Schwartz, Landsbergis, Warren, & Pickering, 1992; Theorell, Ahlberg-Hulten, Jodko, Sigala, & Torre, 1993; Theorell et al., 1991). To use cardiovascular parameters as an indicator of health, both the situation of exposure to workload and the process of recovery after exposure to workload should be taken into account. The process of recovery can be considered as an indicator of good health. An indication of good health is when a person can recover completely from workload within the timeframe between two working days (Rau, 2004). This definition is supported by the model of allostasis and allostatic load (McEwen, 1998; Sterling & Eyer, 1988). Allostasis describes the process of how the physiological system adjusts from one level of activation to the other, including the change from activity to rest (Sterling, 2004). The physiological system is continuously changing in order to adapt to the change in circumstances. Through this continuous change, the system tries to achieve a level of stability. A healthy response of an allostatic system (such as the central and vegetative nervous system, the endocrine and immune system, the cardiovascular system etc.) to exposure of load consists of three steps (a) initiate a response to adapt to the current demanding situation, (b) sustaining this response reaction until the demanding situation comes to an end and the load ends, and (c) shutting off the response after the demand is no longer imposed on the system. The system will then enter a state of rest (McEwen, 1998). For example, an adaptive response to workload could be an increase in heart rate and blood pressure for the duration of the demanding situation. Once the demands are gone and the person no longer faces the workload, heart rate and blood pressure must be reset, i.e., enter a state of rest (Pickering, 1997). However, allostatic load situations occur when the initial adaptive response fails to be shut off after the load has gone (e.g., blood pressure remains elevated up to the late night). Allostatic load is thus considered to be a pathophysiological outcome (McEwen, 1998; Sterling & Eyer, 1988).

HOW IS RECOVERY CONCEPTUALIZED?

Recovery has been defined in several ways, but most definitions have in common that recovery occurs after strain when the stressor is no longer present (Sonnentag & Geurts, this volume). It represents the process that repairs the negative strain effects. More specifically, recovery refers to the process during which an individual's functioning returns to its pre-stressor level and in which strain is reduced (Sonnentag & Natter, 2004).

Put differently, recovery refers to activities that might reduce fatigue to restore a status of physiological and psychological performance readiness. One way in which recovery has been captured empirically is to ask participants to report their level of recovery before starting to work (Sonnentag, 2003). In this research tradition, participants respond to items like "because of the leisure activities pursued yesterday, I feel recovered/relaxed/in a good mood." This operationalization of recovery has been successful in predicting work engagement, personal initiative, and pursuit of learning as reported later that day.

Sonnentag and Natter (2004) used a more specific way to capture the *recovery experience*. Recovery experience refers to the degree to which the individual perceives that the activities he/she pursues during non-work time helps him/her to restore energy resources (Sonnentag & Natter, 2004). Participants had to indicate next to the amount of time they spent one specific evening on off-job time activities, also the degree to which they felt recovered after having performed these activities. In this respect, recovery experiences indicate the strategies that people use to avoid negative effects of stressful situations (Sonnentag & Fritz, 2007). The advantage of this method is that it refers to the recovery effect of each activity separately, providing rich information about what activities potentially enhance recovery. Moreover, these specific (versus global) reports on recovery are provided the same evening as the activity was carried out. Therefore, recalling errors are minimized. However, what is still missing is information about sleep.

Yet another way to operationalize recovery is to use self-report measures of fatigue as a proxy (Rook & Zijlstra, 2006; Sonnentag & Geurts, this volume). The assumption is that elevated levels of fatigue can be used to identify individuals who have failed to recover from the short-term effects of a workday. Therefore, also reductions in the level of fatigue may indicate recovery. Because subjective experiences of fatigue are believed to encompass a strong motivational component rather than feelings of physical fatigue (Meijman, 1991; Rook & Zijlstra, 2006), it is questionable whether such measures really capture the unwinding component and the replenishing of resources which is crucial for recovery. Moreover, fatigue and lack of recovery are related but not identical constructs. According to Sonnentag and Zijlstra (2006), "fatigue is a *state* that results from being active in order to deal with the work demands, and recovery is the *process* of replenishing depleted resources or rebalancing suboptimal systems" (p. 331). Thus, fatigue is more a consequence of lack of recovery, rather than a concept referring to the recovery process or problems within the recovery process.

When fatigue builds up people feel a sense of urgency to take a break from the demands. This sense of urgency is called *need for recovery* (Sonnentag & Zijlstra, 2006) and has also been used as an indicator of (in)sufficient recovery. Need for recovery is an emotional state characterized by a reluctance to continue the present demands or to accept new demands. Owing to conceptual similarity with fatigue and psychological distress researchers have tried to show that need for recovery is something different than these other established constructs. The study of Jansen, Kant, and van den Brandt (2002) on a large Dutch population ($N > 12,000$) showed that although need for recovery, fatigue, and psychological distress were frequently co-morbid, they also clearly occurred as separate entities.

Poor recovery may also manifest itself in elevated levels of neuroendocrine activity during non-work time, such as elevated levels of catecholamines (adrenaline and noradrenaline) and cortisol during after-work hours (Sonnentag & Geurts, this volume). A recent systematic literature review (Sonnentag & Fritz, 2006) has shown that after highly intensified work periods, catecholamine levels remain elevated, indicating poor physiological recovery. For instance, in a classic field experiment among driving examiners with varying degrees of workload, elevated adrenaline levels persisted during after-work hours on workdays with intensive workload, whereas on workdays with relatively low or medium workload, adrenaline levels returned to predemand levels within a few off-job hours (Meijman, Mulder, van Dormolen, & Cremer, 1992). As these neuroendocrine hormones initiate sympathetic activation, elevated cardiovascular activation (accelerated heart rate and elevated blood pressure levels) after exposure to job stressors may also be used as indicators of poor physiological recovery after work. For instance, in an experimental study, Glynn, Christenfeld, and Gerin (2002) provided evidence for poor cardiovascular recovery (i.e., delayed blood pressure recovery) after exposure to an emotional stressor.

In a recent study among couples, Saxbe, Repetti, and Nishina (2008) examined after-work recovery, by exploring associations between self-reported daily work stress and evening cortisol levels. Participants sampled saliva four times per day during three days. Wives who had less satisfying marriages excreted higher evening cortisol at home following days with higher than usual afternoon cortisol, but this continuation of elevated cortisol from work to home was not observed in women with higher levels of marital satisfaction. For both men and women, evening cortisol was lower than usual on higher-workload days, and marital satisfaction augmented this association among women. Men showed higher evening cortisol after more distressing social experiences at work, an association that was strongest among men with higher marital satisfaction.

OUTCOMES OF (LACK OF) RECOVERY

As indicated above, recovery refers to the process during which an individual's functioning returns to its prestressor level and in which strain is reduced. Several studies have examined the outcomes of (lack of) recovery on a day-to-day basis, comparing levels of recovery indicators at a later point in time (typically before going to bed or after waking up in the morning) to scores on the same variables at an earlier point in time (e.g., after waking up in the morning or the previous day, before going to bed). In this section, we provide a short overview of these studies and discuss their main findings in relation to the type of outcome studied. Our aim is to (i) emphasize the importance of recovery in predicting valuable outcomes for organizations, individuals, and families, and (ii) show the differences between recovery processes and outcomes that seem conceptual similar to recovery (e.g., fatigue).

Study selection. As a first step, we conducted an automated search in the PsycInfo and MedLine databases. We searched for entries that met the criterion that the abstract or title of papers include the following terms: (i) either "Day," "Diary," or "Daily," in combination with (ii) "recovery" or "fatigue" and (iii) either "work," "worker(s)," "working," "employed," or "employment." In this way, we aimed to retrieve studies that studied daily recovery in a work context. This search returned 388 potentially relevant studies.

The abstract of these 388 studies were examined by one of the authors for relevance. Oftentimes, the abstract revealed that studies were irrelevant, for example, that they did not study recovery in the work context or on a day-to-day basis, or because the antecedents, rather than the consequences of recovery were studied. Further, studies had to present original empirical evidence on the relationship between recovery and outcomes thereof. Review papers and conceptual papers were excluded. In all, 35 studies were retained. These studies were read in detail by one of the authors, after which six studies remained. This number is fairly small, but our inclusion criteria were rather narrow, explicitly focusing on research that considered research that examined the consequences of *recovery* or lack thereof. This means that research examining the same consequences within related but different theoretical frameworks (e.g., research on the effects of working overtime, shift work, or sleep deprivation) was not included.

Description of studies. Table 1 presents descriptive information on the studies included in our overview. As regards the samples used, these were usually small, ranging from 19 to 166. This may be due to the fact that data collection was quite demanding: all six studies employed some form of diary design, in which participants completed diaries at several occasions during the study. The studies covered up to five consecutive work days (usually a working week).

As regards the recovery indicators included in these studies, five of these (Studies 2–6) focused on the activities conducted after work and before going to bed, e.g., in the form of the time spent on these activities, the subjective experience of these activities, or the degree to which one felt recovered due to doing these activities. Study 5 included a measure of sleep quality, whereas Study 1 considered the length of the layover time between two consecutive flights among airline pilots; what these pilots did during this time was not recorded in detail (it seems likely that they will have spent at least part of this time sleeping). In fourth section, we discuss these activities in more detail, in relation to the outcomes thereof.

The outcomes considered in the six studies vary considerably, and may be roughly classified as either covering motivation and performance, or health and well-being. All outcomes were measured after a period of recovery, e.g., before going to bed (Studies 2, 4, 6), after a night's sleep (Studies 3 and 5), or after a period of inactivity in-between two work shifts (Study 1). As regards *motivation and performance*, one study (Study 1) focused on an objective performance measure, namely response time during playing a game on a hand-held computer. All other recovery outcomes were measured through self-reports. Study 3 examined personal initiative and pursuit of learning as recovery outcomes. With respect to *health and well-being*, fatigue and mood were relatively often examined (fatigue: Studies 4–6; mood: Studies 2–5). Two other studies examined one dimension of engagement: Studies 3 and 6 (both focusing on vigor, i.e., energy – this concept may be considered an alternative way of tapping fatigue as well). Finally, Study 6 employed feelings of depression as the focal variable. All in all, it seems that subjective well-being (especially mood and fatigue) has relatively often been examined in diary research on the effects of recovery, whereas especially studies examining performance are rare.

Table 1. Description of Studies on the Effects of Day-to-Day Recovery.

	Study	Sample	Design	Recovery Indicator	Recovery Outcome
(1)	Lamont, Dawson, and Roach (2006)	19 international airline pilots	Diary study (2 consecutive flights)	Layover time between flights (sleep)	Computerized psychomotor vigilance task: response time
(2)	Sonnentag (2001)	100 teachers	Diary study (5 consecutive work days)	Evening activities: work-related, household chores, low-effort, social, physical	Well-being before going to sleep: feeling tense, mood
(3)	Sonnentag (2003)	147 employees of public service organizations	Diary study (5 consecutive work days)	Feelings of being recovered due to leisure activities	Work engagement, personal initiative, pursuit of learning
(4)	Sonnentag and Bayer (2005)	87 workers, various occupations	Diary study (3 consecutive work days)	Psychological detachment during five evening activities: work-related, household chores, low-effort, social, physical; General psychological detachment	Well-being before going to sleep: fatigue, mood
(5)	Sonnentag, Binnewies, and Mojza (2008)	166 public administration employees	Diary study (5 consecutive work days)	Psychological detachment, relaxation; Mastery experiences, sleep quality	Morning affect: (i) positive effect, (ii) negative effect, (iii) serenity, (iv) fatigue
(6)	Sonnentag and Natter (2004)	47 flight attendants	Diary study (4 work days)	Time spent on five activities before going to bed: work-related, household chores, low-effort, social, physical; Feelings of recovery	Well-being before going to sleep: vigor, depression, fatigue

ACTIVITIES DURING RECOVERY

Activities with a Potential for Recovery

Basically, the present chapter assumes that what one does after work may affect the degree to which one recovers from the effort expended at work. On the basis of the work of Sonnentag and colleagues (e.g., Sonnentag, 2001; Sonnentag & Bayer, 2005), we distinguish among activities promoting (see section "Activities with a potential for recovery") and activities impeding recovery (see section "Activities potentially inhibiting recovery"). Table 2 presents the findings of the six studies discussed in the previous section. These are discussed hereafter.

Table 2.   Findings of Studies on the Effects of Day-to-Day Recovery.

	Study	Recovery Indicator	Effects
(1)	Lamont et al. (2006)	Layover time between flights (sleep)	Response time (−)
(2)	Sonnentag (2001)	Work-related activities	Well-being (−)
		Low-effort, social, physical activities	Well-being (+)
(3)	Sonnentag (2003)	Feelings of being recovered due to various activities	Engagement (+), personal initiative (+), pursuit of learning (+)
(4)	Sonnentag and Bayer (2005)	Psychological detachment during social activities	Mood (+)
		Psychological detachment during physical activities	Mood (+), fatigue (−)
		General psychological detachment	Mood (+), fatigue (−)
(5)	Sonnentag et al. (2008)	Sleep quality	Positive activation (+), serenity (+), negative activation (−), fatigue (−)
		Feelings of mastery	Positive activation (+)
		Relaxation	Serenity (+)
		Psychological detachment	Negative activation (−), morning fatigue (−)
(6)	Sonnentag and Natter (2004)	Feelings of recovery	Vigor (+), depression (−), fatigue (−)
		Time spent on social activities	Depression (+)
		Time spent on physical activities	Vigor (+), depression (−)

Note: "+" denotes a positive effect (more of A is associated with more of B); "−" denotes a negative effect.

Sleep

Studies on daily recovery have consistently ignored the role of sleep as an activity important for recovery in its own right. Because sleep has a restorative function and maintains performance (Campbell, 1992; Horne, 2001), it is necessary to consider sleep in the phenomenon of daily recovery. Research by Zijlstra and de Vries (2000) has indicated that sleep is important for recovery. Van Hooff, Geurts, Kompier, and Taris (2007) found among faculty members that those who invested much effort in their work during work hours did not differ in sleep time from those expending less effort on work, but reported more sleep complaints during the workweek, indicating poor recovery. Individuals with high levels of fatigue typically have fewer hours of sleep and require extra effort to conduct their work in comparison to individuals with low levels of fatigue. Moreover, there is strong evidence that cognitive arousal at bedtime is associated with increased sleep disturbance. For instance, Cropley, Dijk, and Stanley (2006) found that ruminating about work issues in the hour preceding bedtime was associated with greater sleep disturbance.

Adults need on average 7–9 h sleep per night, whereas children need about 9–10 h per night (Carskadon & Dement, 2005). Several studies have shown that a day nap of 15–20 min is very beneficial for recovery (Takahashi, Fukuda, & Arito, 1998). However, too much or too little sleep can affect performance in a negative way. Moreover, not only the quantity but also the quality of sleep is important for recovery and performance (e.g., Craig & Cooper, 1992). It has been shown that deep sleep (75–80%) has a positive influence on growth and repair, whereas rapid eye movement (REM) sleep (20–25%) has a neutral function. These impressions are confirmed by the findings presented in Table 2. Lamont et al. (2006; Study 2) reported that layover time between flights positively affected the performance (i.e., response time on a computer game) of flight attendants, whereas Sonnentag et al. (2008; Study 6) found that sleep quality was positively associated with mood (positive affect, serenity) and negatively with negative effect and fatigue.

Low-Effort Activities

Low-effort activities represent passive activities that by definition require hardly any effort on the part of the individual and therefore pose no demands on the psychobiological system (Sonnentag, 2001; Sonnentag & Natter, 2004). Examples of such activities are watching television, listening to music, or just relaxing on the sofa and doing nothing (Kleiber, Larson, & Csikszentmihalyi, 1986). These activities have a recovery function because they do not occupy resources that are normally required to accomplish work

tasks (Sonnentag, 2001). Consequently, psychobiological systems will return
to their normal prestressor state (Meijman & Mulder, 1998). Although it
seems plausible that low-effort activities will have a recovery effect, some
authors have doubted such an effect. Accordingly, low-effort activities mean
that people spend their time in passive leisure activities and passive activities
are detrimental for well-being because they are related to free-time boredom
and apathy (cf. Iso-Ahola, 1997). However, according to Sonnentag (2001),
such a relationship between passive leisure activities and poor well-being
might be a spurious one that can be explained by third variables. One such a
third variable could be the work environment, for example, a job with low
demands and low autonomy (or passive jobs in terms of Karasek (1998)).

Empirical findings regarding the effect of low-effort activities on daily
recovery and well-being have been mixed (cf. Table 2). Consistent with the
predictions of the effort-recovery model, Sonnentag (2001) found that time
spent on low-effort activities was favorably related to well-being at bedtime
among teachers. However, Sonnentag and Natter (2004) found that low-
effort activities had no effect on well-being (operationalized as recovery
experience, fatigue, vigor, and depression) during bedtime among flight
attendants. In a similar vein, Rook and Zijlstra (2006) showed that low-
effort activities had little or no effect on recovery.

Relaxation Activities
A related category of activities are those that enhance relaxation (Sonnentag
& Fritz, 2007). Relaxation can also be viewed as a state which is
characterized by positive affect and low activation. In the present section,
however, we review activities that may lead to relaxation rather than the
state of relaxation. Examples of such relaxation activities are meditation
(Grossman, Niemann, Schmidt, & Walach, 2004), yoga (Oken et al., 2004),
listening to music (Pelletier, 2004), taking a walk in a natural environment
(Hartig, Evans, Jamner, Davis, & Gärling, 2003), taking a long-hot bath
(Bourne, 2000), progressive muscle relaxation, and breathing exercises
(Calder, 2003a, 2003b). These activities have in common that they are not
demanding and do not require any kind of effort from the individual.
However, the individual is actively involved in a pleasurable activity. The
role that relaxation plays to increase recovery is according to Sonnentag and
Fritz (2007) two-fold. First, because relaxation experiences reduce psychophysiological activation, sustained activation is inhibited, and the psychobiological system can return to the prestressor state. This helps that the
stressor does not translate into illnesses. Second, the fact that the relaxation
activities are pleasurable and can increase positive effects has also favorable

effects on the individual's well-being. According to Fredrickson (2001), positive emotions help individuals to build resources including energy which they can use in the future to minimize the influence of negative emotions and stress.

There is indeed some evidence for the recovery function of relaxation (Table 2), although the relationship between relaxation and recovery has been more extensively studied among athletes (Calder, 2003a, 2003b). In the study of Sonnentag and Fritz (2007), relaxation was negatively correlated with health complaints, exhaustion, sleep problems, and need for recovery, and positively correlated with life satisfaction. Furthermore, in their seven-day diary study among workers from an Australian supermarket, Garrick, Winwood, and Bakker (2008) found that previous day meditation/prayer increased sleep quality and inter-shift recovery. Moreover, they found that daily recovery mediated the relationship between meditation/prayer and acute fatigue. This means that meditation and prayer had a favorable impact on recovery. Finally, Sonnentag et al. (2008) reported that relaxation had a positive effect on mood (specifically, serenity).

Social Activities

Social activities refer to activities that focus on social contact including going to a party, dining, or phoning other people (Sonnentag, 2001). During such activities people meet and spend time with others that they like such as family members, friends, or other individuals or groups (Fritz & Sonnentag, 2005; Sonnentag, 2001). Sonnentag (2001) proposes two mechanisms through which social activities can have a recovery function. The first possible function of social activities is that by meeting other people we open channels of social support. Social support has been found to reduce the negative influence of job demands on well-being (e.g., Bakker, Demerouti, & Euwema, 2005). The second possible function is that social activities draw on different resources than those necessary for work-related tasks. Consequently, recovery processes can take place. Note that there is a difference between the social contact we have when employed in human service occupations and the social contacts during leisure time. Work-related social interactions, e.g., with customers, often require emotion regulation or "emotion work" (Zapf, 2002). Emotion regulation is an effortful process in which employees have to show emotions that do not feel but that are according to the rules of the organization. That kind of emotion regulation may not be necessary for social interactions during leisure time (Sonnentag, 2001).

There is some evidence that engagement in social activities has a beneficial effect on recovery (Table 2). Sonnentag and Zijlstra (2006) found in their dairy study that social activities were positively related to well-being at bedtime and negatively related to need for recovery. In contrast, the study of Sonnentag and Bayer (2005) found that social activities were unrelated to positive mood as well as to fatigue at bedtime. Moreover, Sonnentag and Natter (2004) found that involvement in social activities was related to *higher* feelings of depression at bedtime. An explanation that these authors offered is that social activities might include deliberate preoccupation with job-related thoughts as is the case when meeting friends and talking with them about work. Another possible explanation could be that social activities are relaxing for some people but not for everybody. For instance, extraverts might profit more from social activities in terms of unwinding than introverts (Trougakos & Hideg, this volume).

Physical Activities
Physical activities refer to behaviors including exercise, physical training, sports etc. Physical exercise is important to maintain fitness and is found to contribute to physical and mental health (McAuley, Kramer, & Colcombe, 2004). It seems a paradox to claim that physical activity during leisure time can promote recovery. Both physiological and psychological explanations have been suggested to account for the recovery enhancing effects of exercise (Sonnentag, 2001; Yeung, 1996). Of the physiological mechanisms, most attention has been given to the action of endorphins within the central nervous system. Numerous studies have shown that levels of endorphins are elevated following exercise (Grossman et al., 1984), but attempts to relate endorphin levels to positive mood changes have generally failed – probably due to methodological problems of these studies (Thoren, Floras, Hoffman, & Seals, 1990). A second physiological explanation is the thermogenic hypothesis of exercise suggesting that an elevation of body temperature is responsible for subjectively increased mood following exercise (Raglin & Morgan, 1985). The monoamine hypothesis is a third physiological explanation referring to the enhanced secretion of noradrenalin, serotonin, and dopamine that have an antidepressant effect (for an overview, see Cox, 2002). Next to these physiological mechanisms, the distraction hypothesis asserts that it is not the exercise as such that enhances mood and recovery, but rather the respite or "time out" that it provides from worrisome thoughts and daily stressors (Raglin & Morgan, 1985; Yeung, 1996). Finally, the completion of an important and effortful task (including exercise) brings about a sense of mastery or achievement and self-efficacy beliefs, thereby enhancing positive mood and well-being.

As Table 2 shows, there is consistent evidence supporting that well-being at bedtime is improved on days when individuals spend time on physical activities (Sonnentag, 2001; Sonnentag & Bayer, 2003; Sonnentag & Natter, 2004). More specifically, physical activities have a positive effect on vigor and mood, and a negative effect on depression. However, physical activities were unrelated to fatigue experienced at bedtime in each of these studies. This can be explained by the fact that physical activities increase physical fatigue, which may mask the positive effects on other aspects of fatigue (Sonnentag & Natter, 2004).

Creative Activities

Hobbies, or creative activity, have received very little research in the field of work fatigue and recovery, but initial studies suggest that they can have an important restorative function. Hobbies provide opportunities for personal fulfillment, skills acquisition, and emotionally rewarding "mastery" experiences. In addition, these activities arguably stimulate the pleasure/reward brain center (Winwood, Bakker, & Winefield, 2007). We could locate only two studies that examined the relationship between hobbies and recovery. In their study among a heterogeneous sample of workers, Winwood et al. (2007) found that employees reporting higher levels of creative (hobby) activity reported significantly better sleep, recovery between work periods, and lower chronic maladaptive fatigue. In addition, in their diary study, Garrick et al. (2008) found that engagement in hobbies increased recovery, which in turn had a positive effect on next days' work engagement.

Psychological Experiences with a Potential for Recovery

In this section, we review two psychological experiences that can enhance recovery, namely psychological detachment from work and humor. These do not represent activities per se but are merely ways of thinking that, as we will see in the review, facilitate daily recovery.

Psychological Detachment

Psychological detachment is used to describe individual's sense of being away from work (Etzion, Eden, & Lapidot, 1998). Detachment implies more than just being away from work physically. In contrast to the activities mentioned in the previous section, psychological detachment does not represent an activity but is psychological in nature. It suggests that the individual stops thinking about work and disengages his/herself mentally from work (Sonnentag & Bayer, 2005; Sonnentag & Fritz, 2007; Sonnentag & Kruel, 2006). Further, it suggests that the individual switches off from work-related matters and problems but also from positive aspects of work. Thus, just being physically away from work is not sufficient to experience *psychological* detachment. The underlying mechanisms that explain why psychological detachment helps to recover has to do with whether resources that people use when they are active at work are still occupied while at home. When individuals do not detach and thus think about their work issues during non-work time (negative or positive), they are cognitively aroused (cf. Cropley et al., 2006). Therefore, the functional systems that are activated during work are still activated during non-work time in this way inhibiting the recovery process. In contrast, when individuals detach psychologically from their work, no further functional demands tax their psychobiological system (Sonnentag & Fritz, 2007).

The results of diary studies (Table 2) suggest that individuals who experienced psychological detachment from work during leisure time reported better mood, less negative effect, and less fatigue at the end of the evening and in the next morning (Sonnentag & Bayer, 2005; Sonnentag et al., 2008) and had more sleep disturbances (Cropley et al., 2006). It is important to note that psychological detachment is particularly useful after stressful and demanding working days (Sonnentag & Bayer, 2005). During such days, individuals might continue working at home, might continue thinking about the tasks that remained unfinished, or they might anticipate the workload of the next day. Thus, it appears that experiences on the job and the nature of job-related cognitions when being off work determines the level of recovery and recovery-related outcomes.

Humor

It has been demonstrated that humor states and associated laughter can benefit stress and coping, as well as various other health-related outcomes, such as cardiac rehabilitation and pain threshold (Healy & McKay, 2000). Hence, engagement in humorous activities outside of work can be expected to result in decreased fatigue, increased recovery and higher subsequent work engagement. This hypothesis was tested in the diary study of Garrick et al. (2008). They found that time spent laughing or being engaged in humor stimulating activities inducing laughter was significantly related to inter-shift recovery and sleep quality. However, laughing did not influence next day's levels of fatigue and work engagement.

Activities Potentially Inhibiting Recovery

Work-Related Activities

The traditional work–rest cycle including 8 h work, 8 h time for personal needs and free time, and 8 h sleep is based on the idea that the time between two work periods is sufficient to recover from work. Normally people feel fatigued after work, but this fatigue is not a problem since it is reversible by changing tasks or by stopping the fatigue-inducing activity (Meijman & Mulder, 1998). If the psychobiological systems used during work are activated during recovery time, a cumulative process involving prolonged fatigue, sleep, and psychosomatic complaints may ensue (Rook & Zijlstra, 2006). Work-related activities refer not only to activities related to work but also to other task-related activities similar to those conducted at work like paying bills or arranging private bureaucracy. Such activities have an compulsory character (they have to be done) and they draw on resources similar to those already called on during working time (Sonnentag & Natter, 2004). Continuously drawing on the same resources during the evening can empty the resource reservoir and increase strain. Therefore, work-related activities carried out after work can impair recovery (e.g., overtime work; for a review, see Taris, Beckers, Dahlgren, Geurts, & Tucker, 2007).

Sonnentag and Natter (2004) found in their diary study that time spent on work-related activities resulted in somewhat lower levels of vigor and higher levels of fatigue at bedtime, although the effects were marginal. Similarly, Sonnentag and Zijlstra (2006) found that the time individuals devoted to work-related activities during off-work time was positively related to their need for recovery and negatively to their well-being during bedtime. As Table 2 shows, Sonnentag (2001) reported similar findings.

Household and Child-Care Activities

Household and child-care activities normally draw on different resources than those needed for work, except for occupations in the cleaning services industry or child care (Sonnentag, 2001). Therefore, it could be assumed that these activities offer the possibility to recover from work-related demands. However, another aspect of household and child-care activities is that they require physical and psychological effort and that they have an obligatory character since most of these activities cannot be skipped or postponed. Thus, while the nature of household and child-care activities could facilitate recovery, their obligatory character inhibits recovery. This is because people must accomplish these tasks and spend effort on them when they are already fatigued after a working day.

The suggested detrimental effect of household and child-care activities on recovery has however not been confirmed empirically (cf. Table 2). Time spent on household and child-care activities was unrelated to fatigue and well-being at bedtime in the diary studies of Sonnentag (2001) and Sonnentag and Bayer (2005). Similar findings were reported by Sonnentag and Zijlstra (2006) as well as by Sonnentag and Natter (2004). Several explanations have been provided for the zero effects of household and child-care activities on the recovery process and outcomes. One explanation is that these activities are always studied together making it difficult to separate their unique effect. For instance, it is conceivable that household activities impede recovery and that child-care activities facilitate recovery. Another explanation is that there might be individual differences suggesting that some individuals experience these as positive and other individuals as negative (Sonnentag, 2001). Rook and Zijlstra (2006) (who also found no effect of such activities on subjective fatigue) suggest that because household activities and in particular caring for children require active involvement they help individuals to disengage from the daily strains at work. Therefore, they might be even beneficial for recovery.

FACTORS FACILITATING RECOVERY

Although work generally depletes the energy reserves of employees, it may also contain aspects that minimize the detrimental effects of work. These concern mainly job resources such as job control, feedback, and learning opportunities. Why can such aspects at work help recovery when being at home? This is well illustrated by Rau (2006), who examined the influence of learning opportunities at work on recovery. Learning opportunities included procedural and temporal degrees of freedom, decision authority, responsibility, information about results and feedback. Note that these aspects were measured independent of the job incumbent's perception, by means of a job analysis instrument filled in by an expert analyst. Moreover, recovery was measured using physiological (blood pressure and heart rates) and psychological (self-rated ability to relax) indicators. The findings of the 24-h measures indicated that learning opportunities were favorably associated with nocturnal recovery of heart rate and blood pressure but unrelated with self-rated assessments of recovery. According to Rau (2006), the underlying mechanism for these relationships is that jobs with learning opportunities can be considered as intrinsically motivating and positively challenging for employees (Csikszentmihalyi, 1990). People in such jobs usually are highly activated, but not stressed (Karasek, 1998; Taris & Kompier, 2005) – a state that Dienstbier (1989) calls toughening. When employees have control over their work, they can decide themselves how to deal with problems, and when to stop working. Apparently this helps them to better switch off from work (Cropley et al., 2006), and consequently to unwind.

This positive influence of in particular job control on recovery was confirmed in another diary study by Sonnentag and Zijlstra (2006). They found that next to job demands, job control contributed to explaining variance in need for recovery at bedtime – beyond the effect of negative affectivity and the particularly strong effect of well-being when returning home from work.

Everybody would agree that recovery mainly takes place after work when people are at home. Therefore, it is ironical that we could find no study that examined factors from the home situation that can facilitate recovery. Our expectation is that home resources like autonomy, social support, and feedback will facilitate recovery just like job resources do. However, there is no evidence to support this assumption. Future research should strive to provide more insight into such factors. It should be noted here that in order to achieve this, future research should improve the conceptualization and measurement of the characteristics of the home domain (Geurts & Demerouti, 2003).

FACTORS INHIBITING RECOVERY

Work-Related

Every working day, employees are exposed to a certain amount of *job demands*. These job demands (particularly workload) often vary from day to day (Butler, Grzywacz, Bass, & Linney, 2005), and may determine our daily mood or effect (Zohar, Tzischinski, & Epstein, 2003). Studies using a within-person design have shown that periods of high workload coincide with impaired well-being, suggesting a depletion of employees' energy resources during high workload periods (Teuchmann, Totterdell, & Parker, 1999; Totterdell, Wood, & Wall, 2006).

The diary study by Sonnentag and Bayer (2005) suggests that with high demands on a specific day the risk of not being able to relax and detach from work increases. This result is in line with findings by Cropley and Purvis (2003), who found in their diary study a positive relationship between job demands and rumination, and by Appels (1997), who demonstrated that high demands are related to inability to relax and to exhaustion. Also,

Rau (2006) found that job demands were related to disturbed ability to relax at home although they were not related to blood pressure during night.

Another important work characteristic that influences daily recovery is *overtime*. As Rau and Triemer (2004) argue, overtime acts as a stressor because it increases the demands on employees attempting to maintain their performance levels in the face of increasing fatigue. Additionally, employees working longer hours are exposed to other sources of workplace stress for a greater amount of time. Because working overtime implies that the working day is prolonged, whereas the time left for recovery is curtailed, a large proportion of overtime research has concentrated on poor recovery (e.g., Van der Hulst & Geurts, 2001).

Rau and Triemer (2004) followed participants for 24 h with a computerized diary and ambulant monitoring of blood pressure to test the relationship between overtime and recovery. As expected, overtime impacted both the organization of after-work activities and nocturnal recovery. Men and women working overtime had less leisure time, and men also reported less time for household, childcare etc. than those working regular hours. Although those working overtime had higher systolic and diastolic blood pressure during work than those working regular times, it was unrelated to blood pressure during non-work time. Significantly more participants in the group of men and women working overtime were found to have a disturbed ability to recover and to display clinically relevant sleep disturbances than in the group working regular hours. Furthermore, working overtime was associated with less positive effect after work in men, and with more negative effect during work and before going to bed in men and women.

Non-Work Hassles

Non-work hassles refer to on-going stressors experienced in day-to-day life (Lepore & Evans, 1996). Such stressors are positioned in the private life domain and concern situations that deviate from the normal state like sudden problems with the car, conflicts with a family member, accumulated household duties, moving to another house or repairing one's own house. As the diary study of Bolger, DeLongis, Kessler, and Schilling (1989) showed, such hassles appear regularly and therefore they can influence individual's daily recovery. In addition to hindering the replenishment of resources because they interrupt the recovery process, non-work hassles may also drain emotional resources because they put additional load on the individual (Fritz & Sonnentag, 2005). Thus, non-work hassles represent additional demands for individuals because they have to invest effort to deal with them. Another reason why non-work hassles are demanding is that they are unpredictable and unexpected and therefore individuals do not necessarily know to deal adequately with them (cf. Taris & Kompier, 2005). This means again that the recovery during non-work time is disturbed.

Bolger et al. (1989) found that non-work hassles including transportation, financial problems, and interpersonal conflict with people at home explained about 20% of the variance in daily mood. Interestingly, interpersonal conflicts, because of their emotional impact were far most important in explaining variance in daily mood. Further, Fritz and Sonnentag (2005) found in their diary study that non-work hassles during the weekend significantly contributed to poor general well-being, poor task performance, higher disengagement from work, lower levels of personal initiative, and lower pursuit of learning after the weekend.

NEED FOR RECOVERY

Results for Need for Recovery: Predictors

Although working toward a conceptual model of daily recovery, we reviewed several diary studies that examined relationships between aspects involved in the process of recovery. Because there are not so many diary studies that examined the process of recovery on a daily level and in order to make a more inclusive picture of recovery, we reviewed studies on need for recovery as well. Thus, the aim of this section is to present findings on need for recovery such that we can conclude whether these parallel the findings of daily recovery.

Need for recovery is the *sense of urgency* that people feel to take a break from their demands, when fatigue builds up. Inherent in the experience of need for recovery is a temporal reluctance to continue with the present demands or even to accept new demands (Schaufeli & Taris, 2005). Therefore, need for recovery from work can be viewed as an early stage of a long-term strain process leading to prolonged fatigue, psychological distress, and cardiovascular complaints (e.g., Jansen et al., 2002; Kivimaki et al., 2006). Typical examples of need for recovery experiences are that employees find it difficult to relax at the end of a working day, cannot concentrate during their free time after work, need free days to rest, and feel tired when they start a new work day (cf. Van Veldhoven & Meijman, 1994; Winwood, Winefield, & Lushington, 2006).

High need for recovery during non-work time implies that employees are strained due to dealing with work demands; otherwise recovery would not be necessary. When people have the time and the opportunity to satisfy their need for recovery (by resting or by engaging in appropriate leisure activities), their need for recovery will be fulfilled (Sonnentag & Zijlstra, 2006). This will be the case in the absence of work demands during a respite, which allows one to invest in new resources and to initiate a resource gain (Eden, 2001).

Several studies have examined the relationship between job demands and need for recovery. Job demands refer to those physical, social, or organizational aspects of the job that require sustained physical and mental efforts and are therefore associated with certain physiological and psychological costs (e.g., fatigue; Demerouti, Bakker, Nachreiner & Schaufeli, 2001). To avoid these costs or the negative consequences of demands individuals need to recover (Meijman & Mulder, 1998). Therefore, individuals exposed to highly demanding work situations experience higher need for recovery than those who have not been exposed to these situations (Sonnentag & Zijlstra, 2006). The same kind of argumentation applies to home demands since they also require the investment of effort in order to fulfill them.

Results confirm that there is a positive relationship between demands and need for recovery. In the diary study of Sonnentag and Zijlstra (2006), chronic job demands significantly predicted need for recovery during bedtime. In a longitudinal study, De Raeve, Vasse, Jansen, van den Brandt, and Kant (2007) found that increasing job demands were a significant predictor of a subsequent increase in need for recovery. Similarly, De Croon, Sluiter, Blonk, Broersen, and Frings-Dresen (2004) found in a two-year follow-up study among truck drivers that physical, psychological, and supervisor demands were positively related to need for recovery. Work schedule is considered to be an important factor influencing need for recovery. Using a 32-months follow up study, Van Amelsvoort, Jansen, Swaen, van den Brandt, and Kant (2004) found that backward rotation (night–evening–morning) shift schedule was prospectively related to an increased need for recovery. Additionally, Jansen et al. (2002) found that higher working hours a day and working hours a week coincided with more need for recovery from work. However, it seemed that the effect of working hours and overtime were interrelated with other work-related factors like demanding working conditions. Moreover, in a cross-sectional study in a representative sample of the Dutch working population, Sonnentag and Zijlstra (2006) found that quantity of work, responsibility, temporal demands, overtime, and hazards were positively related, whereas household and care responsibilities were unrelated to need for recovery. Similar findings have been reported by other cross-sectional studies using comparable job demands among specific occupational groups (e.g., Eriksen, Ihlebaek, Jansen, & Burdorf, 2006).

Next to job demands also job resources like job control and social support have been related to need for recovery. Job resources refer to those physical, psychological, social, or organizational aspects of the job that are functional in achieving work goals or reducing job demands at the associated physiological and psychological costs (Demerouti et al., 2001). Since job resources per definition help individuals during their task execution such that they will achieve their work goals and reduce the unfavorable impact of demands on them, they will have to exert low levels of effort. Consequently, need for recovery will not increase.

Several studies found that job resources are indeed negatively related to need for recovery. Specifically, job control was significantly related to lower need for recovery during bedtime in the diary study of Sonnentag and Zijlstra (2006). The longitudinal study of De Raeve et al. (2007) confirmed that an increase in decision latitude predicted a subsequent decrease in need for recovery. Similarly, de Croon et al. (2004) found a negative relationship between job control and need for recovery over time.

Moreover, negative affectivity and well-being when returning home were significant predictors of need for recovery during bedtime. Additionally, daily activities have also been found to influence daily need for recovery. People who spent a high amount of time on work-related activities had a stronger need for recovery at bedtime, whereas high amounts of time spent on social activities and physical activities had negative effects on need for recovery (Sonnentag & Zijlstra, 2006).

Results for Need for Recovery: Outcomes

Daily need for recovery has been found a highly significant predictor of daily well-being at bedtime (Sonnentag & Zijlstra, 2006). Need for recovery was also positively related to employee voluntary turnover in a two-year follow-up study among truck drivers (De Croon et al., 2004), whereas the longitudinal study of Swaen, Kant, Van Amelsfoort, and Beurskens (2002) showed that changing jobs led among others to reduced need for recovery. In the longitudinal study of van Amelsvoort et al. (2004), high levels of need for recovery were associated with an increased risk of leaving shift work during the follow-up two years later. High need for recovery after work increased the risk of subsequent sickness absence that is not explained by relevant (non-) work-related factors in the longitudinal study of De Croon, Sluiter, and Frings-Dresen (2003). Finally, Sluiter, Van der Beek, and Frings-Dresen (1999) found that need for recovery was a major predictor of psychosomatic complaints, sleep complaints, and complaints of emotional exhaustion in coach drivers. Need for recovery was found in this study to be even more important in predicting health problems than job demands and job control. These findings draw attention to the role of need for recovery as a sign of occupationally induced fatigue and predictor of health complaints.

Taken together, need for recovery has been suggested to represent a mediator in the relationship between demanding working conditions and health problems (De Croon et al., 2004). However, the results did not testify that need for recovery after work mediates between the exposure to stressful working conditions and the subsequent occurrence of sickness absence in this study.

RECOVERY MODEL

Fig. 1 displays our model on the process of daily recovery from work. The model departs from the work domain because we found several studies

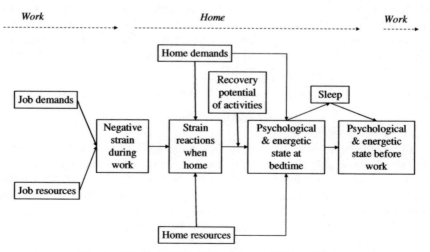

Fig. 1.   The Model of Daily Recovery from Work.

suggesting that what happens at work largely influences the recovery process during non-work time. Similar to the effort-recovery model (Meijman & Mulder, 1998), job demands are crucial factors for recovery because they represent the external load that causes load reactions within individuals (i.e., negative strain during and after work). It is these load reactions that need to be alleviated during non-work time. Although job demands will be positively related to negative strain during and after work, job resources will be negatively related to strain: the more resources, the less negative strain. Such relationships have been confirmed in the diary studies included in the present review (e.g., Sonnentag & Zijlstra, 2006) as well as studies beyond the daily level (e.g., Demerouti et al., 2001). An additional function of job resources (not displayed in the figure for simplicity) is that they may moderate the relationship between job demands and negative strain, such that job demands are more strongly related to negative strain when resources are low than when they are high (e.g., Bakker et al., 2005).

When conditions at work are such that employees develop negative strain (e.g., fatigue which builds up when demands are high), they will be inclined to react to this strain when they are at home. Think for instance of a day that you came home disappointed because of a critical remark made by your supervisor. The more disappointed you are the more likely it is that you will talk about it with your partner or the stronger your inclination to behave distant from family contact. Irrespectively of what the reaction will be, it can be assumed that the higher the level of negative strain after work, the higher the level of strain reactions at home. In support with this contention, Ilies et al. (2007) found in an experience sampling study that workload influenced affective states at work and consequently at home which eventually led to reduced social activities with the spouse and children through work–family conflict. The type of reaction or activity that people will be involved in will also depend on the existing demands and resources in the home domain. In principle, demands and resources in the home domain may have a similar function as demands and resources in the work domain; in both domains demands will inhibit recovery, whereas resources will facilitate it. Note that these hypotheses still need empirical testing because we have seen, for instance, that household and child-care activities did not have a deteriorating impact on the recovery process. Moreover, we found no study examining home characteristics with a facilitating effect on recovery. Similar to the function of demands and resources at work, we expect that demands and resources in the home domain will be directly related to the psychological and energetic state at bedtime, such that demands will have detrimental and resources will have favorable effects.

Now the question is whether the activities that people engage in when at home will lead to the recovery experience. As the review showed and as displayed in the figure, the type of activities will moderate the relationship between the strain reactions and the psychological and energetic state at bedtime. For instance, when a person is involved in activities with potential for recovery (e.g., physical or social activities) the unfavorable effect of strain reactions on psychological and energetic state at bedtime will be weaker than when one is not involved in such activities. In contrast, when a person is involved in activities inhibiting recovery (e.g., work-related activities), conducting such activities will have detrimental effects on psychological and energetic state compared to when one is not involved in such activities.

Note that what is crucial for the state at bedtime is not that the person is necessary fit to work again, but rather that the person has increased his/her ability to relax and to recover from work. In terms of physiological indicators, it means that blood pressure and heart rate are reduced in the evening (Rau, 2006). In terms of psychological indicators, the recovery process during non-work time has to do with less rumination (Cropley et al., 2006), or better well-being before going to bed (Sonnentag, 2001). Of course, it has to be taken into account that the constructs of rumination and situational well-being before going to bed are related to the ability to relax, but they are not similar. What is important for recovery though is that after the non-work activities the person feels ready and able to sleep. The better an individual's physiological and psychological state at bedtime, the longer and better the quality of sleep she/he will have. A better quality and quantity of sleep in turn leads to a better psychological and energetic state the next morning before going to work.

SUGGESTIONS FOR FUTURE RESEARCH

As the present chapter demonstrated, the phenomenon of daily recovery from work stress is a highly complex phenomenon that can be linked to a wide variety of antecedents (both in the work and home domains), processes (both psychological and physiological), and outcomes (including subjective experiences, but also behavior/performance). Empirical studies examining recovery vary strongly in their scope, theoretical bases, methodological approaches, and types of outcomes studied. To shed some light in this somewhat confusing findings, ideas and (methodological) approaches, it is desirable that these are integrated in an overarching theoretical framework.

An attempt to develop such a model has been presented in this chapter. We suggest a model including work and home characteristics that facilitate or inhibit recovery, type of activities with recovery potential and experienced states. These activities and states may affect recovery in two ways, i.e., a behavioral pathway (referring to after-work activities) and a psychological pathway (referring to the degree to which detaches psychologically from work). However, this model is still preliminary and tentative, and primarily intends to serve as a heuristic framework within which follow-up research on recovery can be conducted. On the basis of this model, we offer here a number of suggestions and directions for future research.

1. First, the *behavioral* pathway that links work experiences/effort to recovery draws on the type of activities people pursue after work. The recovering potential of these activities depends on the degree to which they draw on the same resources used during the workday. Basically, working overtime should not contribute to recovery, as it will deplete the same energetic resources as those used during the workday. Conversely, active leisure activities or relaxation draw on different resources, meaning that engaging in such activities should enhance recovery from work. However, at present it is unknown whether and how the *quality* of these after-work activities is related to their potential for recovery. For example, previous research has revealed that working a moderate amount of overtime does not necessarily coincide with negative load effects; rather, it seems that working overtime may well coincide with relatively *low* levels of fatigue, contingent on the degree to which these after-work activities are considered pleasurable and rewarding (Beckers et al., 2008). Conversely, it is conceivable that engaging in particular leisure activities is not found to be rewarding or pleasurable, and it is possible that in such cases these activities will not contribute to recovery. Thus, it seems that the recovery potential of after-work activities may not only depend on what one does, but also on one's subjective evaluation of these activities. A tentative hypothesis to be addressed in future research could be that any type of after-work activity could contribute to recovery, as long as these activities are conducted voluntarily and do not involve unpleasant effect (Van Hooff et al., 2007).

2. Similarly, the *psychological* pathway that links effort expenditure at work to recovery involves the degree to which workers can disengage psychologically from work. Ruminating about unpleasant experiences and events at work in the evening does obviously not promote the recovery process. Interestingly, it appears that thinking about positive

work experiences *does* have the potential to contribute to recovery from
work (Fritz & Sonnentag, 2005). Thus, not detaching psychologically
from the job during leisure time does not always impede recovery; this
also depends on the quality of one's experiences at work. Indeed, it seems
possible that not detaching psychologically from work can contribute to
recovery, as long as the associated thoughts are positive and involve
pleasant mood states.

3. Previous research on day-to-day recovery has primarily focused on
   affective states, mood, and fatigue. However, the practical relevance of
   this research could be greatly enhanced if it were possible to show that
   motivation and job performance depends substantially on the degree to
   which one has recovered from the previous workday. There is some
   research that indicates that recovery covaries positively with self-reported
   job performance (e.g., Binnewies, Sonnentag, & Mojza, 2009). However,
   self-reported performance may not be a valid indicator of objective
   performance (cf. Taris, 2006), meaning that it is imperative to validate
   and extend this research using objective measures of job performance.

4. Recovery from physical strain within the musculoskeletal system begins
   as soon as the physical stress demands are removed. Thereafter, rest and
   adequate nutrition alone, i.e., an essentially spontaneous and passive
   process, is sufficient to allow full recovery to baseline levels of physical
   strength. Although we have proposed an equivalency of this process for
   psycho-social strain recovery, such strain shows a pronounced tendency
   to *spill over* into the non-work time recovery period between work
   sequences. For example, co-worker conflict, bullying, anxieties about job
   security, and worry about the management of anticipated work problems
   in the next work period may all result in the continued activation of the
   stress response mechanism well into the non-work time period. This has
   been shown compellingly to affect sleep quality adversely, thereby
   diminishing spontaneous recovery obtainable from this source (Garrick
   et al., 2008). It would be interesting and important to examine which
   types of daily work-related stressors have the strongest tendency to spill
   over to the home domain, since strain-based work–family conflict seems
   an important barrier to daily recovery.

5. One intriguing finding in the recovery literature is the zero effects of
   household and child-care activities on the recovery process and outcomes.
   Rook and Zijlstra (2006) have suggested that because household activities
   and caring for children require active involvement, they help individuals
   to disengage from the daily strains at work. Therefore, although these

activities demand effort, they might be beneficial for recovery. This suggests that it would be important for future research on recovery to simultaneously consider energy replenishment and psychological detachment from work. Again, such research should consider the degree to which household and child-care activities are considered pleasurable (cf. suggestions 1 and 2 earlier).

6. What constitutes successful recovery may ultimately differ across individuals (Rook & Zijlstra, 2006). Indeed, Selye (1976, p. 413) argued that "Activity and rest must be judiciously balanced, and every person has his own characteristic requirements for rest and activity." This means that individuals need to discover their own thresholds and live at a pace of life suited to their personal needs. Some individuals may maintain health and avoid deleterious outcomes by taking regular short breaks or holidays (Cartwright & Cooper, 1997); others may require episodes of recovery on a daily basis involving physical activity (Rook & Zijlstra, 2006). This links to our suggestions 1 and 2; basically, this reasoning suggests that the recovery potential of after-work activities depends on personal characteristics and preferences. It would be an interesting and challenging task for future research to identify these characteristics and preferences; yet, it would seem that doing so would greatly enhance our understanding of the recovery process.

7. Finally, much research on daily recovery draws on diary designs, i.e., study designs in which the participants must provide data on their feelings, moods and activities at least once a day during a series of consecutive days. Although such a design is imperative for mapping day-to-day variations in health and well-being and for linking these variations to daily experiences, it is difficult to connect these (typically minor) day-to-day variations to serious health problems. For example, it is interesting to see that expending much effort at work may lead to sleep problems during the following night, but practically and scientifically it would be at least as important to see how these day-to-day experiences and activities contribute to, say, mental health problems such as burnout or depression. Such problems typically evolve during a longer period, and it is difficult to capture this period using a standard diary design. Thus, at present the link between serious illness and day-to-day recovery is still to be established. It appears that long-term diary designs, covering several months or even years, are needed to establish this link. Of course, the effort investment asked from the participant should be reduced accordingly; few people will be willing to take the trouble to complete

even a short diary every day for several months. It may be more feasible to ask the participants to provide diary-like data for a limited number of instances (e.g., once every month). This would allow researchers to establish typical individual-level patterns of after-work activities, and these could be linked to major changes of status in health and well-being.

CONCLUSION

The goal of this chapter was to provide insight in the process of daily recovery by discussing theories and research that help us understand the process of recovery, and its outcomes. On the basis of our literature review, we proposed an overall framework from which daily recovery during non-work time can be understood. We hope that this framework will encourage researchers to conduct the diary studies necessary to further increase our understanding of recovery and its effects.

REFERENCES

*Studies denoted with an asterisk have been included in the review.

Appels, A. (1997). Exhausted subjects, exhausted systems. *Acta Physiologica Scandinavica, Supplementum, 640,* 153–154.
Bakker, A. B. (2009). Building engagement in the workplace. In: C. Cooper & R. Burke (Eds), *The peak performing organization* (pp. 50–72). London: Routledge.
Bakker, A. B., & Demerouti, E. (2007). The job demands-resources model: State of the art. *Journal of Managerial Psychology, 22,* 309–328.
Bakker, A. B., Demerouti, E., & Euwema, M. C. (2005). Job resources buffer the impact of job demands on burnout. *Journal of Occupational Health Psychology, 10,* 170–180.
Bakker, A. B., van Emmerik, IJ. H., Geurts, S. A. E., & Demerouti, E. (2008). *Recovery turns job demands into challenges: A diary study on work engagement and performance.* Working paper. Erasmus University Rotterdam.
Beckers, D. G. J., Van der Linden, D., Smulders, P. G. W., Kompier, M. A. J., Taris, T. W., & Geurts, S. A. E. (2008). Voluntary or involuntary? Control over overtime and rewards for overtime in relation to fatigue and work-satisfaction. *Work & Stress, 22,* 33–50.
Belkic, K. L., Landsbergis, P. A., Schnall, P. L., & Baker, D. (2004). Is job strain a major source of cardiovascular disease risk? A critical review of the empirical evidence, with a clinical perspective. *Scandinavian Journal of Work, Environment & Health, 30,* 85–128.
Binnewies, C., Sonnentag, S., & Mojza, E. (2009). Daily performance at work: Feeling recovered in the morning as a predictor of day-level job performance. *Journal of Organizational Behavior, 30,* 67–93.

Bolger, N., DeLongis, A., Kessler, R. C., & Schilling, E. A. (1989). Effects of daily stress on negative mood. *Journal of Personality and Social Psychology, 57,* 808–818.

Bourne, E. J. (2000). *The anxiety and phobia work book* (3rd ed.). Oakland, CA: New Harbinger.

Brosschot, J. F., Pieper, S., & Thayer, J. F. (2005). Expanding stress theory: Prolonged activation and perseverative cognition. *Psychoneuroendocrinology, 30,* 1043–1049.

Butler, A. B., Grzywacz, J. G., Bass, B. L., & Linney, K. D. (2005). Extending the demands-control model: A daily diary study of job characteristics, work–family conflict and work–family facilitation. *Journal of Occupational and Organizational Psychology, 78,* 155–169.

Calder, A. (2003a). Recovery. In: M. Reid, A. Quinn & M. Crespo (Eds), *Strength and conditioning for tennis* (Chapter 14). Roehampton, London: International Tennis Federation.

Calder, A. (2003b). Recovery strategies for sports performance. *USOC Olympic Coach E-magazine,* September 2003. Available at http://coaching.usolympicteam.com/coaching/kpub.nsf/v/3Sept03. Retrieved on June 4, 2008.

Campbell, S. S. (1992). Effects of sleep and circadian rhythms of performance. In: A. P. Smith & D. M. Jones (Eds), *Handbook of human performance: Vol. 3. State and trait* (pp. 195–235). London: Academic Press.

Carskadon, M. A., & Dement, W. C. (2005). Normal human sleep overview. In: M. H. Kryger, T. Roth & W. C. Dement (Eds), *Principles and practice of sleep medicine* (4th ed., pp. 13–23). Philadelphia, PA: Elsevier/Saunders.

Cartwright, S., & Cooper, C. L. (1997). *Managing workplace stress.* London: Sage.

Clow, A. (2001). The physiology of stress. In: F. Jones & J. Bright (Eds), *Stress, myth, theory, and research* (pp. 47–61). Harlow, UK: Prentice Hall.

Cox, R. C. (2002). Exercise psychology. In: R. C. Cox (Ed.), *Sports psychology, concepts and applications* (5th ed, pp. 366–389). Boston: McGraw Hill.

Craig, A., & Cooper, R. E. (1992). Symptoms of acute and chronic fatigue. In: A. P. Smith & D. M. Jones (Eds), *Handbook of human performance: Vol. 3. State and trait* (pp. 289–339). London: Academic Press.

Cropley, M., Dijk, D.-J., & Stanley, N. (2006). Job strain, work rumination and sleep in school teachers. *European Journal of Work and Organizational Psychology, 15,* 181–196.

Cropley, M., & Purvis, L. J. (2003). Job strain and rumination about work issues during leisure time: A diary study. *European Journal of Work and Organizational Psychology, 12,* 195–207.

Csikszentmihalyi, M. (1990). *Flow: The psychology of optimal experience.* New York: HarperCollins.

De Bloom, J., Kompier, M. A. J., Geurts, S. A. E., De Weerth, C., Taris, T. W., & Sonnentag, S. (2009). Do we recover from vacation? Meta-analysis of vacation effects on health and well-being. *Journal of Occupational Health, 51,* 13–25.

De Croon, E. M., Sluiter, J. K., & Frings-Dresen, M. H. (2003). Need for recovery after work predicts sickness absence: A 2-year prospective cohort study in truck drivers. *Journal of Psychosomatic Research, 55,* 331–339.

De Croon, E. M., Sluiter, J. K., Blonk, R. W. B., Broersen, J. P. J., & Frings-Dresen, M. H. W. (2004). Stressful work, psychological strain, and turnover: A 2-year prospective cohort of truck drivers. *Journal of Applied Psychology, 89,* 442–454.

De Lange, A. H., Taris, T. W., Kompier, M. A. J., Houtman, I. L. D., & Bongers, P. M. (2003). The very best of the millennium: Longitudinal research and the demand-control(-support) model. *Journal of Occupational Health Psychology, 8,* 282–307.

Demerouti, E., Bakker, A. B., Nachreiner, F., & Schaufeli, W. B. (2001). The job demands-resources model of burnout. *Journal of Applied Psychology, 86*, 499–512.

Demerouti, E., & Cropanzano, R. (2009). From thought to action: Employee work engagement and job performance. In: A. B. Bakker & M. P. Leiter (Eds), *Work engagement: A handbook of essential theory and research*. New York: Psychology Press.

De Raeve, L., Vasse, R. M., Jansen, N. W. H., van den Brandt, P. A., & Kant, I. (2007). Mental health effects of changes in psychosocial work characteristics: A prospective cohort study. *Journal of Occupational Environmental Medicine, 49*, 890–899.

Dienstbier, R. A. (1989). Arousal and physiological toughness: Implications for mental and physical health. *Psychological Review, 96*, 84–100.

Eden, D. (2001). Vacations and other respites: Studying stress on and off the job. In: C. L. Cooper & I. T. Robertson (Eds), *Well-being in organisations: A reader for students and practitioners* (pp. 121–146). Chichester, UK: Wiley.

Eriksen, H. R., Ihlebaek, C., Jansen, J. P., & Burdorf, A. (2006). The relations between psychosocial factors at work and health status among workers in home care organizations. *International Journal of Behavioral Medicine, 13*, 183–192.

Etzion, D., Eden, D., & Lapidot, Y. (1998). Relief from job stressors and burnout: Reserve service as a respite. *Journal of Applied Psychology, 83*, 577–585.

Fredrickson, B. L. (2001). The role of positive emotions in positive psychology: The broaden-and-build theory of positive emotions. *American Psychologist, 56*, 218–226.

Fritz, C., & Sonnentag, S. (2005). Recovery, health, and job performance: Effects of weekend experiences. *Journal of Occupational Health Psychology, 10*, 187–199.

Garrick, A. J., Winwood, P. C., & Bakker, A. B. (2008). *Leisure-time activities, recovery, and fatigue: A diary study*. Internal Report, University of South Australia, Adelaide.

Geurts, S. A. E., & Demerouti, E. (2003). Work/non-work interface: A review of theories and findings. In: M. Schabracq, J. Winnubst & C. L. Cooper (Eds), *The handbook of work and health psychology* (2nd ed., pp. 279–312). Chichester: Wiley.

Geurts, S. A. E., & Sonnentag, S. (2006). Recovery as an explanatory mechanism in the relation between acute stress reactions and chronic health impairment. *Scandinavian Journal of Work, Environment & Health, 32*, 482–492.

Glynn, L. M., Christenfeld, N., & Gerin, W. (2002). The role of rumination in recovery from reactivity: Cardiovascular consequences of emotional states. *Psychosomatic Medicine, 64*, 714–726.

Grossman, A., Bouloux, P., Price, P., Drury, P. L., Lam, K. S., Turner, T., Thomas, J., Besser, G. M., & Sutton, J. (1984). The role of opioid peptides in the hormonal responses to acute exercise in man. *Clinical Science, 67*, 483–491.

Grossman, P., Niemann, L., Schmidt, S., & Walach, H. (2004). Mindfulness-based stress reduction and health benefits: A meta-analysis. *Journal of Psychosomatic Research, 57*, 35–43.

Hartig, T., Evans, G. W., Jamner, L. D., Davis, D. S., & Gärling, T. (2003). Tracking restoration in natural and urban field settings. *Journal of Environmental Psychology, 23*, 109–123.

Healy, C. M., & McKay, M. F. (2000). Nursing stress: The effects of coping strategies and job satisfaction in a sample of Australian nurses. *Journal of Advanced Nursing, 31*, 681–688.

Hobfoll, S. E. (1998). *Stress, culture and community. The psychology and philosophy of stress*. New York: Plenum.

Hobfoll, S. E. (2002). Social and psychological resources and adaptation. *Review of General Psychology, 6*, 307–324.

Horne, J. A. (2001). State of the art: Sleep. *The Psychologist, 14*, 302–306.

Ilies, R., Schwind, K. M., Wagner, D. T., Johnson, M. D. D., DeRue, S., & Ilgen, D. R. (2007). When can employees have a family life? The effects of daily workload and affect on work–family conflict and social behaviors at home. *Journal of Applied Psychology, 92*, 1368–1379.

Iso-Ahola, S. (1997). A psychological analysis of leisure and health. In: J. Haworth (Ed.), *Work, leisure and well-being* (pp. 131–144). London, UK: Routledge.

Jansen, N. W. H., Kant, I. J., & van den Brandt, P. A. (2002). Need for recovery in the working population: Description and associations with fatigue and psychological distress. *International Journal of Behavioral Medicine, 9*, 322–340.

Karasek, R. A. (1998). Demand/control model: A social, emotional, and psychological approach to stress risk and active behaviour development. In: J. M. Stellman (Ed.), *Encyclopaedia of occupational health and safety* (pp. 34.6–34.14). Geneva, Switzerland: International Labour Office.

Kivimaki, M., Leino-Arjas, P., Kaila-Kangas, L., Luukkonen, R., Vahtera, J., Elovainio, M., Härmä, M., & Kirjonen, J. (2006). Is incomplete recovery from work a risk marker of cardiovascular dealth? Prospective evidence from industrial employees. *Psychosomatic Medicine, 68*, 402–407.

Kleiber, D., Larson, R., & Csikszentmihalyi, M. (1986). The experience of leisure in adolescence. *Journal of Leisure Research, 18*, 169–176.

*Lamont, N., Dawson, D., & Roach, G. D. (2006). Do short international layovers allow sufficient opportunity for pilots to recover? *Chronobiology International, 23*, 1285–1294.

Lee, R. T., & Ashforth, B. E. (1996). A meta-analytic examination of the correlates of the three dimensions of job burnout. *Journal of Applied Psychology, 81*, 123–133.

Lepore, S. J., & Evans, G. W. (1996). Coping with multiple stressors in the environment. In: M. Zeidner & N. Endler (Eds), *Handbook of coping: Theory, research and applications* (pp. 350–377). New York: Wiley.

Luczak, H. (1987). Psychophysiologische Methoden zur Erfassung psychophysischer Beanspruchungszustaende. [Psychophysiological methods for the assessment of psycho-physical strain.] In: U. Kleinbeck & J. Rutenfranz (Eds), *Enzyklopaedie der Psychologie*, Themenbereich D, Praxisgebiete, Serie III, Wirtschafts-, Organisations- und Arbeitspsychologie, Band 1 (pp. 185–259). Göttingen, Germany: Hogrefe.

McAuley, E., Kramer, A. F., & Colcombe, S. J. (2004). Cardiovascular fitness and neurocognitive function in older adults: A brief review. *Brain, Behavior, & Immunity, 18*, 214–220.

McEwen, B. S. (1998). Stress, adaptation, and disease: Allostasis and allostatic load. *Annals of the New York Academy of Science, 840*, 33–44.

Meijman, T., Mulder, G., van Dormolen, M., & Cremer, R. (1992). Workload of driving examiners: A psychophysiological field study. In: H. Kragt (Ed.), *Enhancing industrial performance* (pp. 245–259). London: Taylor & Francis.

Meijman, T. F. (1991). *Over vermoeidheid: Arbeidspsychologische studies naar de beleving van belastingseffecten. [Fatigue: Studies on the perception of workload effects.]* (Doctoral dissertation, University of Groningen, Groningen, The Netherlands).

Meijman, T. F., & Mulder, G. (1998). Psychological aspects of workload. In: P. J. D. Drenth & H. Thierry (Eds), *Handbook of work and organizational psychology* (Vol. 2, pp. 5–33). Hove: Psychology Press.

Oken, B. S., Kishiyama, S., Zajdel, D., Bourdette, D., Carlsen, J., Haas, M., Hugos, C., Kraemer, D. F., Lawrence, J., & Mass, M. (2004). Randomized controlled trial of yoga and exercise in multiple sclerosis. *Neurology, 62,* 2058–2064.

Pelletier, C. L. (2004). The effect of music on decreasing arousal due to stress: A meta-analysis. *Journal of Music Therapy, 41,* 192–214.

Pickering, T. (1997). Cardiovascular measures of allostatic load. In: J. D. MacArthur & C. T. MacArthur (Eds), *Research network on socioeconomic status and health.* Available at http://www.macses.ucsf.edu/Research/Allostatic/notebook/allostatic.html. Retrieved on June 6, 2008.

Raglin, J. S., & Morgan, W. P. (1985). Influence of vigorous exercise on mood state. *Behavior Therapy, 8,* 179–183.

Rau, R. (2004). Job strain or healthy work: A question of task design. *Journal of Occupational Health Psychology, 9,* 322–338.

Rau, R. (2006). Learning opportunities at work as predictor for recovery and health. *European Journal of Work and Organizational Psychology, 15,* 181–196.

Rau, R., & Triemer, A. (2004). Overtime in relation to blood pressure and mood during work, leisure, and night time. *Social Indicators Research, 67,* 51–73.

Rook, J., & Zijlstra, F. (2006). The contribution of various types of activities to recovery. *European Journal of Work and Organizational Psychology, 15,* 218–240.

Saxbe, D. E., Repetti, R. L., & Nishina, A. (2008). Marital satisfaction, recovery from work, and diurnal cortisol among men and women. *Health Psychology, 27,* 15–25.

Schaufeli, W. B., & Taris, T. W. (2005). Conceptualization and measurement of burnout: Common ground and worlds apart. *Work & Stress, 19,* 256–262.

Schnall, P. L., Schwartz, J. E., Landsbergis, P. A., Warren, K., & Pickering, T. G. (1992). Relation between job strain, alcohol, and ambulatory blood pressure. *Hypertension, 19,* 488–494.

Selye, H. (1976). *The stress of life* (Revised Edition). New York: McGraw-Hill.

Sluiter, J. K., Frings-Dresen, M. H. W., van der Beek, A. J., & Meijman, T. F. (2001). The relation between work-induced neuroendocrine reactivity and recovery, subjective need for recovery, and health status. *Journal of Psychosomatic Research, 50,* 29–37.

Sluiter, J. K., Van der Beek, A. J., & Frings-Dresen, M. H. W. (1999). The influence of work characteristics on the need for recovery and experienced health: A study on coach drivers. *Ergonomics, 42,* 573–583.

*Sonnentag, S. (2001). Work, recovery activities, and individual well-being: A diary study. *Journal of Occupational Health Psychology, 6,* 196–210.

*Sonnentag, S. (2003). Recovery, work engagement, and proactive behavior: A new look at the interface between nonwork and work. *Journal of Applied Psychology, 88,* 518–528.

*Sonnentag, S., & Bayer, U. V. (2005). Switching off mentally: Predictors and consequences of psychological detachment from work during off-job time. *Journal of Occupational Health Psychology, 10,* 393–414.

*Sonnentag, S., Binnewies, C., & Mojza, A. J. (2008). Did you have a nice evening? A day-level study on recovery experiences, sleep, and affect. *Journal of Applied Psychology, 93,* 674–684.

Sonnentag, S., & Fritz, C. (2006). Endocrinological processes associated with job stress: Catecholamine and cortisol responses to acute and chronic stressors. In: P. L. Perrewé & D. C. Ganster (Eds), *Research in organizational stress and well-being: Employee health, coping, and methodologies* (pp. 1–59). Amsterdam: Elsevier.

Sonnentag, S., & Fritz, C. (2007). The recovery experience questionnaire: Development and validation of a measure for assessing recuperation and unwinding from work. *Journal of Occupational Health Psychology, 12,* 204–221.

Sonnentag, S., & Geurts, S. A. E. (this volume). Methodological issues in recovery research. In: P. Perrewé, D. Ganster & S. Sonnentag (Eds), *Research in occupational stress and well being* (Vol. 7). US: JAI Press/Elsevier.

Sonnentag, S., & Kruel, U. (2006). Psychological detachment from work during off-job time: The role of job stressors, job involvement, and recovery-related self-efficacy. *European Journal of Work and Organizational Psychology, 15,* 197–217.

*Sonnentag, S., & Natter, E. (2004). Flight attendants' daily recovery from work: Is there no place like home? *International Journal of Stress Management, 11,* 366–391.

Sonnentag, S., & Zijlstra, F. R. H. (2006). Job characteristics and off-job activities as predictors of need for recovery, well-being, and fatigue. *Journal of Applied Psychology, 91,* 330–350.

Sterling, P. (2004). Principles of allostasis: Optimal design, predictive regulation, pathophysiology and rational therapeutics. In: J. Schulkin (Ed.), *Allostasis, homeostasis, and the costs of adaptation* (pp. 2–36). Cambridge, UK: Cambridge University Press.

Sterling, P., & Eyer, J. (1988). Allostasis: A new paradigm to explain arousal pathology. In: S. Fisher & J. Reason (Eds), *Handbook of life stress, cognition and health* (pp. 629–649). New York: Wiley.

Stewart, J. C., Janicki, D. L., & Kamarck, T. W. (2006). Cardiovascular reactivity to and recovery from psychological challenge as predictors of 3-year change in blood pressure. *Health Psychology, 25,* 111–118.

Swaen, G. M. H., Kant, I. J., Van Amelsfoort, L. G. P. M., & Beurskens, A. J. H. M. (2002). Job mobility, its determinants, and its effects: Longitudinal data from the Maastricht Cohort Study. *Journal of Occupational Health Psychology, 7,* 121–129.

Takahashi, M., Fukuda, H., & Arito, H. (1998). Brief naps during post-lunch rest: Effects on alertness, performance, and autonomic balance. *European Journal of Applied Physiology and Occupational Physiology, 78,* 93–98.

Taris, T. W. (2006). Burnout and objectively recorded performance: A critical review of 16 studies. *Work & Stress, 20,* 316–334.

Taris, T. W., Beckers, D. G. J., Dahlgren, A., Geurts, S. A. E., & Tucker, P. (2007). Overtime work and well-being: Prevalence, conceptualization and effects of working overtime. In: S. McIntyre & J. Houdmont (Eds), *Occupational health psychology: European perspectives on research, education and practice* (Vol. 2, pp. 21–40). Maia, Portugal: ISMAI.

Taris, T. W., & Kompier, M. A. J. (2005). Job characteristics and learning behavior. In: P. L. Perrewé & D. C. Ganster (Eds), *Research in occupational stress and well-being: Exploring interpersonal dynamics* (Vol. 4, pp. 127–166). Amsterdam: JAI Press.

Teuchmann, K., Totterdell, P., & Parker, S. K. (1999). Rushed, unhappy, and drained: An experience sampling study of relations between time pressure, perceived control, mood, and emotional exhaustion in a group of accountants. *Journal of Occupational Health Psychology, 4,* 37–54.

Theorell, T., Ahlberg-Hulten, G., Jodko, M., Sigala, F., & de la Torre, B. (1993). Influence of job strain and emotion on blood pressure in female hospital personnel during work-hours. *Scandinavian Journal of Work Environment and Health, 19*, 313–318.

Theorell, T., de Faire, U., Johnson, J., Hall, E., Perski, A., & Stewart, W. (1991). Job strain and ambulatory blood pressure profiles. *Scandinavian Journal of Work, Environment and Health, 17*, 380–385.

Thoren, P., Floras, F. S., Hoffman, P., & Seals, D. R. (1990). Endorphins and exercise: Physiological mechanisms and clinical implications. *Medicine & Science in Sports & Exercise, 22*, 417–428.

Totterdell, P., Spelten, E., Smith, L., Barton, J., & Folkard, S. (1995). Recovery from work shifts: How long does it take? *Journal of Applied Psychology, 80*, 43–57.

Totterdell, P., Wood, S. J., & Wall, T. D. (2006). An intra-individual test of the demands-control model: A weekly diary study of job strain in portfolio workers. *Journal of Occupational and Organizational Psychology, 78*, 1–23.

Trougakos, J. P., & Hideg, I. (this volume). Momentary work recovery: The role of within-day work breaks. In: P. Perrewé, D. Ganster & S. Sonnentag (Eds), *Research in occupational stress and well being* (Vol. 7). US: JAI Press/Elsevier.

Van Amelsvoort, L. G., Jansen, N. W., Swaen, G. M., van den Brandt, P. A., & Kant, I. (2004). Direction of shift rotation among three-shift workers in relation to psychological health and work–family conflict. *Scandinavian Journal of Work, Environment and Health, 30*, 149–156.

Van der Hulst, M., & Geurts, S. A. E. (2001). Associations between overtime and psychological health in high and low reward jobs. *Work & Stress, 15*, 227–240.

Van Hooff, M. L. M., Geurts, S. A. E., Kompier, M. A. J., & Taris, T. W. (2007). Workdays, in-between workdays, and the weekend: A diary study on effort and recovery. *International Archives of Occupational and Environmental Health, 80*, 599–613.

van Veldhoven, M., & Meijman, T. F. (1994). *Het meten van psychosociale arbeidsbelasting met een vragenlijst: de vragenlijst beleving en beoordeling van de arbeid (VBBA). [The measurement of psychosocial job demands with a questionnaire: The questionnaire on the experience and evaluation of work (QEEW).]*. Amsterdam: Nederlands Instituut voor Arbeidsomstandigheden.

Westman, M., & Eden, D. (1997). Effects of a respite from work on burnout: Vacation relief and fade-out. *Journal of Applied Psychology, 82*, 516–527.

Westman, M., & Etzion, D. (2001). The impact of vacation and job stress on burnout and absenteeism. *Psychology and Health, 16*, 595–606.

Winwood, P. C., Bakker, A. B., & Winefield, A. H. (2007). An investigation of the role of non-work-time behavior in buffering the effects of work-strain. *Journal of Occupational and Environmental Medicine, 49*, 862–871.

Winwood, P. C., Winefield,, A. H., & Lushington, K. (2006). The contribution of age, domestic responsibilities and shiftwork to work-related fatigue and recovery within a sample of full-time Australian nurses. *Journal of Advanced Nursing, 56*, 438–449.

Yeung, R. R. (1996). The acute effects of exercise on mood state. *Journal of Psychosomatic Research, 40*, 123–141.

Zapf, D. (2002). Emotion work and psychological well-being. A review of the literature and some conceptual considerations. *Human Resource Management Review, 12*, 237–268.

Zijlstra, F. R. H., & de Vries, J. (2000). Burnout en de bijdrage van socio-demografische en werkgebonden variabelen. [Burnout and the contribution of socio-demographic and work related variables.]. In: I. L. D. Houtman, W. B. Schaufeli & T. Taris (Eds), *Psychische vermoeidheid en werk: Cijfers, trends en analyses* (pp. 83–95). Alphen a/d Rijn, The Netherlands: Samsom.

Zohar, D., Tzischinski, O., & Epstein, R. (2003). Effects of energy availability on immediate and delayed emotional reactions to work events. *Journal of Applied Psychology, 88,* 1082–1093.

RECOVERY AND THE WORK–FAMILY INTERFACE

Fabienne T. Amstad and Norbert K. Semmer

INTRODUCTION

Recovery seems to be one of the most important mechanisms explaining the relationship between acute stress reactions and chronic health complaints (Geurts & Sonnentag, 2006). Moreover, insufficient recovery may be the linking mechanism that turns daily stress experiences into chronic stress. Given this role recovery has in the stress process, it is important to ask in which contexts and under what circumstances recovery takes place.

Obviously, recovery may occur in many different contexts. Probably the most basic distinction refers to the nonwork context vs. work context (Geurts & Sonnentag, 2006). The effect of recovery during working time (e.g., breaks, mini-breaks), is discussed by Trougakos and Hideg in this volume. The focus of this chapter will be on recovery during nonwork time.

The nonwork domain constitutes a very broad category, as it contains all life domains except the work domain. So, it would be helpful to categorize this nonwork context to investigate the effect of different nonwork activities on recovery. One possibility to categorize off-job time is by differentiating the time with respect to one's obligation during this time. Following this, nonwork time has been classified into four different categories (Thierry & Jansen, 1998). The first category of *work-related time* refers to time spent on activities such as commuting or finishing work at home. The second

Current Perspectives on Job-Stress Recovery
Research in Occupational Stress and Well Being, Volume 7, 125–166
Copyright © 2009 by Emerald Group Publishing Limited
ISSN: 1479-3555/doi:10.1108/S1479-3555(2009)0000007007

category refers to *existence time* during which individuals use time for meals, sleep, or personal care. *Semi-leisure time* refers to activities with a somewhat committing nature, such as household activities and childcare. The last category is called *leisure time* and means time that is completely free of obligations.

Considering the effect of these different types of activities on recovery, clear results have been shown for work-related and leisure time activities: Work-related activities are negatively related to recovery, whereas leisure time activities, especially physical activities like sports (Rook & Zijlstra, 2006), are positively related to recovery (Sonnentag, 2001; Sonnentag & Zijlstra, 2006). Semi-leisure time activities (household chores, childcare) show somewhat ambiguous results. One would expect some negative correlations with recovery, but interestingly Sonnentag and Zijlstra (2006) did not find any association. These results suggest that the quality of recovery time may play an important role in the recovery process not solely the recovery activity itself.

Especially for working parents, it is quite obvious that many of these nonwork time activities take place in the family. Hence, recovery opportunities are to a large degree located in the family domain. Furthermore, family life also influences recovery by being an important source of additional demands, and people have less discretion in accepting or avoiding these demands than they do in "pure" leisure time. The family therefore suggests itself as an especially important domain when recovery is the focus of attention.

Work and family have often been considered as independent life domains (Dubin, 1976). But work influences the family in several ways. First, work influences *what* one is doing at home. This is, for example, shown by the first category of nonwork time: if somebody has tight deadlines at work, he or she may work at home, which is likely to impair recovery. Second, work influences how individuals *feel* at home. After an exhausting or upsetting workday one is likely to feel tired, depressed, and irritated, and one may ruminate about one's work experiences (e.g., Judge & Ilies, 2004). These reactions are likely to impair the process of recovery, and they are likely to influence his or her family. The family may react with empathy and support – which may alleviate or solve the problem, but may also see these behaviors as a burden for the family, leading to feelings of inequity, or the like. Third, work may influence *how* one is doing something at home. Thus, being tired and in a bad mood may affect one's way of interacting with family members. For instance, one may react to minor hassles, such as the children being noisy, with more irritation than after a "good" day, or one may be more prone to enter into an argument with one's spouse. Finally, not only does the work domain influence the family, but also the family influences the work domain. For example, if a family evening was very demanding, because a child was ill and was crying the whole night, one feels exhausted at work the next day and might work less efficiently than if he or she would have slept well during that night.

These considerations show how important it is to include the work–family interface when recovery processes are of interest. Therefore, the aim of the present chapter is to discuss the relationships between these different life domains, hoping to contribute to a better understanding of the process of recovery.

First, we discuss work and family as primary life domains. Second, different mechanisms linking work and family and their relationship to recovery are discussed. Third, we focus on antecedents and consequences of the work–family interface, with a special emphasis on exhaustion and need for recovery as possible consequences. Although these considerations imply a "macro-perspective" in that variables and processes are discussed in general, our fourth point relates to micro-processes in terms of sequences of events, and a micro-process model is proposed that might serve as a guide for investigating the pertinent processes. Because issues of the work–family interface are intrinsically linked to gender roles, gender issues have been an important part of theory-building and research in this area (Greenhaus & Parasuraman, 1999). Our fifth section deals with this issue. The chapter finishes with some concluding remarks.

WORK AND FAMILY AS INDIVIDUAL'S PRIMARY LIFE DOMAINS

As our previous examples have shown, it seems obvious that work and family are influencing each other, and that the recovery process is influenced by the interface of these life domains. Before discussing these mutual influences, it is important to define the two life domains and to see what constitutes these domains.

The basic distinction in the literature refers to work and nonwork, or private life, as distinct life domains; and to work and nonwork activities (Geurts & Sonnentag, 2006). However, no consistent position exists concerning the constitutive and distinctive elements of these domains. Mostly, work is defined as paid work, whereas private life or nonwork consists of all other life domains, such as family, spare time, hobbies, sports, clubs etc. To define work in terms of paid work is not without problems, as it is plausible also to define work in terms of tasks that is, exerting energy for goal-related activity. From such a perspective, household chores also constitute "work" (Resch, 1999), as do many voluntary activities (voluntary work, e.g., Thoits & Hewitt, 2001). Nevertheless, the labor market, which is the domain where paid work is delivered, certainly constitutes a domain that has distinctive features separating it from other domains, and this domain is easily distinguished and recognized by society and its members. Actually, many people spontaneously divide their lives into the work and nonwork domain, and studies that focus on the meaning of work (MOW, 1987), or the centrality of work (Dubin, 1956), have followed this line of thinking. Unless indicated otherwise, we therefore will use the term "work" as a synonym for "paid work" throughout this chapter.

A weak point of this gross classification of work vs. nonwork is that nonwork itself includes several life domains. Voydanoff (2001) distinguishes three life domains: work, family, and community; Kirchmeyer (1993) refers to four domains: work, parenthood, community, spare time. These approaches represent an Anglo-Saxon tradition, as they include community life as a life domain, which is less dominant in European traditions (Mieg & Wehner, 2002). Within the family domain, further distinctions are possible. Caring for others often is mentioned as a separate subdomain, focusing on caring for children, but also for elders (cf. Penning, 1998; Reid & Hardy, 1999; Stephens & Franks, 1995). Distinguishing these subdomains is not easy; however, as different aspects of private life, such as relationship, parenthood, friendship etc., tend to be especially closely interwoven. It is probably for this reason that most research on the topic of work/nonwork interface is restricted to the two basic life domains of work and family.

However, clear boundaries do not exist between work and family, either. In many cases, it is possible, and customary, to make private phone calls at work or to have private interactions with coworkers (cf. Tschan, Semmer, & Inversin, 2004), and to do some work-related activities at home and on the way to and from work. One aspect of teleworking that is often discussed actually refers to the problem that people cannot separate work and family domains anymore and that this may lead to problems (Standen, Daniels, & Lamond, 1999). And for owners of little shops, farms etc., the boundaries have always been blurred, and oftentimes this involves the whole family.

But even where a clear separation seems possible, it may depend on one's perspective where the boundary is drawn. When I spend some spare time with my work colleagues just after work (e.g., going for a drink), I may see this as "private," but my spouse might see it as "belonging to work." People also differ in the degree to which they desire to separate their work and nonwork lives (Rothbard, Phillips, & Dumas, 2005). Nevertheless, the differentiation between work and family seems to be less problematic than differentiations within the private family domain. Therefore, we will mostly talk about two life domains – work and family – which interact with each other and influence the recovery process.

Work Family Balance and Recovery

If the relationship between work and family is important for recovery, it is plausible to assume that some form of "balance" between the two domains is conducive to restore one's energy. Basically, there are two approaches to study work–family balance. One approach focuses on the balance of resources that are invested in each domain. For example, time invested in work is compared with time invested in the family, such as household chores and childcare. More generally, the investment of all kinds of personal resources is taken into account, such as attentiveness, involvement, or commitment. Considering recovery as the process of replenishing resources (Zijlstra & Sonnentag, 2006), the importance of work–family balance for the recovery process seems evident.

The question remains, however, what constitutes "balance" in this case. At first sight, balance may be given by an equality of investments in both life domains. Depending on the importance attributed to each domain and on norms governing each partner's contribution, balance may well depart from equality. For example, a study by Greenhaus, Collins, and Shaw (2003) showed that individuals investing more resources (e.g., time or involvement) into the family as compared to work experienced a higher quality of life than individuals investing equal resources in both domains or favoring work over family. This result, which may be interpreted in terms of inequality in favor of the family indicating "balance," held especially for individuals who invested a high amount of resources in both life domains (Greenhaus et al., 2003). Furthermore, not only does the investment in work as compared to the family seem to be important, but also one's investment in the family as compared to the partner's investment (Klumb, Hoppmann, & Staats, 2006).

It therefore seems difficult to determine balance strictly on the basis of quantity, and further research is needed to clarify the criteria that determine balance. This leads to the second approach to work–family balance. This approach focuses more on quality than on quantity, and focuses on the question of harmony vs. conflict between life domains. Thus, Greenhaus and Beutell (1985) defined work–family imbalance as "[...] a form of interrole conflict in which the role pressures from the work and family domains are mutually incompatible in some respect. That is, participation in the work (family) role is made more difficult by virtue of participation in the family (work) role" (p. 77). This qualitative perspective is dominant in the field of work–family interface.

From such a qualitative perspective, conflict represents the negative reciprocal influence of life domains, and facilitation or enhancement represents the positive influence. Individuals feel harmony between their life domains when they experience few conflicts between their life domains and when these life domains enhance each other. Furthermore, there may be an interaction, in that positive effects may buffer the negative ones (cf. Fredrickson, Mancuso, Branigan, & Tugade, 2000). Research so far has mainly concentrated on the negative side of the interface, i.e., the conflict between work and family (for reviews, see Frone, 2003; Geurts & Demerouti, 2003). The importance of positive work–family interactions was shown by Grzywacz and Bass (2003), where family–work facilitation was a protective factor in the relationship between work–family conflict and psychological health.

With respect to recovery, feeling harmony between work and family may indicate (a) that, in general, no domain imposes undue demands on the person that require an unusual amount of recovery, or (b) that very high demands of one domain can be offset in the other one by providing opportunity for recovery and reassurance, or by providing positive experiences. In contrast, conflict would indicate that not enough recovery opportunities of demands from one domain are available in the other domain, and that the other domain contains additional demands that impede recovery or even aggravate the situation. We will discuss such processes later in this chapter.

Influences that create an imbalance between two life domains can be bi-directional (Barnett, 1998; Frone, 2003; Frone, Russell, & Cooper, 1992a), and can proceed from work-to-family or from family-to-work. Demands from work can intrude on the family, but also demands from the family can intrude on work. With regard to negative influences, several studies show that work-to-family conflict has a greater prevalence than family-to-work conflict (Eagle, Miles, & Icenogle, 1997; Frone, Russell, & Cooper, 1992a; Gutek, Searle, & Klepa, 1991). Furthermore, the boundaries between work and family seem to be asymmetrically permeable. This means that working life influences the family more strongly than the other way around (Frone, Russel, & Cooper, 1992b; Rothbard & Edwards, 2003). With regard to positive influences, both prevalence and influence seem to be reversed. Thus, Kirchmeyer (1993) as well as Grzywacz and coworkers (Grzywacz & Bass, 2003; Grzywacz & Marks, 2000a, 2000b) found a higher prevalence for family-to-work facilitation than for work-to-family facilitation. Grzywacz and Bass (2003) conclude that "it appears as though work–family fit is optimized when work is protected from family disruptions and when family contributes to productivity at work" (p. 258).

The Linkage between Work and Family: General Models

It has become clear that, theoretically as well as empirically, work and family are not independent life domains. The nature of the link between the two domains has been the focus of theoretical models that were developed in the 1960s. They represent three different approaches to the relationship between work and family: segmentation, also called segregation (no relationship), compensation (negative relationship), and spillover (positive relationship). We present these approaches and then discuss their relationship to recovery.

Segmentation/Segregation

The first model of segmentation/segregation says that there is no relationship between the different life domains (Dubin, 1956). This position was abandoned rather early because it quickly became clear that there is a relationship between work and family (Burke & Greenglass, 1987; Voydanoff, 1987). Hence, it is no longer advocated in its original form. However, more recent literature (e.g., Edwards & Rothbard, 2000) describes segmentation as an active process. This process is seen as a type of coping strategy, where individuals consciously and actively try to set boundaries between their different life domains (Eckenrode & Gore, 1990; Lambert, 1990). The advantage of such a strategy may be seen in an enhanced ability to detach from work psychologically. Psychological detachment from work is highly relevant for recovery to occur (Sonnentag & Bayer, 2005; Sonnentag & Kruel, 2006). For most people, there is a physical distance between work and family, which may facilitate psychological detachment. However, a certain degree of active psychological segmentation is likely to represent the best strategy to achieve detachment from work. Thus, active segmentation seems to be crucial for the recovery process.

Edwards and Rothbard (1999) showed that active segmentation has a positive relationship with well-being, as long as it is not conducted in an excessive way. If segmentation gets very strong, a negative effect on well-being results. This study shows that a possible curvilinear relationship exists between active segmentation and well-being.

Clark (2000) also emphasizes that balance results from an active and skillful "border management." She regards segmentation as one pole of a continuum, with "integration" at the other end, implying that one does not really distinguish the two domains. In her approach, there is no general optimum of segmentation/integration; rather, the optimum depends on how each domain can fulfill the needs it is supposed to fulfill (e.g., accomplishment at work, close relationships at home). What successful border management means and how it is achieved depends on a host of factors, such as the centrality of each domain for the person, the "other domain awareness" of members of each domain, the strength of the borders, and the like. When people cross borders, they "travel" (often literally, but also psychologically) through a "borderland" that represents a blending of both domains.

The importance of segmentation as an active process is demonstrated in a study with double income parents by Amstad, Tschudi, Zimmermann, and Semmer (2006). In this study, participants reported two types of segmentation strategies that they used in order to protect one domain from negative impacts of the other domain: The first strategy has the focus on the transition between work and family (Clark's "border land"). Individuals use the way to home or the way to work deliberately to detach psychologically from work or from their families. The second strategy is applied within a given domain. One tries to concentrate on the domain one is in, and not to think of the other domain. It was called the "here and now" strategy. Both strategies aim at a psychological detachment of the other domain. Analyses showed that the second strategy of "here and now" had a protective effect, in that it moderated the association between stressors from one domain with well-being in the other domain. For instance, a high level of social stressors at work was associated with a low family satisfaction, and a high level of social stressors in the family was associated with a low level of job satisfaction, but these relationships held only for people who did not report a high level of the "here and now" strategy, and it was absent for those who did.

Compensation/Resource Drain
The second classical model, compensation, postulates a statistically negative relationship between life domains (Wilensky, 1960). According to this model

dissatisfaction in one domain leads to a higher investment of energy and commitment in the second domain; this in turn leads to more satisfaction in the second domain. Thus, unhappiness at work can be compensated by paying more attention to the family, resulting in greater happiness in the family.

A related model, which also postulates a negative relationship between life domains, is the resource drain model. This approach takes account of limited resources, such as time, money, or energy. If such resources are drawn on too often in one domain, they are missing in the other domain (Frone, 2003). A typical example is a lack of energy because of demanding work, which constrains an active family life (cf. Bamberg, 1992).

Recovery plays a crucial role in the conception of the resource drain model. Recovery is usually indicated as the process of replenishing resources (Zijlstra & Sonnentag, 2006) and energy is one important type of resource (Hobfoll, 1998). So, if energy is mostly used in one life domain, and therefore is lacking in the other domain, this other domain will suffer. Quite often, it is family life that is then "degraded" to help restore one's energy resources. To the extent that this is associated with passive recovery, an active family life suffers. However, an active family life is an important resource in itself that may have positive effects on recovery (Sonnentag & Zijlstra, 2006; Winwood, Bakker, & Winefield, 2007). If resource drain, therefore, is compensated by reduced activity, a resource loss spiral may result (Demerouti, Bakker, & Bulters, 2004; Hobfoll, 2001).

Spillover and Crossover
The third model, which has received the highest amount of attention, is the spillover, or generalization, model (cf. Wilensky, 1960). Spillover refers to the "transmission" of behavior, emotions, and attitudes from one domain to another (Geurts & Demerouti, 2003; Meissner, 1971). Statistically, this implies a positive relationship between life domains. Spillover refers to an impact of positive as well as negative states on the other domain. An example for such a process would be a tense family atmosphere in the evening because one parent is in a bad mood because of problems he or she encountered during work.

Two main approaches are found with regard to spillover. The role strain theory sees the work–family interface from a stress perspective. It emphasizes that performing several roles can lead to role conflicts and, therefore, to stress (Kahn, Wolfe, Quinn, Snoek, & Rosenthal, 1964). In this case, we talk of negative spillover. The role enhancement hypothesis postulates the converse effect and is also known as positive spillover.

This approach was advocated by Marks (1977), who studied the relationship between multiple role fulfillment and life energy. He found the combination of several roles (e.g., work and family) to be profitable for individuals. For example, women and men in his study reported that the combination of different roles enabled them to be better parents. More recent studies support this hypothesis (Barnett & Hyde, 2001; Marshall & Barnett, 1993).

The classic spillover approach focuses on intra-individual transmission processes. Westman (2002a) extends this approach with her model of crossover, which represents an interpersonal transmission. For instance, stress experienced at work can be transferred to one's spouse, inducing stress in the spouse as well. Westman and Vinokur (1998) describe three main mechanisms of crossover. The first mechanism is called direct empathic crossover and occurs between very close persons, like couples, who share a great part of their lives. Several studies have found that work-related stress factors of men not only correlate with their own well-being, but also with the well-being of their wives (Jones & Fletcher, 1993; Westman, Etzion, & Danon, 2001). The reverse effect, that is, the transmission of women's stress to their male partners, seems to be weaker. This result corresponds with the classic role allocation regarding care and support, and is compatible with results showing that women tend to react more strongly to the strain of significant others than do men (Doumas, Margolin, & John, 2003; cf. "network stress," Kessler & McLeod, 1984). Amstad and Semmer (2006b) found similar results in a study with double income parents. Controlling men's work-related stressors, men's work-related well-being (resentments) was related to women's family-related well-being. In contrast, the corresponding association between women's work-related and men's family-related resentments was not found. These results suggest that such gender differences in work–family research might be related to traditional role models.

Thompson and Bolger (1999) focused on time effects of emotional transmission. The transmission of negative emotions with regard to a stressful event (examination) of one partner occurred before the event took place. But on the day of the event, when the person was the most stressed, no transmission was reported. It "appears that the couples were able to temporarily halt the transmission of negative emotions between the examinee and partner, a process that probably helped partners be supportive when examinees needed it most" (p. 47).

The second mechanism described by Westman and Vinokur (1998) is spurious crossover. In this case, an association exists but there is no underlying "real" relationship (no causal relationship) between stress reactions of both partners. The spurious association stems from stressors the partners share in their common environment, such as an accident involving a child.

The last type of crossover Westman (2002b) describes is called "indirect crossover." This indirect crossover emerges through the mediating influence of coping mechanisms, communication characteristics, social support, or social undermining. For example, social support may help a supported person deal with a difficult and stressful situation. But this support draws on the resources of the supporting person. As a result of resource depletion, the supporting person may be stressed himself or herself (Hobfoll, 2001). This effect is well known among individuals who care for an older family member (Kiecolt-Glaser et al., 2003).

Preliminary Conclusion
All three models – segmentation, compensation, and spillover – are on a very general level. In each case, these models postulate "the" relationship between life domains. They neglect that the relationship between life domains does not have to be the same for all aspects (e.g., energy, time, emotions), nor does it have to be constant over time for a given individual, nor does it have to be identical with regard to all family members (e.g., spouse vs. children). Furthermore, the three processes may well occur in parallel, referring to different aspects of possible transmissions. Nevertheless, the models had an important impact on work–family research in that they served as a starting point for a more differentiated consideration of the processes involved, including their consequences for (in)adequate recovery.

Thus, the segmentation model certainly cannot be regarded as adequately describing the relationship between work and family. However, it stimulated theorizing about segmentation as an active process (e.g., Edwards & Rothbard, 2000) and about optimal amounts of segmentation for a given individual (e.g., Clark, 2000), and research related to these issues. With regard to recovery, the pertinent research has shown that active segmentation strategies can prevent (or attenuate) negative spillover, in the sense of "perseverative cognitions" (Brosschot, Pieper, & Thayer, 2005), thus promoting psychological detachment and, therefore, recovery.

Likewise, the compensation model cannot claim to be adequate in general. Nevertheless, in this tradition, resource drain has been fruitfully investigated, often drawing on Hobfoll's (e.g., 2001) Conservation of Resources model (e.g., Grandey & Cropanzano, 1999). Although compensation through "passive recovery" does not exactly represent the type of compensation envisaged in the original model, this research tradition has shown how demands from one domain may induce attempts at recovery that (a) are not the most effective in terms of actually achieving recovery (Sonnentag & Zijlstra, 2006) and (b) may induce further problems, leading to loss spirals (Demerouti et al., 2004).

The spillover model probably comes closest to representing a general framework for further theorizing, and it has led to such extensions as the crossover model by Westman (2002b). In particular, the intra- and interindividual transmission of emotions can be regarded as processes that occur very often.

Nevertheless, the challenge is to uncover when which process occurs for whom, what circumstances favor one or the other, and how individuals actively manage these processes. Bamberg (1992) postulated that a compensation model is plausible with regard to quantitative strain and energy: long working hours or high workload drain energetic resources, which are missing in spare time, inducing passive recovery. In terms of a qualitative perspective, however, a generalization seems likely: challenging working tasks promote challenging spare time activities (for the promotion of intellectual flexibility, cf. Kohn and Schooler (1978) and Schooler, Mulatu, and Oates (1999)). Research on the active management of segmentation (e.g., Amstad et al., 2006) shows how individuals can regulate the processes involved, and research by Sonnentag and Jelden (in press) shows how high work demands may undermine the very resources that are needed to exercise this self-regulation. In sum, although unsatisfactory by themselves, the three large models have stimulated valuable developments that help to better understand the processes involved in the work–family interface, and their effect on recovery.

A MACRO-PERSPECTIVE OF WORK–FAMILY INTERFACE: ANTECEDENTS AND CONSEQUENCES

Previous research has concentrated mainly on three issues of the relationship between work and family (cf. Eby, Casper, Lockwood, Bordeaux, & Brinley, 2005). First, the degree to which work–family balance or conflict is experienced was investigated. Second, antecedents that trigger work–family conflicts (and, albeit much less, work–family facilitation), were studied. Third, potential consequences of work–family facilitation or conflicts were investigated, such as indicators of health or well-being.

It is important to consider the work–family balance as a process. This process can be studied from a "macro-perspective," that is, the general, or chronic, conditions in work and family life that can be regarded as antecedents of work–family conflict or facilitation, and the general indicators of health and well-being that can be regarded as consequences. In this section, we focus on this macro-perspective. The micro-perspective that focuses on the daily processes involved will be dealt with in the section to follow.

Fig. 1 depicts this macro-process. Chronic life conditions of each domain are predictors of work–family conflict or facilitation, and these, in turn, affect chronic conditions in the other domain.

Although work–family conflict and facilitation can be investigated both as a consequence (of conditions in the two domains) and as a predictor (of health and well-being), most studies confined themselves to studying either antecedents *or* consequences (cf. Eby et al., 2005). The number of studies that investigated both and that focused on a mediator role of the work–family interface is rather small.

Furthermore, a majority of studies focused on the negative work–family interface, that is, the conflict between work and family. Predictors and consequences of work–family facilitation, or work–family enhancement, have been investigated only sporadically (Parasuraman & Greenhaus, 2002).

We first discuss predictors of work–family conflict. Then, we deal with consequences of work–family conflict, focusing, wherever possible, on variables that are related to fatigue and lack of recovery. Then, we discuss studies that include both, investigating work–family conflict as a mediator. Finally, we discuss work–family facilitation, or enrichment.

Fig. 1. Macro-Process Model of the Work–Family Interface.

Antecedents of Work–Family Conflict

Greenhaus and Beutell (1985) postulate three kinds of role conflicts: First, time-based conflict means that time that is dedicated to one life domain cannot be invested in the second life domain, which may cause conflicts between the two domains. Second, strain-based conflict refers to spillover of stress from one domain into the other one. Finally, behavior-based conflict refers to behavior that is adequate in one life domain, but not in the other domain. This classification can be seen as triggers of such role conflicts.

The aspect of time is emphasized by a number of authors, such as Gutek et al. (1991), and Frone et al. (1992a; Frone, 2003, talks of behavioral involvement). Time as an antecedent is immediately plausible, because time is a finite resource. Time, which is dedicated to one life domain, cannot be dedicated to another domain. Furthermore, if both domains are highly demanding a tension between these domains is obvious. It therefore is not surprising that time has been studied very frequently as a predictor of work–family conflict. Studies showed, indeed, that time invested in work correlates with work-to-family conflicts, and time invested in the family correlates with family-to-work conflicts (cf. Eby et al., 2005; Frone, 2003; Geurts & Demerouti, 2003; Gutek et al., 1991; Smith Major, Klein, & Ehrhart, 2002; van der Hulst, & Geurts, 2001; Wallace, 1997). However, in many cases it may not be time per se that is of pivotal importance (cf. Barnett, 2006). Thus, in a study by Greenhaus and Parasuraman (2002), time allocated to work was unrelated to time devoted to the family, and neither produced extensive life stress. One reason for such a result might be that people invest time in work and family at the cost of other activities (e.g., going to the cinema). Furthermore, such results point to the importance of how efficiently the work–family interface is being managed (e.g., the amount of active segmentation). At least until the time invested is extremely high, therefore, the amount of time itself may be a less than ideal proxy for the problems and processes involved.

Besides the time actually spent in the "other" domain (behavioral involvement), Frone (2003) and Greenhaus and Parasuraman (1999) postulate psychological involvement as a potential trigger of work–family conflicts (Greenhaus and Parasuraman (1999) summarize behavioral and psychological involvement as role involvement). A high psychological involvement in a domain makes "psychological presence" in the second domain difficult, even if the person is physically present (Frone, 2003, p. 150). A study by Cropley and Purvis (2003) illustrated this effect. In their study, stressed teachers thought more often about work-related topics than less stressed teachers, even in the presence of family members or friends.

Empirical findings about psychological involvement of one domain as a direct antecedent of work–family conflict are rather inconsistent – sometimes an effect is found, sometimes not (e.g., Aryee, Field, & Luk, 1999; Frone et al., 1992a). Psychological involvement was, therefore, studied as a moderator variable between other antecedents and life domain conflicts, postulating that high psychological involvement should enhance the effects of domain-specific stressors, such as high work demands (cf. the concept of identity relevant stressors; Thoits, 1991). Such an enhancing effect was found in several studies (Amstad, Jacobshagen, & Semmer, 2008; Fox & Dwyer, 1999; Martire, Parris Stephens, & Townsend, 2000; Wickrama, Conger, Lorenz, & Matthews, 1995).

When psychological involvement enhances the effects of stressors from a given domain on the work–family interface; however, it is not appropriate anymore to talk of time-based conflicts between the two domains. Rather, the issue is one of strain-based conflicts, where the strain induced by domain-specific stressors is carried over into the other domain. It is a case of spillover, where the specific quality of experiences in the "triggering" domain is decisive. Any stressor in one domain therefore becomes a potential trigger of work–family conflict. It is therefore not surprising that "domain-specific" stressors typically are regarded as potential triggers of conflicts between that domain and the other one. These qualitative aspects often are more important than the mere amount of time (for a meta-analysis, see Byron, 2005). For example, a study by van der Hulst and Geurts (2001) showed that working overtime had an effect on poor recovery and home-work interference. But this effect was not very strong in general. Rather, it was strong for individuals working in low reward jobs, who felt under pressure to work overtime.

The third category of Greenhaus and Beutell (1985), behavior-based conflict, is often cited but seldom investigated: This category refers to behavior that is appropriate in one life domain is also shown in the other domain, but there it is seen as inappropriate. An example for such a conflict is when a police officer talks to his family members in a commanding tone; or when a person, who works in a dangerous work environment emphasizes strict compliance with all rules at home. We will not deal with that type of conflict in any detail, not only because it has seldom been investigated but also because there is no obvious association to fatigue and recovery for this type of conflict.

Altogether, triggering factors of work–family conflict should not be studied separately and in isolation, as they often overlap and may appear together (Amstad & Semmer, 2006a). Time and stress often are closely related, partly because many stressors are related to demands on the investment of time (e.g., work overload), and partly because the investment of time may be a mechanism for coping with high work demands. Where psychological involvement is concerned, the distinction between time and stress is also blurred, because the psychological involvement in a domain other than the one where one is present physically is likely to indicate a spillover of stress from that other domain. Therefore, domain-specific variables are the best predictors for life domain conflicts (for an overview, see Eby et al., 2005). Domain-specific time demands (Aryee et al., 1999; Frone et al., 1992a), domain-specific involvement (Barnett & Baruch, 1985; Carlson & Frone, 2003; Frone et al., 1992a), and domain-specific stress (Fox & Dwyer, 1999; Greenhaus & Parasuraman, 2002) have been found to be antecedents of work–family conflicts (cf. a meta analysis by Byron (2005)).

Work–Family Conflict and Well-being

As recovery is also related to other well-being indicators, especially to chronic load reactions (Geurts & Sonnentag, 2006), it might be interesting to see results concerning work–family conflict and such well-being indicators.

For both directions of work–family conflict – work-to-family and family-to-work – relationships with a large number of indicators of well-being have been found, for instance, with work satisfaction (Kossek & Ozeki, 1998), organizational commitment (Netemeyer, Boles, & McMurrian, 1996), turnover intentions (Allen, 2001; Boyar, Maertz, Pearson, & Keough, 2003), absenteeism (Hammer, Bauer, & Grandey, 2003), work performance (Aryee, 1992), and family/marital satisfaction (Aryee et al., 1999), depression (Frone et al., 1992a; Netemeyer et al., 1996; Schieman, McBrier, & Van Gundy, 2003), psychosomatic complaints (Kinnunen & Mauno, 1998), substance and alcohol abuse (Frone et al., 1992b), or work-related and family-related strain (Grandey & Cropanzano, 1999; Parasuraman & Simmers, 2001). These results were confirmed in the meta-analysis by Allen, Herst, Bruck, and Sutton (2000), which, however, only covered work-to-family conflict. Ford, Heinen, and Langkamer (2007) found in their meta-analysis a consistent relationship of work-to-family conflict with family satisfaction, and of family-to-work conflict with job satisfaction. Finally, a meta-analysis of Kossek and Ozeki (1998) found consistent negative relationships between work-to-family conflict and family-to-work conflict with life satisfaction. Most of these studies are, however, cross-sectional.

These studies did not specifically deal with issues of fatigue and recovery, although these variables are likely to be involved in some of the indicators investigated, most notably psychosomatic complaints, which often are assessed with scales containing items on sleep quality. Especially pertinent for issues of recovery, however, is research on burnout, since exhaustion is the core variable of this construct (cf. Schaufeli & Enzmann, 1998). And there are, indeed, a number of studies that found an association between work–family conflict and burnout (e.g., Kossek & Ozeki, 1999). The meta-analysis by Allen et al. (2000) yielded a weighted mean correlation of $r_w = .42$ between work–family conflict and burnout.

The authors found only one study that specifically focused on the relationship between a chronic negative work–family interface and recovery. Demerouti, Taris, and Bakker (2007) investigated the reciprocal influence of home-work interference and need for recovery over time (time lag was 1 month). Need for recovery was conceptualized as "the need for recovery in the sense of urgency that people feel to take a break from their demands, when fatigue builds up" (Demerouti et al., 2007, p. 205). They found that home-work interference led to a higher need for recovery, and also that need for recovery led to increased home-work interference, suggesting a negative loss spiral. Summarizing these results, it is apparent that work–family conflicts have serious impacts on individual's health and well-being.

Work–family Conflict as a Mediator

Given that domain-specific variables predict work–family conflict, and that work–family conflict predicts well-being, models have been developed in which the conflict between life domains is seen as an intervening variable (mediator) between stressors and subjective well-being (Aryee et al., 1999; Demerouti et al., 2004; Frone et al., 1992a; Geurts, Kompier, Roxburgh, & Houtman, 2003; Geurts, Rutte, & Peeters, 1999).

In a study by Frone and colleagues (1992a), family involvement and family stressors were related to depression through two mediators: family distress and family-to-work conflict. For the corresponding work variables, only job distress could be confirmed as a mediator, but not work-to-family conflict. The latter was found to be a mediator, however, by Aryee and colleagues (1999), although only for the relationship between work variables and life satisfaction, but not depression. Geurts et al. (1999) found four stressors as antecedents of work-to-family conflict: first, overtime of the partner; second, the focal person's unfavorable work time; third, quantitative overload; and fourth, a negative relationship with the supervisor. These stressors were associated with general health indicators, such as psychosomatic complaints and sleep disturbance, as well as with work-related health indicators, such as emotional exhaustion and depersonalization; and this association was mediated by work–family conflict (cf. results of burnout research, e.g., Demerouti, Bakker, Nachreiner, and Schaufeli (2001)). Similar results were found by the same research team (Geurts et al., 2003) with four different samples: work overload had an effect on depressive mood and health complaints, which was mediated by work-to-family conflict. This research team concluded that workload exerts its negative effect on well-being mainly through a process of work–family spillover that impedes recovery during the nonworking hours. So again, the close linkage between the work–family process and recovery is shown by these findings.

Also, Jacobshagen, Amstad, Semmer, and Kuster (2005) found work-to-family conflict to mediate the association between work stressors (work overload, insecurity, hours of work) and well-being (irritation, psychosomatic complaints, and depression) in a sample of top managers. The same picture was found in two other samples, where work-to-family conflict mediated the relationship between task-related work stressors and exhaustion (Amstad, Jacobshagen, & Semmer, 2004).

This mediating effect has been found in different samples in several studies. One can therefore conclude that it seems to be a rather robust effect (Amstad et al., 2004; Geurts et al., 2003). However, little can be said about the causality of these effects, because all these findings about work–family conflict as a mediator have been obtained in cross-sectional studies. A longitudinal study by Demerouti and colleagues (2004), which involved three waves, found a reciprocal influence of work demands, work-to-family conflict, and reduced well-being, especially exhaustion, over time. It therefore may be more adequate to speak about a loss spiral, implying a vicious circle, where exhaustion, work pressure, and work–family conflict reinforce each other over time.

Consequences and Antecedents of Positive Work–Family Interactions

We have mentioned several times that the positive interaction of work and family also is important but has been studied only rarely (for an overview, see Greenhaus & Powell, 2006). However, positive consequences of multiple roles (Kotler & Wingard, 1989) especially if they are of high quality (Hibbard & Pope, 1993), have been found since the 1980s. In a longitudinal study, Ross and Mirowsky (1995) showed that, for men as well as for women, being employed has a positive effect on their health compared to unemployed persons and house keepers.[1] Barnett, Marshall, and Singer (1992) found in another longitudinal study that changes in the quality of one's employment role were associated with changes in psychological distress only among women that were not living in a stable relationship or had children. Both parenthood and living in a relationship had buffering functions in the relationship between changes in job-role quality and experienced stress.

Positive effects of performing multiple roles (e.g., employment, marriage, parenthood) have been shown in several studies (for overviews, see Barnett & Hyde, 2001; Repetti, Matthews, & Waldron, 1989). Different assumptions considering the processes that explain such results have been presented. Barnett and Hyde (2001) postulate eight potential processes that explain why multiple roles lead to positive consequences for individuals. First, they speak of a *buffering impact* of multiple roles; negative experiences of one life domain may be buffered by positive experiences or success in another life domain (Barnett et al., 1992). Second, an *additional income* has a positive effect on a couple's well-being (Conger, Rueter, & Elder, 1999). Third, the probability to experience *social support* is enhanced when a person acts in different roles; the positive effect of social support is well supported in research (Leppin & Schwarzer, 1997; Viswesvaran, Sanchez, & Fisher, 1999). Social support acts as a mediator or moderator between multiple roles and health (cf. Granrose, Parasuraman, & Greenhaus, 1992). Fourth, multiple roles offer more *opportunities to experience success*, which implies a confirmation of one's self-efficacy and self-confidence. Fifth, multiple roles provide an *expanded frame of reference*. Sixth, one's *self-concept* is more *complex*, which acts as a buffer for experienced stress (Linville, 1987). Seventh, the *everyday lives* of spouses become more *similar*, which facilitates communication and understanding of each other. Finally, besides these environmental aspects, the authors also postulate *gender-role ideology* as an explanatory mechanism. Individuals with a liberal attitude toward role allocation profit more from multiple roles than individuals with a more traditional view. Barnett and colleagues (Barnett, Marshall, & Sayer, 1992; Barnett et al., 1992) could confirm several of these processes empirically, most notably the first three. Further research is needed for the last five processes.

Although the principles enumerated by Barnett and Hyde (2001) are not specifically oriented toward the enrichment of family life, they do refer to mechanisms that may indeed have that effect. For instance, one domain may buffer the effects of the other one, as when a supportive family helps to cope with work stress, or a supportive supervisor supports coping with family stress. Many of Barnett and Hyde's principles can be found in Greenhaus and Powell's (2006) theoretical model, which focuses specifically on "the extent to which experiences in one role improve the quality of life in the other role" (p. 73). They see work–family enrichment as a transfer of resources from one domain to another. Possible resources are (1) skills and perspectives, (2) psychological and physical resources, (3) social capital, (4) flexibility, and (5) material resources. These resources affect one's performance in the other role, either directly (instrumental path) or indirectly through positive effects (affective path). High performance in that domain, in turn, increases positive effects. Possible moderators are the salience (or involvement) of a specific role as well as the relevance and consistency of specific resources referred to specific roles.

Obviously, many of these postulated mechanisms are related to recovery. Drawing on skills that have been acquired in the other domain may facilitate problem solving and performance, implying less spending of energy. The same applies to high psychological resources, as when self-esteem counters ruminating after stress (cf. perseverative cognitions in Brosschot et al. (2005)). Similarly, social capital means that there are social resources to draw upon, implying less stress, better coping with stress, and less use of energy.

Empirical studies that test the reciprocal positive influence of multiple roles are scarce (Grzywacz & Marks, 2000a; Kirchmeyer, 1993), and typically cross-sectional. A study by Kirchmeyer (1993) shows a strong relationship between work-to-family and family-to-work facilitation and satisfaction in the respective other life domain. Moreover, Grzywacz (2000) found a relationship of positive spillover from work-to-family and family-to-work with fewer chronic health problems and other strain indicators (e.g., depression). Positive spillover from family-to-work also was positively related to well-being indicators, such as autonomy and personal development (Grzywacz, 2000) and less alcohol abuse (Grzywacz & Marks, 2000b). A study of Williams, Franche, Ibrahim, Mustard, and Layton (2006) showed that positive (but not negative) family-to-work spillover was associated with sleep quality, after controlling for age, physical health, depressive symptoms, the work situation, and the number of children.

Concerning antecedents of a positive work–family interface, longitudinal studies are almost absent. But results of cross-sectional studies of Grzywacz and Marks (2000a) show a positive association of job control and work-related social support with work-to-family facilitation. Furthermore, a lack of spouse and family support was the best predictor for low family-to-work facilitation. Not surprisingly, family-to-work facilitation was related to marital status, being less common among unmarried individuals. Interestingly, work conditions showed an impact on family-to-work facilitation as well; it seems that job control and work-related social support play a significant role for this kind of facilitation. Summarizing these findings, they show that work–family facilitation can be seen as a kind of resource process. Resources from one domain are transferred to another domain. This process, however, has direct and buffering positive effects on individual's health and well-being.

Research and theory presented in this section has reached a much higher level of specificity compared with the original models of segmentation, compensation, and spillover. Mechanisms that are involved in the transmission between life domains are specified in terms of being time or strain related. Nevertheless, these mechanisms are investigated in a rather general way. This is reflected in questionnaire items such as "How often does it happen that a successful day at work puts you in a good mood to handle family responsibilities?" The question of what exactly happens when such an effect occurs remains open. To investigate such micro-processes that are involved in the day-to-day transmission between life domains, a more episodic approach is necessary that focuses on daily experiences, using time or event sampling methods or interview techniques. It is this type of approach that we now turn to.

MICRO-PROCESSES

Micro-process models focus on the issue of how exactly work and family interact with each other and where and how recovery plays a role in this process. We will first present a framework of micro-processes with respect to the work–family interface, and then discuss some examples of micro-process studies. In third part, we will discuss recovery in such micro-processes.

A Framework for the Work–Family Interface on a Micro-Level

Only a few studies have been conducted in the area of life domain balance that focus on micro-processes. These studies concentrate on specific events, their development, and their consequences. Such studies can complement research that is more macro-oriented, and help to better understand *how, why, and under which circumstances* work and family interact (Eby et al., 2005).

On the basis of the considerations above, we developed a framework for studying the work–family interface at a micro-level. The basic idea is to start with a triggering event in one domain and to follow it through into the respective other domain, to learn what happens there and how people feel about it. It applies to both positive and negative events, and to both directions work-to-family and family-to-work.

The framework contains four successive stages (Fig. 2), depicting the following course of events: (1) an event occurs in life domain one (work or family). This event can be either positive or negative. For instance, someone has to finish a report under time pressure, and on that day of all days the printer is broken. If the event is negative, as in our example, (2) first and foremost the person is likely to cope with the situation in the domain in which the event occurred (e.g., try to fix the printer, ask the supervisor if the report can be postponed etc.; see Zohar, 1999). Note that coping, by most common definitions (e.g., Lazarus, 1999), does not imply that these attempts are successful. Thereafter the framework focuses on the person entering the second life domain (the family in our example). Before examining the impact that the event has on the second life domain, (3) the specific conditions of this domain have to be considered. More precisely, we hypothesize that it matters who is present, what these persons are doing, and in which mood these persons are. Oftentimes, it may be enough to find out if the current circumstances in the other domain are "as usual" or not. With regard to our example, the moment one arrives at home and sees the youngest child making his/her first steps, one might will forget about the strenuous

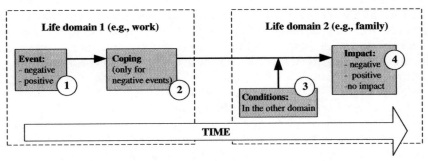

Fig. 2.   Micro-Process Model of the Work–Family Interface.

workday. A similar effect is likely when someone has fallen ill or had a really bad experience. But if it is an evening like any other, there is enough room for the negative (or also positive) work event to intrude into family life. (4) Finally, like the event itself, its impact on the affected life domain can be either positive or negative. In our example, the impact is likely to be negative. Coming home in the evening, one may not be in the mood to play with the children, because one's thoughts are still circling around the report. Note, however, that spillover does not necessarily occur. Coping attempts at work may have been successful, positive events at work, such as a positive feedback about one's last report, may have compensated for it, or one might have calmed down on the way home and not be bothered by the incident any more by the time one arrives at home. If the problem is still on one's mind, this may spoil the evening, but it also may trigger a sympathetic reaction by one's partner, which may restore calmness and self-esteem, and even result in a positive self-confirmation. Depending on these circumstances, the event might (at least temporarily) lose its saliency, or even be turned into a rewarding experience, or it may be aggravated or lead to further consequences (e.g., an argument) that create additional stress. In the first case, one is likely to recover and to rebuild resources; in the second case, further depletion of resources is likely.

If and to what extent long-term consequences occur, depends on a host of different factors. Such factors may be, how often such stressful or joyful events occur, what the proportion of positive to negative events is, how intensively they are experienced, both in terms of absolute and relative frequency (proportion of positive to negative events), and how the individual copes with it (phase 2). Furthermore, it depends on the general nature of the circumstances (e.g., stable relationship, basically satisfactory work conditions), in which they occur, such as quality of working conditions, material resources, additional family demands (e.g., caring for an ill child or an aging parent). The amount of recovery vs. additional depletion of resources that is typically possible after negative events and the ratio of such events to positive events will then determine to what extent long-term consequences are likely to occur. At this point, this approach converges with the macro-approach, and it will be an empirical question to what extent the issues studied from the more general, macro, approach are basically proxies for the accumulation of such experiences, and to what extent they represent background characteristics that codetermine the impact of single experiences (cf. Semmer, Grebner, & Elfering, 2004).

Examples of Micro-Process Studies

Studies that have, in one way or other, tried to investigate micro-processes that correspond to the proposed framework, are quite rare. Usually, they focus on parts of the framework.

The relationship between daily hassles and end-of-day variables has been analyzed in some empirical studies (e.g., Zohar, 1999). Stressful events had an impact on negative mood and fatigue the same evening. Furthermore, in a diary study, Bolger, DeLongis, Kessler, and Wethington (1990) found that overload at home and work, as well as arguments with the spouse, with children, and coworkers had a significant impact on the amount of distress (negative mood) experienced on the same day. Interestingly, the mood on the day after the stressful event was better than on days without experienced stressors. So, mood effects seem to be temporary, which is plausible, given the high sensitivity of mood to stressful events (Bolger, DeLongis, Kessler, & Schilling, 1989; DeLongis, Folkman, & Lazarus, 1988). Furthermore, they even tend to turn into positive mood as a kind of relief, when the stress was over. This seems to be different for psychosomatic complaints: Psychosomatic complaints as stress reaction stay stable during several days after an experienced stressful event (DeLongis et al., 1988).

Spillover of mood from one life domain (e.g., work) to another domain (e.g., family) was shown by Williams and Alliger (1994) in a diary study. They provided evidence for spillover effects in both directions (work-to-family and family-to-work), but the effects were much stronger for negative than for positive mood. Similar results were found by Judge and Ilies (2004) for the relationship of job satisfaction with positive and negative mood after work. Heller and Watson (2005) found daily and lagged effects of job satisfaction on family satisfaction. These authors found evidence for a mediator effect of mood (especially positive mood) in the relationship between work and family satisfaction.

The relationship between stressors and experienced work-to-family conflict has been confirmed on a situational level as well: Stressful work events or negative mood during the workday predicted experienced work-to-family conflicts in the evening (Butler, Grzywacz, Bass, & Linney, 2005; Williams & Alliger, 1994). Moreover, Sonnentag and Zijlstra (2006) demonstrated that chronic high work stressors and low job control showed an impact on a day level. Specifically, these stressful general aspects of participants' job showed an effect in the evening: Individuals reported a higher need of recovery and lower situational well-being.

These studies show that results found on a macro-level can be replicated on a situational level. Furthermore, in these studies, stressful events were assessed in quite some detail, allowing for analyses of specific types of spillover. Thus, Bolger et al. (1990) report that overload at work predicts overload at home, which, in turn, predicts overload at work the next day. The same pattern applied to arguments at work and at home. In general, however, specificity with regard to impacts is not very high. Positive and negative moods as well as daily life domain conflicts are just a few of many possible impacts that may occur in this context.

Also dealing with the situational level, but focusing on a specific kind of impact, Pearlin and McCall (1990) investigated the process involved in providing social support for stressful work situations in couples. Their results show how support may fail because of inappropriate advice, which may be due to lack of understanding of the problem but also to poor timing, i.e., giving advice too early.

Another example for specific micro-processes with regard to the work–family interface is Repetti's finding that mothers tend to withdraw after a stressful workday (Repetti, 1992; Repetti & Wood, 1997). If they are provided with this opportunity – usually by their spouse – the mothers had less conflicting interactions with their children (this strategy of "shielding" the partner from additional stress is also mentioned by Pearlin and McCall (1990) as one of the forms of social support).

These latter researchers asked for different kinds of impacts in detail, but did not specify the stressful events in the other life domain. Moreover, processes were only described unidirectionally, for work-to-family conflicts. The framework we presented suggests considering (a) both the triggering event and the type of impact, (b) both work-to-family and family-to-work interactions, and (c) both the negative and positive quality of the triggering event.

Amstad and Semmer (2006a) conducted an interview study that was inspired by the framework presented. A 112 working parents were asked to describe one positive and one negative incident from each domain, resulting in 448 incidents. People then were asked to describe what happened after the incident had occurred, and the chain of events was "followed through" into the other domain. The authors then tried to identify typical chains of events. Results indicate that two specific negative micro-processes seem to exist (1) work-related organizational problems (e.g., lack of job control) trigger problem focused coping with this stressful event. In the evening, at home, people are tired, and their thoughts are absorbed by the work-related problem experienced during the day. This effect is similar to that reported by Sonnentag and Bayer (2005). In their diary study, a high amount of workload (hours of work during the specific day) led to less work-related psychological detachment, diminishing positive mood, and increasing tiredness at bedtime. The second micro-process in the study by Amstad and Semmer (2006a) was the following: (2) social stressors (e.g., conflicts, lack of appreciation) triggered emotion focused coping at work. At home, individuals tried to get social support. This second micro-process was dependent on the conditions in the second life domain being familiar and not exceptional. Both micro-processes were found predominantly for the direction of work-to-family – the first one emerged only, the second predominantly for this direction. Interestingly, no positive prototypical micro-process emerged in this study. The authors explain these results by the tendency of positive events to broaden the focus of individuals (Fredrickson & Branigan, 2005), opening up a broad repertoire of possible behaviors. This might be the explanation, why positive events do not result in specific impacts. In contrast, individuals tend to focus on negative elements in order to be able to cope with it better. This may explain why negative events may have more specific impacts.

A study that investigated the relationship between levels of distress and different types of activities after work was conducted by Crouter, Perry-Jenkins, Huston, and Crawford (1989). In an interview study of 29 married men, they found that high levels of experienced distress (like feeling under pressure or unable to relax) and fatigue were associated with low involvement in housework as well as with more negative marital interactions. Also Fritz and Sonnentag (2005) showed that hours spent with family work or conflicts with the spouse at weekends were related to a lower general well-being and less productivity at the beginning of the work week.

The Role of Recovery in the Micro-Process Model

It has become clear that the management of the work–family interface is closely connected with issues of resources and recovery. Demands on resources in one domain, additional demands in the other domain, or restoration of resources in the other domain, have emerged as crucial aspects.

On the one hand, demands on resources may be conceived in quantitative terms (e.g., hours of work, breaks, or concentration demands). But also, the qualitative nature of these demands plays a crucial role, in that negative experiences place demands on cognitive resources. This occurs, for example, by demanding attention (and thus reducing the mental capacity that is available for dealing with tasks at work or at home), by requiring additional effort for cognitive (planning) and behavioral (implementing) attempts to cope, and possibly by developing perseverative cognitions (Brosschot et al., 2005) after an event. On the other hand, activities that are physically demanding may restore resources, or at least mitigate depletion of resources, if experienced as positive but not (or less) when experienced as negative (cf. Sonnentag & Zijlstra, 2006; Zohar, 1999; Zohar, Tzischinski, & Epstein, 2003). Finally, positive experiences may not only reduce effort, and thus the need for recovery; they also can enhance the capacity of recovery periods to actually achieve recovery, because people are not ruminating about problems but are fully concentrating on restoring and relaxing activities, or simply sleeping better.

It follows that depletion, and restoration of resources, or recovery, can occur through two pathways, one involving the effort required by a given task, the other one indirectly through affective reactions, which require mental resources by themselves and may induce additional requirements, such as coping (cf. Zohar, 1999). For the energetic component, effort–recovery cycles are pivotal (Meijman & Mulder, 1998). Such cycles can exist at various levels – from a micro-level that concern the ratio of work and rest breaks, to a meso-level that concerns effort and rest over the day and the week (Fritz & Sonnentag, 2006), to a macro-level that concerns vacations in the course of a year (Eden, 2001). Research has shown that recovery is best achieved by not letting fatigue accumulate by inserting frequent short breaks (cf. Geurts & Sonnentag, 2006; Tucker, 2003).

For the affective pathway, the number of negative and positive experiences encountered seems crucial, as well as their ratio (Fredrickson & Losada, 2005). Such experiences have been covered in this section. These considerations imply that recovery can occur at various stages of an unfolding event (Fig. 3).

First, recovery may occur in life domain one, where the triggering event occurs. In our example of the negative work-to-family process, where the report has to be submitted, but the printer is broken, recovery potentially occurs at work. An example for such a recovery phase is inserting a little pause, in order to calm down the negative emotions and to get some new energy to attack the problem constructively. This would be equivalent to palliative coping (cf. Kälin & Semmer, 2002; Semmer, 2003). Note that instrumental coping, such as fixing the printer, or finding an alternative, would have quite different implications. Although it helps to solve the problem (and thus have positive effects through the affective pathway), it requires additional energy in and of itself, constituting "costs of coping"

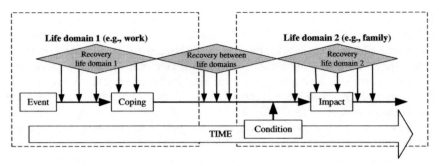

Fig. 3. Recovery in the Micro-Process Model of the Negative Work–Family Interface.

(Schönpflug & Battmann, 1988), so that additional recovery is needed after engaging in such coping behaviors.

Second, recovery might take place between life domains, for example, on the way home. You walk home instead of taking the overcrowded bus, or you go for a drink with colleagues or friends in order to detach from work. These recovery activities focus on the borderland. The purpose of these recovery phases may be seen two-fold. First, boundaries between life domains are strengthened as detachment from one life domain is facilitated (Amstad et al., 2006). Second, the moment of entry into the second life domain is postponed in order to replenish one's resources first, so that the individual feels prepared to face family-related demands.

Finally, there is a third stage in the micro-process model, where recovery might occur – this is the second life domain. For example, you play with your children, perhaps a little bit absent-minded at first, but after a while you get "drawn in," and you start to think of other things than work. Another example is that you drink a cup of tea alone in your garden at home. These examples show that recovery activities in the second life domain are interwoven with the impacts events have on the second life domain. The first example shows the work-to-family impact of ruminating over a work event, which impacts the interaction with family members. But after a while the individual successfully detaches while engaging in social activities. The second example shows the impact of withdrawal from other family members while engaging in a relaxing recovery activity. However, recovery or especially the need of recovery might be seen as an impact on the other life domain, because the individual is not available for the family for a while (which also implies that this withdrawal behavior cannot be continued indefinitely without causing new problems; cf. Repetti, 1992; Repetti & Wood, 1997).

Considering the positive work–family micro-process, it makes less sense to define recovery stages, except that positive experiences can, like the negative ones, occur at any of the three stages. Rather the whole process implies a lower need for recovery, as it reduces additional requirements and may have energizing effects. For example, the study of Crouter, Perry-Jenkins, Huston, and Crawford (1989) gives some clues about the relationship of positive work–family interface and recovery. They found that low levels of distress and high levels of arousal were associated with greater involvement in active leisure. And Sonnentag (2001) found that active leisure activities are positively related to recovery. This may indicate that the positive influence of work and family is crucial for recovery processes. However, further research is needed to make a precise statement about the relationship between positive work–family processes and recovery.

GENDER DIFFERENCES

Gender issues have attracted great interest in the area of the work–family interface (Greenhaus & Parasuraman, 1999, 2002; Perrewé & Carlson, 2002; Westman, 2002a). This is understandable, as, traditionally, work is the primary domain of men, and family is the primary domain of women. These differences have been interpreted from an evolutionary perspective and from a socialization perspective (Pleck, 1977). However, they lead to the assumption that one's identity is tied to the family role more for women, and to the work role for men. This should have an impact on the amount of resources a person invests in a role (Greenhaus & Parasuraman, 2002). This holds for behavioral involvement. In the studies by Gutek and colleagues (1991), where hours worked per week included not only hours paid work but also hours worked at home, female managers worked, on average, 7.4 h more per week than male managers. Corresponding with this finding, Frankenhaeuser, Lundberg, Fredrikson, Melin et al. (1989) found a lagged reduction of high physiological parameters, such as cortisol. Whereas men's cortisol level reduced after work, women's cortisol level reduced a few hours later, at about bedtime of their children. Elevated cortisol levels indicate a lack of physiological recovery in nonwork time (Frankenhaeuser et al., 1989). Therefore, the results of Frankenhaeuser and colleagues (1989) indicate that women's work finishes only after their children are in bed, whereas men's workdays finish after they have left their work places.

Considering psychological involvement, Greenhaus and Parasuraman (1999) found no clear differences, when specific circumstances like parenthood were controlled. On the other hand, Greenhaus and Parasuraman (2002) reported higher family salience for women, and higher work salience for men. Simon (1995, 1997) conducted interviews about the meaning of various roles, and the costs and benefits associated with them. Men profited more from the combination of several roles than women. Simon found that the perceived benefits were greater than the costs in all three life domains studied (work, relationship, and parenthood). In the role of being a spouse both, men and women, see only positive sides. As parents men and women see benefits but also costs, this means positive and negative aspects. Gender differences were found with respect to the third life domain – the work domain: Most notably, among the implications of the work role, "not being available for children and partner" was mentioned by none of the men, but by 75% of the women. Other studies demonstrate that women give more support to their spouse than men do (e.g., Liebler & Sandefur, 2001), and that men are given more opportunities by their female partners to withdraw after a stressful working day than the other way around (Repetti, 1992). Note that withdrawal from family obligations represents one possible recovery opportunity.

Such gender differences would suggest that there also are gender differences with regard to work–family conflict and facilitation. Specifically, it has often been assumed that work-to-family conflict should be more prevalent among women. In contrast, family-to-work conflict should be more prevalent among men. On the other hand, gender may moderate the relationship between time that is allocated to a certain domain and the perceived conflict between work and family. This means that time that is invested in the primary domain (family for women, work for men) is seen as less problematic than time invested in the other domain. Both hypotheses were not confirmed in a study by Gutek et al. (1991), and this is in line with many other findings (e.g., Greenhaus & Parasuraman, 2002). There are some findings in favor of gender differences. For instance, Rothbard and Edwards (2003) found in a study with 623 employees that boundaries between work and family were asymmetrically permeable with respect to the invested time resource for men, but not for women. Greenhaus and Parasuraman (2002) reported that work–family conflict shows a stronger relationship with life stress for women than for men. But in general, there is astonishingly little support for gender differences in the perception, and the effects, of work–family conflict (Frone, 2003; Geurts & Demerouti, 2003).

The same pattern is found for the positive side of the work–family interface. Grzywacz and Marks (2000a) found no substantial gender differences. Even if statistically significant differences were found in large samples, they are not substantial enough to be interpreted (Grzywacz & Marks, 2000a), because they often disappear when socio-demographical factors are controlled for, such as marital or family status (Frone, 2003).

Given these differences in the meaning of work and family roles for men and women, and the gender differences in time allocated to work and family, it seems surprising that there are no consistent findings of gender differences with regard to work–family conflict or facilitation. So far, we can only speculate why this is the case. We see several possible explanations. Thus, a work–family conflict may have different meaning (and different thresholds) for men and women. For instance, men who come home from work may see it as normal and legitimate to have time for recovery (and expect their wives to "shield" them). As a consequence, they may perceive having to indulge in household matters immediately more as an "illegitimate task" (Semmer, Jacobshagen, Meier, & Elfering, 2007), which they attribute to a work–family conflict. In contrast, women might see an immediate focus on household chores and children upon coming home as legitimate. As a consequence, they might feel tired and not very motivated, but without attributing this to a work–family conflict. Furthermore, the main difference may lie in the way of preventing a work–family conflict. Thus, part-time work is one way of reducing the risk of not being available for the family when needed – and part-time work is mainly for female. This may imply that many women work more in part-time arrangements just because they would be more susceptible to work–family conflicts and want to do everything they can to prevent them. The result by Simon (1997) that only women perceive work as a hindrance to time spent with children and spouse would fit into this explanation. Also, remember that Greenhaus and Parasuraman (2002) report that time invested in work was uncorrelated with time invested in the family. This suggests that people may find other ways of coping, such as reducing time for personal needs (cinema, reading, seeing friends). Although this may have negative consequences in the long run, it may not be attributed to a work–family conflict, and therefore not appear in pertinent research. Thus, a variety of interpretations and coping mechanisms are conceivable that would lead to the result of no gender difference in prevalence, and effects, of work–family conflict despite differences in *vulnerability* to such conflicts. For a better understanding of such processes, we think it is important to consider the *meaning* of roles, and of conflicts between them, more than is typically done (cf. the research by

Simon (1995, 1997)). Furthermore, research should focus more on the micro-processes involved, which implies diary-type studies on the one hand, and more qualitative studies on the other hand. The model of micro-processes we presented may offer a framework in which to conduct such studies.

CONCLUSIONS

Except for the "pure" segmentation model, all models we presented imply that work and family are interdependent life domains. Furthermore, in all models the importance of recovery seems crucial. On the one hand, the models assume that the relationship between work and private life may lead to problems. On the other hand, positive spillover and enhancing effects are increasingly emphasized. In contrast with the original global models about the linkage of work and family, newer models postulate that these effects can emerge in parallel.

A number of empirical studies have confirmed that stressors, invested time, and involvement in a certain domain are potential antecedents of subjective conflicts between life domains. Furthermore, psychological and behavioral involvement were found to moderate the association between such domain-specific stressors and an imbalance between work and family (e.g., Fox & Dwyer, 1999; Greenhaus, Parasuraman, & Collings, 2001). Numerous studies confirmed consequences of work–family conflicts on well-being in general, and on exhaustion in particular, and this has been confirmed by meta-analyses (e.g., Allen et al., 2000; Ford et al., 2007; Kossek & Ozeki, 1998). However, most of this research is cross-sectional, and only few longitudinal studies have been conducted (Demerouti et al., 2004).

We emphasized that the investigation of work–family conflict and facilitation in general (the macro-approach) should be, and increasingly is, complemented by studies of micro-processes. Such studies focus on specific events, the way people cope with them, and the way they spillover into the other life domain (or are prevented from spilling over), and thus help to better understand the mechanisms involved, including the active attempts at managing the work–family interface. This is illustrated by the identification of prototypical "process types" by Amstad and Semmer (2006a), showing that social events are associated with emotional coping, and impact the family in a social way, whereas stressors related to task fulfillment had a more intra-psychic impact.

On both levels, issues of recovery are pertinent. Resource drain, restoring resources, and generating new resources are issues of central importance.

Both energetic and affective processes have to be considered in this context. Their relationship needs clarification in further research, and micro-analyses certainly are especially important for this issue (cf. Zohar, 1999). Our modified micro-process model, which highlights the role of recovery, may be promising. Moreover, we might conclude that when talking about recovery in work–family processes, not only recovery opportunities and recovery activities are important but also the quality of recovery, in terms of the quality of activities and the affective experience during times devoted to recovery (cf. Sonnentag & Zijlstra, 2006).

We feel that a broad multi-method approach would be helpful for better understanding the topic of work–family and recovery. Macro-studies typically involve questionnaires, whereas micro-studies typically involve diaries. There are some, but not many studies that use expert assessments (e.g., Zohar, 1999). Some studies use interviews, and we feel this approach should be used more often. Repetti's (1992; Repetti & Wood, 1997) observations about withdrawal behavior in the family after stressful working days are a good example. Also Pearlin and McCall (1990) with their interview study unraveled interesting mechanisms in the process of giving social support. Moreover, to incorporate a broad array of methods may also be enlightening for the discussion about gender differences, where issues of meaning and how they relates to daily coping as well as to interpretations of events seem to be crucial.

A multi-method approach might also study micro-processes while paying attention to macro conditions (Amstad, Demerouti, & Semmer, 2008). For instance, the review by Gump and Matthews (1999) showed that background stressors often are associated with increased reactivity to acute stressors and with slow recovery following exposure to acute stressors. Gross et al. (2008) showed that the impact of negative and positive events at work on fatigue was moderated by social climate at the workplace. We therefore, think that the role of background stressors on micro-processes should not be underestimated (cf. Semmer et al., 2004).

All in all, we feel that our understanding of the processes involved in establishing, and maintaining, a balance between life domains has greatly increased during recent years. As is typical, however, many questions remain, and many additional ones have come up. Investigating these issues is not only challenging intellectually and scientifically. It also is of considerable practical importance – for the individuals involved, for the organizations they work for and, through the consequences of a good vs. poor work–family balance for health, well-being, and productivity, also for society in general.

NOTE

1. Also the reverse effect was found that healthy persons stay employed longer.

REFERENCES

Allen, T. D. (2001). Family-supportive work environments: The role of organizational perceptions. *Journal of Vocational Behavior, 58*, 414–435.

Allen, T. D., Herst, D. E. L., Bruck, C. S., & Sutton, M. (2000). Consequences associated with work-to-family conflict: A review and agenda for future research. *Journal of Occupational Health Psychology, 5*, 278–308.

Amstad, F. T., Demerouti, E., & Semmer, N. K. (2008). Situational and general contextual predictors of social work-to-family impact. March 6–8, 2008. Paper presented at the Conference on Work, Stress, and Health, Washington.

Amstad, F. T., Jacobshagen, N., & Semmer, N. K. (2004). Arbeitsbezogene Belastungen – Work-Family Conflict – Erschöpfung. [*Work related stress – work-family conflict – exhaustion.*] Paper presented at the 44th Conference of the German Association of Psychology, Göttingen, Germany.

Amstad, F. T., Jacobshagen, N., & Semmer, N. K. (2008). *Not only business in mind: The effect of multiple role centrality on the relationship between work-family conflict and burnout among managers.* Manuscript submitted for publication.

Amstad, F. T., & Semmer, N. K. (2006a). Daily hassles and uplifts in work and family: An analysis of spillover processes. In: F. T. Amstad (Ed.), *Unpublished doctoral dissertation.* Switzerland: University of Bern.

Amstad, F. T., & Semmer, N. K. (2006b). *Spillover and crossover of work- and family-related negative emotions in couples.* Manuscript submitted for publication.

Amstad, F. T., Tschudi, C., Zimmermann, R., & Semmer, N. K. (2006). Boundary management: Effective strategies to prevent work–family conflicts. Paper presented at the Conference of the Work- and Organizational Association of Psychology, Nürnberg, Germany.

Aryee, S. (1992). Antecedents and outcomes of work–family conflict among married professional women: Evidence from Singapore. *Human Relations, 45*(8), 813–837.

Aryee, S., Field, D., & Luk, V. (1999). A cross-cultural test of the work–family interface. *Journal of Management, 25*(4), 491–511.

Bamberg, E. (1992). Stressoren in der Erwerbsarbeit und in der Freizeit: Zusammenhänge mit psychischen Befindensbeeinträchtigungen. [Stressors at work and in leisure time: Relationships with strain reactions.]. *Zeitschrift für Arbeits- und Organisationspsychologie, 36*, 84–91.

Barnett, R. C. (1998). Toward a review and reconceptualization of the work/family literature. *Genetic, Social and General Psychology Monographs, 124*, 125–182.

Barnett, R. C. (2006). Relationship of the number and distribution of work hours to health and quality-of-life (QOL) outcomes. In: P. L. Perrewé & D. C. Ganster (Eds), *Research in occupational stress and well being: Employee health, coping, and methodologies* (Vol. 5, pp. 99–138). Oxford: Elsevier Science.

Barnett, R. S., & Baruch, G. K. (1985). Women's involvement in multiple roles and psychological distress. *Journal of Personality and Social Psychology, 49,* 135–145.

Barnett, R. S., & Hyde, J. S. (2001). Women, men, work, and family. *American Psychologist, 56,* 781–796.

Barnett, R. S., Marshall, N. L., & Sayer, A. (1992). Positive-spillover effects from job to home: A closer look. *Women & Health, 19,* 13–41.

Barnett, R. S., Marshall, N. L., & Singer, J. D. (1992). Job experience over time, multiple roles, and women's mental health: A longitudinal study. *Journal of Personality and Social Psychology, 62,* 634–644.

Bolger, N., DeLongis, A., Kessler, R. C., & Schilling, E. A. (1989). Effects of daily stress on negative mood. *Journal of Personality and Social Psychology, 57,* 808–818.

Bolger, N., DeLongis, A., Kessler, R. C., & Wethington, E. (1990). The microstructure of daily role-related stress in married couples. In: J. Eckenrode & S. Gore (Eds), *Stress between work and family* (pp. 95–115). New York: Plenum Press.

Boyar, S. L., Maertz, C. P., Pearson, A. W., & Keough, S. (2003). Work–family conflict: A model of linkages between work and family domain variables and turnover intentions. *Journal of Managerial Issues, 15,* 175–190.

Brosschot, J. F., Pieper, S., & Thayer, J. F. (2005). Expanding stress theory: Prolonged activation and perseverative cognition. *Psychoneuroendocrinology, 30,* 1043–1049.

Burke, R. J., & Greenglass, E. R. (1987). Work and family. In: C. L. Cooper & I. T. Robertson (Eds), *International review of industrial and organizational psychology 1987* (pp. 273–320). New York: Wiley.

Butler, A. B., Grzywacz, J. G., Bass, B. L., & Linney, K. D. (2005). Extending the demands-control model: A daily diary study of job characteristics, work–family conflict and work–family facilitation. *Journal of Occupational and Organizational Psychology, 78,* 155–169.

Byron, K. (2005). A meta-analytic review of work–family conflict and its antecedents. *Journal of Vocational Behavior, 67,* 169–198.

Carlson, D. S., & Frone, M. R. (2003). Relation of behavioral and psychological involvement to a new four-factor conceptualisation of work–family interference. *Journal of Business and Psychology, 17,* 515–535.

Clark, S. C. (2000). Work/family border theory: A new theory of work/family balance. *Human Relations, 53*(6), 747–770.

Conger, G. H., Rueter, M. A., & Elder, G. H. (1999). Couple resilience to economic pressure. *Journal of Personality and Social Psychology, 76,* 54–71.

Cropley, M., & Purvis, L. M. (2003). Job strain and rumination about work issues during leisure time: A diary study. *European Journal of Work and Organizational Psychology, 12,* 195–207.

Crouter, A. C., Perry-Jenkins, M., Huston, T. L., & Crawford, D. W. (1989). The influence of work-induced psychological stress on behavior at home. *Basic and Applied Social Psychology, 10,* 273–292.

DeLongis, A., Folkman, S., & Lazarus, R. S. (1988). The impact of daily stress on health and mood: Psychological and social resources as mediators. *Journal of Personality and Social Psychology, 54,* 486–495.

Demerouti, E., Bakker, A. G., & Bulters, A. J. (2004). The loss spiral of work pressure, work-home interference and exhaustion: Reciprocal relations in a three-wave study. *Journal of Vocational Behavior, 64,* 131–149.

Demerouti, E., Bakker, A. B., Nachreiner, F., & Schaufeli, W. B. (2001). The job demands-resources model of burnout. *Journal of Applied Psychology, 86*, 499–512.

Demerouti, E., Taris, W. T., & Bakker, A. B. (2007). Need for recovery, home–work interference and performance: Is lack of concentration the link? *Journal of Vocational Behavior, 71*, 204–220.

Doumas, D. M., Margolin, G., & John, R. S. (2003). The relationship between daily marital interaction, work, and health-promoting behaviors in dual-earner couples. *Journal of Family Issues, 24*, 3–20.

Dubin, R. (1956). Industrial workers' world: A study in the central life interests of industrial workers. *Social Problems, 4*, 3–13.

Dubin, R. (1976). Work in modern society. In: R. Dubin (Ed.), *Handbook of work, organization, and society* (pp. 5–35). Chicago: Ran McNally College Publishing Company.

Eagle, B. W., Miles, E. W., & Icenogle, M. L. (1997). Interrole conflicts and the permeability of work and family domains: Are there gender differences? *Journal of Vocational Behavior, 50*, 168–184.

Eby, L. T., Casper, W. J., Lockwood, A., Bordeaux, C., & Brinley, A. (2005). Work and family research in IO/OB: Content analysis and review of the literature (1980–2002). *Journal of Vocational Behavior, 66*, 124–197.

Eckenrode, J., & Gore, S. (Eds). (1990). *Stress between work and family*. New York: Plenum Press.

Eden, D. (2001). Vacations and other respites: Studying stress on and off the job. In: C. L. Cooper & I. T. Robertson (Eds), *International review of industrial and organizational psychology 2001* (Vol. 16, pp. 121–146). Chichester: Wiley.

Edwards, J. R., & Rothbard, N. P. (1999). Work and family stress and well-being: An examination of person-environment fit in the work and family domains. *Organizational Behavior and Human Decision Processes, 77*, 85–129.

Edwards, J. R., & Rothbard, N. P. (2000). Mechanisms linking work and family: Clarifying the relationship between work and family constructs. *Academy of Management Review, 25*(1), 178–199.

Ford, M. T., Heinen, B. A., & Langkamer, K. L. (2007). Work and family satisfaction and conflict: A meta-analysis of cross-domain relations. *Journal of Applied Psychology, 92*, 57–80.

Fox, M. L., & Dwyer, D. J. (1999). An investigation of the effects of time and involvement in the relationship between stressors and work–family conflict. *Journal of Occupational Health Psychology, 4*, 164–174.

Frankenhaeuser, M., Lundberg, U., Fredrikson, M., Melin, B., Tuomisto, M., Myrsten, A. L., Hedman, M., Bergman-Losman, B., & Wallin, L. (1989). Stress on and off the job as related to sex and occupational status in white-collar workers. *Journal of Organizational Behavior, 10*, 321–346.

Fredrickson, B. L., & Branigan, C. (2005). Positive emotions broaden the scope of attention and thought-action repertoires. *Cognition and Emotion, 19*, 313–332.

Fredrickson, B. L., & Losada, M. F. (2005). Positive affect and the complex dynamics of human flourishing. *American Psychologist, 60*, 678–686.

Fredrickson, B. L., Mancuso, R. A., Branigan, C., & Tugade, M. M. (2000). The undoing effect of positive emotions. *Motivation and Emotion, 24*, 237–258.

Fritz, C., & Sonnentag, S. (2005). Recovery, health, and job performance: Effects of weekend experiences. *Journal of Occupational Health Psychology, 10*, 187–199.

Fritz, C., & Sonnentag, S. (2006). Recovery, well-being, and performance-related outcomes: The role of work load and vacation experiences. *Journal of Applied Psychology, 91*, 936–945.

Frone, M. R. (2003). Work–family balance. In: J. Campbell Quick & L. E. Tetrick (Eds), *Handbook of occupational health psychology* (pp. 143–162). Washington, DC: APA.

Frone, M. R., Russell, M., & Cooper, M. L. (1992a). Antecedents and outcomes of work–family conflict: Testing a model of the work–family interface. *Journal of Applied Psychology, 77*, 65–78.

Frone, M. R., Russell, M., & Cooper, M. L. (1992b). Prevalence of work–family conflict: Are work and family boundaries asymmetrical permeable? *Journal of Organizational Behavior, 13*, 723–729.

Geurts, S. A. E., & Demerouti, E. (2003). Work/non-work interface: A review of theories and findings. In: M. J. Schabracq, J. A. M. Winnubst & C. L. Cooper (Eds), *Handbook of work and health psychology* (pp. 279–312). Chinester: Wiley.

Geurts, S. A. E., Kompier, M. A. J., Roxburgh, S., & Houtman, I. L. D. (2003). Does work–home interference mediate the relationship between workload and well-being? *Journal of Vocational Behavior, 63*, 532–559.

Geurts, S., Rutte, C., & Peeters, M. (1999). Antecedents and consequences of work–home interference among medical residents. *Social Science & Medicine, 48*, 1135–1148.

Geurts, S. A. E., & Sonnentag, S. (2006). Recovery as an explanatory mechanism in the relation between acute stress reactions and chronic health impairment. *Scandinavian Journal of Work Environmental Health, 32*, 482–492.

Grandey, A. A., & Cropanzano, R. (1999). The conservation of resources model applied to work–family conflict and strain. *Journal of Vocational Behavior, 54*, 350–370.

Granrose, C. S., Parasuraman, S., & Greenhaus, J. H. (1992). A proposed model of support provided by two-earner couples. *Human Relations, 45*, 1367–1392.

Greenhaus, J. H., & Beutell, N. J. (1985). Sources of conflict between work and family roles. *Academy of Management Review, 10*, 76–88.

Greenhaus, J. H., Collins, K. M., & Shaw, J. D. (2003). The relation between work–family balance and quality of life. *Journal of Vocational Behavior, 63*, 510–531.

Greenhaus, J. H., & Parasuraman, S. (1999). Research on work, family, and gender: Current status and future directions. In: G. N. Powell (Ed.), *Handbook of gender and work* (pp. 391–412). Thousand Oakes: Sage.

Greenhaus, J. H., & Parasuraman, S. (2002). The allocation of time to work and family roles. In: D. L. Nelson & R. J. Burke (Eds), *Gender, work stress and health* (pp. 115–128). Washington, DC: APA.

Greenhaus, J. H., Parasuraman, S., & Collings, K. M. (2001). Career involvement and family involvement as moderators of relationships between work–family conflict and withdrawal from a profession. *Journal of Occupational Health Psychology, 6*, 91–100.

Greenhaus, J. H., & Powell, G. N. (2006). When work and family are allies: A theory of work–family enrichment. *Academy of Management Review, 31*, 72–92.

Gross, S., Semmer, N. K., Meier, L. L., Kälin, W., Jacobshagen, N., & Tschan, F. (2008). The impact of positive and negative events at work on fatigue after work: The moderating role of social climate. November 12–14, 2008. Paper presented at the 2008 conference of the European Academy of Occupational Health Psychology, Valencia, Spain.

Grzywacz, J. G. (2000). Work–family spillover and health during midlife: Is managing conflict everything? *American Journal of Health Promotion, 14*(4), 236–243.

Grzywacz, J. G., & Bass, B. L. (2003). Work, family, and mental health: Testing different models of work–family fit. *Journal of Marriage and Family, 65,* 248–262.

Grzywacz, J. G., & Marks, N. F. (2000a). Reconceptualizing the work–family interface: An ecological perspective on the correlates of positive and negative spillover between work and family. *Journal of Occupational Health Psychology, 5*(1), 111–126.

Grzywacz, J. G., & Marks, N. F. (2000b). Family, work, work–family spillover and problem drinking during midlife. *Journal of Marriage and the Family, 62*(2), 336–348.

Gump, B. B., & Matthews, K. A. (1999). Do background stressors influence reactivity to and recovery from acute stressors? *Journal of Applied Social Psychology, 29,* 469–494.

Gutek, B. A., Searle, S., & Klepa, L. (1991). Rational versus gender role explanations for work–family conflict. *Journal of Applied Psychology, 76,* 560–568.

Hammer, L. B., Bauer, T. N., & Grandey, A. A. (2003). Work–family conflict and work-related withdrawal behaviors. *Journal of Business and Psychology, 17,* 419–436.

Heller, D., & Watson, D. (2005). The dynamic spillover of satisfaction between work and marriage: The role of time and mood. *Journal of Applied Psychology, 90,* 1273–1279.

Hibbard, J. H., & Pope, C. R. (1993). The quality of social roles as predictors of morbidity and mortality. *Social Sciences and Medicine, 36,* 217–225.

Hobfoll, S. E. (1998). *Stress, culture, and community: The psychology and philosophy of stress.* New York: Plenum Press.

Hobfoll, S. E. (2001). The influence of culture, community, and the nested-self in the stress process: Advancing conservation of resources theory. *Applied Psychology: An International Review, 50,* 337–421.

Jacobshagen, N., Amstad, F. T., Semmer, N. K., & Kuster, M. (2005). Work-family-balance in top management: Konflikt zwischen Arbeit und Familie als Mediator der Beziehung zwischen Stressoren und Befinden. *Zeitschrift für Arbeits- und Organisationspsychologie, 49,* 208–219.

Jones, F., & Fletcher, B. (1993). An empirical study of occupations stress transmissions in working couples. *Human Relations, 46,* 881–903.

Judge, T. A., & Ilies, R. (2004). Affect and job satisfaction: A study of their relationship at work and at home. *Journal of Applied Psychology, 89,* 661–673.

Kahn, R. L., Wolfe, D., Quinn, R., Snoek, J., & Rosenthal, R. (1964). *Organizational stress: Studies in role conflict and ambiguity.* New York: Wiley.

Kälin, W., & Semmer, N. K. (2002). Arbeitsmerkmale und emotionales Coping als Prädiktoren Positiver Lebenseinstellung. [*Work characteristics and emotional coping as predictors of a positive outlook on life.*] September 22–26, 2002. Paper presented at the 43rd Congress of the German Psychological Society, Berlin.

Kessler, R. D., & McLeod, J. (1984). Sex differences in vulnerability to undesirable events. *American Sociological Review, 47,* 217–227.

Kiecolt-Glaser, J. K., Preacher, K. J., MacCallum, R. C., Atkinson, C., Malarkey, W. B., & Glaser, R. (2003). Chronic stress and age-related increases in the proinflammatory cytokine IL-6. *Proceedings of the National Academy of Sciences of the United States of America, 100,* 9090–9095.

Kinnunen, U., & Mauno, S. (1998). Antecedents and outcomes of work–family conflict among employed women and men in Finland. *Human Relations, 51,* 157–177.

Kirchmeyer, C. (1993). Nonwork to work spillover: A more blatant view of the experiences and coping of professional women and men. *Sex roles, 28,* 1–22.

Klumb, P., Hoppmann, C., & Staats, M. (2006). Division of labor in German dual-earner families: Testing equity theoretical hypotheses. *Journal of Marriage and the Family, 68*, 870–882.

Kohn, M. L., & Schooler, C. (1978). The reciprocal effects of the substantive complexity of work and intellectual flexibility: A longitudinal assessment. *American Journal of Sociology, 84*, 24–52.

Kossek, E. E., & Ozeki, C. (1998). Work–family conflict, policies, and the job-life satisfaction relationship: A review and directions for organization behavior. *Journal of Applied Psychology, 83*(2), 139–149.

Kossek, E. E., & Ozeki, C. (1999). Bridging the work–family policy and productivity gap: A literature review. *Community, Work & Family, 2*, 7–32.

Kotler, P., & Wingard, D. L. (1989). The effect of occupational, marital and parental roles on mortality: The Alameda County Study. *American Journal of Public Health, 79*, 607–612.

Lambert, S. J. (1990). Processes linking work and family: A critical review and research agenda. *Human Relations, 43*, 239–257.

Lazarus, R. S. (1999). *Stress and emotion. A new synthesis*. New York: Springer.

Leppin, A., & Schwarzer, R. (1997). Sozialer Rückhalt, Krankheit und Gesundheitsverhalten. In: R. Schwarzer (Hrsg.), *Gesundheitspsychologie: Ein Lehrbuch* (2. Aufl., S. 349–373). Göttingen: Hogrefe.

Liebler, C. A., & Sandefur, G. D. (2001). *Gender differences in the exchange of social support with friends, neighbors, and coworkers at midlife.* CDE Working Paper No. 2001-12. Center for Demography and Ecology, Wisconsin-Madison.

Linville, P. W. (1987). Self-complexity as a cognitive buffer against stress-related illness and depression. *Journal of Personality and Social Psychology, 52*, 663–676.

Marks, S. R. (1977). Multiple roles and role strain: Some notes on human energy, time and commitment. *American Sociological Review, 42*, 921–936.

Marshall, N. L., & Barnett, R. C. (1993). Work–family strains and gains among two-earner-couples. *Journal of Community Psychology, 21*, 64–78.

Martire, L. M., Parris Stephens, M. A., & Townsend, A. L. (2000). Centrality of women's multiple roles: Beneficial and detrimental consequences for psychological well-being. *Psychology and Aging, 15*, 148–156.

Meijman, T. F., & Mulder, G. (1998). Psychological aspects of workload. In: P. J. D. Drenth, H. Thierry & C. J. de Wolff (Eds), *Handbook of work and organizational psychology* (2nd ed., Vol. 2, pp. 5–33). Hove, UK: Psychology Press.

Meissner, M. (1971). The long arm of the job: A study of work and leisure. *Industrial Relations, 10*, 239–260.

Mieg, H. A., & Wehner, T. (2002). Frei-gemeinnützige Arbeit. Eine Analyse aus Sicht der Arbeits- und Organisationspsychologie. *Hamburger Beiträge, 33*, 4–30.

MOW – International Research Team. (1987). *The meaning of working*. London: Academic Press.

Netemeyer, R. G., Boles, J. S., & McMurrian, R. (1996). Development and validation of work–family conflict scales. *Journal of Applied Psychology, 81*, 400–410.

Parasuraman, S., & Greenhaus, J. H. (2002). Toward reducing some critical gaps in work–family research. *Human Resource Management Review, 12*, 299–312.

Parasuraman, S., & Simmers, C. A. (2001). Type of employment, work–family conflict and well-being: A comparative study. *Journal of Organizational Behavior, 22*, 551–568.

Pearlin, L. I., & McCall, M. E. (1990). Occupational stress and marital support: A description of micro processes. In: J. Eckenrode & S. Gore (Eds), *Stress between work and family*. New York: Plenum Press.

Penning, M. J. (1998). In the middle: Parental caregiving in the context of other roles. *Journal of Gerontology: Social Sciences, 53B*, S188–S197.

Perrewé, P. L., & Carlson, D. S. (2002). Do man and women benefit from social support equally? Results from a field examination within the work and family context. In: D. L. Nelson & R. J. Burke (Eds), *Gender, work stress and health* (pp. 101–114). Washington: APA.

Pleck, J. H. (1977). The work–family role system. *Social Problems, 24*, 417–427.

Reid, J., & Hardy, M. (1999). Multiple roles and well-being among midlife women: Testing role strain and role enhancement theories. *Journal of Gerontology: Social Sciences, 54B*, S329–S338.

Repetti, R. L. (1992). Social withdrawal as a short-term coping response to daily stressors. In: H. S. Friedman (Ed.), *Hostility Coping & Health*. Washington: APA.

Repetti, R. L., Matthews, K., & Waldron, I. (1989). Employment and women's health: Effects of paid employment on women's mental and physical health. *American Psychologist, 44*, 1394–1401.

Repetti, R. L., & Wood, J. (1997). Effects of daily stress at work on mothers' interactions with preschoolers. *Journal of Family Psychology, 11*(1), 90–108.

Resch, M. (1999). *Arbeitsanalyse im Haushalt*. Zürich: Verlag der Fachvereine.

Rook, J. W., & Zijlstra, F. R. H. (2006). The contribution of various types of activities to recovery. *European Journal of Work and Organizational Psychology, 15*, 218–240.

Ross, C. E., & Mirowsky, J. (1995). Does employment affect health? *Journal of Health and Social Behavior, 36*, 230–243.

Rothbard, N. P., & Edwards, J. R. (2003). Investment in work and family roles: A test of identity and utilitarian motives. *Personnel Psychology, 56*, 699–730.

Rothbard, N. P., Phillips, K. W., & Dumas, T. L. (2005). Managing multiple roles: Work–family policies and individuals' desires for segmentation. *Organization Science, 16*, 243–258.

Schaufeli, W., & Enzmann, D. (1998). *The burnout companion to study and practice: A critical analysis*. London: Taylor & Francis.

Schieman, S., McBrier, D. B., & Van Gundy, K. (2003). Home-to-work conflict, work qualities, and emotional distress. *Sociological Forum, 18*, 137–164.

Schönpflug, W., & Battmann, W. (1988). The costs and benefits of coping. In: S. Fisher & J. Reason (Eds), *Handbook of life stress, cognition and health* (pp. 699–713). New York, NY: Wiley.

Schooler, C., Mulatu, M. S., & Oates, G. (1999). The continuing effects of substantively complex work on intellectual functioning of older workers. *Psychology and Aging, 14*, 483–506.

Semmer, N. K. (2003). Individual differences, work stress and health. In: M. J. Schabracq, J. A. Winnubst & C. L. Cooper (Eds), *Handbook of work and health psychology* (2nd ed, pp. 83–120). Chichester: Wiley.

Semmer, N. K., Grebner, S., & Elfering, A. (2004). Beyond self-report: Using observational, physiological, and situation-based measures in research on occupational stress. In: P. L. Perrewé & D. C. Ganster (Eds), *Research in occupational stress and well-being: Emotional and physiological processes and positive intervention strategies* (Vol. 3, pp. 207–263). Amsterdam: JAI.

Semmer, N. K., Jacobshagen, N., Meier, L. L., & Elfering, A. (2007). Occupational stress research: The "Stress-as-Offense-to-Self" perspective. In: J. Houdmont & S. McIntyre (Eds), *Occupational health psychology: European perspectives on research, education and practice* (Vol. 2, pp. 43–60). ISMAI: Avioso S. Pedro.

Simon, R. W. (1995). Gender, multiple roles, role meaning, and mental health. *Journal of Health and Social Behavior, 36*, 182–194.

Simon, R. W. (1997). The meanings individuals attach to role identities and their implications for mental health. *Journal of Health and Social Behavior, 38*, 256–274.

Smith Major, V., Klein, K. J., & Ehrhart, M. G. (2002). Work time, work interference with family, and psychological distress. *Journal of Applied Psychology, 87*, 427–436.

Sonnentag, S. (2001). Work, recovery activities, and individual well-being: A diary study. *Journal of Occupational Health Psychology, 6*, 196–210.

Sonnentag, S., & Bayer, U.-V. (2005). Switching off mentally: Predictors and consequences of psychological detachment from work during off-job time. *Journal of Occupational Health Psychology, 10*, 393–414.

Sonnentag, S., & Jelden, S. (in press). Job stressors and the pursuit of sport activities: A day-level perspective. *Journal of Occupational Health Psychology*.

Sonnentag, S., & Kruel, U. (2006). Psychological detachment from work during off-job time: The role of job stressors, job involvement, and recovery-related self-efficacy. *European Journal of Work and Organizational Psychology, 15*, 197–217.

Sonnentag, S., & Zijlstra, F. R. H. (2006). Job characteristics and off-job activities as predictors of need for recovery, well-being, and fatigue. *Journal of Applied Psychology, 91*, 330–350.

Standen, P., Daniels, K., & Lamond, D. (1999). The home as a workplace: Work–family interaction and psychological well-being in telework. *Journal of Occupational Health Psychology, 4*, 368–381.

Stephens, M. A. P., & Franks, M. M. (1995). Spillover between daughters' roles as caregiver and wife: Interference or enhancement? *Journal of Gerontology: Psychological Sciences, 50B*, P9–P17.

Thierry, H., & Jansen, B. (1998). Work time and behaviour at work. In: P. J. D. Drenth, H. Thierry & C. J. de Wolff (Eds), *Handbook of work and organizational psychology* (pp. 89–119). Sussex: Taylor & Francis.

Thoits, P. A. (1991). On merging identity theory and stress research. *Social Psychology Quarterly, 54*, 101–112.

Thoits, P. A., & Hewitt, L. N. (2001). Volunteer work and well-being. *Journal of Health and Social Behavior, 42*, 115–131.

Thompson, A., & Bolger, N. (1999). Emotional transmission in couples under stress. *Journal of Marriage and Family, 61*, 38–48.

Tschan, F., Semmer, N. K., & Inversin, L. (2004). Work related and "private" social interactions at work. *Social Indicators Research, 67*, 145–182.

Tucker, P. (2003). The impact of rest breaks upon accident risk, fatigue and performance: A review. *Work and Stress, 17*, 123–137.

Van der Hulst, M., & Geurts, S. (2001). Associations between overtime and psychological health in high and low reward jobs. *Work & Stress, 15*, 227–240.

Visweswaran, C., Sanchez, J., & Fisher, J. (1999). The role of social support in the process of work stress: A meta-analysis. *Journal of Vocational Behavior, 54*, 314–334.

Voydanoff, P. (1987). *Work and family life*. Newbury Pork, CA: Sage.

Voydanoff, P. (2001). Incorporating community into work and family research: A review of basic relationships. *Human Relations, 54*(12), 1609–1637.

Wallace, J. E. (1997). It's about time: A study of hours worked and work spillover among law firm lawyers. *Journal of Vocational Behavior, 50*(2), 227–248.

Westman, M. (2002a). Gender asymmetry in crossover research. In: D. L. Nelson & R. J. Burke (Eds), *Gender, work stress and health*. Washington: APA.

Westman, M. (2002b). Crossover of stress and strain in the family and workplace. In: P. L. Perrewé & D. C. Ganster (Eds), *Research in occupational stress and well being: Historical and current perspectives on stress and health* (Vol. 2, pp. 142–181). Oxford: Elsevier Science.

Westman, M., Etzion, D., & Danon, E. (2001). Job insecurity and crossover of burnout in married couples. *Journal of Organizational Behavior, 22*, 467–481.

Westman, M., & Vinokur, A. (1998). Unraveling the relationship of distress levels in couples: Common stressors, emphatic reactions, or crossover via social interactions? *Human Relations, 51*, 137–156.

Wickrama, K., Conger, R. D., Lorenz, F. O., & Matthews, L. (1995). Role identity, role satisfaction, and perceived physical health. *Social Psychology Quarterly, 58*, 270–283.

Wilensky, H. (1960). Work, careers and social integration. *International Social Science Journal, 12*, 543–560.

Williams, K. J., & Alliger, G. M. (1994). Role stressors, mood spillover, and perceptions of work–family conflict in employed parents. *Academy of Management Journal, 37*, 837–868.

Williams, A., Franche, R.-L., Ibrahim, S., Mustard, C., & Layton, F. R. (2006). Examining the relationship between work–family spillover and sleep quality. *Journal of Occupational Health Psychology, 11*, 27–37.

Winwood, P. C., Bakker, A. B., & Winefield, A. H. (2007). An investigation of the role of non-work time behaviour in buffering the effects of work strain. *Journal of Occupational and Environmental Medicine, 49*, 862–871.

Zijlstra, F. R. H., & Sonnentag, S. (2006). After work is done: Psychological perspectives on recovery from work. *European Journal of Work and Organizational Psychology, 15*, 129–138.

Zohar, D. (1999). When things go wrong: The effect of daily work hassles on effort, exertion and negative mood. *Journal of Occupational and Organizational Psychology, 72*, 265–283.

Zohar, D., Tzischinski, O., & Epstein, R. (2003). Effects of energy availability on immediate and delayed emotional reactions to work events. *Journal of Applied Psychology, 88*, 1082–1093.

ARE BUSINESS TRIPS A UNIQUE KIND OF RESPITE?

Mina Westman, Dalia Etzion and Shoshi Chen

ABSTRACT

In this chapter, we discuss the impact of business trips on travelers and their families from the perspective of respite, thus embedding business trips in stress theories. We begin by reviewing the literature on respite and recovery. Focusing on the role of travelers' resources, we relate the phenomenon of business trips to conservation of resources (COR) and job demands-resource (JD-R) theories. We then discuss the negative and positive characteristics and outcomes of business trips. We offer evidence from interviews with business travelers regarding the special characteristics and consequences of business trips. We summarize by addressing the question of whether business trips are a special kind of respite.

In this chapter, we define business trips as short-term international travel performed as part of one's job. Such trips have become common in the global economy, due in no small part to the economic benefits to the employing organization: which include establishing new contacts, obtaining new contracts, retaining existing customers, and participating in conferences and exhibitions. Gustafson (2006) states that business trips occur in a wide range of jobs (e.g., managers, consultants, IT specialists, financiers, and government people), and are conducted for very different reasons (coordination,

Current Perspectives on Job-Stress Recovery
Research in Occupational Stress and Well Being, Volume 7, 167–204
Copyright © 2009 by Emerald Group Publishing Limited
All rights of reproduction in any form reserved
ISSN: 1479-3555/doi:10.1108/S1479-3555(2009)0000007008

consultation, negotiation, and personal relations). Some researchers believe that in addition to their financial costs, business trips incur potential human costs such as deterioration in the well-being and performance of frequently traveling employees. Despite their prevalence, there is presently very little research on business trips and their impact on travelers, their families, and their organization. Most researchers of business trips regard such trips as a source of stress to travelers (e.g., DeFrank, Konopaske, & Ivancevich, 2000; Dimberg et al., 2002) and their families (Espino, Sundstorm, Frick, Jacobs, & Peters, 2002; Dimberg et al., 2002), although several studies have also demonstrated positive effects of business trips (Westman & Etzion, 2002; Westman, Etzion, & Chen, 2009). It seems that business trips are a dual experience, consisting of demands and resources, losses and gains, all impacting on the well-being of travelers and their families.

In the present chapter, we examine the negative and positive effects of business trips on travelers' personal lives, family life, and work performance, based on stress theories. Westman (2004) embedded business trip research in Hobfoll's (1989) conservation of resources (COR) theory. In this chapter, we go one step further to embed business trip research in the job demands-resource (JD-R) model (Bakker & Demerouti, 2007), and discuss the question of whether business trips are a special kind of respite.

RESPITE AND RECOVERY: DEFINITIONS AND LITERATURE REVIEW

The term "respite" has become central in addressing the issues of how employees in organizations recover from occupational stress and burnout. Following Kahn, Wolfe, Quinn, Snoek, and Rosenthal (1964), most scholars define job stress in terms of role demands originating in the work environment. The stress aroused by stressors such as conflict, overload, and responsibility is hypothesized to cause strain. Strains are reactions or outcomes resulting from the experience of stressors (Jex & Beehr, 1991). Thus, in the present chapter, we relate to stressors as job and environment characteristics that potentially cause stress, which leads to strains such as anxiety and burnout.

According to COR (Hobfoll, 1989) theory, psychological stress occurs when individual resources are depleted or threatened, or when individuals fail to gain resources following resource investment. Lazarus and Folkman's (1984) definition of stress emphasizes appraisal "Psychological stress is a relationship between a person and the environment that is appraised by the person as taxing or exceeding his or her resources and endangering his or her well-being" (p. 21). Burnout is perceived by most researchers as a psychological strain resulting from continuous daily stress. According to Westman and Eden (1997), "a respite from work may be a day off, a weekend, a vacation, or some other form of absence from the work setting when the everyday regular pressures of the job are absent" (p. 516). Thus, by respite we mean time off from work, such as an annual vacation, holiday leave, or even a stint of military reserve duty or a business trip. Occupational experts maintain that time off work helps employees recover from stress, replenish depleting energy, and contain burnout development (e.g., Cunningham, 1997, p. 245). Because one of the main factors impacting burnout is believed to be continuous exposure to daily stress, many burnout experts too subscribe to COR theory and see an occasional "time-out" from work as a means of "recharging one's batteries" and renewing one's strength (Chernis, 1981; Freudenberger, 1974; Maslach, 1976; Pines & Aronson with Kafry, 1981).

Another line of research that has merged into the respite literature is recovery from strain and restoration of physical and psychological resources. The basic contention of recovery scholars is that our personal resources weaken or diminish in the effort of meeting the demands of everyday life. According to Sonnentag (2003), recovery experiences during off-job periods help reduce symptoms of stress and strain. Being in a recovered state helps individuals to actively approach work tasks without having to mobilize extra efforts that may deplete energy resources. COR theory assumes that resource levels are restored (i.e., recovery occurs) by refraining from activities that are similar to the activities that originally caused the strain. Moreover, COR theory assumes that additional resources can be gained by investing free time in personal development and positive experiences.

If we do not periodically restore our resources, we run the risk of negative consequences to our well-being and work performance. Recovery research focuses on the physical conditions of recovery, distinguishing between activity and rest, and detects fluctuations between activity and rest, based on daily diary reports (see Fritz & Sonnentag, 2006; Hartig, 2004; Sonnentag, 2001; Strauss-Blasche, Ekmekcioglu, & Marktl, 2000; Strauss-Blasche, Ekmekcioglu, & Marktl, 2003).

Work, nonwork, and their relations with well-being have been of central theoretical and empirical interests in the past several decades, and research has continuously developed and branched into related issues. Research on respite, which is usually conceptualized as any form of absence from the work setting when job stressors are presumably absent or dimmed (Westman & Etzion, 2002), may be considered such a branch, which has focused on the manifold effects of respite from work on well-being.

Initial studies of respite effect focused on job stress (mainly physiological) symptoms and considered time off work as a "control occasion" to be compared with time on the job (Eden, 2001a). In the past decade, respite research has extended through the integration of physiological, psychological, and behavioral aspects.

Among the physiological strains alleviated by respite are cardiovascular and neuro-endocrine malfunctions, physical pains and complaints, sleep disturbances and other symptoms (see Frankenhaeuser et al., 1989; Strauss-Blasche, Muhry, Lehofer, Moser, & Markl, 2004). Gump and Matthews (2000) found that even mortality rates are influenced by respites. They followed mortality rates of 12,338 middle-aged men at high risk for coronary heart disease (CHD), over a nine-year period. Vacation frequency was reported in the first five years of the study. Results showed that the frequency of annual vacations was associated with a reduced risk of all-cause mortality and, more specifically, mortality attributed to CHD.

The psychological strains alleviated by respite include depression, anxiety, dissatisfaction, ill mood, and burnout. Burnout, or more specifically its exhaustion component, has been the most common indicator of job stress included as a dependent variable in most before–after respite studies (Etzion & Boklis, 2006).

As for methodology, respite research has been conducted through longitudinal, repeated measures designs, enabling job characteristics to be intermittently present and absent, with and without control groups. Measurement occasions have commonly ranged from two (before and after respite) to five, including measurements during the respite period itself.

Length of respites has ranged from a few days to months, relating to different respite types, such as a day off work, a weekend, a lengthy holiday, or annual summer vacation, which may be organization-wide or personal/voluntary, to one-year sabbaticals. Fritz and Sonnentag (2005), for example, investigated weekend experiences of 87 emergency service workers. They focused on three different weekend experiences that have an impact on health and job performance. They examined both negative experiences that draw on the individual's resources and more positive experiences that help individuals regain and build up lost resources. Their results indicated that nonwork hassles, absence of positive work reflection, and low social activity during the weekend predicted different aspects of job performance after the weekend.

In an example of a study concerning a lengthy respite, Davidson, Eden, and Westman (2009) conducted a rigorous quasi-experiment testing the ameliorative effects of the relief from job stress afforded by a sabbatical leave. They gathered data from 258 faculty members; 129 *sabbatees* and 129 matched-controls who experienced no leave during that year. They found that sabbatees' stress and resource loss declined, and resource gain and well-being rose during the sabbatical. The comparison group showed no such change. On return to routine work, most of the beneficial effects of the sabbatical vanished. Moderation analysis revealed that respite self-efficacy, perceived control, psychological detachment from work, and respite quality moderated the impact of stress relief on well-being. Those who reported higher self-efficacy and experienced greater control, were more detached, and had a more positive sabbatical experience and enjoyed more enhanced well-being than others. However, sabbatical length (six or twelve months) did not moderate respite effects.

One of the studies have focused on cross-cultural differences in respite effects, and demonstrated different cultural attitudes and values regarding work and nonwork experiences (Etzion & Dar, 2004). Respite studies have also included absence from work due to military reserve service, business travel, maternity leave, and similar absences from work.

The consistency of empirical findings indicating the ameliorative effect of various forms of respite has raised the need for further comprehension of the nature of respite pursuits that enable psychological and physiological recovery. Hence, daily activities on and off work and their contribution to daily recovery and periodical alleviation of stress have also become important issues for the study of the respite effect. Consequently, findings from leisure research have been integrated into recovery and respite research, highlighting types of activities during time off and their effects on well-being, based on data on daily activities collected through daily diaries and physiological follow-ups (e.g., Repetti, 1993; Sonnentag, 2001, 2003).

Samples in respite research represent a large diversity that encompasses almost every pursuit, job status, and profession, including low- and high-tech workers in various organizational positions, medical staff, teachers, soldiers, flight attendants, and others. Research has even expanded to respite effects on the crossover of stress and strains between life partners before and after a respite (Etzion & Westman, 2001). Moderating effects such as vacation satisfaction, length of respite period, quality of experience, content and activities, personal characteristics, and personality traits have likewise been examined (e.g., Etzion, Eden, & Lapidot, 1998; Etzion, 2003; Strauss-Blasche, Reithofer, Schobersberger, Ekmekcioglu, & Marktl, 2005).

In the vast majority of respite studies, results indicated a decline in both stress and strains (physiological and psychological) off the job and, in most cases, on the postrespite occasion. On further postrespite occasions, a return to prerespite levels of stress and strains was demonstrated. When burnout was examined, the fade-out process was similar to the fade-out of stress, however, in some cases burnout showed a slower fade-out effect than stress (Etzion, 2003).

Rubinstein (1980) suggested that most workers feel that a vacation has positive results, such as tension release, personal growth and satisfaction, and indeed many studies have demonstrated that respite yields positive results for the individual (see review by Eden (2001a) and a meta-analysis by Etzion and Boklis (2006)). Lounsbury and Hoopes (1986) were the first to study the effect of vacation in a longitudinal before–after design. They measured the effect of vacation on six work and nonwork characteristics among 128 workers of 24 industrial organizations. They found that satisfaction from vacation impacts subsequent satisfaction from life and work. Caplan and Jones (1975) studied 73 male computer system users (graduates, undergraduates, and faculty) at the University of Michigan during a planned computer shutdown. The study was longitudinal, with two measurements: three days preceding the scheduled 23-day system shutdown, and five months later. Positive associations were found between role ambiguity and anxiety, between depression and resentment, between subjective work load and anxiety, and between anxiety and heart rate. A decline in subjective work load and in all the strain measures was demonstrated on the second occasion compared to the first.

Eden (1990) replicated the 1975 study by Caplan and Jones by studying a scheduled computer shutdown that created a forced vacation event. He studied 29 computer employees and users at the Tel Aviv University's computer center and found that during the period of the computer shutdown, stress among employees decreased, but measures of strain (e.g., anxiety) remained unchanged from the normal course of work (which was indicative of a state of chronic stress). Eden attributed the results to expectations of a heavy workload awaiting employees on return from the forced vacation.

Westman and Eden (1997), who performed five measurements of perceived job stress and burnout around a forced organizational vacation, found that employees' levels of stress and burnout decreased during the vacation and gradually rose again on their return to work. Within three weeks, job stress and burnout returned to their prevacation levels. Their findings showed that female employees and employees who were satisfied with the vacation benefited more from vacation: The decline in job stress and burnout during vacation was greater for female than for male employees, and for employees who were satisfied with the vacation than for those who were less satisfied.

Westman and Etzion (2001) examined the impact of vacation on psychological (burnout) and behavioral (absenteeism) strains among blue-collar employees in an industrial enterprise. Findings showed that vacation reduced both burnout and absenteeism rates reported by the organization. Etzion (2003) compared job stress and burnout among employees at work and their colleagues who went on individually arranged vacations. The results showed a drop in the stress and burnout of the target group immediately after the vacation in comparison to prevacation levels; one month later, the measure of stress had risen to the prevacation level, but the measure of burnout was still low. In the comparison group, no changes in the levels of either stress or burnout were detected. Etzion suggested that burnout may build up gradually as a result of daily stress. Stress, however, is experienced immediately after the return to work, and sometimes the stress reaction on return may be even more intense than in the prevacation measurement as a result of an accumulated backload.

Etzion and Boklis (2006) conducted a series of meta-analyses on over 30 respite studies (published, unpublished, or in process) that were designed to capture the respite effect using a longitudinal, repeated measures procedure. The studies included in the meta-analyses typically consist of a prerespite measurement, a postrespite measurement, and a third measurement approximately one month after the return to work. The results of the meta-analyses show a drop in the stress and burnout measures of the target groups immediately after the vacation (respite effect). One month later, the measures of stress and burnout rise, usually to the prevacation levels (fade-out effect).

Special Kinds of Respite

In an extensive, long-term research project on burnout in Israel (Etzion, 1984; Etzion, Kafry, & Pines, 1982; Etzion & Pines, 1986), men in managerial and technical professions declared that their annual military reserve duty helped them in contain burnout process. Unlike vacation time, military reserve duty is compulsory; activities during reserve duty are generally also very different from typical vacation activities. However, if military reserve duty is viewed in terms of respite, that is, the experience of detachment from the daily routine, we find that its effect on burnout is similar to the effect of vacation time.

In a large public sector industrial enterprise, Etzion et al. (1998) found a drop in the experience of stress and burnout among men who served in the military reserves during the course of the study, in comparison to a matched group whose members carried on in their normal routines during this time. Stress and burnout were measured by means of self-report questionnaires that were administered to each "pair" of matched participants at two points in time: before the target group member left for military reserve duty, and on his return to work. The researchers also found that the more the reserve service was perceived as a positive experience, the greater the drop in stress and burnout levels on return to work. Furthermore, the greater the level of detachment from the routine of civilian life reported – the greater the fall in reported stress and burnout levels on return to work. They found that military reserve service had positive effects on the individual, on returning to the normal work routine. These positive effects seem to emanate mainly from the legitimacy accorded to the work absence because of military reserve duty, and from the actual detachment from the routine of civilian life.

Similarly, business trips can also be considered a special case of respite, as they share several features with military reserve duty. Like the reservists, business travelers are physically removed from their regular work demands; they experience a kind of (at least physical) detachment from their work and their family tasks; and, their absence from the work site is legitimate in the eyes of colleagues, managers, and family members, since they are performing a task that is deemed necessary by the organization and designed for the benefit of all parties concerned.

In a series of studies, Westman and Etzion (2002, 2005) examined the impact of overseas business trips on job stress and burnout. In fact, Westman and Etzion's (2002) study was the first ever attempt to conceptualize and analyze business trips as a special case of respite. They investigated the impact of overseas business trips on job stress and burnout among 57 employees of Israeli high-tech firms, whose jobs include overseas travel. Participants completed questionnaires on three occasions, ten days prior to travel abroad (pretrip), once during their stay abroad (trip), and one week after returning to their regular workplace (posttrip). As in the reserve duty study, here too a respite effect was hypothesized and confirmed. Results indeed showed a decline in job stress and burnout on the posttrip occasion compared to the pretrip occasion.

Westman and Etzion (2002) detected a significant decline in job stress immediately after the trip; job stress was lower after returning to the permanent work site than it was either before or during the trip. Similarly, posttrip burnout levels were lower than pretrip burnout levels. Burnout also tended to be lower on returning from the trip compared to during the stay abroad, but this difference was not significant. Both the anticipation of the overseas journey and the work abroad itself may have been stressful for these employees. Only later, after they returned to their routine jobs did the level of burnout decrease. Their conclusion was that the decrease in job stress and burnout might be evidence of a delayed respite effect (Westman & Etzion, 2002). Though these travelers experienced a heavy workload and ambiguity during the trip, they also enjoyed the physical detachment from their office and their families. Furthermore, the overseas travel afforded them opportunities for new experiences and as well as an opportunity to gain a sense of personal accomplishment. This is in accord with Leider's (1991) observation that immediately after departure the travelers may find their morale elevated because of the change of scenery and their high expectations from the trip. The findings of Leider's research and other studies that followed demonstrated that business trips have outcomes similar to those of other kinds of respite.

Another support to our contention that business trips are a kind of respite comes from a qualitative study with business travelers (Westman & Etzion, 2004). When asked if they perceived the business trip as a respite, 31% of the respondents reported that they perceived the business trip as a kind of respite. Elaborating on their responses, 41% attributed this perception to the change of atmosphere, 27% attributed it to the break in routine, 14% said the trip added variety to their job, 9% commented on the opportunity to meet new people, and the final 9% reported their relief of not having to deal with day-to-day matters. Of those who did not perceive the trip as a respite, 30% said it was part of their day-to-day job, 33% said it was very intensive, 17% said it caused a backload of work at the office, 13% said it was a change of atmosphere but not a respite, and 7% said they were hooked to their laptops all the time. Altogether, this study demonstrated that approximately one-third of the business travelers perceived business trips as a kind of respite and provided reasons for their answer. On the basis of the above review, we elaborate on the business trip, focusing on relevant theories, on travel characteristics, negative and positive outcomes, and theoretical and practical implications.

EMBEDDING BUSINESS TRIPS IN THE JD-R MODEL AND COR THEORY

Very few researchers have examined business trips from a theoretical perspective. Ivancevich and Konopaske (2003) examined business trips with reference to person–environment (P–E) fit theory, whereas Westman (2004) based her study on COR theory. In the present chapter, we added the JD-R perspective in an attempt to integrate both COR and JD-R theories in analyzing the business trip phenomenon. We believe that these models offer the theoretical framework that is lacking in the business trip literature.

The JD-R model (Bakker & Demerouti, 2007; Demerouti, Bakker, Nachreiner, & Schaufeli, 2001) is a heuristic model that specifies how two specific sets of working conditions (job demands and job resources) contribute to employees' well-being. The basic assumption of the JD-R model (Bakker, Demerouti, & Schaufeli, 2003; Demerouti et al., 2001) is that it can be applied to various occupational settings, including business trips, irrespective of their particular demands and resources. According to the JD-R model, job demands are stressors that may evoke strain if they exceed the employee's adaptive capability. Job resources are those physical, psychological, social, or organizational aspects of the job that (a) reduce job demands and their associated physiological and psychological costs, (b) are functional in achieving work goals, or (c) stimulate personal growth, learning, and development (Demerouti et al., 2001).

COR theory (Hobfoll, 1989, 2001) offers an integrative stress model that considers both environmental and internal processes. As a stress and motivational theory, COR outlines how individuals are likely to be impacted by stressful circumstances, what those stressful circumstances are, and how individuals act in order to accumulate and protect their resources. As we show in the following pages, both theories contribute to the understanding of the business trip phenomenon.

The Role of Resources

In this chapter, we attempt to enrich the theoretical basis of business trip research by embedding it in both Demerouti's JD-R model and Hobfoll's COR theory. Both theories emphasize the importance of resources. At the same time, psychological research has increasingly turned to an examination of the impact of people's resources on their stress resistance and well-being. It is therefore interesting to compare the role of resources in each of these theories in order to better understand business trip issues. According to COR theory (Hobfoll, 2001), people seek to obtain, retain, and protect resources which they value (e.g., material, social, personal, or energetic resources). Resources are those entities that are either centrally valued in their own right (e.g., self-esteem, close attachments, health, and inner peace) or function as a means to obtain centrally valued ends (e.g., money, social support, and credit). Accordingly, stress occurs when individuals (a) lose resources, (b) fail to gain resources following an investment of resources, or (c) are threatened with resource loss. Resource gain can prevent, offset, or forestall resource loss, as the resources accrued can be invested in making further gains and accumulating resource surpluses. Accordingly, a gain cycle generates its own positive energy to promote well-being. In addition, Hobfoll (2001) has argued that resource gain in itself has only a modest effect, but acquires its saliency in the context of resource loss. This implies that job resources gain their motivational potential particularly when employees are confronted with high job demands (and thus face potential resource depletion).

In the same vein, one of the propositions of the JD-R model (Bakker & Demerouti, 2007) is that job resources influence motivation or work engagement especially when job demands are high. According to the JD-R model, job resources may buffer the impact of job demands on strain. Typically, the buffering hypothesis explains interactions between job demands and job resources by proposing that the relationship between job demands and strain is weaker for those enjoying a high degree of job resources. This buffering assumption supports predictions regarding the level of the strain or motivation as a function of levels of demands and resources (Fig. 1).

Focusing on resources, business trips may cause resource loss for the traveler starting at the pretrip phase, due to related trip planning and job demands; through the trip phase, due to physical and psychological demands; and in the posttrip phase, which may be characterized by overload (Westman, 2004). Business trips, however, can help the traveler gain new resources. As Hobfoll and Shirom (2000) suggested, a relaxation period between stress episodes allows for resource gain, and the time away from the work site, even on a business trip, can be regarded as such a period. By leaving the regular working site and distancing themselves from the daily demands, travelers may not only stop the loss of resources resulting from job and family demands, but may also gain resources. Following COR theory principles, business trips can interrupt loss spirals and create gain spirals.

On the basis of these assumptions, we offer several predictions for business trips characterized by different levels of demands and resources. Business trips characterized by high demands and low resources result in a high level of strain and a low level of motivation; low demands and high resources result in a low level of strain and a high level of motivation; low demands and low resources result in a low level of strain and an moderate

		A	B
	High	Low strain High motivation	Average strain High motivation
		C	D
	Low	Low strain Average motivation	High strain Low motivation
		Low	**High**

Business Trip Resources (vertical axis label)

Business Trip Demands

Fig. 1. Predictions of Business Trips Outcomes Based on the Job Demands-Resources Model.

level of motivation; high levels of resources and high demands result in an moderate level of strain and a high level of motivation.

On the basis of the JD-R model, managers can improve employees' adjustment to business trips. Enriching travelers' resources before and during demanding trips will help reduce stress and burnout, and increase motivation and engagement. Understanding the results of the various combinations of demands and resources can help organizations plan business trip in such a way that they become a special type of respite that generates important benefits for travelers' well-being.

In the following section, we elaborate on specific resources such as perceived control, cultural intelligence (CQ), multi-cultural experiences, self-efficacy, and trip self-efficacy, which may be specifically relevant to business trip research.

Perceived Control
Perceived control is the extent to which individuals believes that they can directly affect their work environment (Spector, 1986). There is evidence

that individuals' subjective perception of the extent to which they can control events within their environment plays a more important role in influencing responses than the objective reality of the situation (Averill, 1973; Lazarus & Folkman, 1984). Perceived control has been extensively explored in situations that impose on individuals the need to cope with aversive stimuli, psychological threats or stress (Karasek, 1979; Kushnir & Melamed, 1991; Spector, 1986). The research literature has consistently demonstrated positive effects of perceived control for most people when facing a threatening situation (Averill, 1973; Karasek, 1979; Thompson, 1981; Skinner, 1996). Karasek (1979) argued that the interaction between high job demands and low perceived job control (or job decision latitude) leads to job-related strain. These findings suggest that perceived control is an important resource for business travelers. On the basis of several samples, Westman and Etzion (2004) found a negative relationship between the degree of perceived control over trip schedules (i.e., amount of advance notice) and perceived stress. Furthermore, control over the business trip schedule was related to positive work characteristics.

Cultural Intelligence
CQ is defined as "a person's capability for successful adaptation to new cultural settings" (Earley & Ang, 2003, p. 59). CQ is conceptualized as a complex, multi-factor individual attribute composed of cognitive, meta-cognitive, motivational, and behavioral components. According to Ang et al. (2007), the cognitive factor refers to an individual's level of cultural knowledge or knowledge of the cultural environment. The meta-cognitive factor refers to an individual's mental processes that are used to acquire and understand cultural knowledge and encompass the individual's cultural consciousness and awareness during cross-cultural interactions. The motivational factor refers to an individual's interest and drive to learn and adapt to new cultural surroundings. Finally, the behavioral factor refers to the extent to which an individual acts appropriately (verbally and nonverbally), is flexible and adjusts his or her behaviors to the specifics of each cultural interaction

Studying business travelers from Brazil, Israel, and Singapore, Tay, Westman, and Chia (2008) demonstrated that meta-cognitive, motivational, and behavioral CQ decreased travelers' burnout. This finding is consistent with COR theory, which views personal attributes such as CQ as resources (Hobfoll & Shirom, 2000). In the case of business travelers, CQ is likely to reduce or prevent burnout altogether. Business travelers who have greater cognitive and meta-cognitive CQ, i.e., are better informed and more aware and conscious of the cultural environment in different travel destinations, and thus are expected to be in a better position to cognitively plan and manage the stress that arises from interacting in the different cultural contexts during a business trip.

In the same way, business travelers who feel more efficacious, have greater motivation and drive to interact and work with others in different cultures (i.e., high motivational CQ), possess more psychological resources to address emotional demands and the stress of adjusting to different cultures. Motivation serves as an energy resource and is valued for its ability to add to the acquisition of other kinds of resources (Hobfoll, 1998). Therefore, business travelers, who are high in motivational CQ, can be expected to have greater drive and desire to develop personal and work resources to facilitate their intercultural business tasks and interactions that help ease travel stress. Similarly, travelers with higher behavioral CQ, i.e., those who can display a wide repertoire of verbal and nonverbal behaviors, possess more personal resources to prevent threatened loss of other resources needed to address issues that arise due to different cultural interactions.

One of the facilitators of CQ is *need for control*. Need for control is defined as the individual's desire and intent to exert influence over the situations in which he/she operates (see Burger, 1995). Need for control is conceptualized as an individual disposition and is a basic universal need (Gebhardt & Brosschot, 2002). DeCharms (1968) suggested that people need to feel a sense of mastery and personal competence in their environments. Indeed, Sutton and Kahn (1986) noted that the importance of control in organizational settings is "a persistent theme in the behavioral sciences" (p. 276). Thus, in the case of business travelers, the more intense their desire to control, the greater their desire to take action to understand the environment of the destination – which develops the individual's CQ.

An individual's need for control suggests a desire to minimize uncertainties, plan for contingences, and influence the outcomes or situations in which one finds himself or herself. Moreover, a high need for control tends to increase an individual's responsiveness or attentiveness to available resources, including their prior travel experiences, to their advantage.

Travelers with a high need for control are likely to read more about the destination, engage in serious planning of business trips, and be more motivated to learn about the people with whom they will interact during the trip and about their cultures. Such travelers are likely to have larger stores of cultural information (cognitive CQ), be more mindful of cultures in different travel destinations (meta-cognitive CQ), and more confident in and interested to learn about effective interactions in different destinations (motivational CQ). Travelers with greater need for control may monitor, adjust, and align their verbal and nonverbal behaviors to the cultural expectations of their business partners when visiting them. To minimize unexpected outcomes that may arise from inappropriate behaviors, travelers with a high need for control are more likely to develop broad and enhanced behavioral repertoires to match different cultural situations.

Indeed, Tay et al. (2008) found that need for control was positively associated with all four CQ dimensions (cognitive, meta-cognitive, motivational, and behavioral). This indicates that individuals who have a greater need to control their environment seek more cultural information, plan more extensively, are more motivated to learn and interact, and more extensively develop communication repertoires for socializing and networking with people in new cultural settings.

The expectation that travelers with a high need for control will be more proactive in anticipation of upcoming business trips is consistent with finding that managers with a high need for control used proactive coping before their business trips. Interviews of 36 managers from several high-tech companies showed that managers characterized by a high need for control used proactive coping strategies before their business trips; they assigned specific people to report to them about what was going on at the head office, assigned people to constantly keep in touch with them, and used several communications devices while away. These managers showed a higher tendency to plan the business trip with respect to delegation of tasks and authority to subordinates than managers with a low need for control. Managers with a high need for control also tended to maintain closer communications with the organization and with their subordinates than managers with a low need for control (see Westman & Etzion, 2004)

Multicultural Experiences
Multicultural experiences (MCE) represent business travelers' cultural exposure during their business trips. Thus, MCE can be measured by frequency of trips, number of different destinations, or length and intensity of exposure to different cultures. Thus, MCE is a similar resource to tenure and experience and at the same time helps building other resources. MCE provide the opportunities for business travelers to increase their knowledge of specific cultural environments (i.e., their cognitive CQ). For example, a large number of trips abroad to different destinations expand travelers' knowledge about different business and social cultural norms. Travelers with greater MCE have a larger number of opportunities to acquire and cultivate meta-cognitive strategies and interaction models, and

to develop greater cultural sensitivities to and awareness of cultural differences and norms.

Greater cross-cultural experiences should also build travelers' confidence in their ability to function in different cultures. Thus, MCE may be a source of efficacious beliefs on travelers' capability to interact and work with business partners from different cultures. We expect MCE to enhance traveler's motivational CQ. A greater number of trips abroad should also expose travelers to wider repertoires and deeper understanding of behavioral norms.

Self-Efficacy

Self-efficacy refers to beliefs in one's capabilities to organize and execute the courses of action required to manage prospective situations (Bandura, 1995). Bandura noted that self-efficacy should not be conceptualized or measured in terms of generalized feelings of mastery, but rather should be operationalized in reference to handling a specific situation or performing a specific behavior.

Self-efficacy has been studied widely in organizational contexts (Bandura, 1997). Research has shown that self-efficacy predicts several important work-related outcomes, including job attitudes, training proficiency, and job performance (Chen, Gully, & Eden, 2001). Self-efficacy has been related to more positive physical and emotional well-being, and has been linked in prospective studies to robust stress resistance in a broad spectrum of circumstances, ranging from minor hassles to major tragedies (Bandura, 1997).

Most researchers have conceptualized and studied self-efficacy as task-specific (e.g., Bandura, 1997; Gist & Mitchell, 1992; Lee & Bobko, 1994). In the business trips literature, however, business trip self-efficacy has not been widely studied. Business trip-related self-efficacy can be defined as an employee's perceived ability to function well on the job, despite the demands of a changing work environment when traveling. Travelers who doubt their ability to respond to the demands of a business trip are likely to focus attention on their feelings of incompetence, which will be accompanied by psychological distress and a failure to cope with the situation successfully. In contrast, employees who have high levels of business trip-related efficacy are unlikely to be distressed by feelings of inadequacy and, for this reason, are expected to persist in their efforts to manage the business trip efficiently and effectively. Self-efficacy may be a key resource for business travelers because those who possessed high levels of self-efficacy might be more capable of selecting, altering, and mobilizing other resources to meet stressful demands.

Eden (2001b) defined subjective efficacy as "one's overall assessment of all available resources that may be applied toward successfully performing a job" (p. 73). These may be internal resources, such as knowledge or willpower, or external resources, such as a car, work tools, or an IT system. According to Eden's (2001b) Internal–External Efficacy Beliefs model, *means efficacy* is subjective to external efficacy. It is defined as "the individual's belief in the utility of means available for performing the job" (Eden, 2001b, p. 74). Eden (2001b, p. 78) adds that "means efficacy is as motivating as self-efficacy; a high level of means efficacy motivates a person to use the means." In the context of business trips, means efficacy relates to the traveler's belief in the trip's importance.

BUSINESS TRIP CHARACTERISTICS

Despite technological advances and rapid growth in electronic communications, global managers recognize the significance of face-to-face interactions to close deals, solve problems, negotiate contracts, and develop mutual trust and respect (e.g., Govindarajan & Gupta, 2001). Consequently, with its increasing globalization and growing economic pressures, the twenty-first century is characterized by the increasing incidence of *short business trips* defined in the current study as traveling for the organization for periods of a week or so while crossing international borders. According to survey by the 2007 Chief Financial Officers (CFO), including all the leading firms in Israel, major Israeli companies incurred 972 million dollars in business trip-related expenses. According to US data, one in five of US adults traveled for business at least once in 2004, and US business travel generated an estimated $153.2 billion.

Though generally beneficial to organizations, researchers emphasize the toll these trips have on travelers and their families. DeFrank et al. (2000, p. 59) define travel stress as the "perceptual, emotional, behavioral and physical responses made by an individual to the various problems faced during one or more of the phases of travel." They refer to three specific phases of a business trip – pretrip, trip, and posttrip, and identify specific stressors for each phase. In terms of the JD-R model, these characteristics are business trip demands. Using COR terms, travel stress occurs when travelers' resources are depleted or threatened, or when they fail to gain resources following resource investment.

Pretrip stressors include *trip planning* (e.g., flights, hotels, appointments) and *work arrangements* (e.g., leaving the office in good order, delegating work to subordinates, or dealing with unanswered mail). According to DeFrank et al. (2000), some executives push themselves to tie as many loose ends as possible prior to departure, which may result in frustration and, ultimately, stress. Pretrip stressors also include *home and family issues*. A high percentage of business travelers are married and most find extended absences from home to be difficult. Before the trip, travelers work to make the absence as painless as possible (e.g., planning for unexpected emergencies, completing chores).

Trip stressors include *characteristics of the trip* (e.g., duration and intensity of the trip, unexpected complications) and the air travel itself (anxiety during flight, turbulence, uncomfortable seating, flight delays or cancellations, lost luggage etc.), and travel *logistics* (e.g., quality of accommodations and of communications infrastructure). When an effective communications infrastructure is unavailable and when regular e-mail/voice-mail communication is not possible, travel stress will increase and make effective performance more difficult. Trips stressors also include *job-related factors* (e.g., complex job assignments, worry about the work accumulating at the home office) and *cultural differences* (e.g., culture shock). DeFrank et al. (2000) indicate that unmet expectations and the need for cultural adjustments may lead to stress.

Posttrip issues include *job demands* (e.g., problems that emerged and decisions that were made in the traveler's absence, new projects developed and staffed without the traveler's input, backload of tasks awaiting the traveler on his or her return) and *family demands* (e.g., unfinished household chores, guilt over missing important events, addressing the needs of a spouse).

NEGATIVE IMPACT OF BUSINESS TRIPS

The literature reviewed thus far focuses on the various demands and stressors that might emerge as a consequence of traveling. The following section deals with findings concerning the outcomes of such stressors. There is some evidence that business travelers demonstrate physical and psychological strains (e.g., Rogers, 1998; Striker et al., 1999) as a result of the demands that they encounter.

One of the assumptions in the JD-R model is that two psychological processes play a role in the development of job strain and motivation. The demanding aspects of work (i.e., work overload or emotional demands) lead to depletion of energy, and, in the long run, to exhaustion (e.g., Demerouti et al., 2001). Dimberg et al. (2002) found that the demands of business trips resulted in a high level of stress for many travelers, who subsequently sought psychological treatment. Furthermore, they found that psychological disorders (anxiety, acute reaction to stress, and adjustments disorders) increased linearly with the number of business trips.

Although these studies related to business trips in general, consequences of specific characteristics of business trips have also been identified. Westman and Etzion (2004) demonstrated that length of trip, number of trips, flight delays, busy schedules, language difficulties, and jet lag were related to perceived stress and strain.

Employees who travel frequently must continually adjust to and switch between resident and traveling roles. Furthermore, their families may develop two separate routines – one for when the employee is present, and another for when the employee is absent. Thus, traveling impacts not only the traveler but the spouse and children. According to DeFrank et al. (2000), family stressors are most prominent before and after the trip. In the pretrip phase, these stressors can result from the inability to spend time with the family due to heavy workload, and in the posttrip phase they can result from the conflict between the needs of the tired and overloaded traveler and the family's demands. Leider (1991) also discussed the impact of travel stressors on the family and claimed that the temporary separation can place a strain on family relationships. He argued that as all three phases of the trip affect the family: and the longer the trip – the more intense the stress at each point.

Dennis (1997) reported that approximately 82% of the surveyed business travelers missed family events while away on business. As much as travelers try to maintain frequent contact with the family, even to the point of daily phone calls and help in the children's homework through fax, it hardly ever seems to be enough or to compensate for their physical absence from home. Thus, balancing work and family life has become a very serious issue for many business travelers. Rogers (1998) demonstrated the impact of traveling on the family. On the basis of a study of 140 traveling employees, she found that 73% described their business trips as having a negative impact on their family life.

Liese's (2000) findings demonstrate that the business traveler's experience of increased psychological disorders is mirrored in the family. The two sources of psychological strain experienced by the family are the difficulties caused by frequent absences of the spouse and crossover of the traveler's stress and strain to his/her spouse. Crossover is defined as a transmission of stress and strain between spouses (Westman, 2001), either through empathy or a conflictual interaction process (Westman & Vinokur, 1998).

Several studies suggest that business trips are especially stressful when they become a source of conflict between job and family demands. Business trips characteristics, such as long absences from home, last minutes changes in travel plans, and trips that interfere with special family events or holidays, are stressful for the travelers as for families. Furthermore, research suggests that men and women travelers experience such conflicts differently. Westman, Etzion, and Gortler (2004) examined fluctuations in the experience of work–family conflict (WFC) and burnout in different phases of business trips among 58 male and female business travelers. Travelers completed questionnaires at three points in time: prior to going abroad, during the stay abroad, and after their return. Findings indicated that both WFC and burnout fluctuated during the various phases of the trips, but these fluctuations were significant only when gender was controlled. They found a different pattern of fluctuation of WFC for men and women: Among men, WFC remained constant before and during the trip, but declined significantly in the posttrip phase. Among women, WFC declined from pretrip to mid-trip and then increased significantly on returning home. Thus, of the three phases of business travel, the return home constituted the period of lowest WFC for men, but the period of highest WFC for women. These findings corroborate findings by Liese (2000), who maintained that the return home is the most stressful experience for women.

Similar findings were demonstrated by Westman, Etzion, and Gattenio (2008) who examined fluctuations in the levels of WFC and FWC during the three different stages of international business trips among 66 business travelers. Analysis of variance detected differences in WFC and FWC levels between the three stages of the trip, indicating that the work–family interface is not static and varies according to different job and family demands. These fluctuations were moderated by gender. WFC and FWC remained relatively constant for men during the different stages of the trip, whereas for women, measures were lowest during the trip itself and highest on returning home. Furthermore, whereas for men the lowest levels of WFC and FWC were experienced on returning home, for women, they were the highest at that stage.

These findings do not support DeFrank et al. (2000), who claimed that the highest level of stress is before and after the trip, but they do support Liese (2000), who maintained that the return home is the most stressful experience for women. However, it should be noted that DeFrank et al. (2000) as well as Liese (2000) related to stress in general and not specifically to the conflict between work and family demands.

THE POSITIVE IMPACT OF BUSINESS TRIPS

As most of the reviewed research on business trips has focused on stress and strain, this section begins with theories and research pertaining to positive affects in general, such as positive psychology, COR theory, and the JD-R model. Positive psychology is an umbrella term for the study of positive emotions, positive character traits, and enabling institutions. The aim of positive psychology is to catalyze a shift of focus of psychology, from an exclusive preoccupation with repairing the worst things in life to building positive qualities (Seligman & Csikszentmihalyi, 2000). This section of the chapter focuses on the positive aspects of business trip from the perspective of the COR and JD-R models.

According to the JD-R model, job resources play an important role in producing employee well-being (Bakker & Demerouti, 2007; Demerouti et al., 2001). Resource gain occurs during business travel not only through passively experiencing the positive effects of the trip, but also through proactive behavior. The different ways in which people cope with business travel experiences may represent in proactive behavior, and thus result in minimizing the resource loss and increasing the resource gain. Proactive behavior consists of efforts to build up general resources that facilitate the achievement of challenging goals and promote personal growth. In proactive coping (Greenglass, 2002), people perceive risks, demands, and opportunities as challenges. Proactive coping is based on either acquiring resources or preventing loss of resources (Westman, 2004). Conclusions from Westman's (2004) qualitative study suggest that coping is situation-specific, and a strategy that is instrumental in one phase of the trip is not necessarily instrumental in another phase.

DeFrank et al. (2000) performed a thorough review of the stressors and strains that business trips entail. The proportion of negative versus positive effects in their review is typical of stress research, which until recently has focused primarily on negative outcomes. In their review, only a few sentences are devoted to the possible positive outcomes of business trip stressors and strains

> For many, travel can be very educational, providing exposure to new places and cultures, and even giving insight into new business practices and product ideas. It can lead to individual growth, broadening one's awareness of domestic and global issues and enhancing one's sensitivity to the concerns of other populations (p. 59).

More recent studies have recognized that business trips can bring about positive effects, such as insights into new business practices and productive ideas, individual growth, and respite from routine work demands (Welch & Worm, 2006). Furthermore, Presser and Hermsen (1996) have indicated that business trips often evoke a sense of independence from one's immediate supervisors and colleagues while away. Westman and Etzion (2002) concluded that the decrease in job stress and burnout of their high-tech respondents may be evidence of a delayed respite. Though these travelers experienced a heavy workload and much ambiguity during the trip, they also enjoyed the physical detachment from their office and their families.

Furthermore, business travelers have an opportunity to undergo new experiences and gain a sense of personal accomplishment. Thus, travel that is not routine may be perceived as stimulating and contributing to personal development and initiative, offering a source of variety, challenges, and new experiences. Additionally, several researchers (e.g., Oddou, Mendenhall, & Ritchie, 2000) claim that business trips may be important for future occupational advancement, as personal skills required by leaders in the globalized world are skills acquired during business trips such as initiative, open-mindedness, and ability to adapt to cultural differences.

Although business travelers are away on a business trip, they are not subject to the regular job demands, including the organizational physical character-istics such as environment, boss, and peers. Nor do they have to cope with the daily family demands. In addition, they have the positive experience of gaining new resources in the form of new friends, increased sense of self-efficacy, new cultural experiences, rest, and other pleasurable experiences.

It seems that the better a person copes with business trip demands, the greater the gain in personal and social resources (self-confidence, support from others); as the reservoir of resources at one's disposal increases, one is better able to cope with future situations. In COR theory terms (Hobfoll, 1989), this can be viewed as a spiral of resource gain: General well-being can improve the personal and work results of the business trip, and these results increase the resources available for coping on the next trip. In this sense, the more experience gained in business trips, the higher the chance that such trips will be experienced as positive events that increase well-being.

Change of attitude can transform what used to be a negative, stressful experience into an enjoyable experience that increases the person's well-being. Lazarus and Folkman (1984) and Folkman and Moskowitz (2000) describe the mechanisms that allow for positive coping with stressful experiences to occur. These mechanisms are positive reappraisal (through which the meaning of the situation is changed in a way that allows the person to experience positive emotions and psychological well-being), problem-focused coping (possible even in situations with very little personal control), and creation of positive events (infusion of ordinary events with positive meaning or finding humor in otherwise stressful situations). These mechanisms explain how people can not only survive the stress of a business trip, but even transform the trip into an experience that increases their personal resource reservoir and their well-being.

Business trips are in fact a family experience: The traveler's absence affects the family directly, through his or her physical absence, and indirectly, through the crossover of positive and negative emotional states between spouses (Westman, 2001). Espino et al.'s (2002) findings indicate that frequent travel increases the strain on the family and, as a by-product, contributes significantly to the traveler's stress. This finding may also be a product of crossover of stress and strain from one spouse to the other. At the same time, business trips may also be a positive experience and begin a positive spiral. The positive impact of business trips, such as exposure to new places and cultures, insight into new business practices and product ideas, individual growth, and physical detachment from home and workplace, has rarely been studied. However, in recent years positive psychology has come to the forefront of research, demonstrating very promising findings. If the business trip is perceived as a respite, there is ground for positive crossover to operate between the spouses. Westman et al. (2009), for example, found vigor crossing over from the spouses to the travelers, whereas Etzion and Westman (2001) found that the crossover of burnout detected among couples before a trip abroad vanished when they returned from the trip.

EVIDENCE FROM INTERVIEWS

Characteristics of the Business Trip

We extended previous research by interviewing business travelers, with the aim of obtaining an initial and detailed overview of how business trips affect travelers during the different stages of the trip and how business travelers cope with the stressors that characterize the different stages of the business trip. Interviewees were 75 business travelers,[1] 59 men (average age 42), and 14 women (average age 36). At the next stage, the research team read the transcriptions and for each interview question and each stage of the trip (before, during the journey, during the stay abroad, and after the return) identified: (a) the main themes relating to negative and positive aspects of the trip, (b) the coping strategies employed, (c) available organizational support, and (d) the effects of the trip on the traveler and on the family. A preliminary review of all the interviews yielded a list of themes for each subject. A total of 146 themes were identified. The interviews provide evidence and examples for all the issues we dealt with in the previous section, specifying their occurrence along the various stages of the trip. The interviews were analyzed according to the terms of the JD-R model (Table 1). The list of themes is detailed in the first column. Demands are detailed in the second column and resources are detailed in the third column. We classified four groups of resources according to the typology of resources suggested by COR theory (Hobfoll, 1989). For instance, the COR theory term "objects" includes flight conditions; the term "energy" includes time for myself; the term "conditions" includes professional development; and the term "personal characteristics" includes personal growth.

The first type of resource is classified by the JD-R as resources that are instrumental in achieving work goals, namely organizational support, a sense of control over the trip, time for professional preparations, networking, and trip success. In the following quote, the interviewee addresses organizational

Table 1.   Themes Emerging from the Interviews Listed According to JD-R Model and COR Theory Terms.

Themes[a]	Demands[b]	Resources[c]
Concerns regarding work at home	+	
Difficulty to adapting to a new place	+	
Professional requirements of the work abroad	+	
Difficulties concerning the time of coming back	+	
Conditions during the stay	+	Objects
Free time, leisure activities		Energies
Prestige, reputation		Conditions
Professional development		Conditions
Exposure to new places		Conditions
Regular contact with family and friends		Social support
Receiving organizational support		POS
Happily anticipating the return home		Personal characteristics
Help from the extended family		Personal characteristics
Focusing on work		Personal characteristics
Focusing on the positive aspect of the trip		Personal characteristics
Acceptance of the trip as a part of the job		Personal characteristics
Personal traits that facilitate coping		Personal characteristics

[a]List of themes.
[b]Several kinds of demands.
[c]Resources, classified in COR terms.

support *"My organization has created opportunities – we have developed a ritual whereby country directors can bring their spouses if they like and it becomes a team building and social ritual so that the spouses can become acquainted with the colleagues and the work their spouses are doing and that helps. I think there are many more steps my organization could be taking, but, relative to many organizations, my organization is extremely sensitive and understanding about personal needs and issues. If I can't take a trip because I have an important family event, the organization will be understanding."* Fifteen different themes relating to organizational support were reported by respondents, emphasizing the role of this resource for the traveler.

Other types of resources organizations can supply are resources that reduce job demands and their associated physiological and psychological costs, such as flight conditions or conditions during the journey. *"I run up large telephone bills for my company. But I think that's also an important thing that I do – phone home every day and say hello ..."* or *"Our organization teaches people English which generally helps [us] on the trips."*

The third type of resources that are instrumental in achieving work goals are those that stimulate personal growth, such as learning, breaking out of the routine, making time for oneself, leisure activities, professional development, exposure to a new places. For example *"An advantage of business trips is meeting people, learning about the local culture and other new things that I wasn't aware of; to say nothing of shopping ..."* or *"The business trip helped me understand my job better ... I got a better perspective about the goals and how to achieve them. On a personal level, it helped me get ideas about my career ..."*

Many quotes mention other key resources such as social support or control. *"I talked about the trip with my colleagues. This conversation helped me prepare and cope with my trip.".: "I have quite a bit [of control] in terms of flexibility of dates. My daughter is in a one-act play on Thursday night and I was actually scheduled to be away on a trip. When I discovered the dates, I could just imagine my daughter's face; When I told her [I would be away] she was just so crestfallen and she said 'Are you going to be gone?' and I said 'Is that the day of your play? Well then, no way, I'll just reschedule,' and she was just so-o-o thrilled and her face just lit up."*

Other interviewees mentioned the characteristics of the trips, for example *"There is always a feeling that a very tiring trip is ahead of me. The flight to NY is the most difficult, seats are very narrow, you can't stretch your legs, it's very uncomfortable ..." "If your flight is delayed, you could miss your next connection. It's work related in a way because it upsets your routine when you get to the other end. Maybe you miss a meeting, maybe you have to reschedule it, maybe you won't be able to reschedule."*

Negative and Positive Impact of the Trip on the Traveler and the Family

The main themes that emerged from the interviews were negative and positive experiences, as well as the typical coping strategies used at each stage of the trip: before the trip, during the stay abroad, and after return. In general, travelers mentioned more negative than positive aspects of the trip. For example, interviewees noted the negative aspects during the pretrip stage relating the family *"My youngest daughter, she's nine years old, she's said 'Oh, why you are going away again? You are not around when I need you for my homework.'"* A second interview stated, *"The business trip has a price both in professional and the personal life. The separation from the family is not simple ..."*

On the other hand, some interviewees focused on the positive aspect of the business trips. For example *"breaking the routine, more interesting issues to deal with, meeting new people, gaining new knowledge ..."* or *"It has helped me put a perspective on the wonderful opportunities that we have ..."* and *"To be invited to South Africa to give a talk is in itself an ego boost. To go to Singapore and address senior management in a client company about leadership trends that you are seeing and cultural changes from your perspectives – that is esteem enhancing"* or *"I think travel and cultural experience, including language acquisition have greatly benefited my self-esteem."* Another interviewee focused on yet another positive aspect of the trip *"We do need to travel a lot and my career has flourished because of that, because wherever you travel you exchange ideas with people from different countries, and you share experiences, and that adds to your knowledge."*

The following quotes reflect statements that refer to the negative aspects of the business trip *"I think the main thing is the need to get everything done. On most trips you feel that had you stayed a day longer you would have accomplished what you set out to do." "What do you think causes pressure during the trip? ... the knowledge that work and mail is building up and waiting for me in the office"* and *"Professionally it meant dealing with certain things alone, when it is difficult to consult my team the way I'm used to, because of distance and communication problems. You have to do everything there by yourself, and you have a lot of responsibility."*

Interviewees also noted the negative repercussions on their marriage or relationships *"There's always pressure at home. Whenever I go away for two and a half weeks and my girlfriend expects me to get home early on those few evenings beforehand so that we can spend some time together."* The negative aspects of the trip are also reflected in the following statement by a traveler's wife *"getting his work done so that he feels he can leave and not have everything fall apart. Generally, he ends up spending a lot of extra hours before trips just trying to wrap up projects and getting work done." "When I have to go out on short notice, from one day to the next, there is a stress of making sure I am professionally prepared for the job"* or *"Once I used to stay at the office till three in the morning before a trip clearing my desk."* One traveler went one step further and commented *"The organization should provide professional help to people who are suffering the effects of travel. We have had several divorces, and several very strained marriages."* Another travelers related to the expectations from the organization, for example *" the organization doesn't help … I would like them to fund a nanny three afternoons a week and help my wife with the kids when I am on a business trip."*

BUSINESS TRIPS: A CONCEPTUAL MODEL

On the basis of respite and business travel literature, Westman (2004) developed a theoretical framework for business travels embedded in COR theory.

On the basis of a series of open-ended, in-depth exploratory interviews conducted with 35 professional employees (from Israel, the U.S., and Sweden) who travel between 3 and 28 days as part of their jobs, making 3–24 trips per year, Westman (2004) proposed a meta-model (Fig. 2) for outlining the relationships between the various facets of the business travel process. A basic assumption of the model is that business trips are job events that occur over time, therefore, suggesting that each business trip is an unfolding experience consisting of four phases (1) pretrip; (2) journey (e.g. flight); (3) stay; (4) posttrip, each with distinct gains and losses. Furthermore, such trips are viewed as elements in a cycle, where gains and losses from previous trips impact the experiences and outcomes of the following trips.

Fig. 2 distinguishes between several facets and constructs: job demands, family demands, business trips gains and losses of resources, coping, personal characteristics, family status, trip characteristics, organizational support, and personal and family outcomes. According to the model, job and family demands may cause losses and gains at different phases of the trip (arrows from A and B to C), whereas the gains and losses of the trip affect the perception of job and family demands (arrows from C to A and B). Each phase of the trip (Box C) has unique but also similar negative and positive events, losses, and gains of resources. To illustrate, the pretrip phase is characterized by overload, excitement, and expectations of gain. The journey phase is characterized by good or bad flight conditions; The stay phase is

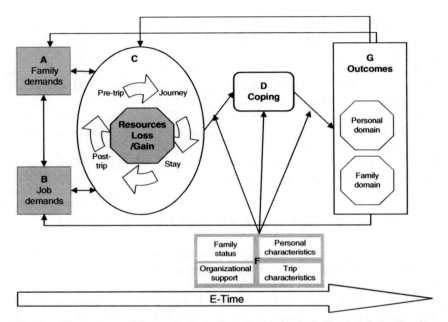

Fig. 2. The Impact of Short Business Travels on the Individual and the Family.

characterized by overload, loneliness, new experiences, detachment, whereas the return phase characterized by overload, success, or failure.

The model also indicates the importance of time (Box E), as each phase of trip affects the others, and each event unfolds and affects other trips and other facets at different points in time. The loss and gain spirals affect the coping process (Box D), which impacts (arrow from D to G) personal and family consequences. Box F includes trip characteristics (length, duration), personal characteristics (age, gender, experience, and self esteem), family status (married, with children), and organizational support: These affect the coping process and moderate the relationship between coping and outcomes.

The findings of the interviews demonstrated that each phase of the trip was characterized by different resources acquired or saved. Across all four business trip phases, the gained resources mentioned most frequently were social support, followed by time, relaxation, control, energies, and objects.

Westman's (2004) study provided insight into the dynamics of business trip demands, resources, and coping behaviors. The model offers a guide for research which aims to determine how experiences and processes in the work and family domain are linked among business travelers and their spouses.

SUMMARY AND CONCLUSIONS

This chapter opened with a literature review on respite and recovery, with the aim of understanding the specific characteristic of business trips. By conceptualizing business trips as a unique kind of "on the job" respite, we provide insight into the dynamics of business trip demands, resources, and outcomes, and focus not only on negative, stressful aspects of business trips, but on the positive aspects as well. Furthermore, we expand the understanding of the business trip phenomenon by basing our reasoning on both COR theory and JD-R model. In this summary section, we also raise several important groups of questions regarding business trips: first, *What is the impact of the separation from the family on the traveler? Is the separation always a stressor or does it also have a positive dimension, namely a sense of detachment? Can we identity the separation conditions that have a negative or positive impact?* Second, *What are the positive impacts of business trips?* The third group of questions concerns the main issue of this chapter *Can a business trip be considered as a unique kind of respite?* Finally, we provide theoretical and practical recommendations.

The Impact of the Separation from Family

As indicated, an important issue in business trips research is the dual effect on the family and the traveler. Although some research findings demonstrate a negative impact of the trip on the traveler and his/her family, other findings that show positive outcomes of business trips to the traveler and to the family. Business trips afford detachment from home, spouse, and children, that serves as a respite to the traveler. As one of the traveler stated in his interview *"When they (the children) were younger it was also nice to be away for a couple of days, because I could relax from all the voices back home and all the noise and all the questions and things like that."* Another traveler indicated that distance makes the hearts grow fonder *"it helps me remember why we decided to get married."*

Thus, though the separation from home may be stressful to travelers, it also releases them from home and family responsibilities. Although they miss their family and may be concerned about how they manage alone, the detachment enables the travelers to temporarily rest from their family responsibilities for a while and regroup resources. The negative or positive impact depends on quality of relationship between partners, age of children, spouse's support, frequency, and length of trip, and other factors.

Positive Impact of the Trip

We suggest that characteristics of the trip (such as destination, length, and purpose), environmental factors, and individual factors (such as control, CQ, and self-efficacy) potentially develop an individual's positive experience of respite during and after a business trip. These individual factors, or resources, are part of a gain spiral in combating burnout and increasing engagement. Another important factor is the perception of the trip as a negative or positive experience. Although this obviously depends on the nature of the experience itself, it is also a function of expectations from the trip and negative and positive effects. Westman and Eden (1997) found that among employees who were satisfied from their vacation, stress and burnout declined more than among employees who were not satisfied. Similarly, Etzion et al. (1998) found that the more military reserve service was perceived by reservists as a positive experience, the greater the drop in the levels of stress and burnout on their return to work. Consistent with COR theory and JD-R model and findings, business travelers who have more resources or gained resources were better able to enjoy the positive impact of the trip.

Business Trips as a Unique Kind of Respite

An appreciation of the dual impact of business trips contributes to our understanding of whether and under what conditions business trips can be considered a unique kind of respite. The contrast between individuals' well-being on and off their regular job is addressed in a general manner in respite research, and addressed more specifically by business trip research literature. Thus, these two lines of research could be mutually enriching. However, the main difference between business trips and other kinds of respite is that people on respite from their job (e.g., vacation) may completely disengage from their jobs, whereas business travelers' detachment is limited to the physical job environment: They may experience a change in venue but not in job overload and responsibility. According to Westman and Eden (1997), "a respite from work ... when the *everyday regular pressures* of the job are absent" (p. 516). Thus, in a business trip, the *everyday regular pressures* of the job are absent, but there is overload, responsibility, and cultural difficulties. Another reason why we may consider business trips as a unique kind of respite is the results from the few before–after studied that demonstrated a decline in job stress and burnout after returning from the trip. As in the case of military reserve service, the change in venue and the physical detachment from the workplace and the home enhance the respite effects of the business trip.

It seems that business trips are dualistic experiences, consisting of demands and resources, or losses and gains, all impacting on the well-being of the travelers and their families. Furthermore, as we saw in the literature review and the interviews, business trips may have different effects on different people. Although some individuals will bloom and find a trip exhilarating, others may be almost debilitated by the same experience. Characteristics such as family status, quality of relationships between partners, need for control and sense of control, self-efficacy, positive and negative affectivity, and CQ impact the perception and experience of the business trip.

Learning what makes business trips a positive experience might help us counsel business travelers on how to benefit more from their time away from their regular work site. It may help managers understand and reinforce some of the resources emerging during business trip that may have an impact on their traveling subordinates. While away, most travelers have some free time for leisure activities including physical exercise, visiting museums and or the theater, going for walks in new places, and other similar activities that offer opportunities for personal growth and engagement.

Haworth (1997) and Iso-Ahola (1997) claim that involvement in leisure activities has a great restorative effect. Being actively involved in activities implies that people have to concentrate and divert attention to that activity, which helps to disengage from the previous activities. Thus, specific trip duties on the one hand, and the exploration of new things on the other hand, may help travelers disengage from the chronic daily hassles at work in the home office, and help "switch off." A logical conclusion from this perspective is that a relaxation period between periods of chronic stress, even if it entails other but different stressors, allows regrouping of resources.

RECOMMENDATIONS

DeFrank et al. (2000) indicated that problems caused by business trips can severely disrupt an executive's ability to perform effectively for the organization while away, and may even adversely influence performance after the return to the office. These difficulties have major implications for the success of organizations and for the physical and emotional health of employees and their families, and highlight the importance to the organization of taking care of the well-being of their employees partaking in business trips. Thus, though we highlighted positive aspects of the trip, we must be cautious and manage the negative aspects.

Korn (1999) recommends two approaches to deal with travel stress – proactive coping, which attempts to reduce demands and stressors before they occur, and reactive coping, which aims to counteract the effects of stressors once they have emerged. These recommendations are consistent with Quick, Quick, Nelson, & Hurrel's (1997) primary and secondary prevention model, which maintains that "Preventive stress management helps one convert stress from a threat into opportunity for health and achievement" (p. 304). According to Striker et al. (1999), organizations should provide more support (resources) for maintaining a balance between work and home demands. Thus, legitimized time off, such as an optional day off prior to or after the trip, whether the option is actually exercised by the traveler or not, might also help relieve stress by giving travelers more of a sense of control. Travelers discussed stress-preventive measures in the interviews. One traveler stated, *"Reducing stressors before they occur (e.g., a day of rest after returning from a trip, long enough notice concerning a trip, support service for families), counteracting the effects of stressors after they occur and maximizing the positive effects of travels can be facilitated by the organization."* Another interviewee stated, *"Executives must recognize the work-family concerns of their 'frequent travelers.'"* The extent to which the organization recognizes the strain that business travel places on its employees and their families, and the extent to which the organization implements countervailing procedures will affect the success or failure of its international operations.

In sum, business trips are a unique kind of respite that contains a work-related component. Similar to the circumstances of other types of respite, business travelers are not in their usual surroundings and not performing their routine jobs. Business trips provide an opportunity to gain resources, which is consistent with one of the most important characteristics of respite. Hence, embedding business trip research in respite research enriches both the respite literature and business trip literature. The main conclusion is that the more elements of respite the business traveler experiences during the trip, the higher the positive impact on the traveler, the family, and the organization. We suggest broadening the scope of respite research by comparing patterns of business trips to learn how different degrees of disengagement (e.g., frequent to no communication with home office, having a spouse join the traveler on the trip, having a vacation after completing the overseas job) relate to indices of stress and strain on the one hand and to engagement on the other hand. This would be a natural extension that would shed light on many of the same issues addressed by respite research.

Knowledge about the impact of the business trips opens new directions for research and applications in organizations. We recommend that additional studies follow this line of research, in an effort to identify additional business trip stressors, resources, and important moderators that will allow us to predict who will benefit from what kind of a respite, using longitudinal designs and embedding the research in theory. Although a number of studies have based their contentions on COR theory (e.g., Westman, 2004; Westman & Etzion, 2002), this chapter proposes adding the JD-R model (Bakker & Demerouti, 2007; Demerouti et al., 2001) to the theoretical grounding of business trip research. This line of theorizing and other avenues should be further investigated.

Finally, on the basis of the accumulated knowledge and acquired understanding, future research on business trips should seek to expand our knowledge about the importance of the characteristics of the trips. What other kinds of resources can impact the travelers' well-being? Which resources are most beneficial to travelers? How can the travelers use these trips as a respite? What can business travelers do to experience these trips as a respite? Knowledge about these issues would strength both COR theory and JD-R model, and their contribution to the business trip field.

NOTE

1. Unfortunately, in two interviews the gender information was missing.

REFERENCES

Ang, S., Van Dyne, L., Koh, C., Ng, K., Templer, K. J., Tay, C., & Chandrasekar, N. A. (2007). Cultural intelligence: Its measurement and effects on cultural judgment and decision making, cultural adaptation, and task performance. *Management and Organization Review, 3*, 335–371.

Averill, J. R. (1973). Personal control over aversive stimuli its relationship to stress. *Psychological Bulletin, 80*, 286–303.

Bakker, A. B., & Demerouti, E. (2007). The job demands-resources model: State of the art. *Journal of Managerial Psychology, 22*, 309–328.

Bakker, A. B., Demerouti, E., & Schaufeli, W. B. (2003). Dual processes at work in a call centre: An application of the job demands-resources model. *European Journal of Work and Organizational Psychology, 12*, 393–417.

Bandura, A. (1995). Exercise of personal and collective efficacy in changing societies. In: A. Bandura (Ed.), *Self-efficacy in changing societies* (pp. 1–45). New York: Cambridge University Press.

Bandura, A. (1997). *Self-efficacy: The exercise of control*. New York: Freeman.

Burger, J. M. (1995). Need for control and self-esteem: Two routes to a high desire for control. In: M. H. Kernis (Ed.), *Efficacy, agency, and self-esteem* (pp. 217–233). New York: Plenum Press.

Caplan, R. D., & Jones, K. W. (1975). Effects of work-load, role ambiguity and Type-A personality on anxiety, depression and heart rate. *Journal of Applied Psychology, 60*, 713–719.

Chen, G., Gully, S. M., & Eden, D. (2001). Validation of a new general self-efficacy scale. *Organizational Research Methods, 4*, 62–83.

Chernis, C. (1981). Preventing burnout: From theory to practice. In: J. W. Jones (Ed.), *The burnout syndrome* (pp. 172–176). London: House Management Press.

Cunningham, J. B. (1997). *The stress management sourcebook*. Los Angeles, CA: Lowell House.

Davidson, O. B., Eden, D., & Westman, M. (2009). *Sabbatical leave relief from job stress: Who gains and how much?* Working Paper no. 9/2009. The Israel Institute of Business Research, Tel Aviv University.

DeCharms, R. (1968). *Personal causation: The internal affective determinants of behavior*. New York: Academic Press.

DeFrank, R. S., Konopaske, R., & Ivancevich, J. M. (2000). Executive travel stress: Perils of the road warrior. *Academy of Management Executive, 14*, 58–71.

Demerouti, E., Bakker, A. B., Nachreiner, F., & Schaufeli, W. B. (2001). The job demands-resources model of burnout. *Journal of Applied Psychology, 86*, 499–512.

Dennis, A. (1997). The life of a road warrior. *Journal of Accountancy, 184*, 89–91.

Dimberg, L. A., Striker, J., Nordanlycke-Yoo, C., Nagy, L., Mundt, K. A., & Sulsky, S. I. (2002). Mental health insurance claims among spouses of frequent business travelers. *Occupational and Environmental Medicine, 59*, 175–181.

Earley, P. C., & Ang, S. (2003). *Cultural intelligence: Individual interactions across cultures*. Palo Alto, CA: Stanford University Press.

Eden, D. (1990). Acute and chronic job stress, strain, and vacation relief. *Organizational Behavior and Human Decision Processes, 45*, 175–193.

Eden, D. (2001a). Vacation and other respites: Studying stress on and off the job. In: C. L. Cooper & I. T. Robertson (Eds), *International review of industrial and organizational psychology* (pp. 121–146). Chichester, UK: Wiley.

Eden, D. (2001b). Means efficacy: External sources of general and specific subjective efficacy. In: M. Erez, U. Kleinbeck & H. Thierry (Eds), *Work motivation in the context of a globalizing economy*. Hillsdale, NJ: Lawrence Erlbaum.

Espino, C. M., Sundstorm, S. M., Frick, H. L., Jacobs, M., & Peters, M. (2002). International business travel: Impact on families and travelers. *Occupational and Environmental Medicine, 59,* 309–322.

Etzion, D. (1984). The moderating effect of social support on the relationship of stress and burnout. *Journal of Applied Psychology, 69,* 619–624.

Etzion, D. (2003). Annual vacation: Duration of relief from job stressors and burnout. *Anxiety, Stress, and Coping, 16,* 213–226.

Etzion, D., & Boklis, V. (2006). Meta-analytic of respite and fade-out effects. Presented at the 26th Annual Convention of STAR, Rethymnon, Crete, Greece.

Etzion, D., & Dar, A. (2004). *Leave and leisure worldwide: A cross-cultural comparison among the USA, the EU, Japan and Israel.* Working Paper No. 21/04. The Henry Crown Institute of Business Research in Israel, Faculty of Management, The Leon Recanati Graduate School of Business Administration, Tel Aviv University.

Etzion, D., Eden, D., & Lapidot, Y. (1998). Relief from job stressors and burnout: Reserve service as a respite. *Journal of Applied Psychology, 83,* 577–585.

Etzion, D., Kafry, D., & Pines, A. (1982). Tedium among managers: A cross-cultural American–Israeli comparison. *Journal of Psychology and Judaism, 7*(1), 30–40.

Etzion, D., & Pines, A. (1986). Sex and culture in burnout and coping among human service professionals: A social psychological perspective. *Journal of Cross-Cultural Psychology, 17*(2), 191–209.

Etzion, D., & Westman, M. (2001). Vacation and the crossover of strain between spouses: Stopping the vicious cycle. *Man and Work, 11,* 106–118.

Folkman, S., & Moskowitz, J. T. (2000). Stress, positive emotion and coping. *Current Directions in Psychological Science, 9,* 115–118.

Frankenhaeuser, M., Lundberg, U., Fredrikson, M., Melin, B., Tuomisto, M., Myrsten, A.-L., Hedman, M., Bergman-Losman, B., & Wallin, L. (1989). Stress on and off the job as related to sex and occupational status in white-collar workers. *Journal of Organizational Behavior, 10,* 321–346.

Freudenberger, H. J. (1974). Staff burnout. *Journal of Social Issues, 30,* 159–165.

Fritz, C., & Sonnentag, S. (2005). Recovery, health, and job performance: Effects of weekend experiences. *Journal of Occupational Health Psychology, 10,* 187–199.

Fritz, C., & Sonnentag, S. (2006). Recovery, well-being, and performance related outcomes: The role of workload and vacation experiences. *Journal of Applied Psychology, 91,* 936–945.

Gebhardt, W. A., & Brosschot, J. F. (2002). Desirability of control: Psychometric properties and relationships with locus of control, personality, coping, and mental and somatic complaints in three Dutch samples. *European Journal of Personality, 16,* 423–438.

Gist, M. E., & Mitchell, T. R. (1992). Self-efficacy: A theoretical analysis of its determinants and malleability. *Academy of Management Review, 17,* 183–211.

Govindarajan, V., & Gupta, A. K. (2001). *The quest for global dominance.* San Francisco, CA: Jossey-Bass.

Greenglass, E. (2002). Proactive coping. In: E. Frydenberg (Ed.), *Beyond coping: Meeting goals, vision, and challenges* (pp. 37–62). London: Oxford University Press.

Gump, B. B., & Matthews, K. A. (2000). Are vacations good for your health? The 9-year mortality experience after the multiple risk factor intervention trial. *Psychosomatic Medicine, 62,* 608–612.

Gustafson, P. (2006). Work-related travel, gender and family obligations. *Work, Employment & Society, 20*, 513–530.

Hartig, T. (2004). Restorative environments. In: C. Spielberger (Ed.), *Encyclopedia of applied psychology* (Vol. 3, pp. 273–279). San Diego, CA: Academic Press.

Haworth, J. T. (1997). *Work, leisure and well-being*. London: Routledge.

Hobfoll, S. E. (1989). Conservation of resources: A new attempt at conceptualizing stress. *American Psychologist, 44*, 513–524.

Hobfoll, S. E. (1998). *Stress, culture and community: The psychology and philosophy of stress*. New York: Plenum.

Hobfoll, S. E. (2001). The influence of culture community and the nested-self in the stress process: Advancing conservation of resources theory. *Applied Psychology: An International Journal, 50*, 337–421.

Hobfoll, S. E., & Shirom, A. (2000). Conservation of resources theory: Applications to stress and management in the workplace. In: R. T. Golembiewski (Ed.), *Handbook of organization behavior* (pp. 57–81). New York: Dekker.

Iso-Ahola, S. (1997). A psychological analysis of leisure and health. In: J. T. Haworth (Ed.), *Work, leisure and well-being*. London: Routledge.

Ivancevich, J. M., & Konopaske, R. S. (2003). Business travel stress: A model, propositions and managerial implications. *Work and Stress, 17*, 138–157.

Jex, S. M., & Beehr, T. H. (1991). Emerging theoretical and methodological issues in the study of work-related stress. *Research in Personnel and Human Resources Management, 9*, 311–365.

Kahn, R. L., Wolfe, D. M., Quinn, R. P., Snoek, J. D., & Rosenthal, R. A. (1964). *Organizational stress: Studies in role conflict and ambiguity*. New York: Wiley.

Karasek, R. A. (1979). Job demands, job decision latitude and mental strain: Implications for job redesign. *Administrative Science Quarterly, 24*, 285–307.

Korn, I. (1999). Stress test. *Successful Meetings, 48*, 42–44.

Kushnir, T., & Melamed, S. (1991). Workload, perceived control and psychological distress in type A/B industrial workers. *Journal of Organizational Behavior, 12*, 155–168.

Lazarus, R. S., & Folkman, S. (1984). *Stress, appraisal and coping*. New York: Springer.

Lee, C., & Bobko, P. (1994). Self-efficacy beliefs: Comparison of five measures. *Journal of Applied Psychology, 79*, 364–369.

Leider, R. J. (1991). Till travel do us part. *Training and Development, 45*(5), 46–51.

Liese, B. (2000). International business travel and stress: Common ground for the individual and the organization. Paper presented at the International Travel health Symposium.

Lounsbury, J. W., & Hoopes, L. L. (1986). A vacation from work: Changes in work and nonwork outcomes. *Journal of Applied Psychology, 71*(3), 392–401.

Maslach, C. (1976). Burnout. *Human Behavior, 5*(9), 16–22.

Oddou, G., Mendenhall, M., & Ritchie, J. (2000). Leveraging travel as a tool for global leadership development. *Human Resource management, 39*, 159–172.

Pines, A., Aronson, E., & with Kafry, D. (1981). *Burnout: From tedium to personal growth*. New York: Free Press.

Presser, H., & Hermsen, J. (1996). Gender differences in determinants of work-related overnight travel among employed Americans. *Work and Occupation, 23*, 87–115.

Quick, J. C., Quick, J. D., Nelson, D., & Hurrel, J. (1997). *Preventive stress management in organizations*. Washington, DC: American Psychological Association.

Repetti, R. L. (1993). Short-term effects of occupational stressors on daily mood and health complaints. *Health Psychology, 12*, 125–131.

Rogers, H. L. (1998). *A survey of the travel health experiences of international business travelers.* A thesis submitted to the Faculty of Graduate Studies of Nursing, Calgary, Alberta.

Rubinstein, C. (1980). Vacations, expectations, satisfactions, frustrations, fantasies. *Psychology Today, 14,* 62–76.

Seligman, M. E. P., & Csikszentmihalyi, M. (2000). Positive psychology: An introduction. *American Psychologist, 55,* 5–14.

Skinner, E. A. (1996). A guide to constructs of control. *Journal of Personality and Social Psychology, 71,* 549–570.

Sonnentag, S. (2001). Work, recovery activities, and individual well-being: A diary study. *Journal of Occupational Health Psychology, 6,* 196–210.

Sonnentag, S. (2003). Recovery, work engagement, and proactive behavior: A new look at the interface between non-work and work. *Journal of Applied Psychology, 88,* 518–528.

Spector, P. E. (1986). Perceived control by employees: A meta-analysis of studies concerning autonomy and participation at work. *Human Relations, 39,* 1005–1016.

Strauss-Blasche, G., Ekmekcioglu, C., & Marktl, W. (2000). Does vacation enable recuperation? Changes in well-being associated with time away from work. *Occupational Medicine, 50,* 167–172.

Strauss-Blasche, G., Ekmekcioglu, C., & Marktl, W. (2003). Serum lipids responses to a respite from occupational and domestic demands in subjects with varying levels of stress. *Journal of Psychosomatic Research, 55,* 521–524.

Strauss-Blasche, G., Muhry, F., Lehofer, M., Moser, M., & Markl, W. (2004). Time course of well-being after a three-week resort-based respite from occupational and domestic demands: Carry-over, contrast and situation effects. *Journal of Leisure Research, 36,* 293–309.

Strauss-Blasche, G., Reithofer, B., Schobersberger, W., Ekmekcioglu, C., & Marktl, W. F. (2005). Effect of vacation on health: Moderating factors of vacation outcome. *Journal of Travel Medicine, 12*(2), 94–101.

Striker, J., Luippold, R. S., Nagy, L., Liese, B., Bigelow, C., & Mundt, K. A. (1999). Risk factors for psychological stress among international business travelers. *Occupational and Environmental Medicine, 56,* 245–252.

Sutton, R. I., & Kahn, R. L. (1986). Prediction, understanding and control as anecdotes to organizational stress. In: J. Lorsch (Ed.), *Handbook of organizational behavior* (pp. 272–285). Englewood Cliffs, NJ: Prentice Hall.

Tay, C., Westman, M., & Chia, A. (2008). Antecedents and consequences of cultural intelligence among short term business travelers. In: S. Ang (Ed.), *Advances in cultural intelligence.* Armonk, NY: M E Sharpe.

Thompson, S. C. (1981). Will it hurt less if I can control it? A complex answer to a simple question. *Psychological Bulletin, 90,* 89–101.

Welch, D. E., & Worm, V. (2006). International business travelers: A challenge for IHRM. In: G. K. Stahl & I. Björkman (Eds), *Handbook of research in international human resource management* (pp. 283–301). Northampton, MA: Edward Elgar Publishing.

Westman, M. (2001). Stress and strain crossover. *Human Relations, 54,* 557–591.

Westman, M. (2004). Strategies for coping with business trips: A qualitative exploratory study. *International Journal of Stress Management, 11,* 167–176.

Westman, M., & Eden, D. (1997). Effects of respite on burnout: Vacation, relief and fade-out. *Journal of Applied Psychology, 82,* 16–527.

Westman, M., & Etzion, D. (2001). The impact of vacation and job stress on burnout and absenteeism. *Psychology and Health, 1,* 95–106.

Westman, M., & Etzion, D. (2002). The impact of short overseas business trips on job stress and burnout. *Applied Psychology: An international Review, 51*, 582–592.

Westman, M., & Etzion, D. (2004). *Characteristics of business trips and their consequences: A summary of recent findings.* Working Paper No. 13/2004. The Israel Institute of Business Research, Tel Aviv University.

Westman, M., & Etzion, D. (2005). The impact of short business trips. In: F. Columbus (Ed.), *Advances in psychology research* (chapter 9). Hauppauge, NY: Nova Science Publishers.

Westman, M., Etzion, D., & Chen, S. (2009). Crossover of positive experiences from business travellers to their spouses. *Journal of Managerial Psychology, 24*, 269–284.

Westman, M., Etzion, D., & Gattenio, E. (2008). Business travels and the work–family interface: A longitudinal study. *Journal of Organizational and Occupational Psychology, 81*, 459–480.

Westman, M., Etzion, D., & Gortler, E. (2004). The work–family interface and burnout. *International Journal of Stress Management, 11*, 413–428.

Westman, M., & Vinokur, A. (1998). Unraveling the relationship of distress levels within couples: Common stressors, emphatic reactions or crossover via social interaction? *Human Relations, 51*, 137–156.

SLEEP AND RECOVERY

Torbjörn Åkerstedt, Peter M. Nilsson and Göran Kecklund

ABSTRACT

This chapter summarizes the knowledge on sleep and restitution. Sleep constitutes the recuperative process of the central nervous system. The use of the brain during wakefulness will lead to depletion of energy in the cortical areas locally responsible for activity. The level of depletion is monitored and sleep is initiated when critical levels are reached. The attempts to initiate sleep are perceived as sleepiness or fatigue. The ensuing sleep then actively restores brain physiology to normal levels. This also results in restored alertness, memory capacity, and mood. Also, peripheral anabolic processes (secretion of growth hormone and testosterone) are strongly enhanced and catabolic process (secretion of cortisol and catecholamines) are strongly suppressed. In the long run, reduced or impaired sleep leads to metabolic diseases, depression, burnout, and mortality. Stress and irregular hours are among the main causes of disturbed sleep.

INTRODUCTION

As is evidenced elsewhere in this volume life is about effort and restitution after effort. However, there has only been modest research on the

Current Perspectives on Job-Stress Recovery
Research in Occupational Stress and Well Being, Volume 7, 205–247
Copyright © 2009 by Emerald Group Publishing Limited
All rights of reproduction in any form reserved
ISSN: 1479-3555/doi:10.1108/S1479-3555(2009)0000007009

importance of restitution, particularly if we consider physiological restitution from everyday mental wear and tear. Stress research often refers to the observation that repeated stress with insufficient restitution in-between will lead to a gradual increase of physiological activation and eventually an allostatic up-regulation of wear and tear (McEwen & Wingfield, 2003). Although the duration or type of rest in-between may be important factors, it is obvious that sleep is one of the major physiological means of restitution (McEwen, 2006). The present chapter will try to summarize some of the knowledge in this area.

First some basic aspects of sleep and sleepiness will be introduced. Then the day-to-day recovery in terms of alertness and performance after sleep loss will be discussed. This will be followed by a discussion of the role of sleep in physiological recovery and its role in morbidity and mortality.

SLEEP AND SLEEPINESS

Sleep

There does not seem to exist a formal consensus definition of sleep but it has been argued that, behaviorally, sleep refers to a reversible condition of altered and decreased awareness (Carskadon & Dement, 2000). One might expect that, for example, body posture should be a part of the definition, but it is clearly possible to sleep sitting or even standing (in many animals). One might also argue that restitution should be part of the definition, but there are situations where sleep lacks restitution. The physiological changes are usually not part of the definition but are certainly used to describe sleep.

Sleep Stages

Sleep is physiologically described using the combined impression from the electroencephalogram (EEG), the electrooculogram (EOG), and electromyogram (EMG). The resulting polysomnogram identifies the stages of sleep across stages 1, 2, 3, 4 and REM sleep (Rechtschaffen & Kales, 1968).

Stage 1 shows 6–8 Hz EEG frequency and low amplitude, relatively high muscle tonus and often the presence of slow rolling eye movements. The recuperative value seems negligible. *Stage 2* is identified by the presence of so called sleep spindles in the EEG (14–16 Hz short bursts) and occasional K-complexes against a background of 4–8 Hz activity. Muscle tonus has fallen further. This stage provides basic recovery and occupies 50% of the sleep period.

Stages 3 and 4, often grouped together under the label Slow Wave Sleep (SWS), show large amounts of 0.5–4 Hz high amplitude waves (present at least 20% of the time for stage 3 and 50% of the time for stage 4). Muscle tonus has decreased further. SWS is considered to represent the daily process of restitution, responds in a quantitative way to the time spent awake, and shows a large increase of growth hormone (GH) secretion, together with a suppression of cortisol secretion. Metabolism falls with the sleep stages and SWS is characterized by slow breathing, low heart rate, and low cerebral blood flow.

Rapid Eye Movement (REM) sleep is a completely different sleep stage characterized by an EEG similar to that of stage 1, but with REMs, a virtual absence of muscle tonus in antigravity muscles and a largely awake brain, particularly the hippocampus, amygdala, and occipital projection areas. Interestingly, the prefrontal areas are not involved in this awakened brain. It is evident that we normally dream in REM sleep (although dream reports may be elicited from other stages), and to prevent the acting-out of dreams the efferent signals to the muscles are blocked.

Development of Sleep Across the Night

The normal development across time involves a rapid descent from waking to stage 4 sleep in 15–25 min, 30–50 min of SWS, followed by a short (5–10 min) period of REM sleep. This cycle is repeated another 3–4 times during the night, but with decreasing amounts of SWS and increasing amounts of REM sleep. The last two sleep cycles usually lack stages 3 and 4. This characteristic pattern is usually interpreted as a high level of recovery during the first hours of sleep, and a gradual reduction in speed of recovery during the later part of sleep, due to less need for sleep with time. This is evident in mathematical models that describe sleep regulation (Borbély, 1982) and its effect on the parallel process of increased subjective and behavioral recovery (Åkerstedt, Folkard, & Portin, 2004).

Brain Metabolism During Sleep

Several studies of brain metabolism have shown that blood flow and metabolic activity is reduced in all areas of the brain during nonrapid eye movement (NREM) sleep, and in particular in SWS. In contrast, the transition to REM sleep is characterized by an increased blood flow in areas of the thalamus, hippocampus, amygdala and areas associated with the visual cortex. The frontal areas of the brain, however, remain quiescent (Maquet, 2000; Nofzinger, 2005).

The physiological mechanism that turns sleep on and off involves a breakdown of adenosine triphosphate (ATP) in the central nervous system (CNS), as ATP is being used to provide energy to the waking brain. The CNS levels of extracellular adenosine will then increase (Porkka-Heiskanen, 1999). The adenosine message is picked up by receptors in the hypothalamus. These receptors, in turn suppress activity in the reticular activating system (the alertness inducer in the CNS). This reduced activity will trigger the hypothalamus to start inducing sleep (Saper, Chou, & Scammell, 2001). Sleep will restore adenosine levels to baseline (Porkka-Heiskanen, 1999).

Sleepiness

The other side of the coin is sleepiness and the related ability to function mentally. It is also the most obvious indicator of insufficient sleep and if sleep was not so crucial in determining sleepiness there would not be much point in studying sleep.

What Is It?

Sleepiness has been defined as a drive to fall asleep (Carskadon & Dement, 1977) and is the main outcome of day-to-day variation of variations in sleep. Sleepiness clearly has a physiological basis (see later), but the most easily accessible indicator of sleepiness is the subjective perception, usually translated into a score on a rating scale. This may have the form of a visual analogue scale that ranges from "very alert" to "very sleepy" usually quantified along a 100 mm line (Monk, 1989). Other scales are of the Likert type, such as the Stanford sleepiness scale which ranges from 1 to 7 (Hoddes, Zarcone, Smythe, Phillips, & Dement, 1973), or the Karolinska Sleepiness Scale (KSS) which ranges from 1 to 9 (Åkerstedt & Gillberg, 1990). Even if it is not clear if it is possible to use absolute values on a scale when comparing individuals or groups, the relation between ratings and EEG or performance measures are usually quite good (Ingre et al., 2006).

If sleepiness represents the drive to fall asleep, then indicators of this speed should be suitable for measuring and defining physiological sleepiness. The most well established, and more or less official measure of sleepiness, is the so-called "multiple sleep latency test" (MSLT) which simply measures (with polysomnography) the time it takes to fall asleep in a dark room (Roehrs & Roth, 1992). Five minutes and shorter latency during daytime is usually seen as excessive sleepiness. EEG activity in the alpha (8–12 Hz) and theta (4–8 Hz) bands are also sensitive physiological indicators of sleepiness, as is slow eye movements (Åkerstedt & Gillberg, 1990) or long eye blinks (Wierwille & Ellsworth, 1994).

Physiological indicators of sleepiness do not seem to have a linear relation to the experience of sleepiness. Rather, physiological changes do not seem to occur until after the midpoint of the scales. For example, the KSS starts to show slight effects in alpha/theta EEG activity and eye movements when level 7 is reached on the scale. This level carries the label "sleepy, but no problem staying awake." Level 9 on the scale usually shows the EEG dominated by alpha, and to some extent theta activity together with slow rolling eye movements and long eye blinks (Torsvall & Åkerstedt, 1988). The label here is "very sleepy, fighting sleep, an effort to remain awake." This of course fits very well with the EEG and EOG indicators. Level 8 is usually in between levels 7 and 9 in terms of physiological changes.

The Physiological Basis of Sleepiness
The physiological basis for sleepiness due to time awake or reduced sleep has not been conclusively identified. At present, we know that extended wakefulness and reduced sleep will reduce the metabolic rate in prefrontal, thalamic, and parietal areas of the brain (Drummond & Brown, 2001). The brain will work at a slower rate. As brought up earlier, wakefulness is also associated with an accumulation of extracellular adenosine, which is a potent sleep inducer (Porkka-Heiskanen, 1999). Through hypothalamic adenosine receptors and the reticular activating system the thalamus starts inducing sleep. It seems probable that these attempts to start sleep are at the basis for the perception of sleepiness – theta activity increases, the eyelids are forced to close, and the eye bulbs are rotated upward (Saper et al., 2001). Incidentally, caffeine is a traditional antagonist of adenosine receptors and will block the effects of circulating adenosine, leading to the need for sleep being hidden from the brain.

Performance
Sleepiness (and fatigue) may also be measured using neuropsychological tests sensitive to sleepiness. If sleepiness is a drive to fall asleep, then tests that demand continuous attention over a longer period of time would be ideal indicators of sleepiness. A ranking list of tests would include simple serial reaction time (long series of monotonous stimuli that invite lapses of attention), vigilance tests (detection of a small deviation in a long series of similar signals), or tracking tests (following a moving target on a screen – including simulated driving) (Balkin et al., 2004). The first is the most widely used one, especially in the form of the "psychomotor vigilance test" or the

"PVT" (Dinges et al., 1997). The common denominator is that these tests require continuous attention and are externally paced. Such tests are usually very susceptible to sleep loss. Another characteristic is that increased duration of the test imposes an extra load, which brings out sleepiness earlier.

The effects of sleepiness include longer reaction times, fewer discovered stimuli, a larger variability of performance, and long response lapses. "State instability" has been used to describe the performance effects of sleepiness (Van Dongen, Vitellaro, & Dinges, 2005). As with physiological measures, the most dramatic performance impairment appears at level 9 of the KSS (Ingre et al., 2006). The effects are not restricted to attention and psychomotor performance − also higher cognitive functioning is affected by sleepiness (Harrison & Horne, 2000). The impression is that higher cognitive functioning takes a longer time to reach impairment during sleep loss, probably because it is stimulating and relatively self-paced. However, less data is available, mainly because higher cognitive functions are difficult to measure repeatedly − learning curves are very steep.

A recent finding of major cognitive significance is the discovery of the role of REM sleep in learning. Apparently, the learning of processes is strongly enhanced by REM sleep (Stickgold, Hobson, Fosse, & Fosse, 2001) and the same brain areas as were used in the learning process are activated in subsequent sleep (Maquet, 2001). However, also SWS seems strongly implicated in learning processes. Thus, it appears that SWS may reflect the high synaptic strength after a day of memory storage and that the reduction in SWS across sleep then reflects the reduction of synaptic strength − the synaptic downscaling (Tononi & Cirelli, 2006). The latter is suggested as a way of getting rid of unwanted memory, making room for new memory.

Fatigue
The concept of *fatigue* is closely related to sleepiness and the two are often used interchangeably. However, in sleep research one tries to distinguish the two and usually consider fatigue to refer to an inability or unwillingness to continue an activity that has been going on for an extended time (Feyer, 2001; Hossain et al., 2005), but there is an ongoing debate on other approaches (Dement, Hall, & Walsh, 2003; Horne, 2003). Åhsberg (2000) identified four different types of fatigue − sleepiness, mental fatigue, physical fatigue, and exhaustion.

Fatigue is the key symptom of the burnout syndrome (Maslach & Leiter, 2005), chronic fatigue (Evengard, Jacks, Pedersen, & Sullivan, 2005) and in disease in general (Wessely et al., 1995). However, in subjects high on burnout scales, sleepiness ratings are similarly increased. Later we will use the concept "sleepiness" in most cases (Söderström, Ekstedt, Åkerstedt, Nilsson, & Axelsson, 2004). Mental/emotional fatigue does not really have an established physiological indicator but there are a large number of scales that combine items like tired, fatiguee, exhausted, listless etc. to form fatigue scales. (Krupp, Larocca, Muir-Nash, & Steinberg, 1989; Taylor, Jason, & Torres, 2000; Maslach, Schaufeli, & Leiter, 2001).

THE DETERMINANTS OF SLEEP AND SLEEPINESS

Sleep and sleepiness are determined by the same homeostatic and circadian factors and are closely interdependent, that is, sleep will affect sleepiness and sleepiness will affect sleep.

The Regulation of Sleep

Homeostatic Regulation
The main determinants of sleep are the duration of time since prior sleep and the amount of prior sleep. Reduced prior sleep normally causes a homeostatic response during the next sleep opportunity, characterized by increased amounts of stages 3 and 4 (SWS) (Webb & Agnew, 1971). This increase occurs at the expense of REM sleep, stage 2 sleep, stage 1 sleep, and stage wake. Also spectral power density in the 0.5–4 Hz band, called "delta power," which essentially corresponds to SWS, increases as SWS does. Recovery sleep becomes deeper and less fragmented. Essentially, there is a linear relation between the amount of prior time awake and SWS. This very early led to the perception of SWS being the major restitutive component of sleep (Horne, 1989). This may be an oversimplification, however.

Circadian Influences
The other factor is circadian influences. The cells of the suprachiasmatic nuclei (SCN) in the hypothalamus produce a pronounced oscillation in most physiological parameters (Saper, Lu, Chou, & Gooley, 2005). These nuclei cause the physiology to oscillate in a cycle of high metabolic rate during nighttime and a low rate during nighttime. The classical physiological indicator of this rhythmicity has been rectal temperature with a peak in the afternoon. Other typical indicators include the stress hormone cortisol, with

a 6 a.m. peak and the hormone melatonin, with a peak around 4 a.m. The latter reduces metabolism and causes a certain amount of sleepiness.

The effect of circadian regulation on sleep is quite strong. The more sleep is postponed from the evening toward noon next day, the more truncated it becomes, and at noon sleep duration is only around 5 h (despite the sleep loss). The trend then reverts and increased sleep is seen again (Foret & Lantin, 1972; Åkerstedt & Gillberg, 1981). Thus, sleep during the morning hours is strongly interfered with, despite the sizeable sleep loss that, logically, should enhance the ability to maintain sleep (Czeisler, Weitzman, Moore-Ede, Zimmerman, & Knauer, 1980).

Homeostatic influences control also sleep taken at the wrong time of day. For example, the expected 4–5 h of daytime sleep, after a night spent awake, will be reduced to 2 h if a normal night's sleep precedes it and to 3.5 h if a 2-h nap is allowed during the night (Åkerstedt & Gillberg, 1986). Thus, the time of sleep termination depends on the balance between the circadian and homeostatic influences. The circadian homeostatic regulation of sleep has also been demonstrated in great detail in studies of forced or spontaneous desynchronization under conditions of temporal isolation and ad lib sleep hours (Czeisler et al., 1980).

The Regulation of Sleepiness

The most obvious restorative aspect of sleep is the return to normal subjective and objective alertness and performance capacity after a full nights sleep – or the response of the same variables after various manipulations of sleep.

Time Awake

With increasing time awake, the subjective alertness and performance capacity will fall in a reverse exponential way toward an asymptote (Fröberg, Karlsson, Levi, & Lidberg, 1972). The process is faster in the beginning and after 24 h it begins to level off. After 48 h there is very little alertness or performance capacity left but a person may be able to stay awake for several days more if adequately stimulated, but the level of functioning would be poor (Kales et al., 1970). Also mood (Franzen, Siegle, & Buysse, 2008) is reduced with time awake, as is judgment (Killgore et al., 2007). The effects are also clearly visible in EEG measures of alpha and theta activity (which increase) (Åkerstedt & Gillberg, 1990). This process of alertness reduction has been quantified and is now built into several mathematical models for prediction of sleepiness and of accident risk during, for example, driving (Akerstedt, Connor, Gray, & Kecklund, 2008). It should be emphasized that sleepiness induced through extension of the time awake is not possible to eliminate through, for example, switching to another activity. The latter is usually possible with fatigue due to long time on task (see later).

Brain Use

The work the brain has carried out has a cost in terms of energy loss. There is not all that much systematic work on this issue, particularly not physiologically. However, it has been shown that local learning will increase SWS during subsequent sleep (Huber, Ghilardi, Massimini, & Tononi, 2004). When an arm is immobilized over a day sleep intensity is reduced, presumably reflecting a lower energy expenditure in the motor areas regulating arm movements (Huber et al., 2006).

Some related changes have been seen also in during weeks with stress – sleepiness is increased toward the end of the day (Dahlgren, Kecklund, & Akerstedt, 2005). The effects are similar in connection with extended work hours (Dahlgren, Kecklund, & Akerstedt, 2006). The effect of work load, and probably also reduced sleep, is very obvious when 3-hourly reports of subjective sleepiness are compared for working days and days off (Söderström et al., 2004). Sleepiness is dramatically higher during the working week. Fatigue reacts in the same way to work load (Konz, 1998; Macdonald & Bendak, 2000), but there does not seem to be any systematic information available on the development process of emotional/mental fatigue in connection with depression or burnout.

Time on Task

An important determinant of sleepiness (and of fatigue) is also the time spent on a particular task. The classical experimental studies are those based on vigilance tests (Mackworth, 1950), showing what is called the "vigilance decrement" – a rapid impairment of the ability to discover small changes in a long stream of repetitive signals. The fact that normal performance is restored after a short break or change in the stimulus situation suggests that the phenomenon reflects habituation. In work physiology, the time to exhaustion has been a thoroughly investigated phenomenon involving depletion of neurotransmitters or increase in lactic acid in muscles (Grandjean, 1970; Borg, 1990).

Sleep Length

Wilkinson, Edwards, and Haines (1966) carried out the first systematic study and found that 1–2 h of sleep loss did not affect performance but that greater sleep truncation did. Similar results were obtained in a dose–response study by Härmä et al. (1998). Jewett, Dijk, Kronauer, and Dinges (1999) used forced desynchronization (living on a non-24 h day/night cycle, causing sleep/wake rhythm to dissociate from the rest of the physiological rhythms) studies to demonstrate the same dose–response relationship. The bottom line is that the first hours of sleep are crucial, whereas the last hours of an 8-h sleep are of little importance.

The question of sleep duration also pertains to the restorative effects of napping. The general impression from the literature is that a short period of sleep, as short as 10 min, has remarkable effects on subjective, behavioral, and physiological sleepiness (Gillberg, Kecklund, Axelsson, & Åkerstedt, 1994; Schweitzer, Randazzo, Stone, Erman, & Walsh, 2006; Lahl, Wispel, Willigens, & Pietrowsky, 2008).

Apart from acute sleep loss we must also consider effects of accumulated sleep loss. This may be more ecologically relevant in today's society. The conclusion from studies of two weeks of partial sleep loss seems to be that gradual performance impairment starts when sleep duration falls below 7 h (Belenky et al., 2003; Van Dongen, Maislin, Mullington, & Dinges, 2003). This appears to function as a lower boundary for sleep duration in order to avoid accumulation of fatigue or behavioral impairment. Six hours of sleep is associated with a small gradual increase of performance impairment, whereas the development is much steeper with 4 h. Presumably, though, the interindividual differences are considerable and some individuals seem to be exceptionally resistant to partial sleep loss (Van Dongen, Baynard, Maislin, & Dinges, 2004).

Sleep Quality

Also the quality of sleep must be of importance for restitution. However, there is no consensus on what constitutes sleep quality. The impression from numerous conference discussions is that it only exists as a subjective phenomenon. Complaints of long sleep latency (>30 min) and high amounts of wakefulness after sleep onset (>30 min) seem to be the most used indicators (Lichstein, Durrence, Taylor, Bush, & Riedel, 2003).

Despite the dominance of subjective complaints in the evaluation of sleep quality there has been a number of attempts to relate subjective complaints to polysomnographical indicators. Sleep efficiency (amount of sleep in percent of the time spent in the bed after the decision to sleep), rate of fragmentation (arousals per hour), and amount of SWS have been among the most central ones. Obviously, sleep efficiency will reflect functioning the next day since it represents the relative amount of sleep. The importance of the rate of fragmentation has been established in several studies of sleep apnea (Roehrs, Zorick, Wittig, Conway, & Roth, 1989) and experimental fragmentation (Bonnet & Arand, 2003a) to be related to next day sleep latency tests and performance. The exact mechanism has not been established but it appears that the discontinuity of the sleep process prevents restorative effects. One alternative interpretation is that it is the amount of low quality stage 1 sleep that is the mechanism of poor recuperation when sleep is fragmented (Wesensten, Balkin, & Belenky, 1999). Also when the EEG does not reach waking levels but only heart rate responds, the effects on the MSLT (a measure of sleepiness based on the time taken to fall asleep) is visible the next day (Roehrs et al., 1989). SWS, which is often seen as a restorative form of sleep has not really been shown to be crucial to next day functioning (Johnson, Naitoh, Moses, & Lubin, 1974; Ferrara, De Gennaro, & Bertini, 1999), but seems to be related to the perception of "good sleep" (Åkerstedt, Hume, Minors, & Waterhouse, 1997).

Circadian Influences

Circadian rhythmicity in itself, and its regulation of sleep has been brought up previously. It also affects sleepiness and performance directly and indirectly (through effects of sleep). The influence of circadian regulation is particularly obvious during continuous wakefulness (Fröberg, Karlsson, Levi, & Lidberg, 1975) and in studies of forced desynchronization (Dijk, Duffy, & Czeisler, 1992). Alertness falls rapidly after awakening, reaches a trough in the early morning and then recovers, through the circadian upswing during the morning. The peak level is, however, lower than that during the previous day. Extension of the time awake will lead to a deeper trough during the next night. Performance capacity describes essentially the same pattern.

The Regulation of Sleepiness and Performance

The observations above have been used to develop mathematical models for the regulation of sleepiness and alertness. The first (two-process) model, however, mainly addressed the question of sleep regulation and by inference, the need for sleep or fatigue/sleepiness (Borbély, 1982). Its main components were the homeostatic effects of time awake and amount of prior sleep, as well as a circadian effect, representing the influence of the biological

clock. The homeostatic factors are usually seen as having an exponential relation to sleepiness. This means, for example, a steep initial fall of alertness (or rise of sleepiness) after awakening, with a gradual flattening out toward an asymptote of very low alertness after 24 h of time awake. The effect of sleep shows a pattern of restitution that increases postsleep alertness. The circadian component is usually represented as a sinusoid function with a 24-h period which results in high alertness during the day/afternoon and lowest alertness around 4 a.m. to 5 a.m. For a review of present models, see Mallis, Mejdal, Nguyen, and Dinges (2004).

Fig. 1 illustrates the factors of the "Sleep/Wake Predictor" (Åkerstedt et al., 2004). The SWP includes a process C that represents sleepiness due to circadian influences and has a sinusoidal form with an afternoon peak. Process S is an exponential function of the time since awakening, is high on awakening, falls rapidly initially and gradually approaches a lower asymptote. At sleep onset process S is reversed and called S' and recovery occurs in an exponential fashion that initially increases very rapidly but subsequently levels off toward an upper asymptote. Total recovery is usually accomplished in 8 h. A final component is the wakeup process W, or sleep inertia (not shown in the figure). The predicted alertness is expressed as the arithmetic sum of the two (W presently excluded) functions above (S+C in Fig. 1). In this example, wakefulness is extended throughout the night and

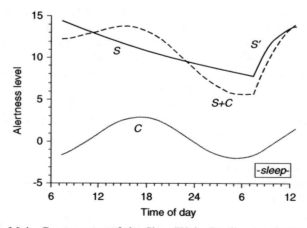

Fig. 1. The Main Components of the Sleep/Wake Predictor – S, S', and C. S+C Describes the Sum of S and C during 24 h of Continuous Wakefulness, Followed by 8 h of Sleep.

the alertness reaches very low levels immediately before the morning bedtime (approximately 06:00 h). The scale of the model ranges from 1 to 21 (and was originally a visual analogue scale), but in practice "3" corresponds to extreme sleepiness and "14" to high alertness and "7" to a sleepiness threshold (Folkard & Åkerstedt, 1991; Åkerstedt & Folkard, 1995). Model output predicts sleep-related road crashes with a high degree of precision. Several other models predict sleepiness or fatigue and most include laboratory performance validations (Belyavin & Spencer, 2004; Hursh et al., 2004; Roach, Fletcher, & Dawson, 2004). The predictive accuracy of each these models is rather similar (Van Dongen, 2004).

PHYSIOLOGY DURING SLEEP

The previous discussion has focused on restoration of alertness and performance capacity. However, these restorative effects are to a great extent due to the physiological changes during sleep and the latter are closely involved in the long-term health effects of sleep or lack thereof. The physiological changes during sleep also actively counteract effects of stress and reduction/disturbance of sleep yield effects very similar to those of stress. Among the early observations on sleep is the reduction of rectal temperature, the rate of breathing, heart rate, blood pressure etc. However, during REM sleep the situation is reversed and levels then exceed those during wakefulness (Parmeggiani, 1995). Below we discuss in more detail the effects on endocrine variables, glucose regulation, the immune system, and brain metabolism.

Endocrine Effects

Profound changes occur in the endocrine system during sleep (Steiger et al., 1998; Steiger, 2002). During sleep an interaction occurs between the electrophysiology and endocrinology. In adults, the first part of sleep is characterized by increased GH release (together with increased SWS and low levels of REM sleep) and suppressed secretion of the hormones of the hypothalamo–pituitary–adrenocortical (HPA) system. This means that the corticotropin-releasing hormone (CRH), the messenger to the adrenal cortex, corticotropin (ACTH), and the cortisol hormone itself are suppressed. These changes directly oppose the effects of stress. GH promotes protein synthesis, which means that it is essential for growing and for repairing tissue. It also prevents glucose from entering brain cells (for storage), which leads to high circulating levels of glucose during the first half of sleep. The reason is to ensure that the brain has a constant supply of energy during sleep, which is a period of fasting. During the second half of the night, the HPA axis dominates and GH secretion is essentially absent. Thus, the first half of sleep is strongly anabolic.

When sleep is prevented cortisol secretion will increase (Spiegel, Leproult, & Van Cauter, 1999) and the rate of sleep fragmentation (microarousals) is related to increased levels of cortisol (Ekstedt, Åkerstedt, & Söderström, 2004). Thus, sleep reduction has effects similar to those of stress. In contrast, GH, secretion is strongly reduced if no sleep occurs, but may to some extent reappear when it normally does not (Van Cauter et al., 2004).

Sleep does not only regulate hormone secretion, it is also affected by it. Thus GH-releasing hormone (GHRH) causes increased SWS and GH secretion, as well as reduced cortisol levels in males (not females) (Steiger, 2002). CRH will exert the opposite effects. It appears that the quality of sleep partly depends on an interaction of GHRH and CRH. Changes in the balance between the two may be part of the sleep problems in depression and aging. Possibly, the differential response to GHRH in males and females can be related to the elevated risk of affective disorders in women. Also elevated glucocorticoid levels may contribute to the sleep EEG changes in depression and CRH antagonism normalizes sleep disturbances.

Glucose Changes

Also insulin and glucose levels are sensitive to manipulations of sleep (Spiegel et al., 1999; Knutson, Spiegel, Penev, & Van Cauter, 2007). In general, glucose levels during sleep are maintained at relatively normal levels and glucose infusion results in dramatically increased levels since insulin effects are impaired during sleep. Furthermore, sleep reduction down to 4 h for 6 days yields decreased glucose tolerance, increased evening cortisol, elevated sympatho-vagal balance, abnormal profiles of nocturnal GH secretion, and markedly decreased leptin levels, as well as a blunted response to influenza vaccination. Short sleepers (<6 h) show results consistent with the experimental results – decreased insulin sensitivity, largely due to the increased GH secretion during sleep. Another observation in relation to experimental sleep reduction is that leptin levels are reduced and hunger markedly increased. The effects suggest links with the metabolic syndrome and may be related to (abdominal) obesity and poor lifestyle, often found in patients of lower socio-economic background.

The Immune System

The immune system shows strong effects of sleep (Bryant, Trinder, & Curtis, 2004). During normal sleep circulating cell counts for most major white blood cells decrease (monocytes, natural killer cells, T and B cells). The latter seem to accumulate in lymphoid tissue during sleep, facilitating local immune responses. However, the sleep process does not seem to affect the production of proinflammatory cytokines like IL-1, IL-6 or TNF-α; but IL-2 is markedly increased (compared to wakefulness) as is also IFNμ (also derived from T-cells).

However, reduced sleep causes increased levels of pro-inflammatory cytokines like IL-1β, IL-6, and TNF-α. These are potent local sleep inducers and, at least the latter two, are elevated in patients with disorders of excessive daytime sleepiness (EDS) (Vgontzas et al., 1997). There seems to be a correlation with the body mass index (BMI) and both cytokines are released by fat tissue. The same cytokines and leptin are increased in sleep apnea, independent of obesity (Vgontzas, Bixler, & Chrousos, 2005). Sleep apnea (frequent awakenings due to respiratory pathways being blocked) is linked to both obesity and diabetes and it appears that insulin resistance, related to visceral obesity, may be partly responsible for sleep apnea. Possibly, sleep apnea, in turn, may accelerate such metabolic changes through elevation of stress hormones and cytokines (cortisol, IL-6, TNF-α).

FACTORS IN SOCIETY THAT INTERFERE WITH SLEEP

Sleep is easily interfered with through various types of activities, states, and circumstances. Stress is one of the most common factors attributed to disturbed sleep, but also irregular work hours and irregular life patterns is an important contributor. We will focus on these factors in this review, but one should also be aware of other circumstances such as many diseases and environmental noise.

Stress and Sleep

One major obstacle to sleep is stress. Here, we will focus on the role of stress in preventing recuperation through sleep. The core problem of stress with regard to sleep is that stress produces significant physiological activation, which is in conflict with the inherent requirement of physiological deactivation during sleep.

The Concept of Stress
From a general perspective psychosocial stress refers to the "the rate of wear and tear in the organism," and the biological definition of stress refers to the nonspecific response to any demand (Selye, 1956) to increase the chances of survival of an individual who is facing a life-threatening situation. More specifically, stress is determined by the balance between the perceived demands from the environment and the individual's resources to meet those demands (Selye, 1956). The Cognitive Activation Theory of Stress (Ursin & Eriksen, 2004) is a recent development of these ideas, focusing on the perception of the gap between the present resources and demands.

Contemporary physiological stress models derive from Cannon (1914) and Selye's (1946) pioneering work. Selye (1946) proposed a model of stress, the general adaptation syndrome (GAS), comprised of three stages: these were alarm, resistance, and exhaustion, and reflected the physiological nonspecific response to a challenge. The resistance stage of GAS has profound energy requirements, which, if persistent over time, depletes the person's capacity and leads to exhaustion.

Cannon (1914) developed the concept of the "fight-flight" response which linked the emotional perception of a "threat" to physiological changes in the periphery. Markers of the fight-flight response are the catecholamines epinephrine and norepinephrine, and other physiological indicators associated with the autonomic nervous system (Dunn & Berridge, 1990; Brown, 1991). Thus, the sympathetic adrenal medullary (SAM) system is activated in situations when the individual feels threatened, irrespective of whether the requirement is to battle or to escape the emergency.

The HPA axis is also fundamental in the stress reaction. When the SAM system is activated and neuropeptides like CRH and vasopressin are released they, in turn, stimulate adrenocorticotropic hormone (ACTH) release into the general blood circulation within the pituitary (Rock et al., 1984; Dunn & Berridge, 1990). An increase or decrease in the HPA axis and SAM system produces abnormal levels of mainly cortisol and catecholamines (epinephrine and norepinephrine) into the blood

(Sapolsky, Krey, & McEwen, 1984; McEwen et al., 1995; Folkow, 1997). These stress systems are interacting with the major endocrine and the gastrointestinal and immune systems through complex stimulatory and inhibitory feedback pathways (Chrousos & Gold, 1992). Note that similar changes are caused also by sleep loss, as discussed earlier.

Long-term effects of stress are described by the term *"allostasis"* referring to the ability of the body to increase or decrease the activation level of vital functions to *new steady states* dependent on the characteristics of the challenge and the person's emotions and appraisal of the event (McEwen & Wingfield, 2003). The resulting *"allostatic load"* represents the cumulative cost to the body when the systems start to malfunction after a stressful event (McEwen, 2004). It is suggested that serious pathophysiology can occur if overload is not relieved in some way (McEwen & Wingfield, 2003). Clearly, one of the outcomes may be insomnia, as discussed later.

The kind of demands that cause stress may result from demands in life and may not even involve increased demands in absolute terms, but may result from decreased capacity to deal with very minor requirements of life. Living up to the needs of family, friends, school etc. are among those (Berntsson, Lundberg, & Krantz, 2006; Eller, Netterstrom, & Hansen, 2006), but there does not seem to exist a systematic theory or model for stress in the private sector. With respect to working life there are such theories, however. One of the leading psychosocial measures in work stress research is the Demand/Control model of Karasek and Theorell (Karasek, 1979; Theorell, 1996). According to this model, high demands and low decision latitude have been found predictive of cardiovascular and other types of stress diseases (Alfredsson, Spetz, & Theorell, 1985; Hammar, Alfredsson, & Theorell, 1994; Toomingas, Theorell, Michélsen, & Nordemar, 1997). A somewhat different approach is that of Siegrist that contrasts between demands and resources (Siegrist, 2000). In this model, "immersion" has an important role, representing major commitment and effort. Another important work-related factor may be the amount of social support received at work. Several studies have indicated the impact of lack of such support on cardiovascular disease, depression, and other outcomes (Theorell, 1996).

The Connection between Stress and Sleep
Considering the physiological activation involved in the stress response it seems logical to expect a connection with sleep. The evidence is, however, surprisingly modest, at least in terms of studies of causal connections. There nevertheless exists a number of cross-sectional

epidemiological studies which point to a strong link between stress and sleep (Ancoli-Israel & Roth, 1999; Morphy, Dunn, Lewis, Boardman, & Croft, 2007; Ribet & Derriennic, 1999; Urponen, Vuori, Hasan, & Partinen, 1988; Åkerstedt et al., 2002c). In fact, stress is considered the primary cause of persistent psychophysiological insomnia (Morin, Rodrigue, & Ivers, 2003). In one study of life events, Cernovsky (1984) demonstrated a clear increase in negative life events before an outbreak of insomnia.

Stress as a predictor of later sleep disturbances has been the topic of rather few studies. One such is that of Jansson and Linton (2006), which showed effects of present stress on later complaints of disturbed sleep. Akerstedt, Kecklund, and Axelsson (2007b) showed that nighttime ratings of stress/ worries at bedtime was related to reduced sleep efficiency, increased waking after sleep onset (WASO), and increased latency to SWS. In other polysomnographic (PSG) studies sleep the night before a big exam, sleep before a day of skydiving, sleep when on call, or sleep before an early awakening (Holdstock & Verschoor, 1974) have been studied. The results indicate a slight reduction of sleep efficiency and the amount of deep sleep. In addition, a number of laboratory studies of stress and sleep have been carried out, but the stressors have been rather artificial (e.g., an unpleasant movie) and the results unclear (Åkerstedt, 1987). It is probably the case that the stressor needs to be of some significance to the individual in order to have any effect.

Sleep disturbances from stress seem to constitute a consistent response pattern. Drake, Richardson, Roehrs, Scofield, and Roth (2004a), for example, have shown that those who report higher habitual sleep vulnerability to stress also show longer sleep latency and lower sleep efficiency on the first night in the sleep laboratory.

The particular reason for a stress-disturbed sleep has been addressed in several studies. Thus, Partinen, Eskelinen, and Tuomi (1984) investigated several occupational groups and found disturbed sleep to be most common among manual workers and much less so among physicians or managing directors. In a retrospective study of older individuals (above the age of 75), Geroldi, Frisoni, Rozzini, De Leo, and Trabucchi (1996) found that former white collar workers reported better sleep than blue collar workers. Kuppermann et al. (1995) reported fewer sleep problems in persons who were satisfied with their work.

In one of the more detailed epidemiological studies so far, Ribet and Derriennic (1999) studied more than 21,000 persons in France, using a sleep disturbance index and logistic regression analysis. It was found that shift work, a long working week, exposure to vibrations, and "having to hurry" appeared to be the main risk factors, controlling for age and gender.

Disturbed sleep was more frequent in women and in older age groups (Bixler, Kales, & Soldatos, 1979).

The work stressor most closely linked to disturbed sleep may be "work under high demands" (Ancoli-Israel & Roth, 1999; Morphy et al., 2007; Ribet & Derriennic, 1999; Urponen et al., 1988; Åkerstedt et al., 2002c). In the study by Åkerstedt et al., it was found that the strongest item of the demand index was "having to exert a lot of effort at work" – not simply "having too much to do" for example. It was also found that when "not being able to stop thinking about work in the evening" was added to the regression this variable took over part of the role of work demands as a predictor. This suggests that it may not be work demands per se that are important, but rather their nonremitting character. It appears that rumination at bedtime may be one of the key factors behind difficulties in sleeping (Harvey, Tang, & Browning, 2005). Hall et al. (2000) have demonstrated in a cross-sectional study that intrusive thoughts at bedtime are related to increased alpha and beta power in the sleep EEG. Similarly, increased cognitive arousal at bedtime is related to increased sleep latency (Haynes, Adams, & Franzen, 1981; Tang & Harvey, 2004), but the former study did not report on other sleep parameters and the latter only included actigraphy, which is only a very approximate indicator of physiological sleep.

Closely related to rumination is worrying and tension before sleep (Kecklund & Åkerstedt, 1997; Kecklund, Åkerstedt, & Lowden, 1997). After times of worry and tension, sleep appears to contain less SWS, which supports the notion that it is the anticipation of difficulties that is important in the stress reaction. This was also found in the previously mentioned study on stress/worries at bedtime (Akerstedt et al., 2007b). In that study sleep recordings preceded by increased (moderately so) subjective "stress/worries" at bedtime were compared with sleep recordings preceded by low such levels (Akerstedt et al., 2007b). The results showed an increased sleep latency, more stage wake, and a longer latency to SWS, all of which were interpreted as indicating slight perturbation of sleep on nights when stress and worries and, by inference, rumination, had been present at bedtime. Mean ratings of stress (every 2 h) during the same day and the day after were also significantly increased.

It has also been shown that sleep is disturbed under threats to national security, for example, after the nuclear accident at the facility at Three Mile Island and during the scud missile attacks on Israel during the Gulf war (Davidson, Fleming, & Baum, 1987; Askenasy & Lewin, 1996). The effect of losing a life partner has in one study been shown to have surprisingly modest effects, and then mainly an increase in REM intensity (Reynolds III et al., 1993).

Lack of social support at work is also a risk indicator for disturbed sleep (Åkerstedt, Fredlund, Gillberg, & Jansson, 2002b; Nordin, Knutsson, & Sundbom, 2008). Poor (general) social support has been associated for instance with sleep complaints in Viet Nam war veterans (Fabsitz, Sholinsky, & Goldberg, 1997), even if the amount of work available is rather limited.

Post-traumatic stress disorder (PTSD) is another well-established cause of disturbed sleep, even if many of the more common indicators of sleep quality (sleep latency, efficiency of sleep, total length of sleep, and amount of stages 3 and 4) are relatively moderately affected (Ross et al., 1994; Dow, Kelsoe, & Gillin, 1996; Mellman, Nolan, Hebding, Kulick-Bell, & Dominguez, 1997; Pillar, Malhotra, & Lavie, 2000). Instead it appears that its major effect is to disturb REM sleep, in particular, by either increasing or reducing its duration, and by increasing its intensity. It also increases the number of awakenings. The unpleasant dreams associated with traumatic memories also tend to produce conditioned avoidance responses in affected individuals, resulting in postponements on a daily basis of retiring or of even entering the sleeping area.

Sleep Disorders

Another major cause of disturbed sleep is the sleep disorders. Among the major categories are insomnia, hypersomnia, and parasomnias (AASM, 2005). Insomnia is usually defined as difficulties in sleeping or complaints of nonrestorative sleep at least half the days of the week and with the problem present for at least three months (APA, 1994). The difficulty in sleeping must be linked to daytime consequences such as sleepiness, fatigue, or performance impairment. The level of complaint must be of "clinical significance." The criteria are not quantitative with respect to specific sleep stages or other aspects of sleep, mainly because of the large overlap between poor and good sleepers. However, authoritative sources suggest a criterion for reported sleep latency of longer duration than 30 min or amount of time awake after sleep onset longer than 30 min (Lichstein et al., 2003). Common criteria also include more than four awakenings per night as an indicator of insomnia. PSG criteria are presently not part of the official criteria, but many researchers use a sleep efficiency (sleep in percent of time in bed) of 85% as a cut-off between good and poor sleep. The international classification of sleep disorders provides more detailed diagnostic criteria (AASM, 2005). A new addition to the diagnostic criteria is also that a complaint of nonrestorative sleep can be used. The definition of this concept is not clear but obviously involves feelings of not having slept well enough to be in good shape in the morning.

In Europe, around 38% of the population suffer from insomnia DSM-IV symptoms and 6% meet the criteria for a diagnosis of insomnia. (Ohayon, Caulet, Priest, & Guilleminault, 1997a). The first figure refers to rather lax criteria of the type "having had difficulty sleeping during the year." Other estimates vary between 5 and 12% (Roth & Drake, 2004; Morphy et al., 2007; Jansson-Frojmark & Linton, 2008). EDS varies between 3.2 and 5.5%, whereas sleep apnea varies between 1.1 and 1.9%. Generally, sleep problems increase with increasing age, female gender, stressful work, and physical workload (Ohayon et al., 1997b; Ancoli-Israel & Roth, 1999; Sateia, Doghramji, Hauri, & Morin, 2000).

In patients with primary insomnia there is an increased incidence of stress markers, including elevated cortisol levels, increased heart rate, and above average body temperature, increased beta EEG intensity, etc. (Monroe, 1967; Adam, Tomeny, & Oswald, 1986; Bonnet & Arand, 1998; Perlis, Merica, Smith, & Giles, 2001). Bonnet and Arand (2003b) have demonstrated increased overall oxygen use in insomnia patients and simulated insomnia by administering 400 mg of caffeine per day for one week. The results show increased uptake of oxygen VO_2, disturbed sleep, increased fatigue and anxiety, but decreased sleepiness, as measured by the MSLTs. The results suggest that insomnia may be more of a metabolic disturbance than a disturbance of the sleep mechanism per se.

Also obstructive sleep apnea has profound effects on the recuperative value of sleep. Since the disease involves a sleep-related relaxation of the muscles of the upper respiratory system, the respiratory pathways become blocked. This requires the sleeper to wake up in order to breath. When this happens repeatedly, as is usually the case sleep becomes interrupted and recuperation may be totally absent depending on the frequency of awakenings. The immediate effects involve fatigue (Wong, Marshall, Grunstein, Dodd, & Rogers, 2008) and an increase in accident risk during the day (Terán-Santos, Jimnénez-Gómez, & Cordero-Guevara, 1999). However, the breathing effort also functions as a powerful stressor and results in increased levels of stress hormones, lipids, proinflammatory cytokines etc. (Lopez-Jimenez & Somers, 2006). Thus, sleep apnea is a contributor to the metabolic syndrome (Lavie, 2004; Vgontzas et al., 2005) and directly related to workability (Mulgrew et al., 2007).

Other types of insomnia include the "Restless legs syndrome," "Periodic limb movements," and those related to psychiatric disease and other medical disorders.

Another type of sleep disorder is that involving the circadian rhythm (Zee & Manthena, 2007). It includes advanced sleep phase disorder (early bedtime/awakening), delayed sleep phase disorder, non-24 h-sleep disorder, irregular sleep disorder, jet lag, and shift work disorder. Advanced sleep phase is very rare and occurs mainly in the elderly. It involves early morning awakenings and results in afternoon/evening sleepiness and performance impairment. Delayed sleep phase is, however, very common. It affects mainly younger individuals and involves an inability to initiate sleep before 3 a.m. It strongly impairs daytime performance for individuals with normal day-oriented working days. The cause is commonly a late night pattern of social activities which involves light exposure too late and the absence of morning light exposure. Both lead to a late setting of the biological clock. A non-24 h circadian rhythm leads to gradual increase in the conflict with the circadian rhythm and results in shortened sleep. It mainly occurs in the blind. An irregular sleep rhythm involves sleep being spread out across the 24 h and a fragmented sleep pattern. It mainly occurs in older, institutionalized individuals who lack exposure to day–night changes of light exposure. Jet lag is another subdiagnosis, but and is usually of short duration. Shift work disorder is discussed later, in connection with shift work.

Shift Work and Sleep/Wakefulness

The key problem with shift work in relation to sleep and wakefulness is that the night shift component of the work schedule requires work when the circadian clock drives the physiology toward deactivation and that sleep is displaced to a time of day when the circadian clock drives the physiology toward activation. This results in a conflict with consequences for disturbed sleep and alertness. Later we first introduce the concept of shift work. Thereafter, we discuss its links to sleep and alertness.

Shift Work

"Shift work" is an imprecise concept, although it usually refers to a work-hour system in which a relay of employees extends the period of production beyond the conventional 8-h day. There are four major types of shift work: day work, permanently displaced work hours, rotating shift work, and roster work.

Day work involves work periods between approximately 7 a.m. and 7 p.m. *Permanently displaced* work hours require the individual to work either in a morning shift (approximately 6 a.m. to 2 p.m.), an afternoon shift (approximately 2 p.m. to 10 p.m.), or a night shift (approximately 10 p.m. to 6 a.m.). *Rotating shift work* involves alternation between two or three shifts. Two-shift work usually involves morning and afternoon shifts, whereas three-shift also includes the night shift. Three-shift work is often subdivided according to the number of teams that are used to cover the 24 h – of work cycle – usually three to six teams, depending on the speed of rotation (number of consecutive shifts of the same type). *Roster work* is similar to rotating shift work but may be less regular, more flexible, and less geared to specific teams. It is used in service-oriented occupations, such as transport, health care, and law enforcement. In most industrialized countries, approximately one-third of the population has some form of "nonday work" (shift work) (Mitler et al., 1988). Approximately 5–10% have shift work that includes night work. In Europe, approximately 20% of the member states of the European Union have work shifts that include night hours (Eurostat, 1997).

Sleep in Shift Work

Early (Graf, Pirtkien, Rutenfranz, & Ulich, 1958; Thiis-Evensen, 1958) as well as more recent questionnaire studies (Ribet & Derriennic, 1999) indicate that the dominant health problem reported by shift workers is disturbed sleep and wakefulness. At least three-fourths of the shift workers are affected (Åkerstedt, 1998) and insufficient sleep is often given as the reason for leaving shift work. The night shift characteristically spans the time between 10 p.m. and 6 a.m., although there is considerable variation. The night sleep *before* the first night shift is usually reported to be rather long (Knauth & Rutenfranz, 1981), starts rather early, and lasts to around 8 o'clock in the morning, or a somewhat further. It is frequently (30–50% prevalence) associated with napping in the afternoon before the first night shift, especially if the preceding main sleep has been short. Sleep after a night shift is usually initiated 1 h after the termination of the shift (Knauth & Rutenfranz, 1981; Tepas, 1982), with very little variation (30–60 min standard deviation) between individuals. The study by Pilcher, Lambert, and Huffcutt (2000) showed that most sleep reduction occurred after rotating night shifts – permanent night work seemed to produce slightly longer sleep.

EEG studies of rotating shift workers and similar groups have shown that duration of sleep during the day sleep is 1–4 h shorter than sleep at night (Foret & Lantin, 1972). The shortening is due to the fact that sleep is terminated after only 4–6 h without the individual being able to return to sleep. The sleep loss is primarily accounted for by reductions in stage 2 sleep and stage REM sleep (dream sleep). Stages 3 and 4 ("deep" sleep) do not seem to be affected. Furthermore, the time taken to fall asleep (sleep latency) is usually shorter. Also night sleep before a morning shift is reduced, but the termination is through artificial means and the awakening usually difficult and unpleasant (Dahlgren, 1981a). Interestingly, day sleep does not seem to improve much across series of night shifts (Foret & Benoit, 1978; Dahlgren, 1981b). It appears, however, that night workers sleep slightly better (longer) than rotating workers on the night shift (Kripke, Cook, & Lewis, 1971; Bryden & Holdstock, 1973).

Approximately one-third of the shift workers add a late afternoon nap between subsequent night shifts (Knauth & Rutenfranz, 1981; Tepas, 1982). The nap duration often exceeds 1 h and the prevalence of napping increases with decreasing length of the prior main sleep (Åkerstedt & Torsvall, 1985; Rosa, 1993). The nap thus seems to be a compensation for insufficient prior sleep.

The long-term effects of shift work on sleep are rather poorly understood. However, Dumont, Montplaisir, and Infante-Rivard (1988) found that the amount of sleep/wake and related disturbances in present day workers were positively related to their previous experience of night work. Guilleminault, Czeisler, Coleman, and Miles (1982) found an overrepresentation of former shift workers with different clinical sleep/wake disturbances appearing at a sleep clinic. Recently, we have shown that in pairs of twins discordant on night work exposure, the exposed twin reports somewhat deteriorated sleep quality and health after retirement (Ingre & Åkerstedt, 2004).

Individual Differences and Shift Work Sleep Disorder
It has often been observed that some shift workers have more difficulties than others. Among the cited factors that are thought to inhibit adjustment to night work are the diurnal "type" of a person (being an evening or morning person), age, and having an excessive need for sleep (Härmä, 1995). The limited findings regarding these influences, however, are limited and prevent firm conclusions. Whatever the causes, the symptoms resulting from an inability to adjust to shift work are excessive fatigue/sleepiness and

nonrestorative sleep (Axelsson, Åkerstedt, Kecklund, Lindqvist, & Attefors, 2003).

The sleep/wake problems in shift work are more pronounced in some individuals and may then fulfill the criteria for the diagnostic classification "Shift Work Sleep Disorder" (SWSD). *The Diagnosis and Statistical Manual of Mental Disorders* (*DSM IV*; APA, 1994) defines SWSD as "report of difficulty falling asleep, staying asleep, or non-restorative sleep for at least one month" and it must be associated with "a work period that occurs during the habitual sleep phase." The recent version of the International Classification of Sleep Disorders (ICSD; AASM, 2001) lists EDS as an additional required criterion for the syndrome. Note that normal night sleep and normal daytime alertness should be present when the individual is not working nights (see also Reid and Zee (2004) for a review).

In one recent attempt to estimate the prevalence of SWSD, the authors arrived at 10% of a population of shift workers (Drake, Roehrs, Richardson, Walsh, & Roth, 2004b). In another study of 400 shift workers, it was found that among the 8% of the sample which had a very negative attitude to work hours there was a greater proportion of sleepiness and sleep complaints (Axelsson, Åkerstedt, Kecklund, & Lowden, 2004).

SOCIETAL EFFECTS OF DISTURBED/SHORT SLEEP

Sleepiness/Accidents

Even if we can show that sleep loss and circadian influences have remarkably strong effects on alertness and behavioral efficiency, the field studies demonstrating the effects on society are relatively few (Philip & Akerstedt, 2006). However, poor or shortened sleep is prospectively related to fatal accidents at work and accident risk is considerably increased in relation to irregular work hours (Åkerstedt, Fredlund, Gillberg, & Jansson, 2002a). Thus, driving at night or short prior sleep are strong predictors of road accidents (Connor et al., 2002). The risk of road accidents is also increased in sleep apneics (Terán-Santos et al., 1999) and in insomniacs (Sagberg, 2006).

As may be surmised, the effects on sleepiness and accidents are largely connected with night or morning work. With respect to the prevalence of perceived sleepiness there is a wealth of questionnaire studies suggesting that the overwhelming majority of shift workers experience sleepiness in connection with night shift work, whereas day work is associated with only marginal or no sleepiness (Andersen, 1970; Menzel, 1962; Mott, Mann,

McLoughlin, & Warwick, 1965; Thiis-Evensen, 1957; Wyatt & Mariott, 1953). In many studies, a majority of shift workers admitted to having experienced involuntary sleep on the night shift, whereas this is rare on day-oriented shifts (Prokop & Prokop, 1955). Between 10 and 20% report falling asleep during night work.

Ambulatory EEG recordings verify that incidents of actual sleep occur during night work in, for example, process operators (Torsvall, Åkerstedt, Gillander, & Knutsson, 1989). Other groups, such as train drivers or truck drivers showed clear signs of falling-asleep incidents while driving at night (Caille & Bassano, 1977; Torsvall & Åkerstedt, 1987). This occurs toward the second half of the night and appears as repeated bursts of alpha and theta EEG activity, together with closed eyes and slow undulating eye movements. As a rule, the bursts are short (1–15 sec) but frequent, and seem to reflect letdowns in the effort to fend off sleep. Approximately one-fourth of the subjects recorded show the EEG/EOG patterns of fighting with sleep. Similar observations have been made for truck drivers (Kecklund & Åkerstedt, 1993; Mitler, Miller, Lipsitz, Walsh, & Wylie, 1997), train drivers (Torsvall & Åkerstedt, 1987), and medical interns (Lockley et al., 2004). Subjective ratings of sleepiness are also strongly increased during the night work or morning work as demonstrated in industrial workers (Axelsson et al., 2004) or truck drivers (Kecklund & Åkerstedt, 1993).

As may be expected, sleepiness on the night shift is reflected in performance. One of the classic studies in this area was carried out by Bjerner, Holm, and Swensson (1955), who showed that errors in meter readings over a period of 20 years in a gas works had a pronounced peak on the night shift. There was also a secondary peak during the afternoon. Similarly, Brown (1949) demonstrated that, compared to daytime performance, the speed with which telephone operators connected calls was considerably slower at night. Hildebrandt, Rohmert, and Rutenfranz (1974) found that train drivers failed to operate their alerting safety devices more often at night than during the day. Most other studies of performance have used laboratory type tests and demonstrated, for example, reduced reaction time or poorer mental arithmetic on the night shift (Tepas, Walsh, Moss, & Armstrong, 1981; Tilley, Wilkinson, Warren, Watson, & Drud, 1982). Flight simulation studies have, furthermore shown that the ability to "fly" a simulator (Klein, Brüner, & Holtman, 1970), or to carry out a performance test (Dawson & Reid, 1997) at night may decrease to a level corresponding to that after moderate alcohol consumption (>0.05% blood alcohol).

The sleepiness induced by irregular work hours also cause increased accident risks. This is particularly obvious in connection with road transport. Thus, Harris (1977) and Hamelin (1987) and others (Langlois, Smolensky, Hsi, & Weir 1985) convincingly demonstrated that single vehicle truck accidents have, by far, the greatest probability of occurring at night (early morning). Similar results have been presented for car accidents (Åkerstedt, Kecklund, & Hörte, 2001). In health care, adverse medical events (wrong diagnoses, for example) are reduced when interns are given possibilities to get at least 6 h of sleep per 24 h (Landrigan et al., 2004).

Furthermore, The US National Transportation Safety board (NTSB) found that 30–40% of all US truck accidents are fatigue related (and grossly underestimated in conventional reports). Recently, the latter investigation was extended to search for the immediate causes of fatigue-induced accidents (NTSB, 1995). It was found that the most important factor was the amount of sleep obtained during the preceding 24 h and split-sleep patterns, whereas the length of time driven seemed to play a minor role. The NTSB also found that the Exxon Valdez accident in 1989 was due to fatigue, caused by reduced sleep and extended work hours (NTSB, 1990). In a new report published by NTSB, the current situation is summarized by the US Department of Transport's investigations into fatigue in the 1990s (NTSB, 1999). The extent of fatal, fatigue-related accidents is considered to be approximately 30%. This is approximately equivalent to the level of incidence in the air traffic sector, whereas similar accidents at sea have an estimated occurrence of slightly less than 20%.

For conventional industrial operations less data are available (Ong, Phoon, Iskandar, & Chia, 1987; Wojtczak-Jaroszowa & Jarosz, 1987) but indicate that overall accidents tend to occur, not surprisingly, when activity is at its peak. These values, however, do not take account of the prevalence of work hours at different times of day .The most carefully executed study, from car manufacturing, seems to indicate a moderate increase (30–50%) in accident risk on night shift work (Smith, Folkard, & Poole, 1994). Most other studies also show an increase in accident rates on the night shift (Menzel, 1950; Andlauer, 1960; Pradhan, 1969; Quaas & Tunsch, 1972; Smith, 1979), but not all.

It is also believed that the (nighttime) nuclear plant meltdown at Chernobyl was due to human error related to work scheduling (Mitler et al., 1988). Similar observations have been made for the Three Mile Island reactor accident and the near miss incidents at the David Beese reactor in Ohio and at the Rancho Seco reactor in California. Several studies have tried to evaluate the costs to society of alertness-related accidents and loss of performance (which does not necessarily reflect only the costs of shift work). One estimate is that the cost of these accidents and performance reductions exceeds $40 billion per year in the US (Leger, 1994). Others have claimed this to be a gross overestimation (Webb, 1995), but the costs are still considerable. Still, it should be emphasized that it is not clear to what extent night shift fatigue may have been the main causal factors.

Morbidity

Poor sleep is also associated with an increased prospective risk of myocardial infarction, particularly when combined with increased resting heart rate – a marker of sympathetic overactivity (Nilsson, Nilsson, Hedblad, & Berglund, 2001). Also hypertension is increased in short and long sleepers (Gottlieb et al., 2006). In women under rehabilitation from a myocardial infarction, the risk of recurrent myocardial events is increased in self-reported poor sleepers (Leineweber, Kecklund, Janszky, Åkerstedt, & Orth-Gomér, 2003). In addition, frequent events of waking-up exhausted in the morning is a predictor of subsequent myocardial infarction (Appels & Schouten, 1991). The exhausted state is also associated with reduced amounts of sleep stages 3 and 4 (van Diest & Appels, 1994).

One new and interesting aspect of sleep loss is the impact on glucose metabolism and diabetes. Previous epidemiological studies have shown that patients with type 2 diabetes report more sleep problems than nondiabetic subjects (Nilsson et al., 2002). This finding could be confounded by obesity or by obstructive sleep apnea. However, in a prospective follow-up study of healthy middle-aged men from Malmö, Sweden, it was recently shown that the 12-year risk of developing type 2 diabetes was independently predicted by self-reported difficulties in falling asleep and by elevated resting heart rate, after full adjustment for obesity, lifestyle factors, and other risk factors (Nilsson, Rööst, Engström, Hedblad, & Berglund, 2004). One possible explanation is obstructive sleep apnea (OSA), which was not measured in the Malmö study, but another possibility would be chronic low-grade inflammation, both linked to insomnia and risk of type 2 diabetes. Also the weakening of insulin efficiency due to loss of sleep might contribute (Knutson et al., 2007).

The presence of a sleep disorder is usually related to many other health problems (Taylor et al., 2007) as well as a higher accident risks, lower self esteem, lower work satisfaction, and less efficiency at work compared to normal sleepers (Leger, Massuel, & Metlaine, 2006). Also sickness absence is increased (Vahtera, Pentti, Helenius, & Kivimaki, 2006; Leger et al., 2006) and complaints of sleep and fatigue one year predicts long-term sickness absence the next year (Akerstedt, Kecklund, Alfredsson, & Selen, 2007a).

Insomnia is a perpetuating factor in depression (Neckelmann, Mykletun, & Dahl, 2007; Pigeon et al., 2008) and increases the risk of developing anxiety (Neckelmann et al., 2007). Sleep duration (short) is also involved in the metabolic syndrome (Hall et al., 2008).

Burnout is another result of long-term stress and a growing health problem in many western countries (Weber & Jaekel-Reinhard, 2000). In Sweden, burnout is estimated to account for most of the doubling of long-term sickness absence since the mid-1990s (RFV, 2003). The characteristic clinical symptoms of the condition are excessive and persistent fatigue, emotional distress, and cognitive dysfunction (Kushnir & Melamed, 1992; Melamed, Kushnir, & Shirom, 1992; Maslach et al., 2001). Self-reports of disturbed sleep are pronounced in subjects scoring high on burnout (Melamed et al., 1999; Grossi et al., 2005). EEG studies have demonstrated increased sleep fragmentation (Söderström et al., 2004; Ekstedt et al., 2006), as well as reduced SWS, long sleep and REM latencies, and other indicators of abnormal sleep (Ekstedt et al., 2006).

Sleep and Mortality

The medical interest in sleep may have begun to increase with the systematic demonstrations of the lethal effects of sleep deprivation in rats, which has been recently summarized (Rechtschaffen & Bergmann, 2002). The mechanism, however, is still unclear. A "vascular collapse" was indicated, even if some authors have found an apparent inability of the immune system to protect against endotoxins (Everson & Toth, 2000). Interesting from a recuperative point of view is also that rats that succeed in getting some REM sleep will survive for a longer time. Also rats, which are taken out of the study before dying, will show strong increases in REM sleep initially. This, obviously, suggests and important function for REM sleep in long-term survival.

In another approach, Lugaresi's group in Bologna demonstrated the first cases of fatal familial insomnia (Lugaresi et al., 1986). This is an autosomal dominant prion disease that involves degeneration of medio-dorsal and antero-ventral nuclei of the thalamus. These overlap with the medial thalamic areas, which are engaged in the synchronization of CNS neurons, particularly SWS, which is the hallmark of sleep. Death ensues in about 7 months to 7 years and the intervening period is characterized by apathy, drowsiness, hallucinations, dream enactment (oneiric stupor), sympathetic over activation, ataxia, and spontaneous myoclonus. Remarkably, only stages 1 and REM remain. This suggests that NREM sleep is necessary for survival.

Another development is the long-term follow up of individuals with different amounts of habitual sleep (Kripke, Simons, Garfinkel, & Hammond, 1979). Large (3–4 h) deviations from the median (8 h) in apparently healthy individuals yielded an increased mortality. This study was recently repeated with approximately the same results, even if the median with lowest risk turned out to be 7 h (Kripke, Garfinkel, Wingard, Klauber, & Marler, 2002). Similar results have been reported by others (Ferrie et al., 2007; Gangwisch et al., 2007; Hublin, Partinen, Koskenvuo, & Kaprio, 2007).

COMMENTS AND CONCLUSIONS

The present review has tried to point out the essential role of sleep in restitution from everyday wear and tear. Sleep will not only reset alertness, mood, and performance capacity to normal levels after a night of sleep. It will also regenerate the CNS, the metabolic system, the endocrine system, and the immune system. Stress, irregular work hours, nighttime social activity, and a number of diseases will interfere with restitution. This leads to increased risks of a number of diseases, accidents, and suboptimal functioning in general. On a positive note, protecting and promoting sleep will have the opposite effects and may even be used as complementary treatment of some diseases. The latter is, however, at very early stages and there is much research needed to develop optimal strategies. We also lack research on the amount of exposure to stress that carries risk and at what levels of exposure the development of disease may be counteracted by improved sleep. Some of this research should also focus on how our 24/7 society should be modified to maintain safe levels of sleep. How many night shifts should be permitted, or how many morning shifts, or how long shifts, or how many successive working days etc? One embarrassing final note is that we do not really know for sure which aspects of sleep are most important for restitution. Although SWS may be a candidate, there is little evidence for a straightforward relation between amounts produced and subsequent health and functioning.

REFERENCES

AASM. (2001). *International classification of sleep disorders – Diagnostic and coding manual.* Chicago, IL: American Academy of Sleep Medicine.

AASM. (2005). *ICSD – International classification of sleep disorders, revised: Diagnostic and coding manual*. Chicago, IL: American Academy of Sleep Medicine.

Adam, K., Tomeny, M., & Oswald, I. (1986). Physiological and psychological differences between good and poor sleepers. *Journal of Psychiatric Research, 20*(4), 301–316.

Åhsberg, E. (2000). Dimensions of fatigue in different working populations. *Scandinavian Journal of Psychology, 41*(3), 231–241.

Åkerstedt, T. (1987). Sleep and stress. In: J. H. Peter, T. Podszus & P. von Wichert (Eds), *Sleep related disorders and internal diseases* (pp. 183–191). Heidelberg: Springer Verlag.

Åkerstedt, T. (1998). Shift work and disturbed sleep/wakefulness. *Sleep Medicine Reviews, 2*, 117–128.

Akerstedt, T., Connor, J., Gray, A., & Kecklund, G. (2008). Predicting road crashes from a mathematical model of alertness regulation – The sleep/wake predictor. *Accident Analysis and Prevention, 40*(4), 1480–1485.

Åkerstedt, T., & Folkard, S. (1995). Validation of the S and C components of the three-process model of alertness regulation. *Sleep, 18*(1), 1–6.

Åkerstedt, T., Folkard, S., & Portin, C. (2004). Predictions from the three-process model of alertness. *Aviation, Space and Environmental Medicine, 75*, A75–A83.

Åkerstedt, T., Fredlund, P., Gillberg, M., & Jansson, B. (2002a). A prospective study of fatal occupational accidents – Relationship to sleeping difficulties and occupational factors. *Journal of Sleep Research, 11*, 69–71.

Åkerstedt, T., Fredlund, P., Gillberg, M., & Jansson, B. (2002b). Work load and work hours in relation to disturbed sleep and fatigue in a large representative sample. *Journal of Psychosomatic Research, 53*, 585–588.

Åkerstedt, T., & Gillberg, M. (1981). The circadian variation of experimentally displaced sleep. *Sleep, 4*, 159–169.

Åkerstedt, T., & Gillberg, M. (1986). A dose–response study of sleep loss and spontaneous sleep termination. *Psychophysiology, 23*, 293–297.

Åkerstedt, T., & Gillberg, M. (1990). Subjective and objective sleepiness in the active individual. *International Journal of Neuroscience, 52*, 29–37.

Åkerstedt, T., Hume, K., Minors, D., & Waterhouse, J. (1997). Good sleep – Its timing and physiological sleep characteristics. *Journal of Sleep Research, 6*, 221–229.

Akerstedt, T., Kecklund, G., Alfredsson, L., & Selen, J. (2007a). Predicting long-term sickness absence from sleep and fatigue. *Journal of Sleep Research, 16*(4), 341–345.

Akerstedt, T., Kecklund, G., & Axelsson, J. (2007b). Impaired sleep after bedtime stress and worries. *Biological Psychology, 76*(3), 170–173.

Åkerstedt, T., Kecklund, G., & Hörte, L.-G. (2001). Night driving, season, and the risk of highway accidents. *Sleep, 24*, 401–406.

Åkerstedt, T., Knutsson, A., Westerholm, P., Theorell, T., Alfredsson, L., & Kecklund, G. (2002c). Sleep disturbances, work stress and work hours. A cross-sectional study. *Journal of Psychosomatic Research, 53*, 741–748.

Åkerstedt, T., & Torsvall, L. (1985). Napping in shift work. *Sleep, 8*, 105–109.

Alfredsson, L., Spetz, C.-L., & Theorell, T. (1985). Type of occupation and near-future hospitalization for myocardial infarction and some other diagnoses. *International Journal of Epidemiology, 14*(3), 378–388.

Ancoli-Israel, S., & Roth, T. (1999). Characteristics of insomnia in the United States: Results of the 1991 National Sleep Foundation survey. I. *Sleep, 22*(Suppl. 2), S347–S353.

Andersen, J. E. (1970). *Three-shift work*. Copenhagen: Socialforskningsinstitutet.

Andlauer, P. (1960). The effect of shift working on the workers' health. European Productivity Agency, TU Information Bulletin, 29.

APA. (1994). *Diagnostic and statistical manual of mental disorders* ((DSM-IV), 4th Ed.). Washington, DC: American Psychiatric Association.

Appels, A., & Schouten, E. (1991). Waking up exhausted as risk indicator of myocardial infarction. *American Journal of Cardiology, 68*(August 1), 395–398.

Askenasy, J. J. M., & Lewin, I. (1996). The impact of missile warfare on self-reported sleep quality. Part 1. *Sleep, 19*, 47–51.

Axelsson, J., Åkerstedt, T., Kecklund, G., Lindqvist, A., & Attefors, R. (2003). Hormonal changes in satisfied and dissatisfied shift workers across a shift cycle. *Journal of Applied Physiology, 95*, 2099–2105.

Axelsson, J., Åkerstedt, T., Kecklund, G., & Lowden, A. (2004). Tolerance to shift work – How does it relate to sleep and wakefullness? *International Archives of Occupational and Environmental Health, 77*, 121–129.

Balkin, T. J., Bliese, P. D., Belenky, G., Sing, H., Thorne, D. R., Thomas, M., et al. (2004). Comparative utility of instruments for monitoring sleepiness-related performance decrements in the operational environment. *Journal of Sleep Research, 13*(3), 219–227.

Belenky, G., Wesensten, N. J., Thorne, D. R., Thomas, M. L., Sing, H. C., Redmond, D. P., et al. (2003). Patterns of performance degradation and restoration during sleep restriction and subsequent recovery: A sleep dose–response study. *Journal of Sleep Research, 12*(1), 1–12.

Belyavin, A. J., & Spencer, M. B. (2004). Modeling performance and alertness: The QinetiQ approach. *Aviation Space and Environmental Medicine, 75*(Suppl. 3), A93–A103; Discussion 104–106.

Berntsson, L., Lundberg, U., & Krantz, G. (2006). Gender differences in work–home interplay and symptom perception among Swedish white-collar employees. *Journal of Epidemiology and Community Health, 60*(12), 1070–1076.

Bixler, E. O., Kales, A., & Soldatos, C. R. (1979). Sleep disorders encountered in medical practice: A national survey of physicians. *Behavioral Medicine, 3*(November), 1–6.

Bjerner, B., Holm, Å., & Swensson, Å. (1955). Diurnal variation of mental performance. A study of three-shift workers. *British Journal of Industrial Medicine, 12*, 103–110.

Bonnet, M. H., & Arand, D. L. (1998). Heart rate variability in insomniacs and matched normal sleepers. *Psychosomatic Medicine, 60*, 610–615.

Bonnet, M. H., & Arand, D. L. (2003a). Clinical effects of sleep fragmentation versus sleep deprivation. *Sleep Medicine Reviews, 7*(4), 297–310.

Bonnet, M. H., & Arand, D. L. (2003b). Insomnia, metabolic rate and sleep restoration. *Journal of Internal Medicine, 254*(1), 23–31.

Borbély, A. A. (1982). A two-process model of sleep regulation. *Human Neurobiology, 1*, 195–204.

Borg, G. (1990). Psychophysical scaling with applications in physical work and the perception of exertion. *Scandinavian Journal of Work, Environment and Health, 16*(Suppl. 1), 55–58.

Brown, M. R. (1991). Neuropeptide-mediated regulation of the neuroendocrine and autonomic responses to stress. In: J. McCubbin, P. Kaufman & C. Nemeroff (Eds), *Stress, neuropeptides, and systemic disease* (pp. 73–93). San Diego: Academic Press.

Brown, R. C. (1949). The day and night performance of teleprinter switchboard operators. *Journal of Occupational Psychology, 23*, 121–126.

Bryant, P. A., Trinder, J., & Curtis, N. (2004). Sick and tired: Does sleep have a vital role in the immune system. *Nature Reviews Immunology, 4*, 457–467.

Bryden, G., & Holdstock, T. L. (1973). Effects of night duty on sleep patterns of nurses. *Psychophysiology, 10*(1), 36–42.

Caille, E. J., & Bassano, J. L. (1977). Validation of a behavior analysis methodology: Variation of vigilance in night driving as a function of the rate of carboxyhemoglobin. In: R. R. Mackie (Ed.), *Vigilance* (pp. 59–72). New York: Plenum Press.

Cannon, W. B. (1914). The emergency function of the adrenal medulla in pain and the major emotions. *American Journal of Physiology, 33,* 356–372.

Carskadon, M., & Dement, W. (1977). Sleep tendency: An objective measure of sleep loss. *Sleep Research, 6,* 200.

Carskadon, M. A., & Dement, W. C. (2000). Normal human sleep: An overview. In: M. H. Kryger, T. Roth & W. C. Dement (Eds), *Prinicples and practice of sleep medicine* (3rd ed., pp. 15–25). Philadelphia: W.B. Saunders Company.

Cernovsky, Z. Z. (1984). Life stress measures and reported frequency of sleep disorders. *Perceptual and Motor Skills, 58,* 39–49.

Chrousos, G. P., & Gold, P. W. (1992). The concepts of stress and stress system disorders. *Journal of the American Medical Association, 267,* 1244–1252.

Connor, J., Norton, R., Ameratunga, S., Robinson, E., Civil, I., Dunn, R., et al. (2002). Driver sleepiness and risk of serious injury to car occupants: Population based case control study. *British Medical Journal, 324*(7346), 1125.

Czeisler, C. A., Weitzman, E. D., Moore-Ede, M. C., Zimmerman, J. C., & Knauer, R. S. (1980). Human sleep: Its duration and organization depend on its circadian phase. *Science, 210,* 1264–1267.

Dahlgren, A., Kecklund, G., & Akerstedt, T. (2005). Different levels of work-related stress and the effects on sleep, fatigue and cortisol. *Scandinavian Journal of Work, Environment and Health, 31*(4), 277–285.

Dahlgren, A., Kecklund, G., & Akerstedt, T. (2006). Overtime work and its effects on sleep, sleepiness, cortisol and blood pressure in an experimental field study. *Scandinavian Journal of Work, Environment and Health, 32*(4), 318–327.

Dahlgren, K. (1981a). Adjustment of circadian rhythms and EEG sleep functions to day and night sleep among permanent night workers and rotating shift workers. *Psychophysiology, 18,* 381–391.

Dahlgren, K. (1981b). Long-term adjustment of circadian rhythms to a rotating shiftwork schedule. *Scandinavian Journal of Work, Environment and Health, 7,* 141–151.

Davidson, L., Fleming, R., & Baum, A. (1987). Chronic stress, catecholamines, and sleep disturbance at Three Mile Island. *Human Stress, 13,* 75–83.

Dawson, D., & Reid, K. (1997). Fatigue, alcohol and performance impairment. *Nature, 388,* p. 235.

Dement, W. C., Hall, J., & Walsh, J. K. (2003). Tiredness versus sleepiness: Semantics or a target for public education? *Sleep, 26*(4), 485–486.

Dijk, D. J., Duffy, J. F., & Czeisler, C. A. (1992). Circadian and sleep-wake dependent aspects of subjective alertness and cognitive performance. *Journal of Sleep Research, 1,* 112–117.

Dinges, D. F., Pack, F., Williams, K., Gillen, K. A., Powell, J. W., Ott, G. E., et al. (1997). Cumulative sleepiness, mood disturbance, and psychomotor vigilance performance decrements during a week of sleep restricted to 4–5 hours per night. *Sleep, 20*(4), 267–277.

Dow, B. M., Kelsoe, J. R., & Gillin, J. C. (1996). Sleep and dreams in Vietnam PTSD and depression. *Biological Psychiatry, 39,* 42–50.

Drake, C., Richardson, G., Roehrs, T., Scofield, H., & Roth, T. (2004a). Vulnerability to stress-related sleep disturbance and hyperarousal. *Sleep, 27*, 285–291.

Drake, C. L., Roehrs, T., Richardson, G., Walsh, J., & Roth, T. (2004b). Shift work sleep disorder: Prevalence and consequences beyond that of symptomatic day workers. *Sleep, 27*(8), 1453–1462.

Drummond, S. P., & Brown, G. G. (2001). The effects of total sleep deprivation on cerebral responses to cognitive performance. *Neuropsychopharmacology, 25*(Suppl. 5), S68–S73.

Dumont, M., Montplaisir, J., & Infante-Rivard, C. (1988). Insomnia symptoms in nurses with former permanent nightwork experience. In: W. P. Koella, F. Obal, H. Schulz & P. Visser (Eds), *Sleep '86* (pp. 405–406). Stuttgart: Gustav Fischer Verlag.

Dunn, A. J., & Berridge, C. W. (1990). Physiological and behavioral responses to corticotropin-releasing factor administration: Is CRF a mediator of anxiety or stress responses? *Brain Research Reviews, 15*, 71–100.

Ekstedt, M., Åkerstedt, T., & Söderström, M. (2004). Microarousals during sleep are associated with increased levels of lipids, cortisol, and blood pressure. *Psychosomatic Medicine, 66*, 925–931.

Ekstedt, M., Söderström, M., Åkerstedt, T., Nilsson, J., Sondergaard, H.-P., & Perski, A. (2006). Disturbed sleep and fatigue in occupational burnout. *Scandinavian Journal of Work, Environment and Health, 32*(2), 121–131.

Eller, N. H., Netterstrom, B., & Hansen, A. M. (2006). Psychosocial factors at home and at work and levels of salivary cortisol. *Biological Psychology, 73*(3), 280–287.

Eurostat. (1997). Employment in Europe 1996: European Commission, Brussels 1996. Eurostat, Labour Force Surveyo (Document Number).

Evengard, B., Jacks, A., Pedersen, N. L., & Sullivan, P. F. (2005). The epidemiology of chronic fatigue in the Swedish Twin Registry. *Psychological Medicine, 35*(9), 1317–1326.

Everson, C. A., & Toth, L. A. (2000). Systemic bacterial invasion induced by sleep deprivation. *American Journal of Physiology. Regulatory, Integrative and Comparative Physiology, 278*, R905–R916.

Fabsitz, R. R., Sholinsky, P., & Goldberg, J. (1997). Correlates of sleep problems among men: The Vietnam era twin registry. *Journal of Sleep Research, 6*, 50–60.

Ferrara, M., De Gennaro, L., & Bertini, M. (1999). The effects of slow-wave sleep (SWS) deprivation and time of night on behavioral performance upon awakening. *Physiology and Behavior, 68*, 55–61.

Ferrie, J. E., Shipley, M. J., Cappuccio, F. P., Brunner, E., Miller, M. A., Kumari, M., et al. (2007). A prospective study of change in sleep duration: Associations with mortality in the Whitehall II cohort. *Sleep, 30*(12), 1659–1666.

Feyer, A.-M. (2001). Fatigue: Time to recognise and deal with an old problem. *British Medical Journal, 322*, 829–830.

Folkard, S., & Åkerstedt, T. (1991). A three process model of the regulation of alertness and sleepiness. In: R. Ogilvie & R. Broughton (Eds), *Sleep, arousal and performance: Problems and promises* (pp. 11–26). Boston: Birkhäuser.

Folkow, B. (1997). Physiological aspects of the "defence" and "defeat" reactions. *Acta Physiologica Scandinavica, 640*, 34–37.

Foret, J., & Benoit, O. (1978). Shiftwork: The level of adjustment to schedule reversal assessed by a sleep study. *Waking and Sleeping, 2*, 107–112.

Foret, J., & Lantin, G. (1972). The sleep of train drivers: An example of the effects of irregular work schedules on sleep. In: W. P. Colquhoun (Ed.), *Aspects of human efficiency*.

Diurnal rhythm and loss of sleep (pp. 273–281). London: The English Universities Press Ltd.

Franzen, P. L., Siegle, G. J., & Buysse, D. J. (2008). Relationships between affect, vigilance, and sleepiness following sleep deprivation. *Journal of Sleep Research, 17*(1), 34–41.

Fröberg, J., Karlsson, C.-G., Levi, L., & Lidberg, L. (1972). Circadian variations in performance, psychological ratings, catecholamine excretion, and diuresis during prolonged sleep deprivation. *International Journal of Psychobiology, 2,* 23–36.

Fröberg, J., Karlsson, C. G., Levi, L., & Lidberg, L. (1975). Circadian variations of catecholamine excretion, shooting range performance and self-ratings of fatigue during sleep deprivation. *Biological Psychology, 2,* 175–188.

Gangwisch, J. E., Heymsfield, S. B., Boden-Albala, B., Buijs, R. M., Kreier, F., Pickering, T. G., et al. (2007). Sleep duration as a risk factor for diabetes incidence in a large U.S. sample. *Sleep, 30*(12), 1667–1673.

Geroldi, C., Frisoni, G. B., Rozzini, R., De Leo, D., & Trabucchi, M. (1996). Principal lifetime occupation and sleep quality in the elderly. *Gerontology, 42,* 163–169.

Gillberg, M., Kecklund, G., Axelsson, J., & Åkerstedt, T. (1994). Counteracting sleepiness with a short nap. *Journal of Sleep Research, 3*(Suppl. 1), 90.

Gottlieb, D. J., Redline, S., Nieto, F. J., Baldwin, C. M., Newman, A. B., Resnick, H. E., et al. (2006). Association of usual sleep duration with hypertension: The sleep heart health study. *Sleep, 29*(8), 1009–1014.

Graf, O., Pirtkien, R., Rutenfranz, J., & Ulich, E. (1958). *Nervose Belastung im Betrieb. I. Nachtarbeit und Nervose Belastung:* Westdeutscher Verlag.

Grandjean, E. P. (1970). Fatigue. *American Industrial Hygiene Association Journal, 31,* 401–411.

Grossi, G., Perski, A., Ekstedt, M., Johansson, T., Lindström, M., & Holm, K. (2005). The morning salivary cortisol response in burnout. *Journal of Psychosomatic Research.*

Guilleminault, C., Czeisler, S., Coleman, R., & Miles, L. (1982). Circadian rhythm disturbances and sleep disorders in shift workers (EEG Suppl no. 36). In: P. A. Buser, W. A. Cobb & T. Okuma (Eds), *Kyoto symposia* (pp. 709–714). Amsterdam: Elsevier.

Hall, M., Buysse, D. J., Nowell, P. D., Nofzinger, E. A., Houck, P., Reynolds, C. F., et al. (2000). Symptoms of stress and depression as correlates of sleep in primary insomnia. *Psychosomatic Medicine, 62,* 227–230.

Hall, M. H., Muldoon, M. F., Jennings, J. R., Buysse, D. J., Flory, J. D., & Manuck, S. B. (2008). Self-reported sleep duration is associated with the metabolic syndrome in midlife adults. *Sleep, 31*(5), 635–643.

Hamelin, P. (1987). Lorry driver's time habits in work and their involvement in traffic accidents. *Ergonomics, 30,* 1323–1333.

Hammar, N., Alfredsson, L., & Theorell, T. (1994). Job characteristics and the incidence of myocardial infarction. *International Journal of Epidemiology, 23*(2), 277–284.

Härmä, M. (1995). Sleepiness and shiftwork: Individual differences. *Journal of Sleep Research, 4*(Suppl. 2), 57–61.

Härmä, M., Suvanto, S., Popkin, S., Pulli, K., Mulder, M., & Hirvonen, K. (1998). A dose–response study of total sleep time and the ability to maintain wakefulness. *Journal of Sleep Research, 7,* 167–174.

Harris, W. (1977). Fatigue, circadian rhythm and truck accidents. In: R. R. Mackie (Ed.), *Vigilance* (pp. 133–146). New York: Plenum Press.

Harrison, Y., & Horne, J. A. (2000). The impact of sleep deprivation on decision making: A review. *Journal of Experimental Psychology: Applied, 6*(3), 236–249.

Harvey, A. G., Tang, N. K., & Browning, L. (2005). Cognitive approaches to insomnia. *Clinical Psychology Review*, *25*(5), 593–611.

Haynes, S. N., Adams, A., & Franzen, M. (1981). The effects of presleep stress on sleep-onset insomnia. *Journal of Abnormal Psychology*, *90*, 601–606.

Hildebrandt, G., Rohmert, W., & Rutenfranz, J. (1974). 12 and 24 hour rhythms in error frequency of locomotive drivers and the influence of tiredness. *International Journal of Chronobiology*, *2*, 175–180.

Hoddes, E., Zarcone, V., Smythe, H., Phillips, R., & Dement, W. (1973). Quantification of sleepiness: A new approach. *Psychophysiology*, *10*, 431–436.

Holdstock, T. L., & Verschoor, G. J. (1974). Student sleep patterns before, during and after an examination period. *Journal of Psychology*, *4*, 16–24.

Horne, J. (2003). The semantics of sleepiness. *Sleep*, *26*(6), 763; Author reply 764.

Horne, J. A. (1989). Functional aspects of human slow wave sleep. In: A. Wauquier, C. Dugovic & M. Radulovacki (Eds), *Slow wave sleep. Physiological, pathophysiological, and functional aspects* (pp. 109–119). New York: Raven Press.

Hossain, J. L., Ahmad, P., Reinish, L. W., Kayumov, L., Hossain, N. K., & Shapiro, C. M. (2005). Subjective fatigue and subjective sleepiness: Two independent consequences of sleep disorders? *Journal of Sleep Research*, *14*(3), 245–253.

Huber, R., Ghilardi, M. F., Massimini, M., Ferrarelli, F., Riedner, B. A., Peterson, M. J., et al. (2006). Arm immobilization causes cortical plastic changes and locally decreases sleep slow wave activity. *Nature Neuroscience*, *9*(9), 1169–1176.

Huber, R., Ghilardi, M. F., Massimini, M., & Tononi, G. (2004). Local sleep and learning. *Nature*, *430*(6995), 78–81.

Hublin, C., Partinen, M., Koskenvuo, M., & Kaprio, J. (2007). Sleep and mortality: A population-based 22-year follow-up study. *Sleep*, *30*(10), 1245–1253.

Hursh, S. R., Redmond, D. P., Johnson, M. L., Thorne, D. R., Belenky, G., Balkin, T. J., et al. (2004). Fatigue models for applied research in warfighting. *Aviation Space and Environmental Medicine*, *75*(Suppl. 3), A44–A53; Discussion A54–A60.

Ingre, M., & Åkerstedt, T. (2004). Effect of accumulated night work during the working lifetime, on subjective health and sleep in monozygotic twins. *Journal of Sleep Research*, *13*, 45–48.

Ingre, M., Akerstedt, T., Peters, B., Anund, A., Kecklund, G., & Pickles, A. (2006). Subjective sleepiness and accident risk avoiding the ecological fallacy. *Journal of Sleep Research*, *15*(2), 142–148.

Jansson, M., & Linton, S. J. (2006). Psychosocial work stressors in the development and maintenance of insomnia: A prospective study. *Journal of Occupational Health Psychology*, *11*(3), 241–248.

Jansson-Frojmark, M., & Linton, S. J. (2008). The course of insomnia over one year: A longitudinal study in the general population in Sweden. *Sleep*, *31*(6), 881–886.

Jewett, M. E., Dijk, D.-J., Kronauer, R. E., & Dinges, D. F. (1999). Dose–response relationship between sleep duration and human psychomotor vigilance and subjective alertness. *Sleep*, *22*, 171–179.

Johnson, L. C., Naitoh, P., Moses, J. M., & Lubin, A. (1974). Interaction of REM deprivation and stage 4 deprivation with total sleep loss: Experiment 2. *Psychophysiology*, *11*, 147–159.

Kales, A., Tjiauw-Ling, T., Kollar, E. J., Naitoh, P., Preston, T. A., & Malmstrom, E. J. (1970). Sleep patterns following 205 hours of sleep deprivation. *Psychosomatic Medicine*, *32*(2), 189–200.

Karasek, R. A. (1979). Job demands, job decision latitude and mental strain. Implications for job redesign. *Administrative Sciences Quarterly, 24,* 285–308.

Kecklund, G., & Åkerstedt, T. (1993). Sleepiness in long distance truck driving: An ambulatory EEG study of night driving. *Ergonomics, 36*(9), 1007–1017.

Kecklund, G., & Åkerstedt, T. (1997). Objective components of individual differences in subjective sleep quality. *Journal of Sleep Research, 6,* 217–220.

Kecklund, G., Åkerstedt, T., & Lowden, A. (1997). Morning work: Effects of early rising on sleep and alertness. *Sleep, 20*(3), 215–223.

Killgore, W. D., Killgore, D. B., Day, L. M., Li, C., Kamimori, G. H., & Balkin, T. J. (2007). The effects of 53 hours of sleep deprivation on moral judgment. *Sleep, 30*(3), 345–352.

Klein, D. E., Brüner, H., & Holtman, H. (1970). Circadian rhythm of pilot's efficiency, and effects of multiple time zone travel. *Aerospace Medicine, 41,* 125–132.

Knauth, P., & Rutenfranz, J. (1981). Duration of sleep related to the type of shift work. In: A. Reinberg, N. Vieux & P. Andlauer (Eds), *Night and shift work: Biological and social aspects.* Oxford: Pergamon Press.

Knutson, K. L., Spiegel, K., Penev, P., & Van Cauter, E. (2007). The metabolic consequences of sleep deprivation. *Sleep Medicine Reviews, 11*(3), 163–178.

Konz, S. (1998). Work/rest: Part II – The scientific basis (knowledge base) for the guide. *International Journal of Industrial Ergonomics, 22,* 73–99.

Kripke, D. F., Cook, B., & Lewis, O. F. (1971). Sleep of night workers: EEG recordings. *Psychophysiology, 7*(3), 377–384.

Kripke, D. F., Garfinkel, L., Wingard, D. L., Klauber, M. R., & Marler, M. R. (2002). Mortality associated with sleep duration and insomnia. *Archives of General Psychiatry, 59,* 131–136.

Kripke, D. F., Simons, R. N., Garfinkel, L., & Hammond, E. C. (1979). Short and long sleep and sleeping pills. *Archives of General Psychiatry, 36,* 103–116.

Krupp, L. B., Larocca, N. G., Muir-Nash, J., & Steinberg, A. D. (1989). The fatigue severity scale. *Archives of Neurology, 46,* 1121–1123.

Kuppermann, M., Lubeck, D. P., Mazonson, P. D., Patrick, D. L., Stewart, A. L., Buesching, D. P., et al. (1995). Sleep problems and their correlates in a working population. *Journal of General Internal Medicine, 10,* 25–32.

Kushnir, T., & Melamed, S. (1992). The Gulf War and its impact on burnout and well-being of working civilians. *Psychological Medicine, 22,* 987–995.

Lahl, O., Wispel, C., Willigens, B., & Pietrowsky, R. (2008). An ultra short episode of sleep is sufficient to promote declarative memory performance. *Journal of Sleep Research, 17*(1), 3–10.

Landrigan, C. P., Rothschild, J. M., Cronin, J. W., Kaushal, R., Burdick, E., Katz, J. T., et al. (2004). Effect of reducing interns' work hours on serious medical errors in intensive care units. *New England Journal of Medicine, 351*(18), 1838–1848.

Langlois, P. H., Smolensky, M. H., Hsi, B. P., & Weir, F. W. (1985). Temporal patterns of reported single-vehicle car and truck accidents in Texas, USA during 1980–1983. *Chronobiology International, 2*(2), 131–146.

Lavie, L. (2004). Sleep apnea syndrome, endothelial dysfunction, and cardiovascular morbidity. *Sleep, 27,* 1053–1055.

Leger, D. (1994). The cost of sleep-related accidents: A report for the National Commission on Sleep Disorders Research. *Sleep, 17*(1), 84–93.

Leger, D., Massuel, M. A., & Metlaine, A. (2006). Professional correlates of insomnia. *Sleep*, *29*(2), 171–178.

Leineweber, C., Kecklund, G., Janszky, I., Åkerstedt, T., & Orth-Gomér, K. (2003). Poor sleep increases the prospective risk for recurrent events in middle-aged women with coronary disease. The Stockholm female coronary risk study. *Journal of Psychosomatic Research*, *54*, 121–127.

Lichstein, K. L., Durrence, H. H., Taylor, D. J., Bush, A. J., & Riedel, B. W. (2003). Quantitative criteria for insomnia. *Behavioral Research & Therapy*, *41*(4), 427–445.

Lockley, S. W., Cronin, J. W., Evans, E. E., Cade, B. E., Lee, C. J., Landrigan, C. P., et al. (2004). Effect of reducing interns' weekly work hours on sleep and attentional failures. *New England Journal of Medicine*, *351*(18), 1829–1837.

Lopez-Jimenez, F., & Somers, V. K. (2006). Stress measures linking sleep apnea, hypertension and diabetes – AHI vs arousals vs hypoxemia. *Sleep*, *29*(6), 743–744.

Lugaresi, E., Medori, R., Baruzzi, A., Cortelli, P., Lugaresi, A., Tinuper, P., et al. (1986). Fatal familial insomnia and dysautonomia with selective degeneration of thalamic nuclei. *New England Journal of Medicine*, *315*, 997–1003.

Macdonald, W., & Bendak, S. (2000). Effects of workload level and 8- versus 12-h workday duration on test battery performance. *International Journal of Industrial Ergonomics*, *26*, 399–416.

Mackworth, N. H. (1950). *Researches on the measurement of human performance: Medical research council special report* (Vol. 268, pp. 1–156). London: His Majesty's Stationery Office.

Mallis, M. M., Mejdal, S., Nguyen, T. T., & Dinges, D. F. (2004). Summary of the key features of seven biomathematical models of human fatigue and performance. *Aviation Space and Environmental Medicine*, *75*(Suppl. 3), A4–A14.

Maquet, P. (2000). Functional neuroimaging of normal human sleep by positron emission tomography. *Journal of Sleep Research*, *9*, 207–231.

Maquet, P. (2001). The role of sleep in learning and memory. *Science*, *294*, 1048–1052.

Maslach, C., & Leiter, M. P. (2005). Stress and burnout: The critical research. In: C. L. Cooper (Ed.), *Handbook of stress medicine and health* (Vol. 2, pp. 155–172). Lancaster, UK: CRC Press.

Maslach, C., Schaufeli, W. B., & Leiter, M. P. (2001). Job burnout. *Annual Review of Psychology*, *52*, 397–422.

McEwen, B., Albeck, D., Cameron, H., Chao, H., Gould, E., Hastings, N., et al. (1995). Stress and the brain: A paradoxical role for adrenal steroids. In: G. Litwack (Ed.), *Vitamins and hormones* (pp. 371–402). New York: Academic Press Inc.

McEwen, B. S. (2004). Protection and damage from acute and chronic stress: Allostasis and allostatic overload and relevance to the pathophysiology of psychiatric disorders. *Annals of the New York Academy of Sciences*, *1032*, 1–7.

McEwen, B. S. (2006). Sleep deprivation as a neurobiologic and physiologic stressor: Allostasis and allostatic load. *Metabolism Clinical and Experimental*, *55*, S20–S23.

McEwen, B. S., & Wingfield, J. C. (2003). The concept of allostasis in biology and biomedicine. *Hormones and Behavior*, *43*(1), 2–15.

Melamed, S., Kushnir, T., & Shirom, A. (1992). Burnout and risk factors for cardiovascular diseases. *Behavioral Medicine*, *18*, 53–60.

Melamed, S., Ugarten, U., Shirom, A., Kahana, L., Lerman, Y., & Froom, P. (1999). Chronic burnout, somatic arousal and elevated salivary cortisol levels. *Journal of Psychosomatic Research*, *46*, 591–598.

Mellman, T. A., Nolan, B., Hebding, J., Kulick-Bell, R., & Dominguez, R. (1997). A polysomnographic comparison of veterans with combat-related PTSD, depressed men, and non-Ill controls. *Sleep, 20,* 46–51.

Menzel, W. (1950). Zur Physiologie und Pathologie des Nacht und Schichtarbeiters. *Arbeitsphysiologie, 14,* 304–318.

Menzel, W. (1962). *Menschliche Tag-Nacht-Rhythmik und Schichtarbeit.* Basel: Schwabe.

Mitler, M. M., Carskadon, M. A., Czeisler, C. A., Dement, W. C., Dinges, D. F., & Graeber, R. C. (1988). Catastrophes, sleep and public policy: Concensus report. *Sleep, 11,* 100–109.

Mitler, M. M., Miller, J. C., Lipsitz, J. J., Walsh, J. K., & Wylie, C. D. (1997). The sleep of long-haul truck drivers. *New England Journal of Medicine, 337,* 755–761.

Monk, T. H. (1989). A visual analogue scale technique to measure global vigor and affect. *Psychiatry Research, 27,* 89–99.

Monroe, L. (1967). Psychological and physiological differences between good and poor sleepers. *Journal of Abnormal Psychology, 72,* 255–264.

Morin, C. M., Rodrigue, S., & Ivers, H. (2003). Role of stress, arousal, and coping skills in primary insomnia. *Psychosomatic Medicine, 65,* 259–267.

Morphy, H., Dunn, K. M., Lewis, M., Boardman, H. F., & Croft, P. R. (2007). Epidemiology of insomnia: A longitudinal study in a UK population. *Sleep, 30*(3), 274–280.

Mott, P. E., Mann, F. C., McLoughlin, Q., & Warwick, D. P. (1965). *Shift work – The social, psychological and physical consequences.* Ann Arbor: University of Michigan Press.

Mulgrew, A. T., Ryan, C. F., Fleetham, J. A., Cheema, R., Fox, N., Koehoorn, M., et al. (2007). The impact of obstructive sleep apnea and daytime sleepiness on work limitation. *Sleep Medicine, 9*(1), 42–53.

Neckelmann, D., Mykletun, A., & Dahl, A. A. (2007). Chronic insomnia as a risk factor for developing anxiety and depression. *Sleep, 30*(7), 873–880.

Nilsson, P., Nilsson, J.-Å., Hedblad, B., & Berglund, G. (2001). Sleep disturbances in association with elevated pulse rate for the prediction of mortality – Consequences of mental strain? *Journal of Internal Medicine, 250,* 521–529.

Nilsson, P., Rööst, M., Engström, G., Hedblad, B., Janzon, L., & Berglund, G. (2002). Incidence of diabetes in middle-aged men is related to resting heart rate and difficulties to fall asleep (Abstract). Paper presented at the 7th International Congress of Behavioural Medicine, Helsinki, Finland.

Nilsson, P. M., Rööst, M., Engström, G., Hedblad, B., & Berglund, G. (2004). Incidence of diabetes in middle-aged men is related to sleep disturbances. *Diabetes Care, 27,* 2464–2469.

Nofzinger, E. A. (2005). Neuroimaging and sleep medicine. *Sleep Medicine Reviews, 9*(3), 157–172.

Nordin, M., Knutsson, A., & Sundbom, E. (2008). Is disturbed sleep a mediator in the association between social support and myocardial infarction? *Journal of Health Psychology, 13*(1), 55–64.

NTSB. (1990). Grounding of the US tankship Exxon Valdez on Bligh Reef, Prince William Sound near Valdez, Alaska, March 24, 1989. National Transportation Safety Board. Maritime Accident Report, NTSB/MAR-90/04.

NTSB. (1995). Factors that affect fatigue in heavy truck accidents. National Transportation Safety Board. Safety Study, NTSB/SS-95/01.

NTSB. (1999). *Evaluation of U.S. Department of Transportation: Efforts in the 1990s to address operation fatigue (No. Safety Report NTSB/SR-99/01).* Washington, DC: National Transportation Safety Board (Document Number).

Ohayon, M., Caulet, M., Priest, R., & Guilleminault, C. (1997a). DSM-IV and ICSD-90 insomnia symptoms and sleep dissatisfaction. *British Journal of Psychiatry, 171*, 382–388.

Ohayon, M. M., Guilleminault, C., Paiva, T., Priest, R. G., Rapoport, D. M., Sagales, T., et al. (1997b). An international study on sleep disorders in the general population: Methosological aspects of the use of the sleep-EVAL system. *Sleep, 20*, 1086–1092.

Ong, C. N., Phoon, W. O., Iskandar, N., & Chia, K. S. (1987). Shiftwork and work injuries in an iron and steel mill. *Applied Ergonomics, 18*, 51–56.

Parmeggiani, P. J. (1995). Brain cooling across wake-sleep behavioral states in homeothermic species: An analysis of the underlying physiological mechanisms. *Reviews in the Neuroscience, 6*, 353–363.

Partinen, M., Eskelinen, L., & Tuomi, K. (1984). Complaints of insomnia in different occupations. *Scandinavian Journal of Work, Environment and Health, 10*, 467–469.

Perlis, M. L., Merica, H., Smith, M. T., & Giles, D. E. (2001). Beta EEG activity and insomnia. *Sleep Medicine Reviews, 5*(5), 365–376.

Philip, P., & Akerstedt, T. (2006). Transport and industrial safety, how are they affected by sleepiness and sleep restriction? *Sleep Medicine Reviews, 10*(5), 347–356.

Pigeon, W. R., Hegel, M., Unutzer, J., Fan, M. Y., Sateia, M. J., Lyness, J. M., et al. (2008). Is insomnia a perpetuating factor for late-life depression in the IMPACT cohort? *Sleep, 31*(4), 481–488.

Pilcher, J. J., Lambert, B. J., & Huffcutt, A. I. (2000). Differential effects of permanent and rotating shifts on self-report sleep length: A meta-analytic review. *Sleep, 23*, 155–163.

Pillar, G., Malhotra, A., & Lavie, P. (2000). Post-traumatic stress disorder and sleep – What a nightmare!. *Sleep Medicine Reviews, 4*, 183–200.

Porkka-Heiskanen, T. (1999). Adenosine in sleep and wakefulness. *Annals of Medicine, 31*(2), 125–129.

Pradhan, S. M. (1969). *Reaction of workers on night shift*. Paper presented at the Proceedings of the XVI International Congress of Occupational Health, Tokyo.

Prokop, O., & Prokop, L. (1955). Ermüdung und Einschlafen am Steuer. *Zentralblatt für Verkehrsmedizin, Verkehrspsychologie und angrenzende Gebiete., 1*, 19–30.

Quaas, M., & Tunsch, R. (1972). Problems of disablement and accident frequency in shift and night work. *Studia Laboris et Salutis, 4*, 52–65.

Rechtschaffen, A., & Bergmann, B. M. (2002). Sleep deprivation in the rat: An update of the 1989 paper. *Sleep, 25*, 18–24.

Rechtschaffen, A., & Kales, A. (1968). *A manual of standardized terminology, techniques and scoring system for sleep stages of human subjects*. Bethesda: US Department of Health, Education and Welfare, Public Health Service.

Reid, K. J., & Zee, P. C. (2004). Circadian rhythm disorders. *Seminars in Neurology, 24*(3), 315–325.

Reynolds III, C. F., Hoch, C. C., Buysse, D. J., Houck, P. R., Schlernitzauer, M., Pasternak, R. E., et al. (1993). Sleep after spousal bereavement: A study of recovery from stress. *Biological Psychiatry, 34*, 791–797.

RFV. (2003). *Långtidssjukskrivna – egenskaper vid 2003 års RFV-LS-undersökning (Redovisning No. 2004:4)*. Stockholm: Riksförsäkringsverketo (Document Number).

Ribet, C., & Derriennic, F. (1999). Age, working conditions, and sleep disorders: A longitudinal analysis in the French cohort E.S.T.E.V. *Sleep, 22*, 491–504.

Roach, G. D., Fletcher, A., & Dawson, D. (2004). A model to predict work-related fatigue based on hours of work. *Aviation Space and Environmental Medicine, 75*(Suppl. 3), A61–A69; Discussion A70–A64.

Rock, J. P., Oldfield, E. H., Schulte, H. M., Gold, P. W., Kornblith, P. L., Loriaux, L., et al. (1984). Corticotropin releasing factor administered into the ventricular CSF stimulates the pituitary-adrenal axis. *Brain Research, 323*(2), 365–368.

Roehrs, T., & Roth, T. (1992). Multiple sleep latency test: Technical aspects and normal values. *Journal of Clinical Neurophysiology, 9*(1), 63–67.

Roehrs, T., Zorick, F., Wittig, R., Conway, W., & Roth, T. (1989). Predictors of objective level of daytime sleepiness in patients with sleep-related breathing disorders. *Chest, 95*, 1202–1206.

Rosa, R. (1993). Napping at home and alertness on the job in rotating shift workers. *Sleep, 16*(8), 727–735.

Ross, R. J., Ball, W. A., Dinges, D. F., Kribbs, N. B., Morrison, A. R., Silver, S. M., et al. (1994). Motor dysfunction during sleep in posttraumatic stress disorder. *Sleep, 17*, 723–732.

Roth, T., & Drake, C. (2004). Evolution of insomnia: Current status and future direction. *Sleep Medicine, 5*(Suppl. 1), S23–S30.

Sagberg, F. (2006). Driver health and crash involvement: A case-control study. *Accident Analysis & Prevention, 38*(1), 28–34.

Saper, C. B., Chou, T. C., & Scammell, T. E. (2001). The sleep switch: Hypothalamic control of sleep and wakefulness. *Trends in Neurosciences, 24*(12), 726–731.

Saper, C. B., Lu, J., Chou, T. C., & Gooley, J. (2005). The hypothalamic integrator for circadian rhythms. *Trends in Neurosciences, 28*(3), 152–157.

Sapolsky, R. M., Krey, L. C., & McEwen, B. S. (1984). Stress down-regulates corticosterone receptors in a site-specific manner in the brain. *Endocrinology, 114*, 287–292.

Sateia, M., Doghramji, K., Hauri, P. J., & Morin, C. M. (2000). Evaluation of chronic insomnia. *Sleep, 23*, 243–263.

Schweitzer, P. K., Randazzo, A. C., Stone, K., Erman, M., & Walsh, J. K. (2006). Laboratory and field studies of naps and caffeine as practical countermeasures for sleep–wake problems associated with night work. *Sleep, 29*(1), 39–50.

Selye, H. (1946). The general adaptation syndrome and the diseases of adaptation. *Journal of Clinical Endocrinology, 6*, 117–231.

Selye, H. (1956). *The stress of life.* New York: McGraw Hill.

Siegrist, J. (2000). A theory of occupational stress. In: J. Dunham (Ed.), *Stress in the workplace. Past, present and future* (pp. 52–65). London: Whurr Publisher.

Smith, L., Folkard, S., & Poole, C. J. M. (1994). Increased injuries on night shift. *The Lancet, 344*, 1137–1139.

Smith, P. (1979). A study of weekly and rapidly rotating shift workers. *International Archives of Occupational and Environmental Health, 43*, 211–220.

Söderström, M., Ekstedt, M., Åkerstedt, T., Nilsson, J., & Axelsson, J. (2004). Sleep and sleepiness in young individuals with high burnout scores. *Sleep, 17*, 1369–1377.

Spiegel, K., Leproult, R., & Van Cauter, E. (1999). Impact of sleep debt on metabolic and endocrine function. *The Lancet, 354*, 1435–1439.

Steiger, A. (2002). Sleep and the hypothalamo–pituitary–adrenocortical system. *Sleep Medicine Reviews, 6*(2), 125–138.

Steiger, A., Antonijevic, I. A., Bohlhalter, S., Frieboes, R. M., Friess, E., & Murck, H. (1998). Effects of hormones on sleep. *Hormone Research, 49*, 125–130.

Stickgold, R., Hobson, J. A., Fosse, R., & Fosse, M. (2001). Sleep, learning, and dreams: Off-line memory reprocessing. *Science*, *294*, 1052–1057.

Tang, N. K. Y., & Harvey, A. G. (2004). Effects of cognitive arousal and physiological arousal on sleep perception. *Sleep*, *27*, 69–78.

Taylor, D. J., Mallory, L. J., Lichstein, K. L., Durrence, H. H., Riedel, B. W., & Bush, A. J. (2007). Comorbidity of chronic insomnia with medical problems. *Sleep*, *30*(2), 213–218.

Taylor, R. R., Jason, L. A., & Torres, A. (2000). Fatigue rating scales: An empirical comparison. *Psychological Medicine*, *30*(4), 849–856.

Tepas, D. I. (1982). Shiftworker sleep strategies. *Journal of Human Ergology*, *11*(Suppl. 1), 325–336.

Tepas, D. I., Walsh, J. K., Moss, P. D., & Armstrong, D. (1981). Polysomnographic correlates of shift worker performance in the laboratory. In: A. Reinberg, N. Vieux & P. Andlauer (Eds), *Night and shift work: Biological and social aspects* (pp. 179–186). Oxford: Pergamon Press.

Terán-Santos, J., Jimnénez-Gómez, A., & Cordero-Guevara, J. (1999). The association between sleep apnea and the risk of traffic accidents. *New England Journal of Medicine*, *240*, 847–851.

Theorell, T. (1996). The demand-control-support model for studying health in relation to the work environment: An interactive model. In: K. Orth-Gomér & N. Schneiderman (Eds), *Behavioral medicine approaches to cardiovascular disease prevention* (pp. 69–85). New Jersey: Lawrence Erlbaum Associates.

Thiis-Evensen, E. (1957). Shift work and health. In: *Proceedings of the XII International Congress of Occupational Health (Helsinki)*. Helsinki. (Vol. 1, pp. 97–105).

Thiis-Evensen, E. (1958). Shift work and health. *Industrial Medicine and Surgery*, *27*, 493–497.

Tilley, A. J., Wilkinson, R. T., Warren, P. S. G., Watson, W. B., & Drud, M. (1982). The sleep and performance of shift workers. *Human Factors*, *24*, 624–641.

Tononi, G., & Cirelli, C. (2006). Sleep function and synaptic homeostasis. *Sleep Medicine*, *10*, 49–62.

Toomingas, A., Theorell, T., Michélsen, H., & Nordemar, R. (1997). Associations between self-rated psychosocial work conditions and musculoskeletal symptoms and signs. *Scandinavian Journal of Work, Environment and Health*, *23*, 130–139.

Torsvall, L., & Åkerstedt, T. (1987). Sleepiness on the job: Continuously measured EEG changes in train drivers. *Electroencephalography and Clinical Neurophysiology*, *66*, 502–511.

Torsvall, L., & Åkerstedt, T. (1988). Extreme sleepiness: Quantification of EOG and spectral EEG parameters. *International Journal of Neuroscience*, *38*, 435–441.

Torsvall, L., Åkerstedt, T., Gillander, K., & Knutsson, A. (1989). Sleep on the night shift: 24-hour EEG monitoring of spontaneous sleep/wake behavior. *Psychophysiology*, *26*(3), 352–358.

Urponen, H., Vuori, I., Hasan, J., & Partinen, M. (1988). Self-evaluations of factors promoting and disturbing sleep: An epidemiological survey in Finland. *Social Science & Medicine*, *26*, 443–450.

Ursin, H., & Eriksen, H. R. (2004). The cognitive activation theory of stress. *Psychoneuroendocrinology*, *29*(5), 567–592.

Vahtera, J., Pentti, J., Helenius, H., & Kivimaki, M. (2006). Sleep disturbances as a predictor of long-term increase in sickness absence among employees after family death or illness. *Sleep*, *29*(5), 673–682.

Van Cauter, E., Latta, F., Nedeltcheva, A., Spiegel, K., Leproult, R., Vandenbril, C., et al. (2004). Reciprocal interactions between the GH axis and sleep. *Growth Hormone & IGF Research, 14,* S10–S17.

van Diest, R., & Appels, A. W. P. M. (1994). Sleep physiological characteristics of exhausted men. *Psychosomatic Medicine, 56,* 28–35.

Van Dongen, H. P. (2004). Comparison of mathematical model predictions to experimental data of fatigue and performance. *Aviation, Space and Environmental Medicine,* 75(Suppl. 3), A15–A36.

Van Dongen, H. P., Maislin, G., Mullington, J. M., & Dinges, D. F. (2003). The cumulative cost of additional wakefulness: Dose–response effects on neurobehavioral functions and sleep physiology from chronic sleep restriction and total sleep deprivation. *Sleep, 26*(2), 117–126.

Van Dongen, H. P. A., Baynard, M. D., Maislin, G., & Dinges, D. F. (2004). Systematic interindividual differences in neurobehavioral impairment from sleep loss: Evidence of trait-like differential vulnerability. *Sleep, 27,* 423–433.

Van Dongen, H. P. A., Vitellaro, K. M., & Dinges, D. F. (2005). Individual differences in adult human sleep and wakefulness: Leitmotif for a research agenda. *Sleep, 28,* 479–496.

Vgontzas, A. N., Bixler, E. O., & Chrousos, G. P. (2005). Sleep apnea is a manifestation of the metabolic syndrome. *Sleep Medicine Reviews, 9,* 211–224.

Vgontzas, A. N., Papanicolaou, D. A., Bixler, E. O., Kales, A., Tyson, K., & Chrousos, G. P. (1997). Elevation of plasma cytokines in disorders of excessive daytime sleepiness: Role of sleep disturbance and obesity. *Journal of Clinical Endocrinology and Metabolism,* 82(5), 1313–1316.

Webb, W. B. (1995). The cost of sleep-related accidents: A reanalysis. *Sleep, 18*(4), 276–280.

Webb, W. B., & Agnew, J. H. W. (1971). Stage 4 sleep: Influence of time course variables. *Science, 174,* 1354–1356.

Weber, A., & Jaekel-Reinhard, A. (2000). Bournout syndrome: A disease of modern societies? *Occupational Medicine, 50,* 512–517.

Wesensten, N. J., Balkin, T. J., & Belenky, G. (1999). Does sleep fragmentation impact recuperation? A review and reanalysis. *Journal of Sleep Research, 8,* 237–245.

Wessely, S., Chalder, T., Hirsch, S., Pawlikowska, T., Wallace, P., & Wright, D. (1995). Postinfectious fatigue: Prospective cohort study in primary care. *The Lancet, 345,* 1333–1338.

Wierwille, W. W., & Ellsworth, L. A. (1994). Evaluation of driver drowsiness by trained raters. *Accident Analysis & Prevention, 26,* 571–581.

Wilkinson, R. T., Edwards, R. S., & Haines, E. (1966). Performance following a night of reduced sleep. *Psychonomic Science, 5,* 471–472.

Wojtczak-Jaroszowa, J., & Jarosz, D. (1987). Time-related distribution of occupational accidents. *Journal of Safety Research, 18,* 33–41.

Wong, K. K., Marshall, N. S., Grunstein, R. R., Dodd, M. J., & Rogers, N. L. (2008). Comparing the neurocognitive effects of 40 h sustained wakefulness in patients with untreated OSA and healthy controls. *Journal of Sleep Research, 17,* 322–330.

Wyatt, S., & Mariott, R. (1953). Night work and shift changes. *British Journal of Industrial Medicine, 10,* 164–177.

Zee, P. C., & Manthena, P. (2007). The brain's master circadian clock: Implications and opportunities for therapy of sleep disorders. *Sleep Medicine Reviews, 11*(1), 59–70.

ANABOLISM AND CATABOLISM AT WORK

Töres Theorell

ABSTRACT

The importance of anabolism and regeneration is related to lack or loss of control. This chapter discusses the psychophysiological basis for such relationships. In the threat of lost control, energy mobilisation is activated and regeneration is inhibited – since regeneration (repairing) has low priority in emergency situations. This pattern can be traced on several psychophysiological levels, from the brain to most of the cells in the body. Such a mechanism explains why the body becomes vulnerable and increasingly sensitive to load when threat of lost control is excessive and long lasting. In several empirical examples, various indicators of anabolism and regeneration have paralleled improvement versus deterioration in psychosocial conditions, in particular lack or loss of control. In these studies, indicators of anabolism and regeneration (such as concentration of sex hormones with anabolic and regenerative functions in blood and saliva) have been followed in subjects going through deteriorating versus improving life conditions. The demand-support model is used as a theoretical basis for the discussion.

Current Perspectives on Job-Stress Recovery
Research in Occupational Stress and Well Being, Volume 7, 249–276
Copyright © 2009 by Emerald Group Publishing Limited
All rights of reproduction in any form reserved
ISSN: 1479-3555/doi:10.1108/S1479-3555(2009)0000007010

INTRODUCTION

The demand-control-support (DCS) model was established by Karasek more than 30 years ago (for reviews, see Karasek & Theorell, 1990; Johnson & Hall, 1988). It has been widely used in epidemiological studies of cardiovascular and mental disease in relation to working conditions ever since (Clays et al., 2007; Landsbergis, Schnall, Pickering, Warren, & Schwartz, 2003; Belkic, Landsbergis, Schnall, & Baker, 2004; Kivimäki, Theorell, Westerlund, Vahtera, & Alfredsson, 2008; Magnusson-Hanson, Theorell, Oxenstierna, Hyde, & Westerlund, 2008). According the DCS theory, excessive psychological demands impose a threat to health mainly when decision latitude and social support levels are inadequate ("isolated strain" according to the DCS terminology). However, when decision latitude and support are adequate, high psychological demands (the combination being labelled "active and supportive work") coping may improve and less threat to health may arise as a consequence of high demands.

An important underlying theory behind the establishment of the initial demand-control model was the theory on anabolism and regeneration which relates to the body's ability to repair and to replace worn-out cells. It constituted an important part of the demand-control formulation for the study of job stressors during the first years after its introduction (Karasek, Russell, & Theorell, 1982). This part of the theory stated that the combination of high job demands and low decision latitude inhibits the regeneration and accordingly increases the vulnerability of the organism to stressors. It also stated that stimulating working conditions, in particular those with high demands and high decision authority could stimulate regeneration and accordingly increase the organism's ability to resist adverse effects of stressors. Surprisingly, a relatively small amount of research has been performed on this part of the theory. Most studies in stress research using the demand-control model (as well as research using other theoretical stress models) have been performed on "arousal" and energy mobilisation (see, for instance Theorell, Perski, & Åkerstedt, 1988; Alderling, Theorell, de la Torre, & Lundberg, 2006; Karasek & Theorell, 1990), whereas the "healthy" anabolism part has been less explored. In this chapter, some examples will be presented which may point at possible future directions for research. Particular focus will be on observations on variations in perceived control and how such variations correlate with indicators of anabolic processes. The chapter will not be limited to the demand-control or DCS model. Similar models for job stress will also be discussed in relation to anabolism and regeneration. Since the published volume on job stress and regeneration is small, I will also use some illustrative examples from rehabilitation and non-work stress research. The first part will be on general stress theory related to anabolism and regeneration; the second will cover the physiology of regeneration. The third part will give an overview of opportunities for regeneration. The fourth part will describe empirical observations made mainly by our own group of researchers. In the discussion section, I will formulate some suggestions about how anabolism and regeneration can be improved in work settings.

THEORETICAL APPROACHES TO ANABOLISM AND REGENERATION

Regeneration of tissues is a central feature of the healthy organism. Regeneration takes place during periods of recovery. Broadly speaking, our body is constructed for swings between effort and recovery. Periods of intense release of energy should be followed by periods of recovery during which energy is being built up and tissues restored. The first psycho-endocrinologist who described systematically the balance between catabolism (release of energy) and anabolism (regeneration) was Mason (1968). In studies of monkeys who were exposed to restraint stress, he found that catabolic hormones were stimulated and anabolic hormones inhibited in this situation. Another study, published in 1998 by Kiecolt Glaser and collaborators, illustrates the importance of regeneration. This study examined the healing of wounds (mucosa injuries) in students facing a major examination period which was very stressful (Marucha, Kiecolt-Glaser, & Favagehi, 1998). In all participants, an experimental wound was inflicted in the mouth during two different periods, one during which they were facing an extensive and stressful examination and one without such a stressful condition. The time needed for total healing of this wound was recorded. It was found that healing was delayed by two days during the examination period compared to the control period. The quite pronounced effect could not be explained by differences in smoking, alcohol consumption or infections. It can be speculated that inhibition of regeneration is likely to occur not only in healing of mucosa injuries, but also in the skin and other bodily organs. Such experiments on healing of physical injuries have been repeated by other authors with similar results

(Weinman, Ebrecht, Scott, Walburn, & Dyson, 2008; Robles, 2007; Godbout & Glaser, 2006).

Later theoretical formulations, for example, the allostatic-load model (McEwen, 1998), also include the regeneration concept. Allostasis theory states that long lasting periods of arousing psychosocial conditions influence the body's regulation of energy mobilisation. If the conditions demand the body to maintain a very high energy level for long periods, the feedback functions are disturbed and the systems will be organised for an increasingly continuous arousal condition. Feedback loops change as a consequence and this means that both decelerator (slowing down) and accelerator (speeding up) mechanisms may be disturbed. In the former case, the body is, for instance, unable to lower the blood concentration of cortisol at night when it should rest. Typical biological assessments of allostasis include measures of regeneration because it is known that a constantly elevated arousal level inhibits anabolism.

Disturbed regulation of energy levels also becomes obvious in a physiologically exhausted state. Ability to mobilise energy in excessively demanding situations is inhibited, "nothing happens when the body pushes the accelerator". This has been observed, for instance, in the chronic fatigue syndrome (Demitrack et al., 1991). However, perhaps even more importantly, if energy regulation is disturbed regeneration is also disturbed. Low regeneration activity has been observed in most of the disorders related to long lasting stress, such as the metabolic syndrome, premature aging, chronic pain, psychiatric depression, burnout syndrome, vital exhaustion and chronic fatigue syndrome (Seeman et al., 2004; Steptoe & Marmot, 2003; von Känel, Bellingrath, & Kudielka, 2008; Björntorp & Rosmond, 2000; Evengård & Klimas, 2002).

How does the anabolism/regeneration process relate to the demand-control theory? According to demand-control theory, the combination of high demands and a good opportunity for an employee to make decisions about his or her own work is associated with an expansion of coping repertoires (Karasek & Theorell, 1990). The widening of options for coping could be assumed to be parallelled by increased physiological regeneration. In general, a positive expectancy arises as a consequence of one's own actions in many situations. This is also consistent with the coping activation theory of stress (CATS; Eriksen, Murison, Pensgaard, & Ursin, 2005).

"Balance between catabolism and anabolism" as a general principle has been applied not only to the body's general endocrinology, but also to psychological processes and it could be applied to whole societies. Societies and communities can tolerate periods of intense rush in emergency situations. However, if support and maintenance are disregarded for long periods in rushed societies they may become sick and even collapse.

PHYSIOLOGY OF ANABOLISM

Release and recovery are being represented by two competing systems in the body, the Hypothalamo–Pituitary–Adrenocortical (HPA) and the Hypothalamo–Pituitary–Gonadal (HPG) axis, respectively. The HPA axis is helping the body in dangerous and challenging situations by facilitating energy mobilisation and preparing the body for physical action. It extends from the hypothalamus through the pituitary to the adrenal cortex. The hypothalamus uses a chemical agent, the peptide corticotrophic releasing factor (CRF), to stimulate the pituitary to release the adrenocorticotrophic hormone (ACTH), which stimulates the adrenal cortex to secrete cortisol and other steroid hormones that are similar in their action to hydrocortisone. In a parallel fashion, the HPG axis extends from the hypothalamus through the pituitary to the gonadal glands. The hypothalamus uses the peptide gonadotrophic releasing factor (GnRF), which stimulates the pituitary to send out hormones that stimulate the gonads, which are producing steroid hormones that stimulate both the reproductive system and regeneration. Regeneration of cells is to a great extent governed by the same hormones that stimulate reproduction, the gonadal system. Another important part of the regenerative system is the pituitary growth hormone. One of the most potent anabolic/regenerative gonadal steroids, testosterone, and growth hormone are well-known in sports as "doping" agents.

Whereas the peripheral endocrine organ representing the facilitation of release of energy is the adrenal cortex, the corresponding peripheral organ representing regeneration is accordingly the testes and the ovaries. Michelson, Licinio, and Gold (1995) have described the relationship between these systems in some detail. There is competition between them on all levels from the central nervous system to the peripheral tissues, from the brain (in particular, the hypothalamus which is a basal part of the brain coordinating several physiological functions) through the endocrine organs to the cells. The central hypothalamic governing CRF inhibits the corresponding GnRF on the same level, whereas glucocorticoids (for instance, cortisol), which are central to the stress reaction, suppress a number of receptor sites in the reproductive endocrine axis including those of testosterone and oestradiol. There is also interplay backwards since glucocorticoids suppress GnRF.

The reproductive steroid hormones are not only produced in gonads. They are also produced in the adrenal cortex and this explains why not only men but also women have testosterone. Furthermore, the adrenal cortex produces precursors of several of these hormones. The commanding factors in the hypothalamus and pituitary are giving complicated orders to the gonads and the adrenal cortex. The system is embedded in a number of complicated interplays with cell receptors in peripheral cells and in the central nervous system. The concentration of steroids in bodily fluids therefore only gives us a very crude estimate of energy release and regeneration. Both cortisol and testosterone are secreted to the blood where they exist both as "free" (solved in the fluid) and bound to proteins. The free part of them is secreted to saliva where fluctuations of concentration can be studied which reflects those in blood.

Several of the steroids also have direct effects on the central nervous system. Such steroids are called *neurosteroids*. De Hydro Epi Androsterone Sulphate (DHEA-s) is one of these neurosteroids, but cortisol testosterone and oestrogene are also examples of neurosteroids.

OPPORTUNITIES FOR REGENERATION

First of all, recovery takes place during sleep. Recent years of research have shown that sleep is of profound importance to the body. During deep sleep (mainly stage 4 sleep), the regenerative activities are maximised and this of course means that loss of deep sleep increases the vulnerability of nearly all bodily tissues. For instance, skeletal muscles become fragile or more easily injured during mechanical strain after long periods (months) of unusually high levels of energy release (Theorell, Hasselhorn, & the MUSIC Norrtälje Study Group, 2002), particularly if there has been insufficient time for sleep (Åkerstedt & Nilsson, 2003). However, recovery in the seven-day cycle is also important. If there has been insufficient sleep during the workdays, this can be compensated for during the weekend. Recovery on a longer time dimension (summer vacation, for instance) has been less studied scientifically but may also be important (Westman & Eden, 1997). It has been shown convincingly that long lasting disturbance of sleep is an important feature of the "burnout syndrome" which is characterised by somatic and mental symptoms. Interestingly, disturbed short-term memory is an important characteristic of burnout and this may be due to lack of regenerative activity in the central nervous system (Ekstedt, 2005). That job strain – the combination of high demands and low decision authority – is a strong predictor of burnout during a two-year follow-up period has been recently shown by our group (Magnusson-Hanson et al., 2008).

To some extent a stimulating environment can compensate for lack of sleep and absence of weekend recovery, at least during shorter periods. This has been insufficiently studied, but it may be due to the ability of the regenerative systems to override the effects of the energy release. For instance, hormones governing regeneration could theoretically, under conditions of joy, counteract some of the effects of the energy releasing processes. How this relates to job stress will be discussed.

Regeneration of cells is absolutely necessary for survival. It has been stated that during an ordinary day a healthy human being gets rid of 1.5 kg of worn-out cells (general theory regarding "programmed cell death", for instance, in Sanders and Wride (1995)). The velocity with which cells are being worn-out and replaced varies between tissues. It is rapid in the skin, the mucosa in the gastrointestinal system and in the immune system and very slow in the skeleton where it takes decades before all the cells have been replaced. Most types of white blood cells have a "half-life" of 10 days. This means that when a person who has no regeneration activity in the body is followed over time, 10 days after the start he or she will only have half the number of white blood cells that he or she had when follow-up started. An inhibition of the regeneration of white blood cells is therefore likely to affect resistance against infections already after some days. It should be pointed out that all organ systems depend on regeneration. To mention a few examples:

Natural killer cells (*NK cells*). Morikawa et al. (2005) studied a specific kind of white blood cells, NK cells, which are of particular importance for the body's defence against infections. Healthy nurses were followed during periods with varying amounts of psychosocial load at work. An increase in quantitative workload was followed by significantly decreased NK cell activity. This finding illustrates that deteriorating working conditions can inhibit the production of NK cells implying that unfavourable working conditions impair regeneration processes.

Muscle cells. Many mechanisms have been discussed which could explain the relationship between psychosocial factors and the course of musculoskeletal disorders. A mechanism that is likely to play an important role is that long lasting periods of adverse psychosocial conditions could inhibit the regeneration of muscle cells. After some time the person develops "bad meat" and will have increased vulnerability to mechanical load (Theorell et al., 2002).

One study by our group (Hasselhorn, Theorell, Vingård, & MUSIC Norrtälje Study Group, 2001) showed that DHEA-s – also the precursor of two other anabolic hormones, testosterone and oestradiol – is strongly correlated with duration of disability after the acute onset of low-back pain in women. Accordingly, low DHEA-s means slow rehabilitation. Similar findings were made in a more recent study by our group (Schell, Theorell, Hasson, Arnetz, & Saraste, 2008). Danish researchers (Kaergaard, Hansen, Rasmussen, & Andersen, 2000) confirmed the relationship between serum testosterone concentration and work-related neck and shoulder pain. That study failed to confirm the prospective relationship, however. A link between a low blood concentration of this anabolic hormone and poor prognosis in subjects with musculoskeletal disorder could be a very concrete indication of the importance of this hormone. The interpretation is that subjects with acute low-back pain who have a low DHEA-s activity will have a longer disability because their muscles do not heal as rapidly as those of other subjects. That disturbed sleep is associated with lowered testosterone excretion in men has been shown by Axelsson, Ingre, Akerstedt, and Holmback (2005).

Central nervous system cells. Regeneration is also important for the health of the central nervous system. It is even important as regeneration may stimulate the formation of new cells in some parts of the brain. During recent years, the importance of regeneration to the survival of nerve cells and formation of new ones has been illustrated in many studies. Just to mention one example, there are specific growth factors produced by the brain's own support system – so-called "glial cells" – that could protect the body against loss of dopamine cells that are of central importance to the development of Parkinson's disease (Ebert, Beres, Barber, & Svendsen, 2008). Another intensive discussion in neurobiology relates to the discussion about loss of nerve cells in the hippocampus during long lasting periods of intensive stress. Since hippocampus is of great importance to short-term memory (see, for instance Emdad et al., 2006) this research is relevant for burnout syndrome which is characterised – among other symptoms – by impaired short-term memory. For a summary of the most recent neurobiological discussion regarding regeneration of hippocampus cells, see Hess and Borlongan (2008). Regardless, however of the discussion on loss of nerve cells, the brain's supporting glial cells are of major importance per se to the function of the nerve cells. Therefore, fluctuations in the body's regenerative activity will be of importance also to brain function regardless of whether there has been loss of nerve cells or not.

General processes – Aging. Our studies have also shown that there are strong negative correlations, particularly in male subjects, between the serum concentration of DHEA-s on one hand, and age on the other. This is central to our discussion since decreased ability to regenerate may be one of the most central features of old age. There is a strongly declining DHEA-s concentration with increasing age (Tables 1A and 1B, unpublished). There are similar correlations for testosterone in male and oestradiol in female subjects in the population. The male DHEA-s – age correlation is the strongest one.

The tables also show, however, that both in men and women there is a significant decrease in the plasma concentration of prolactin with increasing age. Prolactin is an interesting hormone from several points of view. There is some scientific support for the assumption that prolactin which is produced and secreted by the anterior part of the pituitary may have a role in stimulating the organism's anabolism during periods of change combined with powerlessness (Theorell, 1992). This may explain why the serum prolactin concentration increases during such periods both in men and women. However, this hormone does not have the same role as other hormones with predominantly anabolic effects since prolactin seems to serve its protective role mainly in "powerless" situations. Perhaps increased prolactin excretion arises partly as a compensation for decreasing activity in other anabolic systems.

Table 1A. Correlations between Age and the Plasma Concentration of Hormones with Anabolic Effects.

	Women ($n = 169$)	Men ($n = 128$)
Prolactin	$-0.20, p = 0.004$	$-0.19, p = 0.03$
Oestradiol	$-0.25, p = 0.001$	NA
Testosterone	NA	$-0.26, p = 0.006$
DHEA-s	$-0.26, p = 0.0001$	$-0.54, p = 0.0001$

Source: From study of employees in Swedish insurance company (1998, unpublished).

Table 1B. Correlations between Age and Plasma Concentration of Hormones with Anabolic Effects.

	Women ($n = 140$)	Men ($n = 101$)
Prolactin	$-0.10, p = 0.25$	$-0.19, p = 0.06$
DHEA-s	$-0.17, p = 0.04$	$-0.46, p = 0.001$

Source: From the MUSIC Norrtälje Study (Hasselhorn et al., 2001).

EMPIRICAL EXAMPLES FROM RESEARCH ON ANABOLIC PROCESSES

Possible Effects of Sudden Loss of Control on Anabolism

Most research deals with the effects that stressors have on catabolic reactions. Effects of stressors are typically measured quantitatively in terms of increase in cortisol or catecholamine excretion. Of equal potential importance, however, is the inhibition of anabolism that occurs during periods of long lasting adverse conditions requiring energy mobilisation. It seems that particularly loss of control is associated with a decrease in anabolic processes.

A major threat to one member of a cohesive work group could have a strong sociobiological effect resulting in impaired anabolism – according to a recent study of two professional symphony orchestras (Theorell, Liljeholm Johansson, Björk, & Erikson, 2007). These orchestras were followed for two years with observations every six months. In one of the two orchestras, a health threat occurred immediately before the first observation. One of the solo wind players fainted during concert in front of an audience. This happened twice and it also happened during rehearsals on two occasions. The cardiological reason was that this player had a tendency to develop slow heart rhythm (bradycardia) during certain conditions. In particular, the carbon dioxide retention that arose during his playing of long phrases was such a condition. Our cardiological examination showed that he needed a pacemaker, which was installed. However, the other members of the group were also severely affected and it was found that they needed group therapy, which was provided. The situation had calmed down after half a year. The concentration of testosterone in saliva, which is assumed to reflect the serum concentration of "free" testosterone, was dramatically different in the two orchestras at start. The concentration was perfectly normal in the comparison orchestra but strikingly low in the threatened orchestra – with a highly significant two-way interaction in ANOVA. This testosterone process was paralleled in questionnaire data. These data showed that the members of the threatened orchestra reported a low index of influence, which improved significantly after half a year.

Twenty-four hour electrocardiographic analyses were also performed and particular emphasis in these analyses was on heart rate variability. The most interesting finding was that very low frequency power (changes in heart rate occurring twice per minute or less frequently) which is assumed to reflect the activity of the parasymphatic system and in particular the sensitivity of the baroreceptor system – which has an important role in the down-regulation of blood pressure elevation after stress reactions – seems to react in the same way as saliva testosterone with low initial levels in the threatened orchestra. Very low frequency power heart rate variations are likely to be affected by slow changes in the activity of the vagal nerve, a strong component of the parasympathetic nervous system. Although the changes in this parameter were less dramatic than for saliva testosterone, they were still statistically significant with a significant two-way interaction between group and time – the mean very low frequency power developed differently in the two groups. The threatened orchestra started on a low mean level which increased after intervention, whereas the comparison orchestra had a more stable level.

Changes in saliva testosterone and changes in very low frequency power were also correlated and this correlation probably reflects the fact that to some extent both dimensions mirror the activity of the parasympathetic system. In addition, increase in very low frequency power during the first six months was significantly correlated with the improvement in influence. One conclusion of this finding may be that the crisis was followed by inhibited parasympathetic activity. Saliva testosterone and very low frequency power in heart rate variability may represent relatively easily accessible measures of "anabolic" activity. After the solution of the problem, the parasympathetic activity of the orchestra members increased.

Collins, Karasek, and Costas (2006) have recently shown that the part of the heart rate variability that is particularly strongly related to parasympathetic activity (i.e., high frequency power) is associated with a high degree of decision latitude. Similar findings, also for very low frequency power, have been reported in relation to high level of social support in life (Horsten et al., 1999). Support is an important factor in health promotion and is of course also an integral part of the DCS model.

Anabolic Indicators During Regional Intervention for Unemployment: Disappointing Results

Sometimes the follow-up of psychophysiological data may be useful because the development of such data may in fact point in a completely unexpected direction and this could help the researchers to re-interpret findings made by means of questionnaires and interviews. Twenty-one participants in a special regional programme for unemployed persons and for persons on long-term sick leave were followed during a year with repeated observations including indicators of anabolism (Westerlund, Theorell, & Bergström, 2001).

The programme lasted for half a year and the hypothesis was that it would improve health and increase participants' ability to find new jobs. The basic underlying idea was that those who participated would perceive an improved influence over their own lives. Participants were studied before, in the midst and immediately after the end of the programme as well as after a six-month follow-up period. The questionnaires regarding depression, anxiety and control over life showed no significant changes over time, whereas both DHEA-s and prolactin changes over time were significant and opposite to those expected. We had expected DHEA-s (as an indicator of regeneration/anabolism) to increase and prolactin to decrease (corresponding to decreased powerlessness as hypothesised from other studies). Contrary to our expectations and in line with our physiological findings the programme initially triggered unrealistic expectations. During the latter half-year the participants were disappointed that they had had to go back to unemployment. In this case, the anabolic activity mirrored the subjective data. However, the pattern of findings was in the unexpected direction.

Increasing Patient Control in Rehabilitation: Effects on Prolactin Release

High plasma prolactin concentration during powerlessness in change situations may be associated with a low dopamine activity in the brain during such conditions. Dopamine has been regarded as the brain's reward hormone and if our theory is correct, the rise in prolactin excretion during powerlessness periods may be due to lack of reward. Such "powerless" situations could be studied in patients undergoing rehabilitation after the onset of illness causing major limitations in daily activities. Our study was based on patients in a day care stroke rehabilitation centre. They spent three months in the rehabilitation process. We randomised these patients into two groups with 30 persons in each group (Lökk, Theorell, Arnetz, & Eneroth, 1991). In the first group, patients were participating in a group session twice a week under the supervision of an experienced nurse. During the first phase of the group sessions, patients helped one another formulate attainable and reasonable individual rehabilitation goals. During the later phase they helped and supported one another. This was intended to give them an increased feeling of control. In the second (control) group, patients received usual care. Patients in both groups had all recovered from the acute phase of the stroke.

The researchers used the concept of locus of control for assessing the programme's effect on the patients' feeling of mastery and sense of control in this situation. Good rehabilitation aims at increased "internal locus of control" which means the feeling that the individual can take command over situations in daily life himself or herself. A questionnaire-based measure of locus of control was used with "external" in one end (feeling the need to get help from others in most situations in daily life) and "internal" in the other end. Recordings of external locus of control showed that patients in both groups started in the external end (they had suffered a stroke some weeks before). These high scores on external locus of control remained unchanged in the control group, but there was a pronounced movement towards a more internal locus in the control group. The difference between the groups became even more pronounced during the follow-up period, which lasted for three months after the end of the rehabilitation period. As Fig. 1 shows, similar findings were obtained for plasma prolactin. The prolactin concentration increased continuously in the usual care group. In the intervention group, however, plasma prolactin decreased in the first phase and then returned to initial values. The development was statistically different between the two groups.

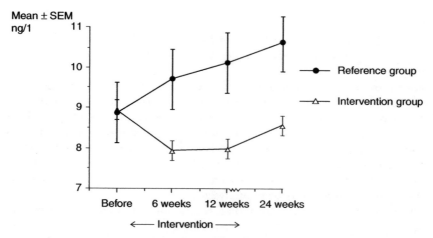

Fig. 1. Serum Prolactin in Patients Belonging to Intervention Group (Regular Group Sessions Aiming at Increased Feeling of Control) and Control Group Within Stroke Rehabilitation Programme in Day Care Centre.

Saliva Testosterone Changes in Patients with Irritable Bowel Syndrome Who Start Singing in a Choir

A more recent experiment (Grape, Wikström, Ekman, & Theorell, 2008) was the intervention study for patients with irritable bowel syndrome (IBS) which manifests itself in abdominal pain, episodes of diarrhoea and constipation, bloating. The hypothesis to be tested was that patients with IBS, the symptoms which are affected by psychosocial processes would benefit from choir singing, which is an activity that strengthens the cohesiveness of a group and also may have anabolic effects in itself. The participants were all suffering from IBS and had a declared interest in starting to sing in choir. They had to accept, however, that they would be randomly allocated to either a choir group or a group with lectures and group talking about IBS. Both groups met once a week during a whole year and symptoms as well as biological parameters were followed. One of the most striking observations was that saliva testosterone concentration increased by 60% in the choir group after a year, whereas no such change was observed in the talk group. This was a small-scale study which has to be repeated with larger samples. However, the study provides first evidence that group singing in a choir is a powerful cohesiveness factor. This knowledge could be utilised not only in treatment of psychosomatic conditions but also in group settings at work.

Anabolic Indicators During a Psychosocial Job Intervention: Computer-Based Individual Stress Management

Indicators of regeneration are of great interest in the evaluation of interventions. If it can be demonstrated that regeneration is strengthened after a psychosocial intervention, such a finding can be a strong argument for that intervention. According to our theory, increased regeneration and anabolism are central to the body's ability to protect itself against stress. An example from an evaluation of the effects of a stress management teaching programme may illustrate this. The results were partly supportive when anabolic indicators were analysed.

The employees in four information technology and two media companies were offered a web-based health promotion and stress management training intervention lasting for six months (Hasson, Anderberg, Theorell, & Arnetz, 2005). A similar control group of employees was established, with 129 persons in the intervention group and 174 in the reference group using random allocation. Participants in the intervention group utilised their own computers when they used the interactive computer programme for stress management adapted for this particular group. They determined themselves when, how often and how many times they used it during the intervention period which lasted for six months. The control subjects did not have access to the programme. In a follow-up examination after six months, there were significant interaction effects (time × group) for DHEA-s and NPY (an antistress hormone secreted in the same domain as noradrenalin). An immunological marker, TNF alpha, (a widely utilised stress sensitive immune marker) was also assessed. This marker has a protective effect during stressful conditions and could thus be regarded as a "healthy" chemical agent during stress conditions. In summary, "protective" factors including regenerating ones were activated in the intervention group.

In the interpretation of the results of this study, it should be taken into account that baseline data were collected during a season with low levels of stress. The six-month follow-up took place during a period with higher levels of stress. It is well-known that the activity of the HPA axis, the immune system and the anabolic functions are all affected by this seasonal variation. We could expect a seasonal lowering of the levels of DHEA-s, TNF alpha and NPY under these circumstances at the six-month follow-up. All the measures developed more favourably in the intervention group than in the control group as was evidenced in significant two-way interactions in analyses of variance. In multivariate analyses, TNF alpha and NPY were the most robust indicators of a beneficial effect of the programme. One interpretation could be that the programme stimulated the production and release of NPY and that this prevented some of the seasonal decrease in TNF alpha. The findings for DHEA-s were in the same direction, supporting the conclusion that the programme stimulated anabolism (or rather prevented seasonal inhibition of anabolism). There were clear beneficial effects of the programme at this stage on questionnaire-based variables such as stress management ability, mental energy and social support. The importance of a control group is vividly illustrated in this example in which the intervention lasted for six months and some of the behavioural and physiological variations were due to seasonal effects – without a control group the results would have been impossible to interpret. It should be pointed out that the effects of the intervention did not last for the next six months; all the intervention effects had disappeared after the half-year following the end of the intervention. This pattern of findings may illustrate that individual computer-based stress management programmes may only have temporal effects. However, an increased sense of mastery and control in the individual may be a stimulus to anabolism although more structural changes are needed for more lasting effects. If the organisation supports the individual programme it is more likely to have sustainable effects. It should be pointed out that exercises in stress management may have to be repeated, just like physical exercises.

Anabolic Indicators During a Psychosocial Job Intervention: Organisational Approach

The health effects on employees of a psychosocial organisation-based intervention programme for offices were studied (Theorell, Ort-Gomér, Moser, Undén, & Eriksson, 1995). Four work sites constituted the intervention group and two work sites a comparison group. The employees in the intervention group reported improved decision authority as well as skill discretion. No such changes were observed in the comparison group. In addition, the cardiovascular risk (ratio between harmful and beneficial blood lipids) improved in the intervention, but not in the comparison group (Orth-Gomér, Eriksson, Moser, Theorell, & Fredlund, 1994). However, when the intervention group was divided into two groups, one in which the managers facilitated and were interested in the intervention and a second in which the managers were not interested or even counteracted the intervention. In the "facilitated" but not in the other group, increasing serum testosterone concentration was observed during the process. This, however, was only observed in female participants. There are differences not only in the total level of serum testosterone concentration in men and women; the pattern of reacting to changes could also be different. It is not possible to know from data collected why men and women reacted differently to "facilitation" from managers. It could be speculated that the facilitation itself might have been more beneficial for the participating women than for their male colleagues.

Effects of Unemployment on Anabolic Indicators

Lack of control and powerlessness are experienced during unemployment, which should therefore be a situation to be studied with an anabolism perspective. Grossi, Theorell, Jürisoo, and Setterlind (1999) conducted a longitudinal study with police officers, who had been fired because of organisational changes in a police district in Stockholm. Blood samples were drawn in the morning before work (and correspondingly during the unemployment period before the time when police officers normally go to work), firstly, during the period of unemployment and secondly, three years later. With regard to catabolism, the results showed that these men had a lowered serum cortisol level during the unemployment period with a clear increase to the second occasion when all of them were working again. This might be due to a low energy level during the unemployment period or to long lasting stress with resulting exhaustion of the HPA axis. Interestingly, total serum testosterone concentration increased significantly (on average 16% increase) after the participants had started working again. There were other statistically significant changes related to unemployment. A statistically significant decrease in serum prolactin (on average a 35% decrease) concentration after re-employment fits the theory presented earlier and presumably indicates a state of powerlessness during unemployment.

Paradoxical Effects in Subjects with Severe Traumatic Experiences

In a longitudinal study of physiological effects of significant life changes on refugees from Iraq (Söndergaard & Theorell, 2003, 2004), fluctuations in DHEA-s were studied. Repeated observations were made during the first year following their permanent permit to stay in Sweden. Negative life events associated with relationships to family members and close relatives were associated with increasing serum concentration of cortisol and thyroid hormone. For the total group positive events occurring during the study year were associated with increasing serum DHEA-s. However, in those refugees who were suffering from post-traumatic stress disorder (PTSD), a deteriorating mental state with increasing PTSD symptoms was associated with rising DHEA-s. The explanation of this finding is complicated. DHEA-s is produced in large amounts in the central nervous system and it may have a role in shutting down the amount of impulses to neurones in certain situations. Rising DHEA-s may accordingly be "protective" for the brain among the mentally troubled participants and therefore may be mobilised in unfavourable situations. Thus, the meaning of increasing serum DHEA-s may differ between PTSD patients and more healthy persons for whom an improving situation is related more active anabolism in general – as has been discussed earlier. This finding again illustrates that steroid excretion in stressful situations may have different roles in different groups of individuals.

Spontaneous Job Variations in Relation to Variations in Anabolism

Periods of uncontrollable conditions at work have been common during the
1990s in Sweden. In health care, downsizing took place in several waves
during the whole decade. Employees were told that downsizing one year
would not be followed by other similar experiences in the future. However,
an increasing sense of hopelessness arose during this 10-year period since
downsizing took place again and again despite promises to the contrary. At
the regional hospital in Örebro, repeated periods of downsizing and
reorganisation were followed by increasing long-term sick leave and feelings
of exhaustion among employees (Arnetz, 2000). Thirty women employed
at this hospital were followed for a year after the final reorganisation
(Hertting & Theorell, 2002). Indicators of anabolism were studied in blood
samples drawn immediately after decisions had been taken and one year
later (1998–1999). The difference between morning and afternoon serum
cortisol decreased which could be evidence of physiological exhaustion. The
oestradiol concentration (adjusted for menstrual cycle and menopause)
decreased on average by 35%. These results are in line with our general
hypothesis that the secretion of steroids with anabolic effects decreases
during periods of long-term negative stress. However, the serum concentration of two other chemical compounds was also studied and significant
changes were found for them as well. The serum concentration of the
protein (apolipoprotein A1) that carries the protective cholesterol (which
decreases the risk of atherosclerosis) decreased by on average 13% and the
concentration of immunoglobulin G (a general marker of activity in the
immune system) decreased by on average 9%. The total picture is thus
indicating loss of protective capacity in the body in these women during this
period of ongoing downsizing and reorganisation.

In another study by our group (Theorell, Karasek, & Eneroth, 1990),
spontaneous variations in job strain were studied in employees in six
different occupations. These variations were followed during one year with
participants starting during different seasons so as to minimise seasonal
effects on biological parameters. Individuals served as their own controls.
There were pronounced variations in job strain as operationalised as the
ratio between psychological demands and decision latitude according to self-
administered questionnaires distributed on four occasions during the year.
Sleep disturbance became more common during peak job strain periods
lasting for some weeks and systolic blood pressure during work hours
increased progressively with increasing job strain in both men and women,

Table 2. Percentage Increase in Mean Plasma Testosterone During "Least" and "Next to Least" Strain Periods Divided by Mean Plasma Testosterone During "Worst" and "Next to Worst" Strain Periods.

	Mean Percent and Standard Errors
Total group ($n = 44$)	14 ± 6
White collar ($n = 23$)	23 ± 9
Blue ($n = 21$)	4 ± 8

Note: Percent change (mean and SEM) of plasma testosterone in relation to lowered job strain.

indicating increased levels of catabolism. The total serum testosterone (which was the measure of anabolic steroids that we used in the male part of this study) decreased with increasing job strain (Table 2). The difference in concentration between the two occasions with the most and the two occasions with the least job strain was on average 14%. In the studied group, there were 23 white-collar workers (air traffic controllers, physicians and symphony musicians) and 21 blue-collar workers (waiters, freight handlers and airplane mechanics). When the analysis was done separately for these two groups it became evident that the findings were much stronger for the white-collar workers than for the blue-collar workers. This may be due to the fact that physically strenuous work in itself causes testosterone fluctuations. Accordingly, this study showed that periods with improved work conditions were associated with elevated regenerative bodily activity, at least in white-collar workers.

Research by Other Groups

Within the strict context of the demand-control model at work very little research has been published on changes in anabolism and regeneration. Our own research projects in this field constitute a large proportion of studies published so far. Using a wider analytical framework, including effects of gain or loss of control, we find more published research however. Arnetz and co-workers have studied the stress of modern technology as well as work organisation factors. One of the conclusions from this research is that leadership with emphasis on employee participation is beneficial to employee health and also that increasing testosterone excretion mirrors improvement in working conditions (Arnetz, 1997; Anderzen & Arnetz, 2005).

GENERAL DISCUSSION

First of all it is striking that there has been a small amount of research on regeneration in relation to beneficial and adverse job conditions (for further research, see Arnetz, 1997; Anderzen & Arnetz, 2005). In the search for possibilities to reduce "negative stressors" most of the research has been focussed on the catabolic energy mobilisation part of the equation, whereas the protection against negative effects has been largely overlooked.

There are many potential measures of anabolism and regeneration. This chapter focussed mainly on anabolic steroids. Testosterone has turned out to be a meaningful indicator of regeneration. Both in men and women, a relatively high testosterone excretion is associated with good social climate in the life situation and with good recovery. Moreover, as described, both in our studies and those of other researchers, testosterone seems to be related to beneficial conditions at work. Although the blood concentration of DHEA-s has documented anabolic effects and is highly negatively correlated with aging particularly in men – and therefore could be expected to have an important role in regeneration – it has worked as an indicator of recovery and improving psychosocial conditions only in some of our studies. In other studies, we have not seen any meaningful associations with DHEA-s. This inconsistency in study findings could be due to technical problems, such as sensitivity to confounding conditions – cigarette smoking, physical activity and alcohol consumption. In addition, as pointed out in a review (Söndergaard & Theorell, 2004), DHEA-s also seems to have a special role in the central nervous system. This could lead to a paradoxical situation in which during extreme long lasting stress (Söndergaard, Hansson, & Theorell, 2002), the production of DHEA-s in the brain increases (possibly influencing the concentration of DHEA-s in peripheral blood), whereas the typical reaction in most situations is that the blood concentration of DHEA-s decreases in the periphery due to the inhibition of the HPG axis during stress. Such antagonistic processes could explain some of the diverging results in DHEA-s research particularly when there have been extremely stressful situations.

Testosterone has been regarded as an interesting "positive" stress hormone for many years. Mason (1968) regarded testosterone as an important protective hormone and in the research performed by Ursin and his co-workers (e.g., Vaernes, Ursin, Darragh, & Lambe, 1982) an elevation of testosterone excretion has also been part of a positive response pattern in stressful situations. However, it has also been known for a long time that an excessively high testosterone excretion is associated with an elevated risk of developing premature cardiovascular disease. From sports medicine, we know that artificially distributed testosterone as well as growth hormone in high dosages is dangerous to health (Bahrke & Yesalis, 2004; Holt & Sönksen, 2008). Therefore, a balance between the HPA and HPG axes is what has to be aspired.

Testosterone concentration could be assessed both in blood and in saliva. On the one hand, the concentration in blood is closer to the concentration in the body's target organs than is the concentration in saliva and therefore concentration in blood is potentially more relevant for biological understanding. On the other hand, saliva testosterone is much easier to measure and therefore many samples can be collected. Such an approach allows the researcher to follow variations during the day and to level out irrelevant variability. In blood, testosterone exists both bound to a specific protein and as a "free" substance. In some of the studies that have been referred, the concentration assessed has been the total one, including both the free and the protein-bound fractions (for instance, Theorell et al., 1990), whereas in others the free concentration has been measured (for instance, those on saliva testosterone such as Theorell et al. (2007)). This difference in assessment procedures might explain some of the diverging results in the literature. Men have much more of the protein-bound fraction than women, whereas the concentration of the free fraction is more similar in men and women. Men usually have 10–20 times higher concentration of the total testosterone in blood than women have. This difference is due to the fact that most of the male testosterone is secreted by the testes and only a portion by the adrenal cortex. In women, all of the blood testosterone is produced by the adrenal cortex. The saliva concentration of testosterone is reflecting the free concentration in blood and as a consequence the concentration is relatively similar in men and women (mostly approximately 50% higher in men). Both from sports and from child psychology there are studies which indicate that well-functioning groups with a good social climate are characterised by high mean saliva testosterone concentration both in males and female (Azurmendi et al., 2006; Edwards, Wetzel, & Wyner, 2006).

The procedures for collecting and analysing saliva testosterone could still be refined. Which tubes and swabs should be used for instance? The wrong materials could increase measurement errors. However, the results that have been obtained so far indicate that saliva testosterone could be a meaningful parameter in the study of regeneration and work environment.

Prolactin represents an interesting riddle. This is a hormone that has an anabolic role but its concentration seems to increase during powerless crisis situations and does not follow the same pattern as the anabolic steroids, for instance.

As mentioned in the introduction, there are many other biological measures that could capture variations in regeneration. Healing of wounds – the most concrete example mentioned – is an interesting possible measure and parasympathetic activity as it is reflected in heart rate variability (mainly the high frequency power component) is also an alternative. The concentration of some of the insulin-like growth factors (IGF) could also be used for follow-up assessments of regeneration (Ebert et al., 2008). Some of the biological indicators that have been used for follow-up assessments of regeneration processes show rapid and wide fluctuations so that it is nearly impossible to use them in practice. One example is growth hormone, which is very important in regeneration, but it cannot be used in follow-up assessment of work site processes.

It could be argued that physiological measures are not needed in the assessment of health consequences of work environment and changes in work environment. However, physiological assessments could serve as a valuable supplement in many such studies. In some situations participants may be exaggerating or underestimating the health consequences in their self-reports based on questionnaires. In such situations, physiological assessments may reveal that the self-reports are misleading. One such example is the above-described study – on anabolic indicators during a regional intervention for unemployment. Although this was a small-scale study, it pointed at a theoretically interesting situation. Both the environment and the individuals were of the opinion that the local programme for unemployed persons "should" be beneficial. However, it turned out that the design of this social experiment was not so good and change "in the wrong direction" in regeneration parameters (in particular DHEA-s) was one of the observations that helped us draw this conclusion.

How do we achieve improved anabolism and regeneration in work settings? The first kind of interventions is related to the reduction of excessive long lasting HPA axis stimulation, "reduced stress". The link between excessive HPA axis activity and inhibition of the HPG axis has been described above. Mostly, however, the biological follow-up of stress is focussed on biological indicators of arousal. It may be even more meaningful to assess fluctuations in regeneration as a consequence of long lasting stress.

The second kind of interventions is related to a more active stimulation of HPG axis activity. Interventions aimed at active improvement of anabolism could be grouped into three obvious areas of action, namely improved conditions for sleep, physical exercise during leisure time and cultural activities. Sleep has an important role in this context. For instance,

Axelsson et al. (2005) have shown that periods of poor sleep have a depressing effect on serum testosterone concentration. The anabolic effects of physical exercise are well documented (see, for instance Joosen, Sluiter, Joling, & Frings-Dresen, 2008). Both sleep and physical exercise could be beneficially affected by organisational interventions in work places. Anabolic effects of cultural activities have not been scientifically established as feasible, although there is indirect evidence indicating that such effects could occur (Bygren, Konlaan, & Johansson, 1996; Grape, Sandgren, Hansson, Ericson, & Theorell, 2003). One example is the small-scale study referred to in this chapter (Grape et al., 2008). But is there any evidence that cultural activity could be related to job stress models? Could cultural activities be related to the health aspects of the demand-control model for instance? In an ongoing epidemiological study of working conditions in Swedish working men and women (Theorell, 2008), the relationship between the demand-control model and cultural activities organised by the work place was examined. A low number of such activities (never or not more than once a year) were reported three times as frequently by female employees who reported low decision authority. Among men, those who reported job strain (high demand and low decision authority) were twice as likely as others to have "few cultural activities" at work. Accordingly, in women "lack of cultural activities" were three times and in men twice as frequently reported as by employees in work situations described as relaxed (low demands and high decision authority). These findings were adjusted for age, education and branch (private/public). Low decision latitude seemed to be the most important component in this pattern of findings.

The regenerative and anabolic perspective on biological processes in the body extends from the nervous system with its cognitive functions through the hypothalamus and the HPG axis to the cells and serves as maintenance and protects against evil effects of negative stress. It interacts on all these levels with the energy providing HPA axis. The interplay between HPG and HPA could serve as a metaphor for the well-functioning organisation or society at large. An organisation that pushes demands extensively and disregards maintenance functions will be able to function for some time but will break down sooner or later. With regard to the staff, the basic functions that we have discussed (sleep, physical activity with variations and cultural activities that stimulate the anabolic functions) have to be facilitated in the organisation.

An anabolic perspective could be of help in job interventions and physiological indicators could help us follow changes in anabolism. There is no doubt that the anabolic perspective can be quite useful in health promotion work. For instance, the improvement of an organisation's function with regard to such factors as performance feedback, participatory management, skills' development and employee health has been shown to correlate with increasing testosterone excretion in employees (Anderzen & Arnetz, 2005). Such correlations give support to the importance of improved organisational function to regenerative bodily functions.

REFERENCES

Åkerstedt, T., & Nilsson, P. M. (2003). Review. Sleep as restitution: An introduction. *Journal of Internal Medicine, 254*(1), 6–12.
Alderling, M., Theorell, T., de la Torre, B., & Lundberg, I. (2006). The demand control model and circadian saliva cortisol variations in a Swedish population based sample (The PART study). *BMC Public Health, 27*(6), 288.
Anderzen, I., & Arnetz, B. B. (2005). The impact of a prospective survey-based workplace intervention program on employee health, biologic stress markers and organizational productivity. *Journal of Occupational and Environmental Medicine, 47*, 671–682.
Arnetz, B. (2000). Rapport från RSÖ:s KAK-uppföljning 1999, resultat, samband, slutsatser (Örebro Medical Centre Hospital RSÖ:s QWC follow-up. Results, connections, conclusions. Örebro Medical Centre Hospital, Örebro).
Arnetz, B. B. (1997). Technological stress: Psychophysiological aspects of working with modern information technology. *Scandinavian Journal of Work, Environment and Health, 23*(Suppl. 3), 97–103.
Axelsson, J., Ingre, M., Akerstedt, T., & Holmback, U. (2005). Effects of acutely displaced sleep on testosterone. *Journal of Clinical Endocrinology and Metabolism, 90*(8), 4530–4535. Epub May 24, 2005.
Azurmendi, A., Braza, F., Garcia, A., Braza, P., Munoz, J. M., & Sanchez-Martin, J. R. (2006). Aggression, dominance, and affiliation: Their relationships with androgen levels and intelligence in 5-year-old children. *Hormones and Behavior, 50*, 132–140.
Bahrke, M. S., & Yesalis, C. E. (2004). Abuse of anabolic androgenic steroids and related substances in sport and exercise. *Current Opinion in Pharmacology, 4*(6), 614–620. Review.
Belkic, K. L., Landsbergis, P. A., Schnall, P. L., & Baker, D. (2004). Is job strain a major source of cardiovascular disease risk? *Scandinavian Journal of Work, Environment and Health, 30*(2), 85–128. Review.
Björntorp, P., & Rosmond, R. (2000). The metabolic syndrome – A neuroendocrine disorder? *British Journal of Nutrition, 83*(Suppl. 1), S49–S57. Review.
Bygren, L. O., Konlaan, B. B., & Johansson, S. E. (1996). Attendance at cultural events, reading books or periodicals and making music or singing in a choir as determinants of survival. *British Medical Journal, 313*, 1577–1580.
Clays, E., De Bacquer, D., Leynen, F., Kornitzer, M., Kittel, F., & De Backer, G. (2007). Job stress and depression symptoms in middle-aged workers – Prospective results from the Belstress study. *Scandinavian Journal of Work, Environment and Health, 33*(4), 252–259.

Collins, S. M., Karasek, R. A., & Costas, K. (2006). Job strain and autonomic indices of cardiovascular disease risk. *American Journal of Industrial Medicine, 48,* 182–193.

Demitrack, M. A., Dale, J. K., Straus, S. E., Laue, L., Listwak, S. J., Kruesi, M. J., Chrousos, G. P., & Gold, P. W. (1991). Evidence for impaired activation of the hypothalamic–pituitary–adrenal axis in patients with chronic fatigue syndrome. *Journal of Clinical Endocrinology and Metabolism, 73*(6), 1224–1234.

Ebert, A. D., Beres, A. J., Barber, A. E., & Svendsen, C. N. (2008). Human neural progenitor cells over-expressing IGF-1 protect dopamine neurons and restore function in a rat model of Parkinson's disease. *Experimental Neurology, 209*(1), 213–223. Epub October 4, 2007.

Edwards, D. A., Wetzel, K., & Wyner, D. R. (2006). Intercollegiate soccer: Saliva cortisol and testosterone are elevated during competition, and testosterone is related to status and social connectedness with team mates. *Physiology and Behavior, 87,* 135–143.

Ekstedt, M. (2005). *Burnout and sleep.* Thesis. Stockholm, Sweden: Karolinska Institutet.

Emdad, R., Bonekamp, D., Sondergaard, H.-P., Bjorklund, T., Agartz, I., Ingvar, M., & Theorell, T. (2006). Morphometric and psychometric comparisons between non-substance-abusing patients with posttraumatic stress disorder and normal controls. *Psychotherapy and Psychosomatics, 75*(2), 122–132.

Eriksen, H. R., Murison, R., Pensgaard, A. M., & Ursin, H. (2005). Cognitive activation theory of stress (CATS): From fish brains to the Olympics. *Psychoneuroendocrinology, 30,* 933–938.

Evengård, B., & Klimas, N. (2002). Chronic fatigue syndrome: Probable pathogenesis and possible treatments. *Drugs, 62*(17), 2433–2446. Review.

Godbout, J. P., & Glaser, R. (2006). Stress-induced immune dysregulation: Implications for wound healing, infectious disease and cancer. *Journal of Neuroimmune Pharmacology, 1,* 421–427.

Grape, C., Sandgren, M., Hansson, L. O., Ericson, M., & Theorell, T. (2003). Does singing promote well-being? An empirical study of professional and amateur singers during a singing lesson. *Integrative Physiological and Behavioral Science, 38*(1), 65–74.

Grape, C., Wikström, B.-M., Ekman, R., & Theorell, T. (2008). *Comparison between choir singing and group discussion with IBS patients during one year.* Manuscript. Stockholm: Institute for Stress Research, Stockholm University.

Grossi, G., Theorell, T., Jürisoo, M., & Setterlind, S. (1999). Psychophysiological correlates of organizational change and threat of unemployment among police inspectors. *Integrative Physiological and Behavioral Science, 1,* 30–42.

Hasselhorn, H.-M., Theorell, T., Vingård, E., & MUSIC Norrtälje Study Group. (2001). Endocrine and immunologic parameters indicative of 6-months prognosis after the onset of low back pain or neck/shoulder pain. *Spine, 26,* 24–29.

Hasson, D., Anderberg, U.-M., Theorell, T., & Arnetz, B. (2005). Psychophysiological effects of a web-based stress management system: A prospective, randomized control intervention study of IT and media workers. *BMC Public Health, 5,* 78. doi: 10.1186/1471-2456-5-78.

Hertting, A., & Theorell, T. (2002). Physiological changes associated with downsizing of personnel and reorganization in the health care sector. *Psychotherapy and Psychosomatics, 71,* 117–122.

Hess, D. C., & Borlongan, C. V. (2008). Stem cells and neurological diseases. *Cell Proliferation, 41*(Suppl. 1), 94–114.

Holt, R. I., & Sönksen, P. H. (2008). Growth hormone, IGF-I and insulin and their abuse in sport. *British Journal of Pharmacology, 154*(3), 542–556.

Horsten, M., Ericson, M., Perski, A., Wamala, S. P., Schenck-Gustafsson, K., & Orth-Gomer, K. (1999). Psychosocial factors and heart rate variability in healthy women. *Psychosomatic Medicine, 61*(1), 49–57.

Johnson, JV., & Hall, E. M. (1988). Job strain, work place social support, and cardiovascular disease: A cross-sectional study of a random sample of the Swedish working population. *American Journal of Public Health, 78*(10), 1336–1342.

Joosen, M., Sluiter, J., Joling, C., & Frings-Dresen, M. (2008). Evaluation of the effects of a training programme for patients with prolonged fatigue on physiological parameters and fatigue complaints. *International Journal of Occupational Medicine and Environmental Health, 8*, 1–10. [Epub ahead of print].

Kaergaard, A., Hansen, A. M., Rasmussen, K., & Andersen, J. H. (2000). Association between plasma testosterone and work-related neck and shoulder disorders among female workers. *Scandinavian Journal of Work, Environment and Health, 26*(4), 292–298.

von Känel, R., Bellingrath, S., & Kudielka, B. M. (2008). Association between burnout and circulating levels of pro- and anti-inflammatory cytokines in schoolteachers. *Journal of Psychosomatic Research, 65*(1), 51–59. Epub May 22, 2008.

Karasek, R., Russell, R. S., & Theorell, T. (1982). Physiology of stress and regeneration in job related cardiovascular illness. *Journal of Human Stress, 8*, 29–42.

Karasek, R. A., & Theorell, T. (1990). *Healthy Work.* New York: Basic Books.

Kivimäki, M., Theorell, T., Westerlund, H., Vahtera, J., & Alfredsson, L. (2008). Job strain and ischaemic disease: Does the inclusion of older employees in the cohort dilute the association? The WOLF Stockholm Study. *Journal of Epidemiology and Community Health, 62*(4), 372–374.

Landsbergis, P. A., Schnall, P. L., Pickering, T. G., Warren, K., & Schwartz, J. E. (2003). Life-course exposure to job strain and ambulatory blood pressure in men. *American Journal of Epidemiology, 157*(11), 998–1006.

Lökk, J., Theorell, T., Arnetz, B., & Eneroth, P. (1991). Physiological concomitants of an "autonomous day care programme" in geriatric day care. *Scandinavian Journal of Rehabilitation Medicine, 23*, 41–46.

Magnusson-Hanson, L., Theorell, T., Oxenstierna, G., Hyde, M., & Westerlund, H. (2008). Demand, control and social climate as predictors of emotional exhaustion symptoms in working Swedish men and women. *Scandinavian Journal of Public Health, 36*(7), 737–743.

Marucha, P. T., Kiecolt-Glaser, J. K., & Favagehi, M. (1998). Mucosal wound healing is impaired by examination stress. *Psychosomatic Medicine, 60*(3), 362–365.

Mason, J. W. (1968). A review of psychoendocrine research on the pituitary–adrenal–cortical system. *Psychosomatic Medicine, 30*, 576–690.

McEwen, B. S. (1998). Protective and damaging effects of stress mediators. *New England Journal of Medicine, 338*(3), 171–179.

Michelson, D., Licinio, J., & Gold, P. W. (1995). Mediation of the stress response by the hypothalamo–pituitary– adrenocortical axis. In: M. M. J. Friedman, D. S. Charney & A. Y. Deutch (Eds), *Neurobiological and clinical consequences of stress.* New York: Lippincott-Raven.

Morikawa, Y., Kitaoka-Higashiguchi, K., Tanimoto, C., Hayashi, M., Oketani, R., Miura, K., Nishijo, M., & Nakagawa, H. (2005). A cross-sectional study on the relationship of job stress with natural killer cell activity and natural killer cell subsets among healthy nurses. *Journal of Occupational Health, 47*(5), 378–383.

Orth-Gomér, K., Eriksson, I., Moser, V., Theorell, T., & Fredlund, P. (1994). Lipid lowering through work stress reduction. *International Journal of Behavior Medicine, 1*(3), 204–214.

Robles, T. F. (2007). Stress, social support, and delayed skin barrier recovery. *Psychosomatic Medicine, 69*(8), 807–815.

Sanders, E. J., & Wride, M. A. (1995). Programmed cell death in development. *International Review of Cytology, 163*, 105–173. Review.

Schell, E., Theorell, T., Hasson, D., Arnetz, B., & Saraste, H. (2008). Stress biomarkers' associations to pain in the neck, shoulder and back in healthy media workers: 12-month prospective follow-up. *European Spine Journal, 17*(3), 393–405.

Seeman, T. E., Crimmins, E., Huang, M. H., Singer, B., Bucur, A., Gruenewald, T., Berkman, L. F., & Reuben, D. B. (2004). Cumulative biological risk and socio-economic differences in mortality: MacArthur studies of successful aging. *Social Science and Medicine, 58*(10), 1985–1997.

Steptoe, A., & Marmot, M. (2003). Burden of psychosocial adversity and vulnerability in middle age: Associations with biobehavioral risk factors and quality of life. *Psychosomatic Medicine, 65*(6), 1029–1037.

Söndergaard, H. P., & Theorell, T. (2004). Review of DHEAS in PTSD: A putative role for dehydroepiandrosterone in posttraumatic stress disorders. In: T. A. Corales (Ed.), *Trends in posttraumatic stress disorder research* (pp. 27–43). New York: Nova Science Publishers, Inc.

Söndergaard, H. P., Hansson, L. O., & Theorell, T. (2002). Elevated blood levels of dehydroepiandrosterone sulphate vary with symptom load in posttraumatic stress disorder: Findings from a longitudinal study of refugees in Sweden. *Psychotherapy and Psychosomatics, 71*, 298–303.

Söndergaard, H. P., & Theorell, T. (2003). A longitudinal study of hormonal reactions accompanying life events in recently resettled refugees. *Psychotherapy and Psychosomatics, 72*, 49–58.

Theorell, T. (1992). Prolactin – A hormone that mirrors passiveness in crisis situations. *Integrative Physiological and Behavioral Science, 27*(1), 2–38.

Theorell, T. (2008). Anabolism and catabolism – Antagonistic partners in stress at work. *Scandinavian Journal of Work, Environment and Health, Suppl. Series*(6), 136–143.

Theorell, T., Hasselhorn, H. M., & the MUSIC Norrtälje Study Group. (2002). Endocrinological and immunological variables sensitive to psychosocial factors of possible relevance to work-related musculoskeletal disorders. *Work and Stress, 16*(2), 154–165.

Theorell, T., Karasek, R. A., & Eneroth, P. (1990). Job strain variations in relation to plasma testosterone fluctuations in working men – A longitudinal study. *Journal of Internal Medicine, 227*(1), 31–36.

Theorell, T., Liljeholm Johansson, Y., Björk, H., & Erikson, M. (2007). Saliva testosterone and heart rate variability in the professional symphony orchestra after "public faintings" of an orchestra member. *Psychoneuroendocrinology, 32*, 660–668.

Theorell, T., Perski, A., Åkerstedt, T., Sigala, F., Ahlberg-Hultèn, G., Svensson, J., & Eneroth, P. (1998). Changes in job strain in relation to changes in physiological state – A longitudinal study. *Scandinavian Journal of Work, Environment and Health, 14*, 189–196.

Theorell, T., Ort-Gomér, K., Moser, V., Undén, A.-L., & Eriksson, I. (1995). Endocrine markers during job intervention. *Work and Stress, 9*(1), 67–76.

Vaernes, R., Ursin, H., Darragh, A., & Lambe, R. (1982). Endocrine response patterns and psychological correlates. *Journal of Psychosomatic Research, 26*, 123–131.

Weinman, J., Ebrecht, M., Scott, S., Walburn, J., & Dyson, M. (2008). Enhanced wound healing after emotional disclosure intervention. *British Journal of Health Psychology*, *13*(Part 1), 95–102.

Westerlund, H., Theorell, T., & Bergström, A. (2001). Psychophysiological effects of temporary alternative employment. *Social Science of Medicine*, *52*, 405–415.

Westman, M., & Eden, D. (1997). Effects of a respite from work on burnout: Vacation relief and fade-out. *Journal of Applied Physiology*, *82*, 516–527.

ABOUT THE AUTHORS

Torbjörn Åkerstedt, Ph.D. in psychology, 1979, is professor of behavioral physiology at Stockholm University and director of the Stress Research Institute, affiliated to Karolinska institute. He has been President of the Scandinavian Research Society, the European Sleep Research Society, and Secretary General of the World Federation of Sleep Research and Sleep Medicine Societies. He has published more than 200 papers in peer-reviewed journals. The focus of his work has been on sleep regulation, sleep quality, sleepiness and risk, effects of shift work, and stress on sleep and sleepiness.

Fabienne T. Amstad is a research fellow of psychology of work and organizations at the University of Bern, Switzerland. She graduated with a Master's degree in social psychology and earned her Ph.D. in work psychology form the University of Bern. Her primary research interests include job stress and well-being with a special emphasis on the work–family interface.

Evangelia Demerouti is an associate professor of social and organizational psychology at Utrecht University, The Netherlands. She studied psychology at the University of Crete and received her Ph.D. in the Job Demands-Resources model of burnout (1999) from the Carl von Ossietzky Universität Oldenburg, Germany. Her main research interests concern topics from the field of work and health including the Job Demands-Resources model, burnout, work–family interface, crossover of strain, flexible working times, and job performance. She has published over 50 national and international papers and book chapters on these topics, serves as a reviewer for various national and international scientific journals. Her articles have been published in journals including *Journal of Vocational Behavior, Journal of Occupational Health Psychology*, and *Journal of Applied Psychology*.

Arnold B. Bakker is full professor of work and organizational psychology at Erasmus University Rotterdam, The Netherlands. He studied social and organizational psychology at the University of Groningen and received his Ph.D. from the same university. Dr. Bakker developed the Utrecht Work Engagement Scale (with Dr. Schaufeli) that is currently used in 25 countries worldwide, and is instigator of the Job Demands-Resources model (with Dr. Demerouti). His research interests include positive organizational behavior, emotional labor, crossover, work engagement, burnout, and work–family interaction. Dr. Bakker published in journals such as the *Journal of Applied Psychology, Journal of Management*, and the *Journal of Occupational Health Psychology*. He serves on editorial boards of several scholarly journals and is editor of the book *Work Engagement: A Handbook of Essential Recent Developments in Theory and Research* (with Michael Leiter).

Shoshi Chen received her Ph.D. in organizational behavior from the Faculty of Management at Tel Aviv University, Israel (2006). Her primary research interests are work and stress, preventive stress management, training in organizations, effects of vacation on psychological and behavioral strain, and the impact of short business trips on the individual, the family, and the organization. As an organizational consultant, over the years Dr. Shoshi Chen has advised a number of large organizations on topics such as learning processes (at both the individual and the organizational level), training, job analysis, technology implementation, leaders and managers training, mentoring, and team development.

Dalia Etzion has been with the Faculty of Management, Tel Aviv University since its establishment. She was one of the founders of the Organizational Behavior Program and headed the program for six years. Prof. Etzion holds a Ph.D. degree in psychology from the Hebrew University, Jerusalem, Israel (1975). She is a certified psychologist and authorized trainer in the areas of social, industrial, and organizational psychology. Her main interests over the years have been: organizational consulting and organization development; gender differences in management and technology; job-stress, burnout, and life/work integration; respite and recovery. Prof. Etzion has held visiting scholar appointments at several US universities, including MIT, UCLA, UC Irvine, and UC Berkeley (Department of Psychology). She serves as a consulting editor of the *Journal of Applied Psychology*, was on the editorial board of *Gestalt Review* and is a reviewer for journals such as *Human Relations* and *Journal of Organizational Behavior*.

Sabine A. E. Geurts is an associate professor in work and organizational psychology at the Radboud University Nijmegen, The Netherlands. She studied neuropsychology as well as work and organizational psychology, and obtained her Ph.D. degree in psychology in 1994 from the Radboud University Nijmegen, The Netherlands. Her expertise as a senior researcher and lecturer is in the field of occupational health psychology. Her scientific work covers a broad area, with special interests in effort and recovery, work–home interaction, work stress, workplace absenteeism, and diary research methods. She has published over 70 national papers and book chapters on these topics, serves as a reviewer for various national and international scientific journals, and works as a consulting editor for the journal *Work & Stress*. Together with Ulla Kinnunen and Saija Mauno, she received the Work & Stress – "Top paper award 2006" for their paper "Work-to-family conflict and its relationship with satisfaction and well-being: a one year longitudinal study on gender differences".

Ivona Hideg is a doctoral student in organizational behavior/human resources management in Rotman School of Management at the University of Toronto. She received her M.A.Sc. degree in industrial/organizational psychology at the University of Waterloo. Her primary research interests include emotions at the workplace, negotiations, and work breaks. She is also interested in the role of culture in perceiving and reacting to emotions of counterparts in negotiations.

Göran Kecklund, Ph.D., is a senior researcher at the Stress Research Institute, Stockholm University. He did his Ph.D. within (biological) work psychology. His main research topics are work hours, sleep/wakefulness, psychosocial stress, and health/safety. He has published 70 papers in peer-reviewed journals and is associate editor of the *Scandinavian Journal of Work Environment and Health*.

Peter M. Nilsson, Ph.D., is professor of clinical cardiovascular research at the Department of Clinical Sciences, Lund University, Sweden. He is mainly involved in research and clinical intervention studies related to the metabolic syndrome, insulin resistance, type-2 diabetes, sleep problems, hypertension, and the early vascular ageing (EVA syndrome). He is chairman of the European Society of Hypertension (ESH) Working Group "*Hypertension in Diabetes*". Dr. Nilsson is also involved in quality assessment of diabetes care as a member of the data group for the National Diabetes Register of Sweden. He has published more than 150 papers in peer-reviewed medical journals.

Norbert K. Semmer is professor of psychology of work and organizations at the University of Bern, Switzerland. He earned his Ph.D. from the Technical University of Berlin and worked for the Technical University of Berlin, and the German Federal Health Office in Berlin before moving to Bern. He has a long-standing interest in stress at work and its relationship to health, in recent years with a special emphasis on low back pain. He has also published about job satisfaction, the development of efficient strategies in groups, on human error, and on the transition of young people into work. He is a member of the editorial board of the *European Journal of Work and Organizational Psychology*, *the Journal of Occupational Health Psychology*, the *Zeitschrift für Arbeits- und Organisationspsychologie*, and the *Scandinavian Journal of Work, Environment and Health*.

Sabine Sonnentag is a full professor of work and organizational psychology at the University of Konstanz, Germany and a visiting professor at the Radboud University Nijmegen, The Netherlands. She studied psychology at the Free University Berlin and received her Ph.D. from the Technical University Braunschweig. In her research, Dr. Sonnentag is mainly interested in how individuals can achieve sustained high performance at work and remain healthy at the same time. She studies recovery from job stress, proactive work behavior, learning, and self-regulation in the job context. Dr. Sonnentag published in journals such as the *Journal of Applied Psychology*, *Journal of Occupational Health Psychology*, and *Personnel Psychology*. She serves on editorial boards of several scholarly journals and is currently the editor of *Applied Psychology: An International Review*. She is Fellow of the *Society for Industrial and Organizational Psychology*.

Toon W. Taris is a full professor of work and organizational psychology at the Radboud Universiteit Nijmegen. He holds an MA in administrative science (1988) and took his Ph.D. in psychology in 1994, both from the Free University of Amsterdam. His research interests include worker well-being, work socialization, work motivation, informal learning at work, psychosocial work stress models, and (longitudinal) research methods. Taris has published extensively on these and other topics in journals such as *Journal of Applied Psychology*, *Journal of Vocational Behavior*, *Personnel Psychology*, *Sociological Methods and Research*, *Journal of Cross-Cultural Research*, and the *Journal of Organizational and Occupational Psychology*. He currently serves on the boards of several Dutch and international journals, including *Work & Stress* (deputy editor), *Psychology & Health*, and the *Scandinavian Journal of Work, Environment and Health*.

Töres Theorell is MD and has worked as a clinician in internal medicine between 1967 and 1978. He made his Ph.D. thesis at the Karolinska Institute on the subject "life events preceding myocardial infarction" in 1971. He has also been working in social medicine and epidemiology between 1978 and 1980. Since 1980 he has been a professor at the National Institute for Psychosocial Factors and Health (IPM). In 1995, he became director of this institute and also a professor of psychosocial medicine at the Karolinska Institute. Since his retirement in 2006 he has been working as a scientific consultant at the Institute for Stress Research at the University of Stockholm (previously IPM). His publications are on psychophysiological stress mechanisms and on the relationship between psychosocial stressors and illnesses such as cardiovascular disease and psychiatric disease.

John P. Trougakos is an assistant professor of management in the Department of Management at the University of Toronto's Scarborough Campus, as well as the Rotman School of Management at the University of Toronto's St. George Campus. He earned his MBA at Oklahoma State University and his Ph.D. at Purdue University. His research interests include work recovery, emotions in the workplace, leadership, interpersonal functioning at work, knowledge management, and work–life balance.

Mina Westman is a professor of organizational behavior at the Faculty of Management, Tel Aviv University. Her primary research interests include job stress, work–family interchange, crossover in the family and the workplace, the effects of vacation on stress and strain, and the impact of short business trips and expatriation on the individual, the family and the organization. She has authored empirical and conceptual articles that have appeared in such journals as the *Journal of Applied Psychology, Academy of Management Review, Human Relations, Journal of Organizational Behavior, Journal of Occupational Health Psychology, Applied Psychology*, and *Journal of Vocational Behavior*. In addition, she has also contributed to several book chapters and presented numerous scholarly papers at international conferences. She is on the editorial board of *Journal of Organizational Behavior; Journal of Occupational Health psychology*, and *Applied Psychology: An International Journal*. She heads the organizational behavior program at the faculty of Management from January 2005.